THE CULTURE VULTURES

THE CULTURE VULTURES

VULTURES

OR

*Whatever Became of the Emperor's
New Clothes?*

by ALAN LEVY

G. P. Putnam's Sons

New York

To MONICA and ERIKA LEVY
"Thank Heaven for Little Girls"

Acknowledgments

W HILE primary and secondary sources of material are credited wherever their contributions occur, neither footnotes
nor attribution can do justice to a handful of people who literally *saved* this book at a number of crucial turning points that
I started toward five years ago. Not all these people will be glad
they did; nevertheless the opportunities and moral support they
gave me are all gratefully acknowledged: Walter J. Minton and
William Targ of G. P. Putnam's Sons; Theron W. Raines; Mr.
and Mrs. Fred Lazarus III and their Manhattan emissary,
Maurice Feldman; Gregory Harney of the Carnegie Commission on Educational Television; Dean and Mrs. Irwin Wladaver
of New York University; Yvonne V. Chabrier, and Hans Christian Andersen.

Contents

The Good, the True, the Beautiful,
These are the things that Pay.
—LEWIS CARROLL

Prologue:
Whatever Became of the
Emperor's New Clothes?

AFTER the flimsiness of the emperor's new clothes was un-
masked by the little boy, who cried out, "But the emperor
has nothing on at all!" there was great consternation throughout the realm. A blue-ribbon panel of Establishment peers in-
vestigated the incident preparatory to drafting a report proving
conclusively that the whole embarrassment had never really
happened and recommending measures to prevent a recurrence.
Even before this, however, the chief master of parades was retired to civilian life, the privy council and lords of the bed-
chamber were reshuffled, and the little boy was summoned to a
private audience with the emperor.

"Where," asked the emperor in all humility, "did my people
go wrong?"

"Your Majesty," piped the little boy, "when a whole culture
starts to go on the rocks, the rocks are in the head."

"Never mind the sociology," the emperor said. "Just tell me
how two men—those so-called weavers—could pull the wool
over a whole people's eyes."

"Are you sure there were just *two* villains, Your Majesty?"

"I *saw* only two," said the emperor, "and what else is there
to believe anymore besides your own two eyes?"

"But even before those two scoundrels appeared at your
court, had you ever been troubled by a slight ache in your
intellectual backbone?"

"Well, yes. I must say that every now and then I had a vague,
nagging feeling that things weren't as good as they were sup-

posed to be. There was a certain sameness about everything. Even the good things somehow seemed disappointing when I got to them, if you know what I'm getting at."

"I think I do," said the little boy, his falsetto suddenly maturing into a murmur reeking of conspiracy. "And I have news for Your Majesty. It is no accident that your—er—people's yearnings were debased and their needs perverted. Their instinct for uplifting themselves made them easy prey for these culture vultures hovering in the smog of contemporary aesthetics."

"Culture vultures?" said the emperor. "Is that who those two villains were—the culture vultures? Now I must confess that I had heard about them, but I never quite knew who they were. If I thought of them at all, it was more as a phrase than a reality. I hadn't even realized that there were just two of them."

"There are more than just two of them," the little boy corrected. "In fact, there are at least three broad general *categories* of culture vultures that I will unmask here today. I will show you not only who they are and how they operate but also the values they live by and how they actually see their victims."

"Very well," said the emperor, clapping his hands commandingly. "But start with the two weavers, for I am indeed most anxious to learn who they really were."

The little boy bowed and then began. "We will take them one at a time. The first weaver, I am told, was extremely likable."

"Bland and unctuous as the day is long on Midsummer's Eve," said the emperor, "but with a smile so sincere, so warm, that I used to think even my silver would melt in his mouth. . . ."

Part I:

THE PIED PIPERS

Pied Piper—2. (*sometimes* l. c.) a person who induces others to imitate his example, esp. by means of false or extravagant promises.

—*The Random House Dictionary of the English Language,* a 1967 Book-of-the-Month Club Book dividend.

The First Commandment of the Culture Vultures:
Just as the cart goeth before the horse, so
shall the tail wag the dog.

I

The Book-Club Business

[1]

FOR a birthday present to itself in the fall of 1966, the Book-of-the-Month Club spent $85,000 on a sixteen-page color supplement that added only slightly to the staggering bulk of one Sunday's New York *Times.* This Section 11 (Advertisement) was labeled "THE FIRST 40 YEARS OF THE BOOK-OF-THE-MONTH CLUB" and subtitled "A List of the Selections for the Years 1926 to 1966." Riffling through the pages with the ruthless abandon that the Sunday *Times* requires, I stumbled across a contrast that gave me some pause. After paring away various "Special Gifts" and a "Canadian Choice," these were the Books-of-the-Month for 1927, the club's first full year of operation, and for 1963:

1927	*1963*
The Heart of Emerson's Journals, edited by Bliss Perry	*The Sand Pebbles,* by Richard Mc-Kenna
Napoleon, by Emil Ludwig	*The Fall of the Dynasties,* by Edmond Taylor
Elmer Gantry, by Sinclair Lewis	
Revolt in the Desert, by T. E. Lawrence	*Face of North America,* by Peter Farb
Marching On, by James Boyd	*Where's Annie?* by Eileen Bassing
Giants in the Earth, by O. E. Rolvaag	*The Living Sea,* by Captain Jacques-Yves Cousteau with James Dugan

1927	*1963*
Your Money's Worth, by Stuart Chase and F. J. Schlink	*Terrible Swift Sword,* by Bruce Catton
Meanwhile, by H. G. Wells	*Francis Bacon: The Temper of a Man,* by Catherine Drinker Bowen
Dusty Answer, by Rosamond Lehmann	
Right Off the Map, by C. E. Montague	*The Road to Huddersfield,* by James Morris
Red Sky at Morning, by Margaret Kennedy	*Caravans,* by James A. Michener
Abraham Lincoln, by Carl Sandburg	*The Age of Louis XIV,* by Will and Ariel Durant
	The Battle of the Villa Fiorita, by Rumer Godden
	The Age of Napoleon, by J. Christopher Herold
	Love, Let Me Not Hunger, by Paul Gallico and *The First Day of Friday,* by Honor Tracy (dual selection)

It seemed incredible that in 1927, five years before I was born, there were more Books-of-the-Month that I'd heard of and would want to buy and read today than there were in 1963. For the 1963 roster was as eminently forgettable a collection as ever cluttered a Marboro remainder counter: second-line works by first-rate (or once first-rate) talents, with the fiction spectacularly poor (or, to put it more kindly, overanticipated and inevitably disappointing). Was 1963 perhaps an off year for quality in contemporary American publishing? Outside research quickly indicated that 1963 was, if anything, better than most. It was the year of James Baldwin's *The Fire Next Time,* Hannah Arendt's *Eichmann in Jerusalem,* Mary McCarthy's *The Group,* Yevgeny Yevtushenko's *A Precocious Autobiography,* William H. McNeill's *The Rise of the West,* and Nathan Glazer's and Daniel Moynihan's *Beyond the Melting Pot.*

With a glance at selection lists for various adjacent years (1928's *Bambi, John Brown's Body* and *The Intelligent Woman's Guide to Socialism and Capitalism* by George Bernard Shaw versus 1964's *Von Ryan's Express, Comrade Don Camillo,* and *Life with Picasso*), it became clear that 1927 versus 1963 was no farfetched comparison. A major artery of book distribution had hardened, clogged, and rusted. I knew that statistics would tell only a fraction of the story. There were six times as many Book-of-the-Month Club members in 1963 as there were in 1927. And in today's best-seller arithmetic, quality seldom equates with quantity.

Rather than consult various cultural witch doctors like Dwight Macdonald (who, sight unseen and in prose smacking with glee, would prescribe instant euthanasia for Book-of-the-Month masscult), I determined to make, at the very least, a firsthand journalistic diagnosis of when, where, why, how, and by whom a worthy innovation was corrupted.

Back in 1926, a thirty-nine-year-old mail-order mogul named Harry Scherman launched a cultural revolution that was to quintuple the nation's 1 million regular book buyers and enable some 40,000 post offices to double as bookstores. By 1953 the Book-of-the-Month Club ranked with the federal government, Montgomery Ward, and Sears Roebuck as the heaviest users of the U.S. mails. And Kiplinger's *Changing Times* estimated that more than one-quarter of the general, or "trade," books published in a year were sold—or "given away"—by book clubs. Five years later, the figure was up to nearly half.

The Eisenhower and Kennedy eras were the zenith of the book-club business—a decade when each major club had its own distinct personality. After five minutes in a man's home, you could tell that his was a Book-of-the-Month family by its formidable array of Churchills and Will Durants, or a Literary Guild family by Frank Yerby dueling for precious shelf space with Agnes Sligh Turnbull, or a Book Find family willing to stand up to McCarthyism by brazenly displaying De Tocqueville's *Democracy in America* cheek by jowl with Harold Laski's *The American Democracy.*

Reader's Digest Condensed Books, which spares the reader the pain of unnecessary reading, entered the lists in April, 1950, with a standing army of 200,000. Its recruits paid $1.88 each for a quarterly volume containing abridged versions of four books. The first quartet included, rather surprisingly, Alan Paton's poetic clarion call of a novel, *Cry, the Beloved Country.* The Pleasantville brand of painless disembowelment was alarmingly skillful, and by 1954—thanks to such overwritten (and thus eminently condensable) entries as Herman Wouk's *The Caine Mutiny* and Whittaker Chambers' *Witness*—there were over 1,400,000 members, slightly more than B-M-C and Literary Guild combined. And Bennett Cerf of Random House was proclaiming the managing editor of Reader's Digest Condensed Books "the most important individual in American book publishing."

Reader's Digest Condensed Books is known in the book-club business as an "automatic" club because it ships in cycles without previous announcement and with no selection privilege offered to the reader. The Book-of-the-Month Club is known as a "nonautomatic" club because its members have an opportunity to reject or substitute in advance. (Neither the automatics nor the nonautomatics will tell you this readily, but the customer may return any book for credit before or after reading it simply by saying, "It didn't live up to your advertising of it." As Kiplinger's *Changing Times* pointed out: "The book clubs aren't particularly happy to have you do this, but you are certainly within your rights.")

Reader's Digest's success spawned its own imitators (Omnibook's Abridged Books) and subsidiaries (Young Readers of America). Doubleday's Best-in-Books was formed, offering eight condensations for $1.49. Every glimmer of a good idea bore its own specialized fallout as the postwar book-club boom swelled past 5 million members and 100 clubs—from the *Christian Herald*'s Family Bookshelf to the Jewish Book Guild, from Doubleday's Fireside Theatre (scripts and anthologies of plays) to the Farmer's Book Club (almanacs?).

Like most booms, the book clubs peaked out, and the mid-sixties were a period of merger, consolidation, diminishing returns, and increasing facelessness. The Marboro Book Club osmosed into the Hudson Book Club and then was absorbed by Grove Press' avant-garde society, Evergreen. Absorption into Evergreen was also the fate of the pretentious Mid-Century Book Society, erected in the late 1950's around the imposing facades of Lionel Trilling, Jacques Barzun, and W. H. Auden. Along the way, the three eminent judges were cashiered, and Mid-Century even selected an Ian Fleming for its members.

The Literary Guild—which had for years been the flagship of the Doubleday book-club empire—was surpassed in size by the Doubleday One Dollar Book Club and promptly moved to upgrade its image by snaring Saul Bellow's *Herzog* and offering James Baldwin's *The Fire Next Time* as a premium for joining.

Besides the clubs already mentioned, the Doubleday mail-order-fulfillment department in Garden City, Long Island, also maintains, at last count, the American Garden Guild; Around the World Program; Best-in-Books; Best-in-Children's Books; Best-Loved-Girls' Books; Book Club Associates; Cook Book Guild; Dollar Book Club; Doubleday Book Service for Women; Family Reading Club; Fireside Theatre; Happy Hollisters; International Collectors Library; Junior Deluxe Editions Club; Junior Literary Guild; Know Your America and Know Your Bible programs; Literary Guild of America; Mainstream Book Club; Mystery Guild; Nature Program; Paint-It-Yourself Art Program; Reading for Men Club; Amy Vanderbilt's and Nelson Doubleday's personal success programs; Science Fiction Book Club; Science Program; Universe Book Club; Wonders of Life Program; and Young World Book Club.

These specialized Doubleday clubs and programs offer books, booklets, and pamphlets of all publishers on a subscription basis supplemented by such premiums as microscopes, arrowheads, and slides. Within the Doubleday corporate structure, which also takes in a publishing house and a bookstore chain, a club that is not doing well may be dropped and replaced by another. Later, it may or may not be reinstated.

Careful scrutiny of the selection list of the Doubleday clubs suggests that one Doubleday organization can serve as a farm club for another where their interests overlap. Doubleday's new current-events club, Mainstream, features a number of Literary Guild selections. Mainstream recently absorbed the Washington, D.C., based Contemporary Affairs Society. The object of this matrimony—as is often the case in the half-billion-dollar-a-year books-by-mail industry*—was mailing lists. Books clubs can always sell these to junk-mail merchandisers at two cents per

---

* Current statistics on book clubs in this section are drawn largely from *What Happens in Book Publishing,* edited by Chandler B. Grannis (New York, Columbia University Press, 1967)—particularly the chapters "Publishing Books to Sell by Mail," by John Tebbel and "Book Club Rights," by Joseph Marks. The books-by-mail statistics also take in such enterprises as Time-Life Books, American Heritage Publishing Company, Great Books and various encyclopedias that are marketed like Fuller brushes.

name per throw. And maybe, along the way, they can peddle some books, too.

In its throes of desperation during the early sixties, the Washington club had coupon merchandised a miraculous self-erasing typewriter ribbon. (The ribbons erased, all right, but they were good for only three or four typings.) Now, three or four years later, disgruntled ex-coupon clippers were startled to receive unsolicited Mainstream selections (concentration-camp memoirs, early Hemingway, *Hell's Angels,* etc.) and bills.

When the dust jackets had been cleared from the book-club upheavals, three giants held the bulk of publishing influence. These were, in descending order of membership, Reader's Digest Condensed Books, the Book-of-the-Month Club, and the Literary Guild.

Their order of prestige, however, was not precisely the same. And since it was Harry Scherman who invented the book-club business, I decided to focus on his Book-of-the-Month Club—without losing sight, however, of its rivals.

The Book-of-the-Month Club was a logical climax of Harry Scherman's checkered past: as a failed free-lance writer, as a direct-mail genius with two advertising agencies, Ruthrauff and Ryan and J. Walter Thompson, and most malodorously, as cofounder of the Little Leather Library.

For a dime apiece at Woolworth's or free with a box of Whitman's Candy, the Little Leather Library had sold some 48 million miniature editions of various Shakespeare plays (e.g., *Romeo and Juliet* for the Valentine's Day assortment) and excerpts from the Bible. Back in his Little Leather days, Scherman had also experimented (unsuccessfully) with a Book-of-the-Week Club, fifty-two little cowhide classics for $5 a year.

After World War I, however, leather prices had soared sky high. The Little Leather Library was forced to cut corners by using inexpensive synthetics in their bindings. Scherman's particular brand of imitation leather perspired so during hot weather that in the good old summertime, a traveling salesman could measure any community's cultural index simply by taking a deep breath on the outskirts of town. Harry Scherman has said succinctly: "They literally stank." But he came away from this ill-starred venture convinced that even "down at the level of dime-store buyers . . . there was a demand for really good literature."

Then, as now, most Americans did not patronize a bookstore. One-third of the nation didn't have any bookstore to patronize. Nevertheless Scherman also detected a great thirst for brand-new books, if only the reader could depend on the knowledgeable guidance that book clerks were then, as now, supposed to give.

From the outset, Scherman felt, "If you are to deal with or think about the American people en masse, you must regard them as little different from yourself in all essentials." But he knew that most Americans had never heard of Harry Scherman (or his partners, ad man Maxwell Sackheim and Robert K. Haas, later co-owner of Random House) and would have no reason to entrust him with choosing their reading.

Scherman therefore approached celebrities from the literary world. H. L. Mencken and William Lyon Phelps declined to serve on the Book-of-the-Month Club's board of taste makers. Five said yes: Henry Seidel Canby, editor of the *Saturday Review of Literature**; Christopher Morley, essayist; William Allen White, editor of the Emporia, Kansas, *Gazette,* house organ of grass-roots America; Dorothy Canfield Fisher, who wrote novels about Yankees; and Heywood Broun, columnist.

This board, Richard H. Rovere once commented, "carried the stamp of culture without being too frighteningly highbrow." It suggested "literature with a strong dash of journalism: bookish taste with the homey Emporia touch. It was a mellow and respectable jury . . . with just a suggestion of intellectual daring in the Broun reputation."

The initial advertising campaign was headlined, "HANDED TO YOU BY THE POSTMAN, THE NEW BOOKS YOU INTEND TO READ." In the beginning, membership involved taking a dozen books a year at a price no higher than $3 each, plus postage. ("And if the book you receive is not one you would have chosen yourself, you may change it for a book you prefer. . . .") After a member had paid for his first twelve books, he would receive a bonus of three free books. Newspaper and magazine advertisements simply explained who the judges were and how the system worked: "YOU CAN NOW SUBSCRIBE TO THE BEST NEW BOOKS,

---

* Later abridged to the *Saturday Review* as we know it now.

JUST AS YOU DO TO A MAGAZINE." A mailing was sent to the *New York Social Register*'s subscribers.

"I went down to that first meeting," judge Dorothy Canfield Fisher recalled, "and found everybody just as uncertain as I was about what it would be possible to do. I remember we assumed that we'd have to send out detective stories to keep people's interest in the new organization. But we hoped we could send out one or two really good works that could be slipped in among the detective stories so that the readers wouldn't know."

Oddly enough, the book that captivated the judges that first month was *Lolly Willowes,* an enigmatic English fantasy by Sylvia Townsend Warner, which Mrs. Fisher and the other judges knew "wouldn't be popular. We suggested it, however, and found that the businessmen were really in earnest about not interfering. So *Lolly Willowes* was chosen and sent out, and I imagine it almost sank the boat. . . ." Returns were quite heavy, though scarcely comparable to the returns a few months later of *The Heart of Emerson's Journals,* which came back in what Harry Scherman calls "carload lots."

The September selection was *Show Boat,* by Edna Ferber. By the end of 1926, *The Orphan Angel,* a novel by Elinor Wylie, was going to 46,539 members. "Within a little more than a year," Scherman has recalled, "one hundred thousand families had subscribed, and altogether since then, more than six million persons all told have subscribed to the Book-of-the-Month Club alone. Don't be misled. This does not mean anything like six million separate families. We have found it most economical to maintain our list around the five hundred thousand level.* In other words, subscribers come and go and come back again, as magazine subscribers do, and interestingly enough, in about the same ratio yearly as the better magazines. About forty percent a year have to be replaced."

---

* Since these remarks were made by Scherman—in a 1960 lecture at the Library of Congress—the cumulative membership total has risen to 8 million members (and 200 million books distributed), and the current list is maintained at between 600,000 and 700,000, according to one 1966 statistic given out by the club, and at 900,000, according to another. This is still a far or near cry from the club's postwar peak of 920,000 members in 1947.

By 1929, the year the club introduced J. B. Priestley (*The Good Companions*) and Erich Maria Remarque (*All Quiet on the Western Front*) to their first large American audiences,** Scherman's creation was a force to be reckoned with in publishing.

The first reckoner was the president of E. P. Dutton & Company, Inc., who fired off a letter to 500 newspapers in which he accused the Book-of-the-Month Club of leading the public "by its nose." But Harry Scherman knew what was irritating Dutton. The judges' March, 1929, selection had been Joan Lowell's "autobiographical" *Cradle of the Deep* instead of a Dutton novel, *The Pathway*, by Henry Williamson. And so Scherman said blandly: "Possibly the thing we most regret in our organization is the inevitable disappointment that we must cause some authors and publishers each month."

Purely by accident, perhaps, Dutton had picked the best of all possible months for attacking the judging system. After close to 100,000 copies had been mailed out, *Cradle of the Deep* proved to possess what the club called "considerably more fiction . . . and less fact than our judges and the publishers had been led to believe." Miss Lowell, whose book was the saga of her girlhood at sea, turned out to have spent most of it in Berkeley, California.

"Any damn fool can be accurate—and dull," the synthetic autobiographer explained.

Blushing manfully, the club insisted, "Fact or fiction, it is still an exciting and interesting yarn." But it admitted that "our judges might not have chosen it, had they known. . . ."

As a matter of fact, three of the judges—Canby, Morley, and Dorothy Fisher—had been dubious of the "autobiography's" literary merits but had eventually voted for it as "an interesting document." Heywood Broun recalled, in the amused recriminations that followed, that when Canby pronounced it readable but undistinguished, "this maddened me to flights of eloquence. It seemed to me that the Book-of-the-Month Club sent out too many worthy books. . . . By dint of talking, I managed to get

** In that otherwise grim year of 1929, the Book-of-the-Month Club also claims credit for *discovering* the young Walter Lippmann (whose *Preface to Morals* was a selection), but this is disputable.

several judges to say that they would vote for *Cradle of the Deep* as their second or third choice."

Since there was no clear agreement on a first choice, this, in Broun's words, "sufficed to put it over." It also helped to dramatize the club's weakness, then and now, of culture by committee.

While defending its choice of *Cradle of the Deep*, the club offered to exchange any copy returned within thirty days. More than half the members, however, liked it enough (either as reading or as a curiosity) to keep it. And the controversy helped sell another 100,000 copies in the bookstores.

The Depression years of the 1930's were among the club's most resourceful and vital. For legal and cost-cutting reasons, the club resorted to manufacturing its own edition of a book on a license from its publisher and paying royalties rather than buying in bulk from the publisher. The only difference between today's Book-of-the-Month and the regular edition of the same book is that the former possesses a club imprint on the jacket and the copyright page. Sometimes a jacket that doesn't appeal to the club's artistic tastes is redesigned for its edition.

The Book-of-the-Month Club still might not have survived the Depression if necessity hadn't mothered another innovation: printing its own editions of "special" books, old and new, and giving them away as "dividends." The first three dividends, all offered in 1931, were *Imperial Palace,* by Arnold Bennett; *Romance of Leonardo da Vinci,* by Dmitri Merejkowski; and *War and Peace,* by Leo Tolstoy.

Book clubs had been springing up in B-M-C's wake, but in the 1930's only the hardiest and the most resourceful survived the national belt-tightening. One club offered free bookshelves as a recruiting come-on; the assumption was that the joiner would have to buy books to fill them. The Book-of-the-Month Club met the challenge to stay alive with economy, dividends and a third secret ingredient—a blend of quality and excitement that could only be called personal taste. In 1931 alone, the selections included Vicki Baum's *Grand Hotel*; Pearl S. Buck's *The Good Earth*; Willa Cather's *Shadows on the Rock*; James Gould Cozzens' *S.S. San Pedro*; and Frederick Lewis Allen's *Only Yesterday*. The following year included Nordhoff and

Hall's *Mutiny on the Bounty* and Antoine de Saint-Exupéry's *Night Flight,* as well as Van Loon's *Geography* and Warden Lawes' *Twenty Thousand Years in Sing Sing.* 1933 was the year of *Anthony Adverse,* just as 1936 was the year of *Gone with the Wind.*

"Probably it's difficult for anyone who remembers the prodigious success of *Gone with the Wind,*" Dorothy Canfield Fisher recalled, "to think how it would have seemed to people who encountered it simply as a very, very long and detailed book about the Civil War and its aftermath. We had never heard of the author and didn't have anyone else's opinion on it. It was chosen with a little difficulty because some of the characterization was not very authentic or convincing. But as a narrative it had the quality which the French call *attention;* it made you want to turn over the page to see what happens next. I remember that someone commented, 'Well, people may not like it very much, but nobody can deny that it gives a lot of reading for your money.' Its tremendous success was, I must say, about as surprising to us as to anybody else. And the same thing happened with *Anthony Adverse.* We were simply stunned by its length, but we finally voted to send it out, not knowing how it was going to be considered."

That the judges even then were unhesitant about their influence on publishing is indicated by Mrs. Fisher's tale of how she found both a publisher and a public in America for Isak Dinesen's *Seven Gothic Tales.*

"The stories were so strange. I thought they were very fine, highly colored like a new kind of fruit or wine. I'd never seen anything like them. I tried them out tentatively on several publishers, who returned them promptly and said, 'We can't make anything out of them. What do they mean?' Then [club co-founder] Robert Haas, who was as puzzled as everybody else, tried them on his colleagues at Random House, and they were all crazy about them, even the salesmen. They felt that their strangeness was something precious."

When the galley proofs came in a few months later, Mrs. Fisher's evangelizing prevailed on her colleagues, and *Seven Gothic Tales* was a 1934 Book-of-the-Month Club selection. Even more remarkably, shortly thereafter, a dual selection paired Henry A. Wallace (*New Frontiers*) with Herbert Hoover (*The Challenge to Liberty*). Culture by committee can beget strange bedfellows indeed.*

In 1935 the club intervened on behalf of *Salah and His American*, by Leland Hall, a 1934 runner-up that had just missed out at a judges' meeting. Despite good reviews, it had sold only 2,000 copies in bookstores. Terming it "the most neglected book of 1934," the club mailed it free to its entire membership. This gift and the talk it generated earned *Salah* a sale of 70,000 copies in bookstores during 1935, when it would otherwise have been hopelessly out of print.

Salah was the first *pro bono publico* book—sent free to members because of its literary or social importance. In recent years this category has included John Hersey's *Hiroshima* and the Warren Commission's official report on the assassination of President Kennedy—both far more fashionable publishing events than *Salah and His American*. In 1965 a book of light verse by Ogden Nash was similarly distributed as a *pro felicitate publica* bonus "primarily for public happiness rather than public good." And there has been another important change. These *pro publico* gift books are sent only to members who have ordered the selection for that particular month. They tend to be timed as added inducements in months when the Book-of-the-Month is particularly weak.

Like any other large company, the Book-of-the-Month Club has diversified, but mostly within the framework of merchandising and distributing culture by mail. At various times, including the present, there have been: Metropolitan Miniatures (somewhat less than adequate gummed reproductions of art treasures in New York's Metropolitan Museum); Metropolitan Museum Art Seminars in the Home—twenty-four portfolios prepared by John Canaday of the New York *Times* under museum supervision

---

* Other memorable B-M-C double features: *National Velvet*, by Enid Bagnold, with *The Road to War*, by Walter Millis; *Christ in Concrete*, by Pietro di Donato, with *You and Heredity*, by Amram Scheinfeld; *Darkness at Noon* with *Junior Miss*; *The Song of Bernadette* with *Victory Through Air Power*; and most recently, Cornelia Otis Skinner's biography of Sarah Bernhardt with Vladimir Nabokov's autobiography.

to meet a widespread intellectual need. Many otherwise cultivated persons seem to have a blind spot so far as painting is concerned. They can stand before a famous or respected work of art and see nothing beyond what the painting is "about"—and frequently they are unsure of that. If asked to comment, they are tongue-tied and embarrassed. They seem to be cut off from a rare form of pleasure they surely ought to be able to enjoy as much as other people.

and for those with a different inferiority complex, a reading-skills-improvement program complete with calibrated timer and automatic pacer, the latter being a metal bar that marches down the page you're reading at preset speeds; globes as well as atlases; spring-action tubular steel book bracers which "keep books upright when shelves are only partly filled [and] simplify the problem of combining books and bric-a-brac for decorative purposes"; Swedish-made antique-auto wall posters; Christmas cards; a rare-Book-of-the-Month subsidiary (*The Book of Hours of Catherine of Cleves*, a facsimile for $13.50, and the three-volume Nonesuch Bible for $30); the Metropolitan Opera Record Club's listless, unimaginative, though technically excellent original-cast condensations; recordings of Chopin, Bach, Handel; actual performances at the piano by Paderewski, Debussy, Ravel, and Mahler; Boris Karloff reading *The Ugly Duckling* and Basil Rathbone reading Poe; John Ciardi and Robert Frost reading their own poetry; flamenco guitar played by the silver hands of gypsy Manitas de Plata; folk songs by Mississippi John Hurt, Lester Flatt, Earl Scruggs and the Foggy Mountain Boys, the Weavers, the Rooftop Singers, Odetta, Ian and Sylvia, and Joan Baez; Roger Tony Peterson's *Field Guide to the Birds*, plus binoculars to bird-watch by; portfolios of Audubon bird prints (made in Holland), Edward Hopper watercolors (made in Switzerland) and Andrew Wyeth prints ("ideal for your guest room or for a reception room"), and children's books ranging in sophistication from Dr. Seuss and Maurice Sendak to Ian Fleming's *Chitty Chitty Bang Bang*.

Culturally speaking, it became possible to go from womb to tomb without ever really leaving the club's automated bowels at 345 Hudson Street, where between 1962 and 1967 a highly sophisticated computer that could "read and reply to" com-

munications from club members had pared the work force from
1,800 to 560.

[II]

About the time I first became interested in the book-club
business, my mailman brought me a bulk-mail packet from
345 Hudson Street. (The club does mailings in quantities of
from 1 million to 8 million.) Inside was a handsome brochure
promoting an internationally coproduced edition (printed and
bound in Milan and dubbed into English there) of *Tutankhamen: The Life and Death of a Pharaoh,* by Christiane Des-
roches-Noblecourt, a $15 volume that "belongs in every public
library and on the shelves of everyone interested in Egyptian
archaeology," according to the New York *Times.*

Although I couldn't care less about Egyptology, I found the
brochure as eminently readable as movie posters advertising
spear-and-sandal movies filmed in Italy and dubbed into English ("SEE THE PAGAN REVELS OF A THOUSAND LOVE-STARVED
VESTAL VIRGINS AND ONE INSATIABLE MONGOL IN LURID ORGY-
COLOR!"). It had everything but a guest appearance by Orson
Welles as King Farouk.

In vivid orange and black, the Book-of-the-Month Club's
brochure shrieked: " 'I SEE WONDERFUL THINGS,' HOWARD CARTER
CRIED OUT WHEN HE FIRST PENETRATED TUTANKHAMEN'S BURIAL
CHAMBER. *The 'wonderful things' he saw appear on almost every
page of the book—75 of them superbly reproduced in full
color."* And three of his favorite things appeared in the brochure: a golden statue resembling a Negroid Elizabeth Taylor,
the king, looking like an Oscar with breasts, and a golden animal
head that could have been M-G-M's Leo the lion on a starvation
diet.

The brochure was virtually irresistible, particularly when it
informed me that I could have this "BEAUTIFUL $15 VOLUME
SENT FREE . . . IN A SHORT TRIAL MEMBERSHIP." Before mailing
off the postpaid four-color business reply card, however, I pe-
rused the accompanying three-page orange and black letter
signed by Warren Lynch, executive vice-president of the Book-
of-the-Month Club. He greeted me in black letters with "Dear
Reader." In quoting further, since I don't have Mr. Lynch's

many-splendored resources, I'm using italics to denote his lapses into orange.

> The extraordinary opportunity announced here—to obtain "one of the most beautiful books in many seasons" *without charge*—should in itself justify the attention of anyone interested in collecting fine volumes for his library.

I made a mental note that Mr. Lynch said "collecting," not "reading."

> There are, however, two aspects of this proposal that could not be spelled out completely in the big Announcement, and it seems advisable—very much in your interest, as well as in ours—to call them especially to your attention.
>
> First, the *extent of the money-saving* made possible by the Book-of-the-Month Club's new Book-Dividend plan. . . .
>
> YOU WILL FIND THAT YOU CAN SAVE AS MUCH AS $92.60 JUST IN THIS EXPERIMENTAL MEMBERSHIP. Hard to believe, but the arithmetical proof will be found on another page of this letter.
>
> No less astonishing, you will discover, this is *not a one-time affair*. Should you decide to continue after the three-book trial, you can enjoy SIMILAR SAVINGS on other beautiful volumes and fine sets (selling for as much as $86, as you will notice in the Announcement). All will be obtainable with the Book-Dividend Certificates you regularly receive, one with each book you buy as a member.
>
> There is still another highly important aspect of this opportunity that bears emphasizing.
>
> During the coming twelve months *more than* ONE HUNDRED *different Club Selections and Alternates* will be made available to you as a member.
>
> Is it conceivable that from this wide choice there won't be *at least three books* that you will be anxious not to miss and would go out and buy anyway (if, indeed, you do not neglect to do so through oversight)?

Oversight is an eye disease one can scarcely avoid in junk-mail America, but hooked by the low-key gentility of Mr. Lynch's two-tone sell, I read on. As promised, there was a page of "ARITHMETIC OF THE POSSIBLE SAVING," which added up thusly:

Category 1: On the beautiful library volume—
TUTANKHAMEN—which you can obtain *without
charge,* the immediate saving would be $15.00
Category 2: On the three books you would engage
to buy later, the average retail price (according
to past experience) would be $6.00 each. Mem-
ber's price would, on the average, be 20% lower,
a saving of $3.60
Category 3: With the three Book-Dividend Certificates you receive during this trial, you could
choose (if you so wished) Will Durant's 8-vol-
ume THE STORY OF CIVILIZATION, which has a total
retail price of $86.00. Since the payment called
for with the Certificates would be $12.00, the
saving would be $74.00
MAXIMUM POSSIBLE SAVING IN THE EXPERIMENTAL
MEMBERSHIP $92.60

What did I have to lose? On a scratch pad, I computed my own personal "Arithmetic of the Possible Saving." By eliminating categories 1 (I didn't really want *Tutankhamen* and probably would never read him) and 3 (I certainly didn't want Will Durant and wouldn't know where to put all eight volumes of him), I credited myself with an immediate cash saving of $12 that I would otherwise have shelled out to the Book-of-the-Month Club.

This left me with Category 2, where the saving is arguable. For one thing, in New York at least, I could buy those same three current $6 books for anywhere from 5 percent to 50 percent off at Macy's or Korvette's or Alexander's. Department stores and discount houses make big buys of major book-club selections and use them as "loss leaders" to lure customers through their revolving doors. But let's assume I can't get to a discount house. Let's assume I pay the full $18 to a bookstore, instead of $14.40 (plus $1.23 for postage and handling) to the Book-of-the-Month Club.

Then I've paid a total of $18 for three books I want. It struck me as a much better bargain than paying $26.40 for the same three books, plus nine books that I didn't want. In plain black and orange, my net saving by *not* joining the Book-of-the-Month Club was *at least* $8.40.

On a strictly green cash basis, therefore, membership in the Book-of-the-Month Club seemed a poor investment. But did it have literary and cultural merits that would compensate? And why was it so appealing, despite various flaws in Mr. Lynch's sentence structure and mathematical logic? And was it conceivable, to rephrase Mr. Lynch's question, that the club wouldn't come up with *at least three books* in a year that I'd otherwise go out and buy? As the 1963 versus 1927 lists of Books-of-the-Month began to dance before my eyes, I decided it was time to beard the literary lion in its lair.

I dialed 924-1300, and the cheeriest switchboard voice I have ever heard sang out: "Book-of-the-Month Club!" I asked for Mr. Lynch, and the warble grew more guarded. "Is it about a subscription?"

When I said, "Not yet, just research," I was connected with Mr. Lynch's secretary. She suggested that I begin at the literary end and work my way into Mr. Lynch's province. Advertising and merchandising are considered only *after* a Book-of-the-Month has been selected. Said she!

[III]

One of the most famous addresses in America, 345 Hudson Street—the citadel of American mail-order culture—is an undistinctive tan brick office building near the North River waterfront and the Holland Tunnel. It is not called the Book-of-the-Month Building, as I'd expected, but the Standard & Poor's Building. Lest this be construed as a comment on the club's selections in recent years, I hasten to add that the building's principal tenant, Standard & Poor's, is an eminent publisher of credit ratings and investment aids. Similarly, the club's intention to move its clerical operation in 1968 to a cornfield near Harrisburg, Pennsylvania, has no ulterior significance. The club's executive headquarters and judges' meetings will remain on the eleventh floor at 345 Hudson Street.

It was there that a motherly receptionist introduced me to Ralph Thompson, the club's chief reader and editor of its monthly *News.* Thompson, a sprightly, professorial man who used to review books for the New York *Times,* told me, "When you work as a reviewer, you're your own boss. The mistakes you make are on your own head. But now it's a much more serious responsibility."

Thompson and his staff were in the throes of preparing for the February judges' meeting, which was two Tuesdays away. Weeks earlier, almost every publisher in the East had submitted galleys (or a finished typescript) of the one or two or three books on his July list that he considered worthy of club selection.

(Some authors won't let their publishers offer manuscripts to the B-M-C. John O'Hara is one, and a club official attributed this decision to a review by B-M-C judge Clifton Fadiman of an O'Hara novel. Ernest Hemingway was another, for the more familiar complaint by authors that the club ignores their best work when they're struggling and leaps at anything of theirs once they're established. Hemingway relented with *The Old Man and the Sea,* a 1952 selection. Posthumously, his *A Moveable Feast* was a 1964 selection, and A. E. Hotchner's *Papa Hemingway* was a 1966 selection.)

Each of some 200 entries had been read by at least two preliminary readers, and on the basis of their one-page reports, Ralph Thompson had graded each book "A," "B," or "C."

A "C" book is seldom heard from again—by the club's members, at least. Once upon a time, the unmistakably unique *Cry, the Beloved Country* passed unnoticed through 345 Hudson Street as a "C" book. Harry Scherman has said, "The publisher himself paid little attention to it. It went to two readers, and there wasn't a thing in their reports to put us on notice."

A "B" book is occasionally sent to one or two of the judges, either at their request or because it might be of particular specialized interest to them. A stir of interest by any judge is enough to upgrade a book from "B" to "A."

The "A" books—from four to a dozen each month—are the finalists, the ones that all judges should have read when the meeting convenes every fourth Tuesday.

A publisher generally knows when his book has made the "A" grade, for an urgent call for more galleys comes from 345 Hudson Street. From that moment on, the publisher frets anxiously, for the spoils of victory are immense and immediate. The first tangible reward is a check from the club to the publisher for $75,000 as an advance against a 10 percent royalty per copy sold by the club. This $75,000 windfall is customarily divided equally between author and publisher.*

It is still winter when the B-M-C goes to press with its own edition of the July selection. This edition would have a first printing of 125,000 to 200,000 copies. And a lucrative chain of events would be set in motion. The winning book for July would be featured in the June Book-of-the-Month Club *News,* which is mailed to all club members. If a member did not take the trouble to reject it (the club neglects, for a perfectly obvious reason, to furnish a business reply card or envelope, thereby requiring the member to fish around for stamps and an envelope and then address his rejection himself), the book and the bill would be sent automatically by mail. On the average, one-third of the members sit back and let the book come to them after receiving the announcement.

Being a Book-of-the-Month is no guarantee of bestsellerdom. But if you will glance at any current national best-seller chart, you are likely to find that three out of four money-makers thereon are B-M-C or Literary Guild selections. And the best-seller charts represent bookstore, not book club, sales.

"A Book-of-the-Month Club selection," judge Clifton Fadiman once boasted, "automatically sets in motion a wave of bookish conversation, for the club members form a mighty army of talkers." But long before a book arrives (and possibly is read) in hundreds of thousands of American homes, its choice has inspired its publisher to spend an average of four times as much money on advertising it as he normally would, the average bookstore to increase its normal order by a third, and the average book-review editor (if there is such a person) to order a review of it. Whether the notice is favorable or unfavorable, that last break is crucial; any less-than-famous author's battle today is simply to be reviewed at all.

---

* The Literary Guild's advance guarantee is $40,000, and Reader's Digest Condensed Books' ranges from $20,000 to $100,000. In recent months, *all* guarantees have proved to be negotiable upward.

Ralph Thompson told me that seven or eight "A" books were up for selection. A ninth book, however—a noncandidate —loomed large over the impending meeting.

The latest *Making of the President* volume by Theodore H. White was to be published that July. Dealing as it would be with the assassination of John F. Kennedy and its aftermath, it was a certain best seller.* Since several of White's lesser works had been B-M-C selections and the first *Making of the President* had been a 1961 selection that achieved what the club calls a high "index of reader satisfaction," the July meeting ought to have been no contest.

But while White was writing his second chronicle of a Presidential campaign,** his energetic publisher had taken the unorthodox step of soliciting bids on the still incomplete book, and the Literary Guild had made off with the prize by virtue of an unprecedented guarantee against royalties in the neighborhood of $100,000. The guild's offer represented almost triple its usual advance as well as a declaration of war. Recognizing that its future did not lie with Frances Parkinson Keyes, the guild was ready to compete for potential B-M-C members. Even the guild's advertising was taking on a staid clublike air. Thanks to a gentleman's agreement that was more of a prisoner-of-war exchange, the club and the guild were sending each other coupons that had been mailed by mistake to 345 Hudson Street instead of Garden City, Long Island, and vice versa.

Out of courtesy to the B-M-C and perhaps in anticipation of a counteroffer, White's publisher had relayed the guild's terms to the club before accepting. But to its credit, the club's parliamentary system of judging proved so inflexible that without a finished manuscript as evidence, it had to pass up its likeliest candidate for July.

At the time, any struggling author had to applaud the B-M-C's courage in declining to bid. Enough blind preselling and star packaging already existed in publishing without rigging the race any further against the unknown hopeful. Sitting lonely at his typewriter, he used to be able to think that he was writing a po-

---

* It went to the head of the best-seller list that very July.
** White is booked for full-length coverage of every Presidential election through 1980.

tential Book-of-the-Month and had a shot—a long shot, perhaps —at going from rags to riches in one Tuesday afternoon. This applause, alas, would quickly turn to hand-wringing. For the club's noble stand on principle in the White matter proved so shattering that months later, Arthur Schlesinger, Jr.'s, and Theodore C. Sorensen's memoirs of Kennedy were chosen even before their authors had completed writing them. For William Manchester's book on the assassination, the club upped its guarantee to a record $250,000. This record lasted less than a year, by which time the club had paid $325,000 for Joseph Stalin's daughter's memoirs, sight unseen. The Literary Guild may have lost more than it won, but its Theodore White coup did force the Book-of-the-Month Club to come down to the crass, commercial level of presold culture merchandising as practiced by its hungrier competitors.

At our first of several meetings, Ralph Thompson was very open in outlining B-M-C procedures but not at all helpful when I pressed for specific examples. Generally I would have to describe my reception at 345 Hudson Street as "arm's-length cooperation": a cordial welcome, frank discussion of superficialities, a supply of pamphlets, brochures and statistics on all matters of open public record, plus the usual gossip and ephemera that pervade the world of books. When, however, I asked to attend a judges' meeting, I was assured that no outsiders (other than Scherman, Lynch, Thompson, and occasionally some other B-M-C official) ever sat in. And when I asked for some sample reports by preliminary readers, I was handed only the blank forms. Surveys that had been alluded to were seldom available. For-instances were off the record.

Nevertheless, if you let a man say no often enough, his answer sometimes comes out yes. After I had pressed Thompson several times for a sample reader's report on some bygone book, he remarked impatiently that even if his answer were yes, which it would never be, he wouldn't be able to show them to me. All the old reports had been shipped to the Library of Congress, and God only knew what had become of them.

At home that afternoon, a phone call to Washington established that not only God but also a number of earthbound librarians knew exactly where they were and would be happy to share their secrets. Within the legal limits of fair quotation, a two-day trip to Washington contributed measurably to this chapter.

By the end of World War II, the club's selection procedures had been refined into a dubious but highly rigid and self-fulfilling science. According to my *Tutankhamen* brochure, the club's screening system is "the most thorough and painstaking in existence." While this was less than true, my Washington browse did impress me with the club's reliance, when its half dozen salaried readers did not feel qualified to evaluate a manuscript, on outside readers like Allan Nevins, Henry Steele Commager, and Gerald W. Johnson.

Nowadays the club uses some thirty outside readers. They include a well-known specialist in Americana, a museum employee, a college English teacher, a story editor for a movie company, a newsmagazine editor, an Englishwoman reared in Argentina, a former foreign correspondent, an assistant professor of philosophy, and, as one club underling confided, "a relative who was forced on us."

(The club, incidentally, makes a policy of not picking books written or edited by its judges, officials, or their relatives as selections. On the other hand, it makes a fetish of offering these books as dividends or alternates for dividend credit. In 1966 there were at least a dozen such books available, five of them by women named Scherman.)

Outside and salaried readers alike fill out the same form. It asks four short-answer questions, plus one essay question requiring a page-long reply. ("If necessary, please finish report on other side of this sheet.") The short-answer questions are:

1. Would you yourself be inclined to VOTE for this book as a Book-of-the-Month?
2. If not, do you at least consider it of sufficient IMPORTANCE to warrant its being read by the judges?
3. Do you think it deserves notice in the *News*?
4. Or may it be disregarded?

(The capitalizations are mine. Later on, for purposes of shorthand in referring back to which key question is being answered, I will use these capitalized labels rather than numbers.)

Finally the ESSAY question specifies: "What we principally want in first-reader reports: A *brief* general characterization of the book and a specific statement of what *you* like and dislike about it . . ."

At the Library of Congress, I concentrated on first-reader reports and subsequent fates of three famous novels of the 1950's:

THE CATCHER IN THE RYE
by J. D. Salinger

One first reader answered NO to both the VOTE and IMPORTANCE questions. His ESSAY read:

"The book is one long monologue, done almost in free-association, so that you learn a great deal about [Holden Caulfield]. He has an unerring eye for a phony, and his world has been full of phonies, and probably because he has too keen an eye for human weakness and too much youthful intolerance of it, he has had no real friends. All this you can comprehend; you know him well enough to feel that in fact you probably wouldn't like him at all, and yet you feel so much sympathy for his essential sincerity and his hopeless floundering that, without liking him, you almost, in the Christian sense, love him. This is quite an achievement. But I don't think this has a wide-enough appeal for consideration as a selection. For one thing, Holden is one of those schoolboys—it is a common type, though not a useful one—who are as foul-mouthed as anybody in *From Here to Eternity*; for another, the book is sometimes a little monotonous and may seem even a little aimless. At the end he is pretty much where he was at the beginning; he is back with his family, but no catharsis has been achieved. Probably if he is lucky he will grow up to be a writer, like J. D. Salinger."

The next "first reader" said YES to the two key questions of VOTE and IMPORTANCE.

"Salinger set himself an extremely difficult task, and he has succeeded at it beautifully. Though the book is written with brittle wit and sardonic humor (the author owes considerable to Ring Lardner, stylistically), the lasting effect of the book is one of tenderness and understanding."

The third "first reader" VOTED NO, but wrote:

"The boy talks obscenely, in the lewd bromides of schoolboy vernacule [*sic*]—and for this reason the book is extraordinarily

THE CULTURE VULTURES [42

candid. But if dirty language is appropriate in *From Here to Eternity*, it is just as appropriate here in that it is used realistically, honestly, and with great effect. Here is a boy who cannot tolerate 'phonys,' and his sure reaction against artifice in the adult world—in society, in the theater, among educators, among debutantes, among cliques like 'for Christ's sake, even the goddam members of the Book-of-the-Month Club'—have a very tonic reaction on the reader. Sometimes the story wears thin, as do the boy's interior monologues. But most of the time, the humor is effective and the analysis of the madness of childhood and adolescence very moving."

On the basis of these mixed notices, the chief reader had classified Catcher in the Rye *a "B" book. But at the behest of two judges—Clifton Fadiman and John P. Marquand—it was upgraded to "A" and chosen as the B-M-C's 1951 summer selection.* The Book-of-the-Month Club's year, incidentally, is a baker's dozen—twelve monthly selections, plus a thirteenth for summer reading.

The readers' emphasis on dirty words in Salinger (never, to some minds, his most notable asset) made one hanker to see their opinions of the slightly earlier novel that two of them had acknowledged as a landmark in foul language:

FROM HERE TO ETERNITY
by James Jones

I blushed when I noted that three of the four "first readers" on file were—ulp!—*females*.

The first female VOTED that she would "consider it strongly" and, in any event, found it IMPORTANT enough to be read by the judges. Her ESSAY said:

"I think this is a greater Army book than *The Naked and the Dead*.* It isn't really war. It is the Army in Hawaii for a year, up to and just barely beyond Pearl Harbor. Its author is rightly James Jones, a sort of anonymous American. This is the story of many men, told straight, no highfalutin' effects. . . . But this is a very hard decision: to send out a book in which every paragraph is filled with filth of soldier talk, where the scenes

---

* Norman Mailer has not yet been and may never be a Book-of-the-Month Club selection.

in whorehouses and bars and in the latrine are never played down. But you feel that this is as it should be."

The second female bore a famous name and a chatty style.

"This falls into the category of *The Naked and the Dead* and *The Young Lions** . . . but it *is* good of its kind. Same language and hard-boiled Army scenes as the two above. It is more of a man's book than a woman's and full of GI passions. . . . It is like a combination of tough Kipling, Thomas Wolfe, and the new rough school. Could James Jones be a pseudonym? He seems an experienced writer."

Thus impressed, she VOTED "A possibility." As to whether it was IMPORTANT enough for the judges to read, she said NO.

The third female VOTED "on its merits, YES" and on its IMPORTANCE, YES. She, too, concentrated on the language.

"The dialogue, as completely unshorn and outspoken as any I have come across anywhere, while it may repel and horrify, nevertheless has justifications in what would seem to be its complete rightness. . . . This is quite a book."

Apparently the club's chief reader was market-testing James Jones for the heavily female membership. The only male member of this first-readers' quartet had one answer for the two key questions of VOTE and IMPORTANT: "Hardly, but I think a couple of judges should see it." His ESSAY read:

"I had to do a rush job on reading this, and I wish I could have had a little more time to evaluate it; it is possible that I am being carried away by its sheer shock value; but I really think it is quite a book." He warned, however, that *From Here to Eternity* "will do little or nothing to raise the morale of our new draftees and their mothers, and if it should be chosen it will keep our correspondents busy with subscribers who think *damn* is a naughty word."

The club apparently was ready to risk a legion of plum-pudding ladies pelting the naughty boys at 345 Hudson Street with homemade pies, for From Here to Eternity *went before the judges as an "A" book. But it was not selected. Later it was chosen as a B-M-C alternate for 1951.* An alternate is a face-saving hedge (usually culled from a judges' meeting's rejects) offered to members along with the monthly selection. If the selec-

---

* Irwin Shaw's war novel was not a B-M-C selection.

tion is fiction, the alternate is likely to be nonfiction, and vice versa. When, however, the club has simply missed the boat on a sudden runaway best seller, it promptly offers it as a "special alternate" with a "flash" announcement stuck in the Book-of-the-Month Club *News*. This disadvantage of being an alternate book is that the member does not receive it automatically; he must request it by name on the rejection form.

THE CAINE MUTINY
by Herman Wouk

The same two readers who had VOTED NO on *The Catcher in the Rye* VOTED NO on Herman Wouk's most famous novel.

Said the one who had predicted that Holden would grow up to be J. D. Salinger:

"What this book needs is a Max Perkins.* It is certainly good, but if it could have some very drastic cutting it could be outstanding." He conceded that the villain, Captain Queeg, was "beautifully drawn. . . . Also, without any underscoring, we have seen the hero develop from a rich, careless, almost spoiled boy to a mature man. All this is excellent stuff. The trouble is that Wouk wants to get in everything about (I assume) his own naval recollections. There is too much about the hero's early experiences before Queeg comes aboard. And there is an affair with a nightclub singer which may be meant to show him rising above Princetonian prejudice but which is really embarrassingly bad."

The "lewd bromides of schoolboy vernacule" man weighed in with this opinion:

"This is a very exciting naval story botched by a very cheap and slick romance, and while the stupid love story could easily be dispensed with, in its present state it contaminates the whole book." Conceding that Captain Queeg and the court-martial were "beautifully done" with "vivid and dramatic writing and wonderful suspense," the reader noted regretfully: "After the trial, however, Wouk doesn't seem to know what to do with the story. He involves it in a bad denouement with another officer who is a novelist, a psychological explanation of Queeg's weak-

---

* Maxwell Perkins (1884–1947) is the Scribner's editor credited with making Thomas Wolfe manageable, Ernest Hemingway salable, F. Scott Fitzgerald readable, and James Jones printable.

ness, and other anticlimactic chapters that are a letdown. And the story of the boy's love for the nightclub singer is absolutely impossible."

Their judgment was heeded by the chief reader, who classified The Caine Mutiny *as a "C" book. It never reached the judges.*

One of the judges it never reached, the late John P. Marquand, cited *The Caine Mutiny* episode as one of the club's major blunders. Harry Scherman called it "quite an oversight on everybody's part" but said it happened "because our first readers' reactions happened to coincide with the original *un*-excitement on the part of the publishers. . . . Fortunately our system of providing alternates to the Book-of-the-Month had by then been established, and we later distributed to subscribers one hundred fifty-eight thousand copies of the book."

Wouk was unknown to the public then, but he should not have passed unnoticed by the Book-of-the-Month Club. Four years earlier, when Wouk was a complete unknown, the club had discovered him by selecting an inferior novel of his, *Aurora Dawn*. After the *Caine* embarrassment, it selected Wouk's *Marjorie Morningstar*, plus two of his lesser works, *Youngblood Hawke* and *Don't Stop the Carnival*. The lesson the club seems to have learned from Herman Wouk's Navy is: Don't miss the boat. But if you do, take any other boat of the same line, and everything will be shipshape.

(The club's traffic with Ernest Hemingway, John Steinbeck, and William Faulkner has been similarly insensitive. "For years," said Clifton Fadiman, "we read Faulkner's books as they came along, with care and respect, and we didn't take them. We didn't take them because we didn't like them. But then *The Reivers* came in, and it seemed delightful, and we took it, though we had turned down all the books that the vanguard critics thought were great. Maybe we were blind." Or were the club's judges rectifying their sins of omission toward Faulkner by choosing a lesser work after ignoring his masterpieces? The Pulitzer Prize juries, which are virtually the last to perceive greatness, were doubly solicitous toward Faulkner by honoring him belatedly for such threadbare treasures as *A Fable* and *The Reivers*.)

After the *Caine Mutiny* fiasco, there was talk of courts-martial at 345 Hudson Street, of scuttling the system, and of awarding all books by previous winners an automatic "B" or better. But no firm new policy emerged, for there were those who, even back in the McCarthy era, were willing to stand up inside or outside the Standard & Poor's Building and say that perhaps the two disgraced readers were right.

I took the Congressional Limited home the next day, eager for a confrontation with the judges. The club, of course, had been unwilling to let me sit in on its meeting or even to identify the candidates for July 1965 selection. Nevertheless, two weeks before the meeting, I had ascertained that there were seven "A" books:*

THOMAS, subtitled "A Novel of the Life, Passion, and Miracles of Becket," by Shelley Mydans. A quality historical novel about a saint made fashionable by Laurence Olivier on the stage and Richard Burton on the screen.

THE LIBERATION OF LORD BYRON JONES, by Jesse Hill Ford. A seething Southern novel that had almost made the grade as the June selection before losing out to *The Source*, by James A. Michener. Its publisher had agreed to postpone publication for a month if *Lord Byron* was selected for July.**

DOG YEARS, by Günter Grass. An uneven but frequently powerful novel by the German author of *The Tin Drum*.

THE STRODE VENTURER, by Hammond Innes. An adventure novel by an English craftsman who turns out fiction like well-made clockwork.

WITH EVERY BREATH YOU TAKE, by Howard Lewis. One of several books of the season about air pollution. Like its competitors, this one was *against* its subject. Unlike almost every other book on the subject, however, this one was stodgy enough to defy reading.

THE PAST THAT WOULD NOT DIE, by Walter Lord. The au-

---

* Their identities were not hard to ferret out. From the demand for galleys to be rushed to 345 Hudson Street, every publishing house involved knew that it had a candidate in the running.

** Most publishers are more than willing to postpone or advance the publication date by as much as eight months to suit the B-M-C's needs. This has helped to make publishing more of a year-round occasion rather than a spring and fall eruption. The only notable case in which a B-M-C request for a new publication date was refused involved Boris Pasternak's *Doctor Zhivago*, where there was an international commitment for simultaneous publication. As a B-M-C alternate, however, *Doctor Zhivago* has sold 365,000 copies thus far to club members.

thor's usual minutia-by-minutia reportage applied to 1962's Battle of Ole Miss, when James Meredith, a Negro, enrolled at the University of Mississippi.

NEVER CALL RETREAT, by Bruce Catton. Volume three in a Civil War trilogy.

Charted from the outside, Lord and Catton ruled as co-favorites. Lord's *Day of Infamy* and *The Good Years* had been successful selections, although his first and best book, *A Night to Remember,* had missed the boat. Catton had even more imposing credentials. The first two volumes of his trilogy had been B-M-C selections. It struck me that the new Lord and the new Catton might make an appropriate dual selection.

On hearing that I was making inquiries about the seven candidates, Ralph Thompson of the B-M-C had mentioned that while he couldn't stop me, he ought to warn me that "there's always the possibility of a last-minute 'A' book being chosen." Nevertheless I contacted each of the five judges, at the time* for his appraisal of the seven candidates.

The judges are paid handsome salaries, plus a substantial bonus, for attending thirteen meetings a year, reading approximately 100 "A" books and several dozen other possibilities, and performing the ceremonial functions of a far less than full-time job. They were not wholly responsive, but I did talk with each.

John K. Hutchens, former book reviewer for the New York *Herald Tribune* and author of *One Man's Montana,* is a baseball fan, theaterlover, and Civil War addict who told me tersely: "I'd really like to stay out of this. I'm a very junior member of the board of judges, and anything that's said should come from my seniors." To no avail, I reminded Hutchens that in a one-man, one-vote parliamentary system, junior opinions were at least as vital as senior opinions.

Gilbert Highet, Anthon Professor of Latin Languages and Literature at Columbia University, returned my call in a severely clipped British accent with a loquacious no.

"I really don't think I ought to talk with you. Partly it's because of my time problem; I'm getting ready for a sabbatical,

---

* One of them, Basil Davenport, subsequently died and has not yet, at this writing, been replaced. There have been only twelve judges in the club's first forty years: Canby, Morley, White, Broun, Mrs. Fisher, Amy Loveman, J. P. Marquand, and the five picking the July 1965 selection.

don't y'know. And it's partly because I don't think you ought to know what happens at our meeting. It's like *any* board of directors' meeting. Letting you in on it would be letting the public in."

I pleaded the public's right to know. Highet, however, was not to be swayed.

"But what if we picked a real turkey?" he asked me. "There are some months when we just don't have a choice of anything worthwhile."

With Theodore White's defection to the Literary Guild, I gathered that Highet's outlook for July was just that. But when I said so, Highet bristled.

"Oh, no. After all, we do have a new Bruce Catton. I'm thinking of the time when we all had a terribly overwritten book by *that Australian writer* practically forced down our throats." After some prodding, Highet identified the writer in question as Patrick White, whose *Voss* was a 1957 selection.

I reminded Highet that I was evaluating the club's forty-year track record, not just its big mistakes.

"No," he said. "It's too much like attending rehearsals of a play and judging it by that."

"But the play will have closed," I argued, "by the time my book appears."

"No," Highet concluded, "too many things can go wrong."

The most to be gleaned about Highet's personal tastes, as expressed at B-M-C judges' meetings, came from a published interview with the otherwise reticent John K. Hutchens, who confessed: "Highet loves violence, sadism, and mutilation, which John [Mason] Brown and I think is his form of escape from the classical disciplines." Highet, incidentally, is married to the Scotch-born novelist Helen MacInnes, whose thirteen mostly tepid chillers (five of them available on the January, 1967, list of B-M-C alternates) have sold over 4 million copies in nineteen languages.

John Mason Brown was the first judge to talk freely. I would scarcely have expected otherwise from the famed drama critic and lecturer who is listed in *Celebrity Register* as the country's number one talker and who has described himself as a "wind instrument."

Tuning Brown in, even by telephone, makes one tingle, like

a women's club getting its annual cultural rubdown from him.
"Half the 'A' books shouldn't have been made 'A,' " he began.
"That applies to this month and any other month. . . . The
Catton? I haven't read it yet, but I know what to expect. I've
been up one hill and down the next with that man, and I feel
like a veteran of Pickett's charge. I'll read it, though. I'm look-
ing forward . . . The air pollution? I don't have to read it. I
can just inhale it. In fact, I'm doing that right now. It's all
around me in New York. I suppose I'll read it, though. . . .
Thomas? I don't like historical novels, but this one begins well.
Then it bogs down, though, in ecclesiastical detail. . . . The
Günter Grass? I liked *The Tin Drum,* and I think he's a good
writer. But for my money, it's a bad translation. . . . The
Southern novel? Enormously, powerfully, gleefully brutal, but
it's got quality, too."

When I asked Brown what went on at the judges' deliberations, he gave a courtly Kentucky chuckle and replied:

"That's a mighty big word for such a simple process. We're
not trying to pick the best book of any month, but a book that
we all like the most. It's not like the Supreme Court."

Still, on the crucial Tuesday, at least seven publishers would
await the judges' verdict amid agony worthy of death row. One
or two might even bolt their lunches, for the verdict would
come as early as 2 P.M.

Brown concluded our chat with a man-to-man tribute to the
Book-of-the-Month Club's tangible rewards.

"The money doesn't hurt a fellow who's been working like a
dog for months and even years."

I assumed he was talking about authors, not judges.

Clifton Fadiman talked freely, too, though nowhere nearly as
glibly as John Mason Brown. The onetime *Information Please*
pundit made me feel like an old friend chatting about books.

"There is nothing sinister or nefarious about our deliberations," he began, using the word Brown had deplored. "It takes
about five seconds to explain. We have a list of the 'A' books.
We go over them and then discuss some of the 'B' books. We
eliminate right away any book that all or most of us didn't like
at all. Then we talk about the ones we liked best. In the discussion, one or two emerge. That's all there is to it. Five judges get
together for four or five hours until one book emerges.

"Last month, I made it clear that one particular book would be taken over my dead body, or at least my resignation. I was angry that it had reached the status it had. I haven't resigned, so you can gather it wasn't taken. I'm sure you'd like to know its name, but I can't tell you that."

Fadiman grew specific.

"The holdover from last month is interesting, I think, with many dramatic episodes, but a little long, and like most Southern novels, somewhat talky. The book about Thomas seems reasonably interesting. I haven't read the book about air pollution or the one by Hammond Innes yet. Bruce Catton is simply more of the same. We've taken two of his books, and this one is just as good. The only question is whether we've had enough Civil War."

I asked Fadiman: "Don't the judges feel any moral obligation to furnish a member with the final third of Catton's trilogy?"

"We can always offer it as an alternate," he replied.

I asked Fadiman about the Walter Lord book.

"It's an excellent attempt to recapitulate the Meredith episode in Mississippi," he remarked. Then he added in a slightly downbeat tone: "Like anything else Mr. Lord has done."

Fadiman concluded by discussing Günter Grass.

"Frankly, he has tremendous talent. Looking back now, I wish we'd taken *The Tin Drum*. This new one is extraordinarily puzzling. But Grass certainly has great energy."

Basil Davenport, the fifth judge, was the only one who suggested I drop up to see him in his chambers. This was most agreeable because I wasn't very certain exactly who Basil Davenport was. He wasn't listed in my almanacs, *Who's Who, Celebrity Register,* directories of authors and writers, *Reader's Guide,* or library indexes. The various literary agents, writers, and editors to whom I popped the name almost invariably replied: "He has something to do with the Book-of-the-Month Club." Three who had met him at parties were able to add that he was a charming man with a prodigious memory and a penchant for ghost stories. All three were certain of one other fact: "He's an Englishman."

The voice that invited me up was veddy Oxonian indeed. And when I bearded the real Basil Davenport, he proved to be a ruddy, cherubic bachelor spouting unvarnished Gilbert and

Sullivan ("Taking one consideration with another, the judges . . ." etc.) and was on his way out "to have my shoes cobbled." I asked him an easy question—where was he from?—and he replied blandly that he, like John Mason Brown, was a native of Louisville, Kentucky.

"I am the only judge who came up through the ranks," he went on. "I was graduated from Yale in 1926, the year the club was founded. . . . I traveled abroad and spent some time at Oxford and then taught classics at Rutgers. While I was there, Henry Seidel Canby sent me books to review. When I came to New York in the fall of 1929 to seek my fortune, the streets were paved with gold—but not for long. Canby offered me a desk and a salary for the pleasurable task of weeding out books."

Basil Davenport, B.A., stayed with the Book-of-the-Month Club for the rest of his life, with time out for Uncle Sam in World War II. He worked his way up to chief reader—Ralph Thompson's present post. In 1956, after the deaths of Amy Loveman and Christopher Morley, their judgeships were awarded to two Kentuckians, Brown and Davenport.

"I always have a problem when I apply for a driver's license," Davenport told me. "Sometimes I give my occupation as editor, and I'm asked, 'What newspaper?' Sometimes I put down *judge*, and I'm asked, 'What court?' "

This judge's chamber would have confounded any jury. It was an office in a corner of the Book-of-the-Month Club's fourteenth-floor addressograph department, where the only other sign of life that day was a lone woman puttering around an arsenal of files.

"I used to be surrounded by a garden of femininity's finest flower," Davenport's resonant voice boomed out wistfully, "but now they've been automated. Ah, progress!"

I asked Davenport what happened every fourth Tuesday, when he left his automated garden and joined the other judges on the eleventh floor. He replied:

"As we state in our advertisements—and goddamit, we tell the truth—all the books we send out are the unanimous choice of the judges. Some books, I must admit, are more unanimous than others.* I liken it to a Quaker meeting and its concluding

---

* In 1955, in the pages of the B-M-C *News*, Amy Loveman divorced herself from the other judges' choice of Robert Ruark's *Something of Value*, which she

question, 'Is it the sense of the meeting that such-and-such?'
Sometimes you get three judges *for* a book and two very unen-
thusiastic, but they get talked around, and then they see more
in the book than when they started out. Whatever the sense of
the meeting, it's always very spirited, and I usually come away
with at least one new joke."

Chuckling all the way, Davenport then regaled me with an
unprintable tale of some lovesick monkeys. I also learned that
he and Highet would sometimes tell jokes with punch lines in
Greek or Latin and then laugh heartily, thereby dumbfounding
their fellow judges.

I asked Davenport if a strong personality ever dominated a
meeting.

"Our personalities are equally strong," he said, "although not
perhaps on first encounter. It is very much like what happens
when a jury of twelve men is locked up together and talk and
talk and talk for two hours or so. In our case, it seldom goes
longer than that. After all, as Disraeli says, there is practically
no question on which two sensible men, smoking cigars, cannot come to an agreement—in time. Only once every three or
four years will I show up prepared to fight to the death for or
against a book—usually *for,* because taking one consideration
with another, we can't hope to come up with thirteen *Huckle-
berry Finns* and *Moby Dicks* a year, can we?"

Instead of answering, I asked Davenport to comment on this
statement by the late John P. Marquand, author of *The Late
George Apley* and B-M-C judge from 1944 to 1960:

. . . There are several faults in the judging system. One,
I think, may be that the judges are too apt to compromise
in the event of a disagreement, and I have seen several
excellent books thrown out for this reason. Another trouble
with the judges is that they know too much about writing.
When they deal with a work of fiction they are apt to tear
its parts to pieces to such an extent that they finally lose
sight of the whole thing. At any rate I think our board is
weak in its selection of novels. We turned down Faulkner's
Intruder in the Dust simply because it made one person

found worthless—"a bad novel and a horrifying story. I've read so much that it
takes a lot to shock me, but that did. . . . I don't want to put my name on the
selection of this book."

nervous. Before my time *The Grapes of Wrath* was turned
down for some similar captious reason. More recently *The
Caine Mutiny* never reached the judges at all. . . . In other
words we are far from being infallible. We do, however,
turn out a fairly conscientious job without being influenced
by commercialism.

By the time I'd finished reading this to him, Basil Davenport,
B.A., had embarked on a classic aside:

"Oh, dear, oh, dear! How shall I answer this? What I need is
a public relations man to tell me how to answer without sounding severe."

He glanced around the deserted fourteenth floor. Seeing no
help in sight, he took a deep breath and went on.

"No one is infallible but the Pope. And nobody knows when
he makes a mistake. We judges find it more difficult to come to
agreement on novels than on nonfiction. A biography of Na-
poleon is either a good one or not. But what about the sensitive
novel of a young girl's awakening?"

What about it? And what about the turbulent Southern
novel, the book about Becket, the Hammond Innes, the Bruce
Catton, the Walter Lord, the Günter Grass, and the polluted
air? What was the outlook for a July selection?

No answer was forthcoming from Basil Davenport (who
dropped dead of a heart attack not long thereafter). He told me
he would rather confine himself to generalities. He concluded
with a whopping one.

"There are a thousand ways in which a book can be good and
tens of thousands of ways a book can be bad."

Having visited the Library of Congress and interviewed the
judges, I knew at least two good reasons why a Book-of-the-
Month is likely to be bad: the dyspepsia of the first readers and
the judges' synthetic, tradesy, nervous disdain for the art they
serve. Or, from jaundiced to jaded.

Clearly the impending meeting would have none of the
spirit of that very first meeting, at which the brand-new judges
flexed their literary muscle with *Lolly Willowes,* or that hun-
dredth-odd meeting, at which Dorothy Canfield Fisher strong-
armed her fellow judges with *Seven Gothic Tales,* or that three-
or four-hundredth meeting, at which Fadiman and Marquand

rammed through *The Catcher in the Rye*. Instead I had found
John Hutchens playing the freshman Congressman, Gilbert
Highet shrouding simple procedure in garrulous mystique,
John Mason Brown treating books and authors like commodities
rather than vessels of talent, Basil Davenport casting around
for a P.R. man, and only the indefatigable Clifton Fadiman
hinting at some reflex of literary zest and relish. Even Fadiman, though, had sounded tinged with culture fatigue—
another Catton, *another* Walter Lord, and, oh, Lord, not an-
othe‡ *Southern* novel!

Put together the conspicuous absence of enthusiasm and the
lack of love I'd encountered, and what have you got? A collection of bibbety-bobbety-boo, like the 1963 roster of Books-of-
the-Month!

[IV]

Recalculating the odds on the forthcoming July selection in
the light of my backstage research, I placed heavy emphasis on
the judges' susceptibility to the inflation and depression that
afflicts people in publishing but should never be allowed to
infect the paying reader. They spoke with such distaste of past
favorites (books *they* had picked)* and with such unenthusiasm
of current contenders (disenchantment with Lord and Catton,
grave reservations about the Southerner and the German,
boredom with Becket, utter uninterest in air pollution or the
storytelling of Hammond Innes) that any kind of synthetic
stampede, I suspected, would win the B-M-C sweepstakes for
July. And as Ralph Thompson kept reminding me, a sudden
"A" book or an upgraded "B" book could storm out of nowhere
and run off with the judges.

There was only one certainty: Whoever won this race would

---

* A splendid sampling of this disenchantment can be found in Charles Lee's
admiring chronology of the club, *The Hidden Public*. On page 180: "Fadiman,
who once raved about *The Story of Mrs. Murphy*, now thinks it was 'not a very
good book.'" On page 182, discussing a 1949 selection, *Hound-Dog Man*: "Fadiman still thinks it is 'an inferior piece of synthetic Americana.'" On page 183,
about a 1950 selection: "Chief advocate of *The Little Princesses* was Dorothy
Canfield Fisher. The other judges would like to forget that they succumbed to
her eloquence. As Fadiman puts it today: 'It is one of the worst books ever
written.'"

certainly lag behind Theodore White, wearing the Literary Guild colors, in the July sweepstakes.* The B-M-C could scarcely hope to compete with this parlay of Teddy White and the Kennedy assassination. But as the front-running club, it would want to make a respectable showing. What was needed at 345 Hudson Street, I concluded prophetically, was a Churchill in a room full of Chamberlains.

For the second Tuesday morning of February, 1965, Clifton Fadiman flew in from Los Angeles. The meeting would start promptly at 11 A.M. A limousine would stand by on Hudson Street, for Fadiman would have to leave by 3:15 P.M. to catch the 4 o'clock jet back to the Coast. John K. Hutchens commuted from his home in Rye, New York, an hour away. Gilbert Highet took a half-hour ride downtown from Columbia. Basil Davenport made a 30-second elevator descent from the fourteenth to the eleventh floor. Only John Mason Brown was absent. He was in Boston, lecturing the Women's Educational and Industrial Union at 11 A.M. But he would phone in from the Ritz-Carlton Hotel two hours later. By then, he was certain, his fellow judges would have reached some consensus.

"We meet with our retinas detached," Brown has said of meetings he attends. "The books tend to arrive in the last week, dim Xerox copies of books that are merciless in length."

The meeting was in the eleventh-floor office of Axel Rosin, president of the club and son-in-law of Harry Scherman. Rosin sits in on the meetings, as do his father-in-law (now chairman of the board), Warren Lynch and Ralph Thompson, but all keep silent unless asked by the judges for factual information.

A long conference table in Rosin's office was set for a business luncheon—silverware and china, plus pencils, pads, a typed list of "A," "B," and "C" books, and a mimeographed list of books scheduled for publication in August, September, and thereafter. (This "futures" list would be taken home by the judges, who might request galleys of any of them prior to the screening by Thompson's staff.)

---

* Book-of-the-Month Club members would scarcely be oblivious to the Literary Guild's rival choice; club surveys show that one-third of its members belong to another book club as well.

Cocktails were served, and toward noon, lunches from Long-champs were wheeled in. Each judge's order had been taken days in advance.

What went on over lunch is a well-guarded secret. But when the cigar smoke had cleared and John Mason Brown had phoned in from Boston and Clifton Fadiman had hurried off to his limousine, one book had emerged from the lunchtime rubble.

It was indeed the dark horse on the outside rail that Ralph Thompson had warned about and I had anticipated.

It all happened as fast as the denouement of a bad murder mystery, in which one crucial clue is withheld or ignored. In this case, however, the clue had been before my eyes for days. It had even lodged itself in a corner of my mind, for in my final computation of the odds, I had used a telltale metaphor.

In the interval between meetings, Sir Winston Churchill had died. The obituaries and headlines and panoply had filled the newspapers and newsmagazines. On the day before his funeral, the Book-of-the-Month Club had mourned him with a full-page advertisement in the New York *Times*. Appearing on the costly back page of the first section, the ad had begun:

"WE WILL BOAST ALL OUR LIVES THAT WE LIVED WHEN WINSTON CHURCHILL WAS ALIVE"
—*The Economist,* London

. . . and his *Legacy of History* can be a treasured memorial in every home. . . .

and had ended with a coupon offering Churchill's *The Second World War* (six volumes, retail value, $39) or his *History of the English-Speaking Peoples* (four volumes, retail value, $24) for $1 a volume with the proverbial "Short Experimental Membership." Even before he was buried, Winston Churchill had been embalmed by the club as thoroughly as Tutankhamen.

It was a crass but fitting send-off for—despite the recent inroads of Michener and Wouk—Churchill, Pearl Buck and John Gunther still rank as the club's big three. Some 6 million books *by* Churchill have been sold as selections (ten in all) or given away as book dividends under the B-M-C imprint.

And now the rich, full life of Winston Churchill was to pay an unexpected dividend to the Book-of-the-Month Club on the second Tuesday of February.

Some years earlier, Lady Violet Bonham Carter, a patroness of the arts in England, had written a memoir of Churchill from 1906 to 1916, when he advanced from Undersecretary for the Colonies to First Lord of the Admiralty. Lady Violet—the daughter of Herbert Henry Asquith, who during those same years advanced from Chancellor of the Exchequer to Prime Minister—describes herself as Churchill's "militant accomplice and confidante" during that decade.

In her *Winston Churchill: An Intimate Portrait,* the unblushing Lady Violet revealed, chattily but tamely, that Sir Winston wore pink silk underwear because of the delicacy of his cuticle. The book had been set in type by an enthusiastic British publisher, but by agreement with Lady Violet, it was not to be published until after its subject's death.

The time was ripe. After ninety glorious years, Sir Winston was dead—but a new Book-of-the-Month author had been born in her eightieth year.* Violet Bonham Carter's first (and thus far, only) book was rushed onto the club's list of "A" books and chosen by the judges. At last the B-M-C stable had a thoroughbred filly, sired by Asquith and befriended by Churchill, to give the Literary Guild's White hope in the Kennedy derby a highly respectable run for the money.**

Of the July candidates, only Hammond Innes and Shelley Mydans went away from 345 Hudson Street empty-handed.*** Of the five other also-rans, the Bruce Catton history later became the August selection, the Southern novel became the summer

---

* Ridiculous though this may sound, the octogenarian Lady Violet is claimed —along with Stephen Vincent Benét, Erich Maria Remarque, André Malraux, and J. D. Salinger—as a club discovery in at least two lists put out by the club on its fortieth birthday in 1966.

** The club's necrophilic passion for books about Churchill continued unabated with a special printing that same July of Jack Fishman's two-year-old biography of Lady Churchill, *My Darling Clementine,* and the subsequent selection, eleven months later, of Churchill's physician's notorious diary, Lord Moran's *Churchill.*

*** *Thomas* later caught on with the Literary Guild and became a popular best seller in the bookstores.

selection, and the Günter Grass, Walter Lord, and air-pollution tomes all became alternates.

Alternates and dividends are not chosen by the judges. They are picked as business decisions by Lynch, Scherman, Rosin, Thompson, and some other club officials who don't sit in on the judges' meetings. While a *selection* merely begins with a first printing of 125,000 or more and can, with listings in the B-M-C *News* over the years, sell close to 1 million through the club (e.g., William Shirer's *Rise and Fall of the Third Reich* and several Churchills), an *alternate* is generally assured of 30,-000 to 60,000 sales in the B-M-C edition. It also counts toward a member's dividend credit.

Because *dividends* are, in effect, given away, the royalty scale is lower than B-M-C's customary 10 percent. But a giveaway total of 150,000 to 200,000 copies can leave a dividend's author and publisher happily dividing some $20,000. And its bookstore fallout is similar to a selection's.

This, then, is the pot of gold to which struggling writers aspire and even knuckle under long after they are established. The Book-of-the-Month Club rewards conformity. For writing the same brand of book over and over, a Walter Lord may not always make the grade as a selection, but he will be looked after as an alternate. And perhaps you wonder why his work shows very little literary growth!

Despite various disclaimers* that B-M-C is not a publishing house, there is a cultural debasement at 345 Hudson Street that occasionally tampers with existing books. In the late 1940's, a decade after swallowing *Gone with the Wind* and *Anthony Adverse* whole, the B-M-C choked when confronted by Ross Lockridge's 1,000-page first novel, *Raintree County*, even though the author had already satisfied the demands of his publisher. The first reader's report recommended it conditionally: "Yes, if cut." The report read:

> This is quite a book. It is inexcusably long, a great, sprawling narrative, bursting at the seams. It contains some of the worst writing produced since Dickens published *The*

---

* "We don't publish *books;* we publish *editions*," the club's secretaries and receptionists explain several times a day to would-be writers seeking shortcuts to fame via direct submissions to the club.

Battle of Life. It bursts into lyrical passages that are mere purple splotches on the page, and it overflows with what in another author would seem to be padding, but in Mr. Lockridge appears to be sheer exuberance of spirit.

The judges took *Raintree County* as their January, 1948, selection but "suggested" certain deletions and changes to Lockridge. The author obliged, thereby surprising one of the judges, who presumed all first novelists to be balky.

Similarly, Thomas Duncan's novel, *Gus the Great,* was selected on the proviso that it would be cut. Duncan delivered the revisions in a matter of days. And *Edwin Booth: Prince of Players* was retitled *Prince of Players: Edwin Booth* on the judges' recommendation.

Anatomy of a Murder, by Robert Traver, offended one judge who selected it; it had an explicitly clinical reference to rape. There was some correspondence between 345 Hudson Street and Ishpeming, Michigan, where Traver (pseudonym for John D. Voelker, himself a judge) resided, and the offending term was voluntarily withdrawn. (Similar excisions have been "suggested" by the Literary Guild on another novel.) But the most steady-handed, clean-cut ritual circumcisions of literature, of course, are performed up near Pleasantville, New York, where Reader's Digest Condensed Books considers and even practices on more books than it will ever abridge. It has been known to seek and obtain postponement of a publication date by plunking down $2,500 for time to make a "trial cut" before determining whether to select. This is almost certainly the vivisection that *Gone with the Wind* would have undergone today, and one wonders what compromises Margaret Mitchell might have had to resist.

It is hardly likely that her publishing house would back her up very emphatically if controversy arose. For as Clifton Fadiman has pointed out: "Today's editor is a confector of books, not an adviser. I don't think we're developing that type anymore. We're developing the shrewd business type. . . . The new operators know that the money isn't to be made in the bound book; it's in the taxidermy rights. So they choose books that will do well in secondary areas," like book clubs. Similarly, Peter Schwed of Simon and Schuster conceded at a trade book clinic,

"Without subsidiary rights, publishers would be out of business." Schwed listed everything from movie sales to wallpaper and scarf rights, but he stressed book clubs as the source of greatest opportunity for extra income.

I had picked a particularly good month to scrutinize the B-M-C's procedures under my journalistic microscope. The July selection, *Winston Churchill: An Intimate Portrait,* was precisely the sort of pallidly gray dark horse that only culture by committee could conjure up. And the "SUGGESTED ALTERNATE for members preferring fiction in place of—or in addition to—the announced Selection" was an absolutely unnecessary two-volume set of *Collected Stories of Sholom Aleichem* ("Retail Price: $10. Price to Members: $5.95. One Book-Dividend Certificate Given With This Purchase")—a nonbargain that owed its very existence to the Book-of-the-Month Club.

Shortly after Tevye the dairyman dawned on Broadway—played by Zero Mostel in the musical *Fiddler on the Roof,* based on several of the stories—the B-M-C contacted a publisher who had laid a small egg with an inexpensive one-volume Sholom Aleichem collection. Would the publisher be interested in redesigning the same stories in an elegant two-volume format featuring Ben Shahn illustrations? If so, the club's sales would make it worth his while.

The publisher said yes, and thus was born another expensive gift book—overpriced for the general consumer, seemingly a bargain for book-club members, and actually a waste of money all around. In the wake of *Fiddler on the Roof,* an astute publisher could easily have unloaded his unsold copies of the original edition and reprinted competently and cheaply if demand warranted.

If the member wanted, he could pay the full $10 to the B-M-C and receive the original-cast album of *Fiddler* as well as the two-volume set. With this package, he would receive *two* book-dividend certificates.

The club was also willing to sell him the album à la carte for $4.98 monaural or $5.98 stereo. With it he would receive *one* book-dividend certificate. With original-cast albums and *Winnie-the-Pooh* record packages, it is already possible to fulfill one's membership obligations to the Book-of-the-Month Club without ever buying a book.

It is even easier to remain a member in good standing without ever *reading* a book. The club once unloaded 26,000 one-volume abridgments of Arnold Toynbee's *A Study of History* in a single month. John P. Marquand, a judge at the time, remarked that he'd spent five hopeless hours with Toynbee before giving it up. At the instant Marquand put Toynbee down and forever after, he couldn't remember a single thing he'd read there.

Discussing the Toynbee syndrome in *Harper's* magazine, novelist Merle Miller once attributed it in part

> to the fact that the book is a beautiful piece of furniture—it is decorative and gives the home an intellectual air as well. After all, you don't *have* to read it; conveniently, the thesis of Dr. Toynbee's many-volume work is still further digested into 11½ pages in the Appendix.

The furniture book—that oversized and undernecessary decorative cornerstone to the heap of culture it takes to make a house a home—may well be the book-club industry's major contribution to American literature. Bear this in mind whenever you see *Tutankhamen* or Toynbee reposing unread on a coffee table, alongside or on top of *American Heritage* or *Réalités,* in a living room lined with Will Durants and Winston Churchills.

As soon as the judges' meeting had ended, Ralph Thompson, Warren Lynch, and Axel Rosin, who had sat in on the deliberations, phoned the seven publishers of "A" books. At six publishing houses, there were curses or back-to-the-drawing-board stoicism or even sober second looks at a losing book's budget. At the seventh, there was rejoicing.

The busiest people that Tuesday afternoon were chief reader Thompson and executive vice-president Lynch, the two key men in the overrating process that was already underway. For even before the judges have left their chamber, the machinery is whirring to package literature (such as it is) and presell it so persuasively to a semicaptive audience that the final product must inevitably disappoint.

Wearing his other hat as editor of the Book-of-the-Month Club *News,* Ralph Thompson had to assign a "selling" review of the Churchill book. He usually approaches the most enthusiastic of the judges. In this case, it was Basil Davenport, who promptly proclaimed that Lady Violet Bonham Carter's book, "written with great style and acuity, is without parallel in Churchill literature." Thompson also began rounding up biographical data on Lady Violet.

Both of these articles had to be in Thompson's hands within two weeks, for the Churchill book would be featured in the June B-M-C *News*. As much as the New York *Times* Sunday Book Review or the *Saturday Review,* the Book-of-the-Month Club *News* can safely be termed one of the most influential book publications in America. It reaches more than half a million book *buyers* (not just book browsers or book lovers or book talkers) who find it compelling for at least one good reason:

If they don't examine the News *when it comes in the mail, they may automatically receive a book they don't want.*

This is the basic ground rule of the topsy-turvy edifice that mail-order science has built at 345 Hudson Street. In doing so, Harry Scherman and his heirs have made book buying a passive act of nonresistance. You sit back and receive the book, either through choice or apathy. That tangible and promising monument to an author's hard work, *the book,* comes no longer as a pleasurable experience but as the ultimate in negation, handed to you by your postman: *your punishment for neglecting to mail in your rejection.*

Critics are paid, in part, to reject books that will waste the public's time. Editors are paid, in part, to reject books that will waste their publishers' money. But only the book-club business makes its public pay for computerized lessons in *how to reject books.* With the average age of B-M-C members plunging downward (in recent years, it has gone from over forty to the mid-twenties), it may soon be possible to go from regarding books as homework to regarding books as rejects without any pleasurable interruption at all.

Once the July selection had passed out of Ralph Thompson's editorial domain with a rave notice in the B-M-C *News,* it entered the territory of Warren Lynch, who is in charge of advertising.

For many years, the club's ad copy simply hewed to Harry

Scherman's initial approach of telling how the system worked (photos of the judges and this title: "THE BEST NEW BOOK EACH MONTH IS SELECTED BY THIS COMMITTEE AND SENT YOU REGULARLY ON APPROVAL"). But now that the club has achieved institutional status and other clubs have copied its procedure, the ad takes a different tone—ready, wheedling, and available to cure the reader's cultural bad breath:

> IN THE NEXT TWO PAGES you will find forty-seven books listed and all together the list presents an excellent opportunity to check up on some bad reading habits you may have been acquiring unconsciously. Perhaps you have been allowing the *sheer busyness of your life* to keep you from reading new books you have been really anxious not to miss. Why not arrange to have these particular books delivered to you infallibly? *If they are actually in your home,* constantly before your eyes, reminding you of your good intentions, sooner or later you will surely find time to read them. *This certain insurance against missing* books you are anxious to read has always been the prime advantage of membership in the *Book-of-the-Month Club.*

But the other side of this two-faced coin was revealed seven years ago in Harry Scherman's lecture at the Library of Congress, where he revealed that the club's annual turnover of members is 40 percent.* Scherman gave this explanation of why members resign:

> . . . they find themselves not reading as much as they had intended. The books pile up, just as unread issues of magazines pile up. So they stop; but then soon again find themselves oppressed by a feeling of intellectual fallowness, by the same sense of missing out on important reading. They then re-subscribe. How many "repeaters" there have been over the . . . years we have never calculated, but the net number is probably somewhere between 2½ and 3 million.

Warren Lynch, who proved to be an affable but wary middle-aged businessman, added to my turnover lore. "The most pro-

---

* No details on this turnover are given out by the club on the grounds that they would "give aid and comfort to our rivals." While some outside estimates range higher than 40 percent, several book-club experts told me that an annual turnover of more than 60 percent could be fatal to a large book club.

ductive mailing list we know of for new offers is our list of old members who canceled." That the Book-of-the-Month Club indeed values its mailing lists is indicated in *The Hidden Public,* Charles Lee's history of the club:

> . . . the enrollee's name goes through a variety of recording processes, is filed according to both a geographical and an alphabetical arrangement, and is listed with other members' names in a special bank vault in northern New Jersey specifically maintained against the possibility of atomic destruction of the company's regular records.

This passage conjures up a sick vision of a book lucking into the role of First Fallout Selection of the Book-of-the-Month Club. I could see hundreds of thousands of copies going out automatically to readers who wouldn't be around to send in their rejection slips—until Lynch informed me: "That was before our computerized data processing. I don't *think* we have the vault anymore. But we do keep one set of membership records in another building in case there's a fire or the building blows up."

While these names are still on the *active* list, the club is constantly surveying them. Dr. George Gallup sits on the club's board of directors. Since 1947, his polling organization has interviewed a cross section of the members every year to ascertain which of the previous year's thirteen selections went unread. They are also asked to rank whichever books they purchased on a scale of descending pleasure. From these polls comes the flowery phrase, "index of satisfaction," which ranges from +246 for *Kon-Tiki* to −7 for *Voss.* Runners-up to *Kon-Tiki* are *The Rise and Fall of the Third Reich* and *Cheaper by the Dozen.* Surprisingly, *The Catcher in the Rye* and Thomas Mann's *Doctor Faustus* have low satisfaction indexes while those of *The Cruel Sea, The Sea Around Us,* and *Endurance: Shackleton's Incredible Voyage* were remarkably high. This may have to do with the nautical theme. More likely, though, it has to do with the contemporary reader's thirst for detailed nonfiction and realistic novels. Only four novels—*Hawaii, Advise and Consent, The Ugly American,* and *The Old Man and the Sea*—rank among Dr. Gallup's top thirty.

Dr. Gallup has also sought to "profile" the club's members, which is no easy task with a heavy annual turnover. But the new hard-core audience of the club seems to be young married couples. In an essay for the Book-of-the-Month Club *News* in April, 1966, social critic William K. Zinsser wrote that *motivation* was the biggest spur to this crowd:

> When they were in college they swallowed books in huge quantities. Later, sprung into the more urgent world of diaper-changing and dishwashing, they gave up all reading except the morning paper and Dr. Spock.
> It is somewhere in this period that guilt comes creeping, often in the guise of a Book-of-the-Month Club ad. . . .

To which Harry Scherman has added: "It is natural for them to turn to us, if only because the sheer convenience makes it seem the best solution to their backsliding."

Sitting in Warren Lynch's office as he plied me with authorized statistics and surveys, I suddenly blurted out an unauthorized question. "What would happen if you made one small change in your procedure: Instead of having to write in to *reject* a book, the member would have to write in to accept it?"

My naïveté gave Lynch such a visible jolt that I felt impelled to add: "What I'm asking isn't terribly farfetched, you know. It's pretty much the way the Book Society operates in England." (I didn't bother to add that the Book Society's sale generally runs between 5,000 and 7,000 for each monthly offering.)

After a long minute, still eyeing me warily, Lynch replied: "The acceptance of our books wouldn't be as great as it is. It takes an effort to send in the form. Frankly, I doubt if any book club would be in existence on a large scale with such a system. Our method is one of the immutable laws that we don't question."

It occurred to me then and there that the "immutable law" I was confronting was that of cart-before-horse, alias tail-wagging dog. It is a doctrine that threatens every art whenever *procedures* (such as choosing a committee of eminent "names") and *externals* (be they marble culture centers or dirty words in J. D. Salinger) take precedence over the art form itself.

The Book-of-the-Month Club was one of the best ideas of the twentieth century, but the symptoms of its current arteriosclerosis were there in infancy. The judges' innate cantankerousness aged into bland consensus. Membership shifted from on approval to automatic shipment. Competition dictated sacrificing individuality to bigness. Adventurousness, surprise, and controversy gave way to the kind of aspiration to adequacy implicit in an index of satisfaction. The old judges grew tired, and the new judges tiptoed onstage timorously. And when, in that chain of events, the book itself was relegated from hero to walk-on, the cart forged ahead of the horse.

The Second Commandment of the Culture Vultures:
Render kind words unto amateurs, and you
will inherit their earthly gratitude.

2

The Would-Be-Writer Industry

[1]

EVEN the Book-of-the-Month Club, which influences it so greatly, cannot forecast what will happen in the literary world later this year. One small prediction can be ventured, however, for it is as inevitable as Santa Claus and New Year's Eve: Toward the end of the year, editors will be stuffing stamped addressed envelopes with rejected manuscripts keyed to such impending events as the 53d birthday of crossword puzzles and the 32d anniversary of King Edward VIII's abdication.

Rehashing the Duke of Windsor's love life is a regular "Idea a Day for December" recipe served up in a would-be writer's trade journal, *Writer's Digest* ("Conduct a public opinion poll in your city—would most have done the same thing? You might query marriage counselors!")

Somewhere between the sublime and the ridiculous lies a vast American industry that manufactures endless lists, mass-produces useless formulas, packages false hope, and offers encouragement to thousands who yearn for self-expression, instant immortality, or easy money through the printed word.

"Live a richer, fuller life . . . enjoy the rewards and prestige of a writer," the Famous Writers School of Westport, Connecticut, implores. "There is no seniority or job prejudice in writing." The Famous Writers School estimates the opportunities open to people who can write at a total of $20 billion a year.

Another correspondence school, the Newspaper Institute of America, proclaims that Mrs. I. M. Sheck of Browning, Montana, "earns $60 each month in spare time—writing the N.I.A. way." The N.I.A. way begins with a three-page aptitude test as any ambitious newcomer's key to the "Hundred-Million-Dollar Free-Lance-Writing Field."

The road to literary fame and fortune, being open to everybody, is naturally a crowded one. A "vanity" publisher, whose authors pay to be printed, has estimated that at least a million Americans have sat down to or seriously intended to write a book. Citing one minor statistic, he added: "At one time, I had an active list of a hundred thirty-five thousand people who write verse."

Any industry whose entrepreneurs include Bennett Cerf, Faith Baldwin, and Bruce Catton (founders of the Famous Writers School) and whose hired hands include Mark Harris, Kurt Vonnegut, Jr., and Nelson Algren (on writers' conference faculties) must have something to recommend it. Some of these "names" have actually earned their livings from good writing. But the would-be-writer industry thrives on the axiom that there are also livings to be made from bad writing.

This gospel is preached for profit by the trade bibles. The editorial tone of *Writer's Digest* is almost identical with its advertising. Both voices insist that *you* can write no matter who you are—and don't let anybody tell you otherwise. Inspiration tumbles over inspiration; exclamation points abound. ("W-h-e-e-e!" begins one cover ad.) One recent issue contained ads for five agents who will read anything legible (for a fee), twelve editors who can fix almost anything (for a fee), five correspondence courses, nine vanity presses, three literary ghosts, one querying service, and nine publishers in desperate need of "song poems."

The largest single advertiser in *Writer's Digest,* however, is *Writer's Digest* itself. That same issue featured thirteen house ads promoting *Writer's Digest's* own Beginner's Individual Course in Short Story Writing; its own manuscript-criticism service ($4 minimum per poem); a $4.95 book, *Freelancer's Treasury of Article Ideas,* and a *Writer's Market Service.* The latter is a loose-leaf directory updated every three or four weeks. For $17 a year, it will tell you that the *National Insider* buys 1,500 articles a year, the *American Weekly* has ceased publication, and the minimum length for novels at Thomas Bouregy and Company is now 50,000 words.

The *Digest*'s rival, the *Writer*, tempers gaudy hopes with a certain amount of grayish caution. Occasionally it even says something relevant about writing, as in an article on the importance of revision ("Don't Lick the Stamp Yet," by Barbara Robinson). The *Writer*'s more spartan philosophy may be one reason why its monthly circulation is only in the vicinity of 30,000 while *Writer's Digest*'s hovers around 50,000. But the *Writer* can be as sappy as its most affluent rival. It, too, compiles absurd rosters: *Oral Hygiene, Safety Education, Dixie Dairyman,* and *Coins* magazines appear on the same market list for manuscripts as *Popular Science* and *Paris Review*.

Every spring both the *Writer* and *Writer's Digest* list summer writers' conferences, and every summer an estimated 5,000 to 8,000 Americans flock to these scenic outposts of the would-be-writer industry much as the ailing converge on Lourdes.

"Bread Loaf is not a how-to-do-it school," said *Saturday Review* poet and lecture-circuit lion John Ciardi, who directs the two-week conference in Vermont. "I sometimes think it is more nearly a confessional in which people who have spent their lives at the writing process itemize their failures while clinging to their hopes."

The American ritual of holding a writers' conference originated at Bread Loaf, in the Green Mountains, only forty-two years ago, around the time of ferment when the Book-of-the-Month Club was born. Today there are more than sixty notches in the borscht belt of literature. Some conferences, notably Bread Loaf's and Indiana University's, boast the loftiest ivory towers on the would-be-writer horizon. A few, such as the Humor and Comedy Writers' Conference at Rosoff's Restaurant in Manhattan, are belligerently trivial. Others (the Pemaquid Seminar in Reading and Writing at Damariscotta, Maine; Pineywoods Writers' Conference in Nacogdoches, Texas; the New York City Writers' Conference on picturesque Staten Island; Writers' Week in Pasadena, etc.) fall somewhere in between.

The writers' conferences' most clearly visible means of support are the Helen Hokinson ladies who turn up with checkbooks, much-thumbed manuscripts, lonely hearts, and vague yearnings to write like Fanny Hurst or Faith Baldwin.

Their pens and pencils dutifully record every pedantic noise made by speakers who ought to know better: "the structural mathematics of plotting," "etymology of words," "thematic dynamics," "the furniture of the book" (i.e., bibliography and index). Their notebooks must chronicle with stenographic realism the memorable moment one summer at Bread Loaf when Professor Theodore Morrison of Harvard harrumphed that Robert Frost "never was a man who 'put on a persona,' to use the popular phrase."

Occasionally a Nelson Algren or even a Brock Brower bares his soul and his creed most eloquently on the conference platform. The ladies listen respectfully and then pepper him with questions about how wide margins should be, the relative advantages of double spacing and triple spacing, and whether permission is needed to quote from Washington's Farewell Address.

"Talk is the Bread Loaf product," said Ciardi, who might have described it more accurately as talk-talk-talk. One hardworking writer's reaction to two weeks of it was apparent when Nelson Algren electrified Bread Loaf's final clinic with this comprehensive advice to would-be writers:

"Never eat at a place called Mom's. Never play cards with a man named Doc. And never sleep with anyone whose troubles are worse than your own."

Algren's remarks may have been more useful than a dozen sermons about writing, for at most conferences the ratio of nontalent to talent is high. Critic Granville Hicks once deplored this after an Antioch Writers' Conference. At Bread Loaf several faculty members estimated (and my own observations would tend to confirm) that 145 people who are not now and never will be writers are subsidizing about 5 who may have some good writing in them.

Almost every conference claims at least one novel that was discovered there. Bread Loaf's pride is *The Big Sky*, by A. B. Guthrie, Jr. Contacts may be more easily made in sylvan settings than in Manhattan reception rooms, but the "discoveries" are needles in haystacks. At Bread Loaf one summer, the first drop-out was a naïve fledgling writer who left in disgust because nobody had offered him a contract. Most writers' conferences make no promises, but perhaps they ought to post the odds.

[II]

While the summer writers' conferences are in hibernation, the year-round creative workshops are in session. These vary in quality from place to place and even from year to year. Currently the fashionable one is Paul Engle's Iowa Writers' Workshop. Because not everyone can make his way to Iowa City, Engle's workshop has hooked up with the most aggressive arm of the would-be-writer industry: the home-study packagers. Now, through *Encyclopaedia Britannica*'s correspondence-course program, you can take an Iowa fiction-writing course "so designed that you will receive a constant, personal criticism of your lessons and manuscripts by the staff that has for so long offered 'hard criticism and decent sympathy' to resident students. Because of the nature of home study, you are their class of one." Thus far, the Iowa sell has been far softer than Famous Writers School's assurance: "We can teach you how to write."

Some mail-order moguls remind you insistently that Margaret Mitchell was a housewife when she dashed off *Gone with the Wind,* Jonathan Swift dean of a cathedral when he scribbled *Gulliver's Travels,* which also made a swell movie, and Zane Grey a dentist.

Other institutes rely on personal persuasion. I used my wife's name in sending for one correspondence school's brochure. My wife received the mail, plus, a few evenings later, a phone call from the school's field representative. (One school, I've learned, gives its salesmen the title of "registrars.") He wished to discuss "your background, your aspirations, and—most important—the depth of your interest in writing." On the basis of a few questions and answers, he was empowered to recommend her for instant enrollment.

It should be noted, however, that most postal academies rely on entrance exams to keep out misfits. The Newspaper Institute's is in three parts. The first is a page of "CONFIDENTIAL— Personal Information," the most personal of which is "What is your age? (optional if over twenty-one but specific answer is desired)." The other confidential questions cover such secrets as what magazines you read regularly, travel, literary aspirations, and abilities. Several of the questions hint at a bright future: "Are you interested in becoming a member of the writing staff of a newspaper or magazine? . . . If so, and should we feel justified in recommending you to an Editor, in what locality would you prefer to work? . . . Are you interested in qualifying as a spare-time local correspondent for an out-of-town newspaper? . . . Do you look to free-lance writing as a means of ( ) adding to your income? ( ) a hobby? ( ) primarily to express yourself? ( ) broadening your cultural horizons?"

My wife was amused by the grammar of "free-lance writing as a means of primarily to express yourself," so she checked it off and went on to Part Two. This starts out with a drawing of a disaster at a railroad crossing. Strewn about the wreckage are a car, a signpost, two men, a gun, a whiskey bottle, and assorted clues. The applicant is supposed to play news reporter and jot down the "Who-What-When-Where-Why-and-How" of the story. "Do not write the complete story now. Just let us have your notes."

The third and final part is a test for "dramatic perception . . . deductive reasoning power and . . . constructive and creative imagination." A story of romance and murder on a lonely country road is told in a style worthy of the old *Look* Photocrimes that could be solved while waiting in barbershops. The story's only rewards are what is left unsaid, such as "Gail Winslow's _____ excited John Clarkson." My wife dutifully followed instructions, read the story through, and then filled in the blanks. At the end, she was allowed space to finish the story for the tired hack who started it. One of his few complete sentences was: "The farm hand came forward to tell of seeing John Clarkson near the scene, with a woman in his car the farm hand had not recognized." The test's final admonition was: "IMPORTANT: Do not attempt to pass judgment on your own work. Mail your Test as soon as possible."

The Famous Writers School gives a more complex eight-part admissions test. At least one professional journalist has been denied admission. In 1962 Gerald Walker, then the president of the Society of Magazine Writers, took the Famous Writers

School test. "I did as bad a job as I could, and they flunked me," Walker told me, "so they must run an honest shop."

Advised of Walker's identity, Gordon Carroll, director of the Famous Writers School, responded ungraciously. "Mr. Walker's experience is not unique; we flunk large numbers of prospective students for a simple and ethical reason. We do not believe that you can teach semiliterates or morons to write, and we consistently refuse to enroll them."

The experience must have taken its toll on Walker, for shortly thereafter he left the "Hundred-Million-Dollar Free-Lance-Writing Field" to go to work as an articles editor at the New York *Times* Magazine.

The lessons offered by the home-study packagers are mostly sound. Some of the criticism the buyer gets is indeed detailed. One student submitted some of Joseph Conrad's better work as his own. He received drastic editing by return mail.

A reputable literary agent who looked into the mail-order method said, however, "Only one percent of would-be writers are *ready* to benefit from such lessons." It is also a badly kept trade secret that most literary correspondence courses barely break even on the diligent student who completes all his lessons. The profits come from the early dropouts.

[III]

For would-be authors who consider themselves ready for marketing (and in his heart of hearts, what alumnus of the Famous Writers School doesn't?), the industry offers more specialized guidance—by literary agents who charge appraisal fees. One of them, A. L. "Lucky" Fierst, not long ago lowered his minimum from $10 to $5 because "this fantastic book market has brought me so many calls that I cannot supply enough good books to meet the demand." Scott Meredith, whose advertising features "29 typical checks" from publishers, is holding the line at $15 for small books under 10,000 words and "$10 per story or article up to 10,000 words, plus $1 per thousand words for additional thousands."

A former employee of an agency that advertises heavily for manuscripts told me:

"We had one submission whose first sentence was: 'Black

Abraham Lincoln S.O.B. in a casket.' From there on, it went downhill.

"It was against company policy to tell the author his work was hopeless. First, I wrote to him that it lacked plotting. Well, he fixed that up with a few more ravings. Then I wrote to him that it had no hero. When it came back again, I wrote to him that it had no point of view. Then no sentence structure, no dialogue, no sex. . . .

"Anyway, when it had been mailed to me fifty times at five dollars a throw, I began to get nervous. I wrote to the man that his work wasn't really very salable and maybe it ought to be retired. Two days later, I got a long-distance call from the man's wife: 'Please don't stop writing to him. Your letters and my visits are all he lives for since we committed him.' "

Another alumnus of one of these agencies—*factories* would be a better word—told me:

"During a good week, I would read and report on as many as forty short stories, articles, TV or radio scripts, and perhaps five book-length manuscripts of fiction, poetry, or save-the-world-before-it's-too-late preachments.

"It was a Niagara of verbiage. Everyone in the world seemed to be writing a book, and a good portion of the authors required our services not only as critics but as confessors, psychotherapists, and pen pals.

"As far as *I* was aware, none were in mental institutions, but many were ripe candidates. And at least two enclosed with their manuscripts little slips from prison censors giving permission for their publication."

All factories have their rules. At one, no manuscript could be returned with less than two single-spaced pages of comment, and book-length manuscripts required at least five pages. Moreover, each had to be read carefully, for a client was likely to write in months later and ask whether Alice should have kissed Freddy there, in that crucial scene in Chapter 12.

"Incredible as it seems," said a man who used to work there, "we learned to remember plots by the hundreds, storing them in our minds like little spools of thread, to be unwound the instant there was need.

"When it came to remembering nonfiction books, however,

we had to rely on formulas. Authors of diatribes and lengthy expositions on such subjects as the need for a revised world calendar received condolences for the backwardness of a public not yet ready for such advanced thinking. Autobiographers required more tact. After all, one couldn't simply inform them that their lives were too dull or their names too insignificant to interest readers.

"We were forever cudgeling our brains to find words enough to fill the required number of pages of commentary, but Everett, a septuagenarian who lived with his son in a small Southern town, was the client who most taxed our imaginations. Everett's specialty was religion in politics, or vice versa; it was difficult to tell where one began and the other left off. It was his brevity that gave us trouble. Once he sent in a manuscript consisting of eleven words. It went something like this: 'The brazen bull came down upon us, bright in the sun.' He was alluding to Eisenhower, as I remember, and the title was *Everett's Thesis, Subhead B.*

"The only time Everett became angry with us was when someone failed to discuss his theses in proper order. It seemed that some imbecile had failed to note that *Everett's Thesis, Subhead C* linked *Subhead B* with *Subhead D*. The world, he feared, would never forgive him for failing to present his ideas with clarity and logic.

"Though I must have written at least ten thousand words of advice and comment to Everett on his magnum opus, I never had the slimmest idea what it was all about. Every installment, however, even the eleven-worder, cost him five dollars."

Why did the clients hang on?

"Some of them simply to have someone to correspond with," was one reply. "There was this California masseur who dropped us a line every now and then, describing his thoughts while kneading the flesh. The fat, rich customers inspired him to his highest peaks of eloquence. But he did well, too, whenever he had an attractive young female on his hands. Too bad he couldn't put his thoughts into anything printable!"

Others responded to faint praise as though it were adrenalin, and I have come upon an interoffice memo that takes cognizance of this.

A good *fee letter* is one with the most sincere-sounding and persuasive balance of criticism and praise. If a first submission, open with kind words for the writer's literary style. If he happens to be semi-literate, suggest mildly that he polish his prose—a mere nothing, it is implied, for a person of his obvious talent.

Next comes the [ostensible] reason why the manuscript has to be returned as unsalable, after which are added a few routine remarks about the proper way to organize an article or story. It is always lack of organization or poor choice of subject matter that forces a submission to be returned—*reluctantly!*

For a close, insert a little pep talk and a line or two expressing admiration for some real or invented merit of the author's style or handling.

Sign off with an exhortation to try again. This last is always built around the metaphor of "hitting the target." Successive letter elaborate on this idea: "you're inching toward the bull's-eye" . . . "you scattered your shots this time" . . . "you got buck fever," etc., etc.

At this particular factory, perhaps 1 manuscript out of 500 was selected for actual *submission* to any kind of publisher. Of all that one alumnus read, only one-tenth of 1 percent—or one book and three articles—ever were sold.

Some factories maintain canned paragraphs of encouragement. A reader will skim a manuscript and scrawl a note to the secretary: "Send him paragraphs A, D, G, and L." Others pay readers on a piecework basis; a while back the going rate was $1 per manuscript read and criticized.

"We must have made a strange and depressing picture," recalls one reader, "we scavengers, in our tiny room with five or six desks cheek by jowl, our typewriters going like machine guns, scanning a manuscript in five minutes, beating out a report, hustling to a file for another armload of manuscripts, lugging bulging briefcases home and back to the office, reading, reading, reading frantically, sixty or seventy hours a week. But it was the only way we could earn a subsistence.

"A good fee man could earn eighty or ninety dollars a week, if he worked at night, and one phenomenon got up to a hundred twenty-five dollars, for which he must have had to read and report on at least eighty short stories at a dollar apiece and nine novels at five dollars. I often wonder if he ended as cracked as some of our clients.

"It wasn't easy for our boss to find and keep good fee men, and few women could stand the pace. One fee man went berserk after a few weeks and, shrieking curses on all writers, scattered a book manuscript all over the room. Another was sacked for being too harsh and acidulous with the clients. Most simply got out while their sanity was intact.

"Oddly enough, there was never any problem getting eager applicants for the jobs. A small advertisement would bring dozens of letters. Some of them came from writers with impressive lists of sales. Most came from college students and schoolteachers."

Ironically, the principal talents to emerge from these boiler rooms have been not the would-be writers but these semistarving *readers!* One of them was the poet Allen Ginsberg, who used to agonize over every manuscript he received. He often wrote just one letter and earned one dollar in a whole afternoon.

Ginsberg's career as a talent scout came to an end not because he was unproductive but because his punctuation was poor. His letters were sent out over the name of the agency chief, who grew embarrassed and let Ginsberg go. If any client still possesses an encouraging letter in which *isn't* is consistently spelled *is'nt* and *don't* is spelled *do'nt,* he may own a collector's item.

Few others who answer the ads will be that amply rewarded. While all agents have the right to charge reading fees, most of the good ones don't. And hardly any of them advertise.*

Manuscript doctoring—or "editing" for a fee—is the custom branch of these assembly-line agenting factories. One, which deals mainly in book-length works, charges a particularly low fee for a first reading. The report that the client receives is almost invariably enthusiastic—but regretful. Alas and alack, it is one of those "almost publishable" efforts—very nearly in shape for submission and probable sale but in need of editing, rewriting, and polishing. For a sum, anywhere from $50 to

---

* A reasonably trustworthy list may be obtained from the Society of Authors' Representatives Inc., 101 Park Avenue, New York City.

$150, an editor will furnish the writer with a lengthy analysis of the book, together with a suggested outline for rewriting it.

The client does indeed receive his outline (often done on a freelance basis for $25 or $30 by a competent, though currently unemployed, editor), but the manuscript is almost always incapable of being brought to anything approaching a publishable state, with or without editorial guidance. About all that such help buys is the assurance that to avoid prosecution for fraud, the agent will later make a token effort to peddle the "finished" manuscript.

Because this work is sporadic, manuscript doctoring is less smoothly administered than the main factory. Thus a client sometimes receives two almost identical "first letters" on two different would-be books and often, but not always, sees the light. Occasionally a manuscript is lost. Or perhaps a client receives two conflicting reports signed by the same person. It is then necessary to invent an ambitious but imbecilic office assistant who took it on himself to deal with matters outside his province. "He was, of course, immediately dismissed." One client even possesses two virtually identical letters about, presumably, the same office assistant. He was fired twice within a month just for his handling of this one client's work.

Every now and then, usually at quitting or firing time, one of the "scavengers" will rebel and send a letter telling all to the client. One young man wrote such a confession to a little old lady in New England with whom he had been corresponding for a year (above his boss' signature). This time, he signed it with his own name and home address. This is the reply he received:

"You are a nasty young man—a disloyal, Satan-hearted employee. [Your former employer] has written to me that I am on the verge of a great literary success, and I'll thank you to remember that I have absolute faith in his opinion."

[IV]

For the would-be-writer industry, there may not be a sucker born every minute, but on the average at least one is published every day. This year, at least 500 hard-cover books will be issued by Pageant, Carlton, Exposition, Vantage, and eight other vanity presses. The Federal Trade Commission estimates the cost borne by each author as ranging "from about $900 up to $6,000, depending upon the book's size and the initial printing order." Forgotten already, most of last year's vanity volumes today clutter warehouses, attics, and remainder counters. Buried beneath their dust jackets are faded hopes, life savings, and hard labors. After all, it usually takes just as much effort to write a bad novel as a good one.

"The 'vanity press' charges a grim price for flattery," says a pamphlet called *Consumer Alert,* issued by the F.T.C. in Washington.

"Yet the price is paid willingly by naïve but determined authors too ready to believe assurances from vanity editors that literary hopes and even fame can be realized—for the payment, in advance, of a 'cooperative' publishing subsidy.

"The F.T.C. has no quarrel with a writer's willingness to pay to have his book published, but it does narrow an eye at flattery and misrepresentations used to exploit him. . . .

"To flatter an author for the sole purpose of taking his money is a deceptive practice which can be halted by an F.T.C. order, but this is small consolation for the victimized writer whose hard work and high hopes have been abused in order to provide the vanity publisher's quick profit. . . ."

The F.T.C. *Consumer Alert* cites this pattern:

"The vanity publisher invites an author (usually through advertising) to submit his manuscript for sincere and constructive evaluation [free of charge] by an impartial expert. Good news is not long in coming. The author is told his manuscript has been accorded 'the most enthusiastic reader reports in many a month. . . .'

"With this bait in the sales trap, there ensues correspondence lathered with literary jargon and sprinkled with breathtaking (but carefully vague) references to promotional advertising, multiple editions, foreign sales, and movie and TV rights, best-seller lists, and literary awards.

"Next comes the contract whose fine print has the effect of requiring the author to pay all costs of the first (and nearly always the last) edition. The same fine print spares the publisher any solid financial responsibility for promoting the book.

"In short, the 'co-operative publishing plan' assures the profits to the vanity publisher and the costs to the author. The cost, incidentally, must be paid in advance."

An F.T.C. attorney cited this list of come-ons and, in italics, what they really mean:

Your book will be copyrighted in your name! *This costs $4 and is standard practice.*

You will receive a 40 percent royalty, which is much higher than the 10 or 15 percent paid by a regular publisher! *You have already paid all publishing expenses, so it is your own money you are receiving, and you will be lucky to recoup even $100 of it.*

Your book will be advertised! *Perhaps once or twice along with several other vanity books. Even if you offer to pay for additional advertising, you will find that many periodicals do not accept advertising of vanity books.* Ironically, even the Famous Writers School's magazine rejects vanity press advertising.

Your book will be sent to reviewers! *At your expense. But it is highly unlikely that major newspapers will review a book with a vanity imprint.*

Your book will be handled by a salesman! *If so, he will be working on commission and selling books of many publishers. You have no guarantee that he will show or even mention your book to those on whom he calls.*

You will appear on radio and TV! *If you yourself can wangle the opportunity.*

You will have autograph parties! *If you can arrange them with local bookstores and agree to invite enough of your own friends.*

Advance publicity releases will be sent to the nation's press! *To newspapers in your hometown, perhaps.*

The F.T.C. tells the story of a minister's widow, who submitted a book-length manuscript that her late husband had written for boys. The vanity publisher's interoffice report on it was: "This is a preposterous, sentimental, badly written adventure story about teen-age boys. The plot makes very little sense."

The same firm's report to the widow was:

I found [the manuscript] the kind of straightforward, clean teen-age boys' book that is a pleasure to read. . . .

There is enough excitement and adventure in this story to make it highly appealing to any red-blooded American youth. . . . I think your husband wrote very well, with an excellent sense of plot development. The mystery unfolds cleverly, sustaining even this much older reader's attention.

Later came the contract, with provision for 40 percent royalties and still later, a "co-operative publishing" bill for $1,320.

"I am very anxious to get my husband's work published because, as you can see, he has put so much of himself into his writing," the widow explained at the time. "I am living on a minister's pension and have two children still at home. . . . I am very ignorant of the cost of printing and didn't realize that it would cost that much. I have friends from whom I could borrow the money, but am a little doubtful as to the wisdom of such a move."

Reassured by her publisher, however, she plunged ahead, and this is her epilogue, as told to the F.T.C.: "I had to do all kinds of odd jobs at the age of sixty-two because I never disclosed the real tragedy to my children until I got every cent of the money repaid." It was small consolation that the F.T.C. put the publisher under an order, backed by a potential fine of $5,000 per day, to stop such misrepresentations for all time.

The F.T.C. contends that "the vanity boys are hard put to refer you to any happy former customers," but this does not appear to be the case. Exposition Press advertises dozens of case histories, including:

> #5. O. W. "BILL" HAYES: *Your Memory—Speedway to Success.* 5th ed. Writing, teaching, lecturing, plus LP record album sale. Author nominated for Lt. Gov. of Texas. 54,000 in print.

The liveliest book that Exposition Press ever published, however, was its founder's own confessional, *The Rogue of Publisher's Row,* by Edward Uhlan (1956). Like most vanity-press authors, Mr. Uhlan didn't receive the editing he needed. But his book offers a revealing insight into the techniques of subsidy or cooperative publishing, as its practitioners insist on calling themselves.

"Much of the censure that subsidy publishing has been subject to has been justified in my opinion, and is mainly due to the built-in larceny of the contract itself," Uhlan admits.

Later he cites this example: "I have before me a subsidy publishing contract similar to the one you may receive. . . . The contract specifies a first edition 'not exceeding 2,500 copies.' This, of course, gives the publisher the *legal* right to print as few as, say, 400 copies, as has happened. Meanwhile, you envision a sale of 2,500 copies, at a dollar royalty per copy."

When I contacted Uhlan, he said I would be naïve to confine my studies of subsidy publishing to the self-confessed vanity houses.

"Virtually every big-name publisher now has a subsidy department," Uhlan insisted. "These all have euphemistic names, such as Business Department, Author Participation Plan, or Industrial Bank Relations Division." From a number of offers that come a free-lance writer's way each year ("The president of the company has placed a prepublication offer for 73,000 copies of a company history, so all we have to do is come up with a writer who'll play it safe, accurate, and readable" . . . "There's a politician who wants a campaign biography, and his people'll prepay," etc.) and from outfits like Books for Business, Inc., and other packagers and publishers, I would guess that Uhlan is not far off target.

Exposition's rival, Pageant Press, advertises "$202,573 TO WRITERS!" paid out in royalties and other earnings over a seven-year period. There is no mention of what was paid in.

Vantage Press takes the prestige approach. Its brochure is studded with quotes from famous persons, such as William James: "The greatest use of a life is to spend it for something that outlasts it."

Vantage also quotes the Association of American University Presses: "Circumstances have forced the scholarly book largely into the non-profit or deficit category, and the commercial publisher cannot afford to underwrite books of this nature." True, but this was scarcely intended to drive the AAUP's audience into the arms of Vantage Press. Similarly, Harrison Smith of *Saturday Review* is cited as urging publishers to consider making "a fair arrangement with writers who can share in the expenses of a first edition and thus gamble on their own books." Without reading Mr. Smith's mind, it can be gathered that he, too, did not mean Vantage Press.

The reader, however, with a manuscript in one hand and a

sheaf of rejection slips in the other, interprets this wisdom in a different light. He sees himself marching with the ghost of William James to tea at the Algonquin with Harrison Smith, and maybe John Ciardi will drop by, too. . . .

There are two pages of questions and answers in Vantage's brochure.

Q: "Do you ever reject manuscripts?

A: "Yes, and on these grounds: (*a*) When the manuscript has neither merit nor sales possibilities; (*b*) When the manuscript is so personal as to be of interest to no one but the author and his family; (*c*) When the manuscript is too short for hard-cover book publication; (*d*) or when the type of material falls outside the scope of our publishing program.

Q: "How can I satisfy myself as to your trade or financial standing?

A: "You may consult our bankers, the Chemical-Corn Exchange Bank, Times Square branch, New York, N.Y. We are listed in such important publishing directories as *Publisher's Trade List Annual, Books in Print, Wilson's Cumulative Book Index, The Book Buyer's Guide,* and *Publisher's Weekly.*" The F.T.C. is not mentioned.

Gilt by association carries over into Vantage's glittering stable of "name" writers, including Dr. Albert Szent-Györgyi, Nobel Prize winner in chemistry; Fulgencio Batista, the dictator who preceded Fidel Castro in Cuba; and the late Eva Perón. ("Why not give yourself a chance to join this select group?" says Vantage's copy.)

If you write to Vantage's editorial director, who has the alluring name of Helen Winner, she will send you a list of authors, "who were compelled to subsidize their maiden efforts" at other houses: Stephen Crane, Edgar Allan Poe, Edwin Arlington Robinson, Willa Cather, Walt Whitman, Vachel Lindsay, Henry David Thoreau, and Edgar Rice Burroughs, among others.

It is an impressive roster, expanded most recently by James Purdy, author of *Color of Darkness* and *Malcolm*. Purdy's first two books were published here on a subsidy basis by William-Frederick Press, but it was in England that the American-born Purdy first achieved recognition.

Vanity publishers come in all sizes. One of the smallest advertises wistfully: "Why wait till eternity to have your poems, stories, articles accepted and published? Save your time, and money, and effort. We publish your poems, stories, articles NOW at a nominal charge of only 20 cents a line for poetry, and 2 cents a word for prose in our pocket magazine *The Poet's Mission*. From one line of poetry to a thousand lines, or up to a thousand words of prose accepted (very few manuscripts refused). Send complete payment with your manuscript. . . ."

Much of this says more about general, or trade book, publishing than it does about vanity publishing. Sylvan H. Stein of Pittsburgh, one of the more articulate vanity press authors (*Creative Living: Life, Man, and Mind*), insists that he wouldn't have it any other way—under what he sees as today's conditions:[*]

"Trade book publishers publish far too many trivial books, far too few worthwhile ones. Their custom is to publish petty books by well-known people; whether these people are writers or television personalities, chronic alcoholics or criminals makes no difference to the publisher as long as they are well known.

"The university presses, most of whose efforts are also trivial, are not trade publishers, as commonly believed, but are subsidized publishers. The fact that they are subsidized by boards and foundations makes them no less subsidized than the so-called vanity press.

"Books by the iconoclast, the social critic, the reformer, are largely ignored by the trade publisher, not necessarily because of poor writing but because the average book buyer shuns a book which exposes his own shortcomings. If a relatively unknown writer has something important to say and wishes to be read, he is compelled to seek out the so-called vanity publisher. This was the situation in the days of Theodore Dreiser, who subsidized his own works, and is still the situation today."

[v]

To all of the exploiters already cited, add ghosting specialists, miscellaneous tipsters, bogus contests, and even travel bureaus. (You don't need to have published to embark on a "Writers'

---

[*] Letter to the author.

Tour of Mexico" and visit the setting of Eileen Bassing's novel, *Where's Annie?*—a Book-of-the-Month Club selection in that melancholy year of 1963—for inspiration.) Add Benson Barrett of Chicago ("MAKE MONEY WRITING SHORT PARAGRAPHS. You don't have to be a trained author to make money writing. . . . Lots of small checks in a hurry bring cash that adds up quickly. No tedious study. Write to sell, right away") and H. W. Gabriel of West Nyack, New York, author of *How to Write for Money*, whose publisher promises: "I'll show you how to write short paragraphs that can be written by anyone who can write plain English that bring as high as 30¢ a word." Add to the list a compact $2 paperback, *Confess for Cash*, by Pauline Smith (Pilot Books), who oozes encouragement: "Someone you know must be having wife or husband trouble, child or financial trouble, extra-marital woes. The kid down the street is probably headed straight for reform school. Or you've had a fight with your husband and wanted to blast out but didn't. Take it out on the typewriter—with profit." Add by all means Mildred Reid of Contoocook, New Hampshire, whose advertising positively purrs: "Why not live with me at my Writers' Colony and receive teacher-at-elbow assistance . . . ? Any length of time. Experience this stimulating meeting of minds amidst beautiful surroundings, ten acres of pine groves."

The would-be writer has been part of the American landscape for more than a century. His prototype was there when Poe, Thoreau, and Whitman were underwriting their own early efforts.

With growing literacy came rising literary aspirations. But there were many more new writers than the legitimate publishing houses could accommodate. From the opening of the West to the dawn of the jet age, the publishing capitals—New York, Boston, and Philadelphia—grew more isolated than ever from the crop of potential writers in the provinces. There were more would-be writers out there but more millions of words to be waded through back home. In such a situation, many of the talented were rebuffed just as impersonally as the untalented.

When creativity became fashionable, the professional writer's image became that of a Cary Grant-like Scotch drinker on a perpetual first-class cruise with a portable typewriter in his lap and an Audrey Hepburn at his beck and call: "As long as you're up, get me a Grant's." Philip Hamburger, the *New Yorker's* man Stanley, says his garage mechanic recently assured him, "It's so easy to make money in the writing game" and charged him accordingly for repairs. All sorts of nonwriters wanted in— from astronauts to nannies, transvestites to defectors—and a few did cash in. But even an old pro like Edna Ferber was taken aback when she "stumbled on a statistic that startled and fascinated me. . . . There are, the proven statistic said, only 250 writers in the United States whose art or profession is that of creating original books, plays, short stories, articles, whose complete working hours are spent solely in the task of writing, and who earn their living by this means only. I, in my ignorance, had thought we numbered many thousands."

Dr. Michael Wyschogrod, a City College of New York philosophy professor, deplores the growing abuse of the term "creativity" * as "a form of occupational therapy that is destructive of the dignity of labor, particularly creative labor. . . . We cannot pretend that dabbling with creativity is the solution to the problem of the housewife and the salesman who find their lives empty."

The would-be-writer industry grew up in this vacuum to fill the needs of vast numbers on the outside looking in. It perpetuated and solidified the myth of a cultural elite, and it even developed what one of its employees calls "a moral casuistry that eventually anesthetizes all scruples. True, we encourage crackpots, semiliterates, and the utterly talentless just as enthusiastically as the few genuinely promising would-be writers. On the other hand, the scraps of praise we toss out are probably the only bright spots in many of their lives."

If only that were all! But in peddling hope indiscriminately to the hopeless and the hopeful, the would-be-writer industry has blurred the distinction between them.

---

* The Manhattan Telephone Directory lists 89 enterprises beginning with the word "creative," including Creative Art Flowers and Creative Money Management.

The Third Commandment of the Culture Vultures:
Revere the almighty presell, for the
name of the game is insurance,
not art.

3
Broadway's Golden Dozen

---

[1]

MISS SANTHA RAMA RAU perched on a piano bench in
a book-lined living room and told the story of E. M.
Forster's *A Passage to India,* which she had adapted into a
drama. Friendship, she concluded gently, is impossible between
those who rule and those who are ruled.

Then her host, a high official of the Theatre Guild, added harrumphingly that Miss Rau's play was as "up to the minute" as
the headlines from Asia, Africa, and our own South. *A Passage
to India,* he went on, had the extra theatrical virtue of focusing
on a hallucination of attempted rape. "If I may say so," said the
man from the Theatre Guild, "a lot of people will buy tickets
to rape even if they won't buy tickets to colonialism."

As the host, a man whose name has been equated with "a com-
mercially and culturally successful theater," rambled on gen-
teelly about rape, there were other ladies present besides Miss
Rau. There was Anne Meacham, the actress, who came on the
arm of her costar, Eric Portman. Both would start rehearsals of
A Passage to India a month later. But the guests of honor that
Tuesday afternoon were seven matronly ladies named Frances
A. Drill, Thelma K. Ellis, Gertrude Fox, Elsa Hoppenfeld,
Mildred Kaplan, Ivy Larric, and Lenore Tobin.

They, plus five others who had been invited but were unable to attend, comprise virtually the entire membership of the Association of Theater Benefit Agents. (One or two of the ladies have male silent partners.) They sell one out of every five Broadway theater tickets and bring more than $8 million to Times Square box offices in a season. As the only link between theater producer and theater party, alias benefit, the ladies are known as Broadway's "Golden Dozen."

A theater party is a social gathering at which a group of people come together not to make merry but to aid a cause by seeing a play. Hospitals, milk funds, homes for unwed mothers and underprivileged children, alumni associations, private schools, fraternal orders, boys' clubs, and churches depend on theater parties to raise several million dollars a year for them. By reselling each ticket at a premium of $1 to $100 (such scalping is legalized when it's for nonprofit fund-raising purposes), a charity can clear a $5,000 to $20,000 profit on one theater party at a hit play.

In the New York area, as one charity's benefit chairman put it, "the theater party is the *fun* way of making money," far less painful and often more palatable than the $50-a-plate roast beef dinner. Broadway's theater-party business, which has increased fiftyfold in the past two decades, may or may not have revolutionized the theater, but it *has* transformed the audience. People used to go to the theater to see shows. Now they go to fight rheumatoid arthritis.

What's more, in addition to being good-hearted, it's a remarkably well-heeled class of theatergoer that the Golden Dozen have attracted. In a recent series of advertisements beamed at advertisers, *Playbill,* the theater program, profiled the kind of self-satisfied, do-not-disturb couple that now pays up to $200 for its seats. His custom-tailored suit "hangs well . . . the wallet contains 6.5 credit cards and $86.32 . . . lighter comes from that fancy place on Fifth Avenue. . . . One of the jingling keys starts the motor of 1.74 cars. . . . Spends $187.20 per year on smokes." Her "scent of expensive fragrance fills the air. . . . Just one of the 4.5 furs she owns . . . Expensive milk farm figure . . . Spent $155 on cosmetics this year . . . 3.60-carat blue-white perfect marquise diamond . . . Evening slippers bill: $34.50 . . . Today's beauty salon bill was $20.50, including tip." Says *Playbill:* "To us they're just plain folks. We got our figures straight from lots of expensive market research findings. It seems this is just about what the average theater-going couple looks like. Smile and all. It seems theater-goers are just about the cheeriest group you can find. No matter how hard you look. Receptive and relaxed and the perfect audience to read just about anything you would put before them. . . ."

Or to see anything you'd put on the stage that wouldn't jar their well-stuffed solar plexus or status quo.

As the pipeline to these people, the twelve theater-party ladies have come—in the minds (or perhaps the imaginations) of various stage businessmen—to embody "Broadway's economic staff of life," "the theater's Florence Nightingales," and "the best insurance we have against financial instability." For better or worse, the Golden Dozen are worshiped and feared and pandered to in some quarters as the true First Ladies of the American theater.

"Many of them are in a position to bid for Fort Knox," said Arthur Cantor, producer, director, and press agent. "They are now courted, cocktailed, and bussed on their motherly cheeks by most producers. Their counsel on scripts, stars, bookings is not only sought but aggressively volunteered. Their power spreads, and if it is somewhat misapplied, why not? . . . The hand that rocks the theater party rules the world of Forty-fourth Street."

The Golden Dozen achieved their status during a busy, well-heeled postwar era, when charities grew competitive and the tax-exempt dollar all-powerful. Today the ladies gross some half million dollars a year in commissions.

To earn their money, they do not work in mysterious ways. For example, the first theater party I ever looked into, more than six years ago, was substantially illustrative of them all.

For a Thursday night performance of *How to Succeed in Business without Really Trying*, the Milk and Egg League of the City of Hope sold all 1,326 seats in the Forty-sixth Street Theater. Several weeks before the Frank Loesser musical's premiere, the Milk and Egg people had contracted with Lenore Tobin, the most businesslike of the Golden Dozen, to buy up the entire house. The Milk and Egg League bought the tickets at list price and later scaled them upward to charitable levels. The producers of *How to Succeed* paid Miss Tobin's commission. Occasionally a producer declines to pay benefit agents' commissions on his show. In such a case, the charity foots the bill. No matter who pays it, the bill almost always comes to 7.5 percent of the list price of the tickets.

If a charity bypassed the Golden Dozen and approached a show's management directly, it almost certainly would be rebuffed. New York City regulations require theaters to verify that all sales of ten or more tickets to unlicensed persons are not for purposes of resale. The Golden Dozen, however, are all certified as ticket brokers by the city's Department of Licenses.

For her commission, each lady arranges dates that are satisfactory to both producer and charity. When she knows how much money an organization wishes to raise, she can advise its officials whether to buy the whole house, just the main floor, or slices of orchestra and balcony.

She does her best to avert mismatches between audience and play. She would, for example, discourage a Jewish group from staking its fund-raising hopes on a play about intermarriage. She did caution a Catholic charity that the musical *Milk and Honey* was set in Israel. She had absolutely no use for John Osborne's *Luther*. "It just wasn't a fundraising thing. The Catholic organizations wouldn't touch a play about Martin Luther. The Jewish organizations couldn't endorse it in any way, of course. And the Protestants warned me, before I ever saw the script, that anything about Luther would be too earthy for their people. Their grapevine must have known that Albert Finney was going to play up Luther's constipation."

She keeps abreast of the theatrical scene by reading scripts, attending auditions, subscribing to *Variety*, chatting with producers and comparing notes with her colleagues. On weekends she goes diligently to Philadelphia or New Haven (occasionally as far as Wilmington) to sit in on pre-Broadway tryouts. In summer she may travel to London and scout the transatlantic candidates. "Going places is a must if you want to do an intelligent selling job and presentation."

On the night of a theater party, she usually stands in the lobby—just in case. Invariably she will have to look after a sheepish husband who sent his suit to the cleaners with his tickets still in a pocket. A smartly dressed couple may strut in, brandishing tickets for another night at another theater.

The most agonizing theater-party flop of them all occurred at the Broadway Theater on a winter night in early 1944. The Bronx Hadassah had bought up the entire balcony for *Carmen Jones*. As a courtesy, the show's management had printed a new set of balcony tickets showing the raised prices for that night. But somebody had neglected to withdraw the original set of balcony tickets, which were sold at the box office. Thus did 1,200 people show up to claim 600 seats. Six hundred heated arguments later, while the band in the pit played "The Star-Spangled Banner" over and over to deter further aggression, a police emergency squad arrived. A detective went onstage to soothe the irate ticket holders by threatening to arrest them all for disorderly conduct.

The show went on—thirty minutes late. The box office made 600 refunds or exchanges. The management ran a two-column apology in the New York *Times*. And the benefit agent lost the lucrative Hadassah account.

On another occasion, an inexperienced benefit chairman took charge of distributing seats for a performance of *On the Town* and gave them out in 1-2-3 order. A couple who wanted two tickets together were given, for example, seats D1 and D2. Theater seats, however, run in 1-3-5-7 and 2-4-6-8 sequences.

A performer who watched that memorable game of musical chairs through a hole in the curtain has recalled: "Shortly before it was time to go on, we heard and felt a dreadful rumbling in the theater, like an earthquake. Our audience was dashing from one side of the theater to the other, shouting. Before we could go on, all the seating had to be rearranged. The cast never got over it."

Ever since then, benefit agents have given their clients cram courses in theater seating and business administration. Some of the Golden Dozen even moonlight as social secretaries of their own theater parties—for a fee.

The Golden Dozen's recurrent nightmare, however, is not seating mix-ups but *empty seats*. When a benefit committee books an *Anya* or a *Jennie* (to name two of the more expensive musical flops of recent times), there are howls of anguish—or, worse still, deep silence.

The twelve ladies are primarily middlemen. Like all servants of two masters, they have cautious instincts, a yen for common denominators, a palate for blandness, and an aversion to frying pans and fires. They want a handle, something they can grab onto, something they can run with, something they can peddle. They want a hit song they can hum, a story sensational enough to *tell* well in a few sentences, and even then, how do they know it'll *play* well? Oh, dear, if only *everything* would be previewed for Broadway in London or Mineola! The kind of experimentation they seek is unveiling a movie idol on the stage for the first time and hoping for the best, or coaxing a classical actress to let down her hair in her first singing part, or persuading a Book-of-the-Month author to try his hand at adapting his best seller into a Play-of-the-Month. Is it any wonder, then, that as subsidiary spawns subsidiary ad infinitum,* each rendering becomes cruder and blurrier, like successive reproductions of a work of art via carbon paper?

One of the ladies, Mildred Kaplan, tapped my lapel while I was interviewing her. "That's a nice suit you're wearing," she remarked. "Where'd you get it?"

"Brooks Brothers," I admitted.

"You see!" she said triumphantly. "When you need a good suit, you don't go to Woolworth's. Well, we shop for the craftsmen surrounding a show. If they have good reputations, we can usually count on them to turn out a good show."

Who could resist making the off-the-cuff observation that all twelve ladies see themselves as cautious comparison shoppers with pious faith in brand names? Mrs. Kaplan didn't disagree.

In one interview, I asked a benefit agent if she'd ever picked a long shot.

---

* A couple of for-instances: A novel called 7½¢ becomes a musical and then movie called *The Pajama Game,* whereupon the author is induced to write a book (that later becomes a play) called *Say, Darling!* about the experience. The Japanese movie *Rashomon,* an art theater success starring Toshiro Mifune, becomes an arty but unnecessary Broadway flop *d'estime* called *Rashomon,* starring Claire Bloom and Rod Steiger. Then, in successive adaptations, it becomes a Paul Newman Western called *The Outrage,* which is novelized into a book called *The Outrage* and also turns up as a Spanish-made Western starring Clint Eastwood, called *A Fistful of Dollars.* Novelized screenplays, incidentally, are one of Hollywood's many contributions to the milking of what are known as "residual assets." When an Edgar Allan Poe short story was made into a low-budget horror movie, it generated a paperback adaptation that was billed on its spine as "*The Pit and the Pendulum,* by Lee Sheridan."

"Well," she said, after a pause, "I was one of the first to like
The Sound of Music."

Part of the Golden Dozen's job is to spot the hidden dissuader
in the shiniest piece of merchandise. There may never have
been a more commercial sex comedy than *The Seven-Year Itch,*
but one theater-party lady's response was, "Who wants to see
an itch?" Her resistance was overcome in the nick of time, she
admits now, when she saw the 11 "other girls gobbling up all
the good dates."

My Fair Lady encountered some initial theater-party flak—
"Who ever heard of Julie Andrews?" "All our people have
seen *Pygmalion* in the movies"—until the ladies met the talent
and heard the songs. *West Side Story* bucked major turbulence.
Leonard Bernstein was only as good as his previous show, the
ambitious but ill-fated *Candide.*

How to Succeed had Rudy Vallee. "That dirty old man!" one
benefit chairman snarled. "Don't try to push *him* down our
throats." A special audition for the ladies was arranged, at which
Vallee not only strutted his stuff but spoke Yiddish to them.

Hello, Dolly! overcame complaints about the star ("Carol
Channing's too cute") and the show's original source, a play by
Thornton Wilder ("He's a little literary, isn't he?") after producer David Merrick held *separate* auditions to woo *each* of
the key ladies and her clients. *Fiorello,* which won the Pulitzer
Prize, lacked names. *The Pajama Game* gave a "lousy audition."

Occasionally an unlikely prospect will reward a lone hunch-
player for a number of wrong reasons. The Golden Dozen's
majority opinion on *A Far Country* was, in effect: "A very beautiful play about Dr. Freud and a paralyzed patient, but so many
people are undergoing psychiatric treatment nowadays that it
brought up unpleasant associations." One dissenter recommended it to her clients anyway, with considerable success.
"You see," she confided later, "it had a miracle in it. Kim Stanley got up off the couch and walked. That's the best kind of
miracle to sell because it isn't a religious miracle."

The membership of the Association of Theater Benefit Agents
is overwhelmingly female, and so are the benefit chairmen they
service. But any natural feminine tendency toward utter recklessness is outweighed by the urge to keep peace between the

sexes. It is the man of the house who will ultimately pay as much as $200 for two seats. Since all women are convinced they understand their men, it is hopeless to argue with the benefit chairman who contended: "Men don't want to see plays about the troubles of the world. They *live* them."

The Golden Dozen hate to sit around saying no. Luckily for the ladies, though not for the rest of us, producers these days bear them in mind when deciding what will be produced and what won't be. The ladies, after all, represent the most solid one-fifth of a dwindling market. Therefore, the other side of the theater-party coin is that they are given many opportunities to say yes. Many a potential clinker owes some degree of success to the Golden Dozen and their clientele despite first-night obituary notices from the drama critics.

When *The World of Suzie Wong* opened to a sour press ("Sophomoric," "On the artistic level of a comic book"), its future was sweetened by 300 theater parties that had been booked and paid for. *Romanoff and Juliet* had three months of theater parties to make the general public forget divided reviews ("A gay little improvisation" versus "As funny as a box on the ears"). In the interim, its publicists peddled author-actor Peter Ustinov's personality instead of his play.

Sometimes the blame for an entirely dismal Broadway season is laid in the ample laps of the ladies. When this happens, the ladies doth protest, most disarmingly, that the cart is indeed being put before the horse: "We girls are the whipping boys!" "We merely reflect the taste of the public." *It would be more accurate, however, to say that the Golden Dozen reflect the public's growing unwillingness and inability to buy its own ticket.* Members of some religious and fraternal organizations know no other way to see the shows than to book a theater party, and so they end up seeing each other.

What is more alarming is the responsibility that theatrical professionals have abdicated to the ladies. If today's Broadway is torn between the smugly sensational and the inane, its Checkpoint Charlie is the Golden Dozen. One of the ladies admitted: "Sometimes a play won't get enough backers if we turn it down." Another said matter-of-factly: "Sometimes a theater owner will call me if he has a choice of two or three plays that might go into one theater. He asks me if I've read the scripts and which play would be best for parties." The ladies' every taste, their every whim, is anticipated (often wrongly), pandered to, and indulged. Even their predominant Jewishness is considered when casting. Why was the soft spot in an otherwise robust *Man of la Mancha* a Yiddish-theater Sancho Panza playing himself? Why did *The Zulu and the Zayda,* an extraordinarily inept but determinedly upbeat comedy about race relations in South Africa, have a respectable run on Broadway? (The *Zayda,* or grandfather, was played by Menasha Skulnik, the Zulu by a Negro actor who spoke Yiddish.) Why did *Chu-Chem,* billed as "The First Zen Buddhist Hebrew Musical," almost get to Broadway? (Starring Molly Picon and Menasha Skulnik, it collapsed in Philadelphia shortly after Miss Picon defected.) Why, for that matter, were those last two plays written at all?

Last season the Golden Dozen nearly achieved immortality on the other side of the footlights. A comedy about their exotic vocation, *The Party Girls,* was being readied for Broadway and heavy benefit bookings when death struck down the star, Gertrude Berg.

The play was by Leonard Spigelgass (author of Miss Berg's previous vehicles, *A Majority of One* and *Dear Me, the Sky Is Falling*), not Arthur Miller. The latter has equated "people representing theater parties who can come into play readings and decide whether the script can be produced" with interfering television sponsors. In both cases, said Miller, "if the deciding voices in any medium are interested in something else before the medium itself, the medium is going to suffer."

The medium *has* suffered, so much so that Arthur Miller's own stage success might have been a different story if our foremost heterosexual dramatist had entered the Broadway lists just a few years later than he did. Miller's first play, *The Man Who Had All the Luck,* expired in three nights during the mid-1940's, which would have been enough to tab him as "failed" and "serious" in today's Golden Dozen shorthand. His second, *All My Sons,* earned a Critics' Prize and a respectable run. His third was *Death of a Salesman,* which the Golden Dozen almost unanimously found "hard to sell." One of the ladies, who pressed in vain for a title change, said, "That downbeat word *death* made my work difficult for me."

Miller's next outings—*The Crucible* and a double bill of *A Memory of Two Mondays* and *A View from the Bridge*—were so badly served by their nervous Broadway productions that Miller (for personal and professional reasons) went unrepresented on Broadway for almost a decade. Finally, at great financial sacrifice, he virtually donated his *After the Fall* and then *Incident at Vichy* to the Repertory Theater of Lincoln Center. In those days of early hope, when the repertory troupe was housed not in its airtight mausoleum at Lincoln Center but in a Quonset hut at New York University downtown, Miller was able, in effect, to buy the kind of production and direction (first by Elia Kazan, then by Harold Clurman) that his plays deserved.

An unflinching autobiographical probe, *After the Fall* would have been sensational enough to make the Broadway grade, if only for its second-act parallels to Arthur Miller's married life with the late Marilyn Monroe. But such is Broadway's dependence on names (plus its inability to see through them) that when *Monocle* magazine made four little changes—the title to *Yes, Dylan, There Is a Virginia*, the hero's name to Dylan, the girl's name to Virginia, and the author's name to Katherine Gregg, a *Monocle* employee—and submitted the otherwise intact script of *After the Fall* to eight Broadway producers, this is what happened:

David Merrick's office returned it unopened because he doesn't read unsolicited material. Alexander Cohen rejected it without comment.

Saint-Subber's office rejected it with some encouragement. "It is not a play, just a nebulous dramatic abstraction," but Miss Gregg did have "a very good feeling for the stage."

Herman Shumlin said, "It is very difficult for me to be of value to you in terms of a rough draft of a play. I am really concerned with reading complete plays."

The Theatre Guild said it didn't meet "our specific needs," and the William Morris Agency was too busy to read it. Only Kermit Bloomgarden (producer of *Death of a Salesman*) and David Susskind recognized it for what it was.

S. N. Behrman, who took the same tack as Arthur Miller by awarding his twenty-fourth play, *But for Whom Charlie*, to the Lincoln Repertory, has remarked ruefully: "It seems to me that people write most modern plays out of a sense of revenge.

There is no more marketable commodity than sadism. . . . The theater once was an adventurous medium, but it isn't anymore." Behrman's scorn for Broadway applies particularly to today's so-called serious drama, where the freakish sensations, piled on with tabloid recklessness, are simultaneously cheap and overpriced. It may be symbolic that only three of the thirty-four playhouses that comprise the Broadway theater are actually on Broadway; all the rest are on the side streets of New York. For the Broadway theater of today has become a sideshow—and a synthetic one at that.

The artistic departure of Broadway from the mainstream of American culture can be charted by following the career of Thomas Lanier "Tennessee" Williams. After *A Streetcar Named Desire*'s climactic rape of Blanche du Bois by her brother-in-law, Stanley Kowalski, perhaps the playwright had nowhere to go but down. But who could have envisioned a responsive audience (let alone a Pulitzer and two Drama Critics' prizes) for *Cat on a Hot Tin Roof*'s impotent athlete, bitchy bedmates, Big Daddy, and no-neck monsters; *Sweet Bird of Youth*'s venereal ingenue, venerable mistress, and blackmailing gigolo doomed to third-act emasculation; or *The Night of the Iguana*'s defrocked minister turned statutory rapist? The decline in Williams' scope and ambition was measurable then, even before the last half decade's steady succession of sterile, grotesque, fatigued, half-written failures from the pen that not so long ago illuminated the stage with *The Glass Menagerie*.

While Tennessee Williams has been tinkering with lobotomy, latent lesbianism, and overt cannibalism, his protégé, William Inge, has been concerning himself with more lifelike problems, such as teen-age marriage (*Where's Daddy?*) and a young man's sexual awakening by his mother's best friend (*A Loss of Roses*). But Inge no longer confronts his crises with the intense poetic reality that makes his *Picnic*, *Come Back, Little Sheba*, and *The Dark at the Top of the Stairs* drama to remember. Instead he faces up to real situations like a *Daily News* rewrite man pushing a deadline. Take the climax of Inge's *Natural Affection*, whose "hero's" mother is living in sin with a car salesman. On learning that his mother loves her lover more than she loves him, the boy kisses her full on the mouth. Mother exits hastily. A drunken woman wanders in from a party next door. The boy stabs her with a carving knife. They disappear necrophilically behind the sofa. The boy reappears, drinking murky symbolic milk. Curtain!

One critic couldn't help marveling: "As the work of a mental patient urged to write for therapeutic reasons, *Natural Affection* would be an understandable though unpalatable experience. As the work of one of America's major playwrights, it is incredible."

In the marketplace that the Golden Dozen have helped to generate, *serious* has become equated with *sensational* just as *frantic* has become equated with *comic*. And Broadway's lighter fare is largely a clutter of Yiddish-accented *Gemütlichkeit*, onanistic bedroom farces, giggle-free family comedies that make you suspect you're watching rehearsals of TV pilots, and tuneless musicals pasted up (sloppily) from undistinguished movies almost before they've finished their half week at the Skyway Drive-In.

The legitimate theater has become so inbred and so shallow that aside from Neil Simon (*Barefoot in the Park*, *The Odd Couple*, etc.), only its best-known technicians of perversion and castration get the practice a playwright needs. The new writer who persists *may* win a hearing, but he must wait his turn in an unrewarding queue. He must, for example, bide his time while Tennessee Williams falls on his face *not once, but twice, with the same play!* In 1963 a Williams passion play about an ancient harridan seeking to seduce a predatory angel, *The Milk Train Doesn't Stop Here Anymore*, lasted sixty-nine performances. Less than a year later, *The Milk Train* was "revived" on Broadway—somewhat revised, its flaws magnified, and expensively mounted in pseudo-Kabuki style by director Tony Richardson. Tallulah Bankhead and Tab Hunter played the leads. *The Milk Train* tarried for five performances. (Now it's being made into an Elizabeth Taylor movie.)

The standard rejoinders from the Times Square side streets are, "This is what the public wants" and "When better plays are written, Broadway will stage them." But any institution that loses somewhere between $5 million and $7 million in a year (as Broadway did recently) and that experienced its smallest season of the twentieth century in 1966–67 (48 openings, as compared to a peak of 263 in 1926–27) clearly is *not* giving its public much of what it wants. While the American population was increasing by 50 percent, Broadway's annual audience was dwindling from 12 million to 8 million.

The other defense, "Where are the playwrights???" is rebutted by Albert C. Bermel, an associate professor of theater arts at Columbia University, whose own plays have been performed in London and at the Phoenix Theater in Manhattan. Recently, seeking to found a nonprofit company to produce new American plays, Bermel reported:

> Over the past two years, I have been reading a fair sampling of unproduced and unpublished drama. Some of the plays were experimental in content and technique; some were conventional; some fell into no recognizable category. Most of them would probably not interest an audience, any audience. Yet I found that on the average, one out of fifteen scripts I saw was well written and deserved to be mounted. . . . Further, one out of the fourteen remaining scripts needed relatively little work to lift it into the first division. But all these plays, good and nearly good, had been rejected by the producers. Reading at my unhurried rate of about three scripts a week (an hour to an hour and a half for each), a producer's reader who knows his job should be able to find ten first-rate plays a year. Where are these plays? Why doesn't anybody do them? Why do most of the interesting plays that appear on Broadway come from Europe? It is comforting to say, as has often been said, that great plays do not go undiscovered; the word "great" neatly begs the question. I have grounds for believing that we are missing out on much of the best theater that America has to offer.

There is an important corollary to Bermel's findings: Classics do not often erupt; they evolve, as Arthur Miller's steady growth toward *Death of a Salesman* would indicate. But today's fledgling playwright is rarely, if ever, given a continuing opportunity to flex his muscles and stretch his wings and even stumble badly as he masters his craft. Too many culture vultures like the Golden Dozen are on hand to write him off early as a bad investment.

* * *

Soon after producing his superfluous and unsuccessful stage version of the Japanese film *Rashomon*, David Susskind publicly characterized the Golden Dozen as a contingent whose "idea of the ideal Broadway production would be something called *Hip, Hip, Hooray!* starring Jayne Mansfield and Rock Hudson." On Susskind's TV talkathon, producer Carmen Capalbo called the ladies "kookie birds" who cause delay and difficulty, and director José Quintero called them "harpies" who decide which shows get on the boards. When one of the ladies phoned to ask for equal time, Susskind replied courteously: "Madam, the worst thing you can do is let yourself be seen by a noncaptive audience."

With enemies like David Susskind, the Golden Dozen need never lack defenders. It was Susskind who in the beginning romanced the ladies with a cocktail party to let them in on the ground floor of *Rashomon*. It was Susskind who wooed Lenore Tobin, she says, with assurances that she should find it easy to peddle parties for *Rashomon* because it was chock full of rape. But, considering the power they wield in Times Square, it is not amiss to scan the ladies' qualifications.

Individually, ten of the Golden Dozen may be described succinctly.

Pauline Hirsch, a sedate widow, was an insurance agent and president of the Brooklyn League of the Hebrew National Orphan Home. (She was billed on the cover of the May, 1936, issue of *The Modern Jewish Woman* as "The Greatest Little Mother of All.") Anne Herschkowitz used to be president of the Yeshivah of Flatbush and is active in Hadassah, Mizrachi, and the East Midwood Jewish Center. ("Most of my business is Jewish, but I sell Gentile, too.") Thelma Ellis danced in the Ziegfeld Follies, and Janet Robinson sang on the old Kraft Music Hall program. Frances Drill, a pert redhead, used to be a professional fund raiser. Elsa Hoppenfeld worked for Macy's as an adjuster, straightening out complaints. ("I learned patience there, the kind of patience you need when you have to explain to people that not every seat in the house is a center seat.") Mildred Kaplan used to be East Coast representative for Sol Lesser, who produced *Tarzan* movies. Gertrude Fox and Bert (short for Bertha) Landsman were housewives. Esther Littauer is a spinster who was "staying home and doing nothing" until she got into the business.

Such an incomplete rundown gives a superficial impression of Helen Hokinson ladies who should be presiding over suburban kitchens rather than dabbling in theater. But the two best-known members of the Association of Theater Benefit Agents —Ivy Larric, its first president, and Lenore Tobin, its second and current president—have more impressive qualifications.

Miss Larric, who played bit parts in two Broadway plays, has been a leader in the theater-party business for a quarter of a century. Miss Tobin studied drama at Cornell and started out to be a great American playwright. She went to work for the Shuberts as a secretary, sold tickets in box offices, handled mail orders, and read scripts. After she had studied a few scripts, she realized that as a playwright, at least, she represented no threat to Lillian Hellman. She did, however, have aptitude for the business side of the theater. When she took over the Shuberts' theater-party bureau, a small operation, she built it up to such proportions that Shubert executives complained she was making more in commissions than they were in salary. Then she went into business for herself.*

Firmed up by Lenore Tobin and Ivy Larric, the composite picture that the Golden Dozen provides is respectable and perhaps even, as one of them has claimed, "knowledgeable." In a theater whose ranks are swelled by real-estate magnates, oil-rich Texans, homosexual dilettantes, and practicing nepotists, the Golden Dozen have little need to apologize for amateurishness. They do their chosen work with professional competence. And they certainly seem to be on the same wavelength as their female clientele. Their customers are, with rare exceptions, satisfied with their work. Male and female theater-partygoers respect them all too unquestioningly as experts on what's good and what isn't. Some of the Golden Dozen's admirers even attribute to them a little of the glamor of the theater.

Across the footlights, the actors know little or nothing about

---

* As a gift for her benefit chairmen, Lenore Tobin once printed a book with seating plans of legitimate theaters. People asked where they could buy extra copies, and that was how Lenore Tobin at last became an author of sorts. Her little guidebook, *Stubs*, has sold more than a million copies.

the Golden Dozen. But they do know the ladies' customers and have very few kind words for them. Anne Bancroft, star of *The Miracle Worker,* which opened with 168 theater parties in the till, said: "It takes actual screaming by actors to quiet a benefit audience." Lauren Bacall observed: "Most of the time they seem more preoccupied with seeing themselves than with seeing the play." In the second act of a benefit performance of *Pygmalion,* the late Gertrude Lawrence almost dropped her H's when she discovered that the theater lovers in the first row were munching sandwiches. And one noisy evening during the brief run of *Silent Night, Lonely Night,* the normally imperturbable Henry Fonda stuck out his tongue at an inattentive theater party.

At a benefit of the two-character musical *I Do! I Do!* in February, 1967, the stentorian bellow of Robert Preston was actually drowned out by an imperative shriek from the balcony: "Harvey, change seats with Gretchen! Shelly can't see!" And Gower Champion, who directed Preston and Mary Martin in *I Do! I Do!,* swears he "heard some guy look over the credits and say, 'You mean I paid a hundred bucks a seat and there's only two people in this show?' He didn't know where he was. He was there because his wife had joined some committee."

Sir Tyrone Guthrie has written of his first encounter with the New York theater-party scene:

> Never have I known such audiences. They came late; they talked loudly all through the performance, often commenting on the actor's personal appearance in tones perfectly audible to the stage. The last twenty minutes of the dialogue used to be rendered totally inaudible by the hubbub in the audience: "How's about it, Mildred?" a gentleman would yell to his wife sitting four seats away on the other side of their guests. "Shall we stick it out or shall we go now while we can get a cab?" If Mildred elected to go, they would stand right up and pull on their overcoats, talking a mile a minute and good and loud so as not to be interrupted by all that gabble on the stage. I suppose the attitude was that Frank and Mildred and four guests amounted, at fifty bucks apiece, to three hundred, and that to be asked to pay, in addition, a little attention, and even a little respect, to the actors—well *that* was just ridiculous.

That was at a successful comedy, *The Matchmaker*. For sheer terror it scarcely compares with the collective snarl emanating from an audience that has gathered in solemn assembly to witness the death throes of a turkey it has subsidized at $50 a head.

John Crosby has denounced benefit audiences as "half-asleep, half-loaded." A few years ago, Lenore Tobin inserted a plea for better behavior into *Playbills* at benefit performances. In it, she exhorted her audiences to "applaud as much as possible" because "a responsive theater party audience will enable you to have a better show." She abandoned her printed pep talks when several of her constituents complained that she was talking down to them. "You can't tell adults how to behave," Miss Tobin remarked to me. But Jessica Tandy, who can recognize theater parties by their I-dare-you-to-entertain-me posture, has an outrageously simple solution. "Instead of being uncomfortable or unhappy, they should make outright donations to whatever charity is in question."

Charity, Miss Tandy implies, begins at home and should stay there. Instead, thanks to the Golden Dozen, it is the disillusioned theater lover who sits at home or settles for the movies. The $7.50 seat you scrimped for is occupied by someone who paid $50 to sit through or snore through a play he didn't wish to see. For our twelve fairy earth mothers have overfattened their deformed son, the theater, with a synthetic audience, a sizable glob of which would rather be somewhere else.

Most of Broadway has learned all too easily to live with benefit audiences. "Just let the actors play to empty houses for a few nights and *then* listen to them howl," says Jack Schlissel, general manager for David Merrick. Hardly anybody bothers nowadays to contemplate the utopian possibility of actors performing in better plays to full houses of enthusiastic patrons who bought their tickets at box-office prices.

Even Tallulah Bankhead, whose contracts used to forbid benefits and who once remarked, "Benefit audiences are cannibalistic monsters who eat their young," has recanted. Having experienced a string of flops, she even invited the Golden Dozen into her home in an effort to bail out one short-lived comedy. Confronted by her past utterances, the reformed Tallulah growled, "I'm not that much of a bully. Times have changed."

Indeed they have. And if the benefit business continues to grow, it will become harder to distinguish between theater parties and the general public. As one of the Golden Dozen asked me: "If eleven hundred of my people fill a theater, aren't they the public? These eleven hundred people just happen to be very civic-minded. They're going to get entertained while they give to a charity they care about."

Theater-party audiences have not yet become THE public, but in shaping our theater, too many producers behave as if they already have. With light comedies and big musicals, the courting of the Golden Dozen achieves farcical proportions. The producer of *What Makes Sammy Run?* sent each lady a statuette worthy of the Olympics. Resembling a gilded marathon runner in action, it was called the Sammy Award. The ladies apparently returned the favor. After Sammy survived its first week and then its first year on Broadway, despite a drubbing from the press, one critic wrote: "What makes *Sammy* run? Theater parties."

Some producers dispatch their actors to drop in at after-the-theater-party parties in Times Square restaurants.

"One night," said Peter Cook of *Beyond the Fringe*, "there were two groups—Cancer and Asthma. They were both to meet at Sardi's afterward, and we were told to show. When we arrived, we found Vincent Sardi at the door, saying, 'Asthma or Cancer?' to everyone who came in. One couple went up to him, and the husband said, 'I'm Cancer and my wife's Asthma, but we'd like to sit together just the same.' It was astonishing. Another man said that he was TB. He was too late, it seemed; TB was the night before. Sardi said, 'Why don't you join Cancer?' "

Jule Styne, composer of *Gypsy* and producer of a notable *Pal Joey* revival, takes theater parties far more seriously. "A musical that costs four hundred thousand dollars to present today used to cost ninety thousand. And the price of tickets has not gone up to compensate, despite what the buyer may think. The economics of the theater have forced producers to compete for parties, to cast not for acting ability but for benefit appeal. It could make you weep." Anyone who has witnessed the Broadway debuts of such miscast TV personalities as Robert Horton,

Richard Chamberlain, Soupy Sales, and Mary Tyler Moore will weep along with Styne.

The Golden Dozen were the most visible means of support for two epic Broadway fiascos—*Jennie,* starring Mary Martin, and Irving Berlin's *Mr. President.*

After unprecedented staggers in Boston and Detroit, *Jennie* blithely plodded onto Broadway, right on schedule. Two members of the Golden Dozen admitted to me that *Jennie* came to town only because million-dollar theater-party advance sales kindled delusions of a miracle on Forty-fourth Street. "An irretrievable bore," said Walter Kerr. Another critic depicted Mary Martin as "the prisoner of her own cockeyed optimism." For ten weeks of theater parties, however, *Jennie* recorded the highest grosses in Broadway history. At the end of the eleventh week, when its party cushion wore thin, it closed.

"I booked all the dates I could get for *Jennie,*" one of the theater-party ladies told me ruefully. "Everybody got stuck up to her eyeballs with empty seats. I lost one big organization because I hadn't been able to get it an early date for *Jennie.* Later on, I lost another organization because I had."

Mr. President was endowed with 385 theater parties (189 for the full house), some uninspired tunes, and the worst lyrics ever credited to Irving Berlin (e.g., a love song called "The Secret Service Makes Me Nervous"). On the one night here and two days there that had somehow been left open to the public between parties, the house was so barren that the show lasted a modest 265 performances, or 7½ months.

What producer, even one trying desperately to salvage an imperfect show, will dare to postpone a premiere and risk giving back those golden presold theater-party shekels? The Golden Dozen fumed when Ray Stark of *Funny Girl* kept his show on the road in a last-ditch bid for betterment, but they ultimately juggled dates and assuaged their charities.

Stark was a novice manager with Barbra Streisand on his team, so he got away with it. More experienced producers wouldn't have the temerity to buck the Golden Dozen. And even the unlikeliest production must kowtow to them, for who knows for sure what the ladies' reaction will be? In 1949, didn't one of them persuade the Beth Jacob School's Ohav Sholom congregation to book Jean Giraudoux's allegorical *Madwoman of Chaillot* for its Lag b'Omer (Arbor Day) theater party? Only a dozen years later, didn't the Golden Dozen's combined resources sell a preview of Harold Pinter's *The Caretaker*? When an off-Broadway charade, which ends in eternity with Billy the Kid committing cunnilingus with Jean Harlow, is booked solid by classload after classload of suburban matrons studying the avant-garde for adult-education credit, who knows where the next hot party ticket may come from? Which is why we have glimpsed such occidental exotica as David Susskind hawking *Rashomon* as a play about rape and, to bring us full circle, the Theatre Guild doing the same for *A Passage to India.*

After Santha Rama Rau's audition of *A Passage to India*, the Golden Dozen listened attentively and then—against a backdrop of martinis, hot and cold hors d'oeuvres, and reprints of the play's London reviews—mixed and mingled. One of them inquired if an impending journey by Jacqueline Kennedy to the Orient might stimulate interest in the play. Another asked an innocent bystander if he'd been introduced to the famous "Santarama Who." Still another complimented Miss Who on her genuine Indian "sarong."

Like good drawing-room comedy, this particular scene had ironies within ironies. Here was a distinguished producer trying to package an important play in a four-letter word. But in peddling *A Passage to India* to Just One Break, Inc., or the National Multiple Sclerosis Society, several of the Golden Dozen might have been capable of transmitting its flavor in a sentence or even a paragraph, if given a chance.

Even a thousand well-chosen words, however, would not have done justice to *A Passage to India*, a drama in which nuances of three principal characters were depicted by their reactions to an elusive collar button. Miss Rau's play did not generate much party support.

[II]

If you hang around the Golden Dozen and their admirers long enough, you begin to speak their language. For a number of pages now, we have been talking about the theater not as an art but in terms of fiscal risk and commodity accessibility. This is hardly coincidental, for the theater has become a remote actuarial table or the form chart of a distant racetrack whose events a lot of people follow but only a select few attend. In the minds of its mentors, there is understandably no business like show business. And their hit-or-flop contagion is carried by various middlemen to the theater's critics and audiences and, worst of all, to its creators. "The theater is one of the great ways man speaks to man," wrote Clive Barnes last fall after just a week as drama critic of the New York *Times.* "Too often in the New York theater, pocketbook is speaking to pocketbook. It wouldn't be so goddam unhealthy if they didn't so often fail to communicate. It makes one very, very angry."

In the disastrous 1962–63 season, when Broadway finished at least $5 million in the red, the producers issued an instant denial of that appalling statistic. Then they huddled with their accountants, who tacked on projected income from movie sales, summer-stock rights, and overseas productions as well as profits of shows held over from previous seasons. Lo and behold, with wondrous feats of self-deception, they ultimately reaffirmed the theater's stature as a house of illusion. Thanks to subsidiary sales, that season went into *their* books in black, not red.

It was a scare, though, and as each season trickled from bad to worse, the Fabulous Invalid took out more insurance and wondered why it wasn't making him any better. Some of the hands in which he placed his coverage included show train-conductors, tour packagers, convention bureaus, ticket brokers, scalpers, expense-account panderers, department-store merchandisers, and other "experts" who buy in bulk and think in volume.

Gaining fast on the Golden Dozen and moving into second place by selling a good 10 percent of the Broadway ticket market in 1967–68 were New York's five theater clubs: Play of the Month Guild, Cue Theater Club, Macy's Theater Club, Critics Choice (started in late 1967 by the Theatre Guild), and the Stubs Preview Club (operated by benefit agent Lenore Tobin's husband, who works out of her office in the St. James Theater Building). The clubs buy up blocks of seats or whole houses at 7.5 percent discount and sell them to their 100,000 members, who pay dues of $5 to $10 a year for the privilege of buying tickets by mail from the clubs at list price (occasionally, less).

The Macy's club, which was inaugurated by the world's largest store in 1962, has been an aggressive competitor and possibly the most serious rival to Play of the Month, the oldest (founded 1941) and perhaps still the largest. From its inception, Macy's Theater Club has engaged in scare advertising ("This is the only way you can be sure of seats") and package deals (to buy Richard Burton's *Hamlet* at a small discount, you also had to buy the same producer's *Rugantino,* a soggy Italian *zuppa*-spectacle) that have led irate consumers to complain to the Federal Trade Commission and the New York State Attorney General.

All this presold insurance is working *against* you when you pick up the Sunday paper and find, in the very first announcement of a play, a long list of "FOLLOWING PERFORMANCES COMPLETELY SOLD OUT." But what I am describing here is not a uniquely Broadway malady. It cuts across the country and across the arts. There are theater clubs in Boston, Chicago, Los Angeles, and Philadelphia (under auspices related to the Macy's club) and Theatre Guild subscribers up and down the land. The richly endowed APA-Phoenix touring repertory troupe won't let you take *The School for Scandal* without taking a concert reading of Walt Whitman, too. Up at Lincoln Center (and in various other shopping centers for the arts in America), the whole economy hinges on the presold subscription. If you want to catch Brecht, you have to settle for Lorca, Ben Jonson, and Leo Lehman's *East Wind,* too. To secure a particularly promising evening of four one-act ballets by George Balanchine's troupe, you have to sit through three other evenings, including one of two full-length ballets: an overstuffed *Midsummer Night's Dream* or an underdanced *Don Quixote.* At the spanking new Metropolitan Opera House, no mail orders are accepted: 80 percent to 95 percent of the seats at all but seven performances a year are filled by subscribers, and the waiting list for subscriptions is 3,000 names long. If you still want to try for a pair of Met tickets at the box office, you have to wait overnight on line five weeks in advance. Next door at the New York State Theater, when Julius Rudel's New York City Opera put out its initial brochure for the 1967 fall season, every performance but one (a Thursday night *Tosca* in the Jewish New

Year) during those nine weeks had the words "SOLD OUT" listed after it.

Are we talking here about art or accessibility? There does seem to be a direct relationship, for every one of the democratic institutions listed above lost some of its vitality when it became the presold preserve of an affluent elite. Balanchine's New York City Ballet even lost some of its coordination. (Although many blamed this ragged footwork on the marble mausoleum that became the troupe's home at Lincoln Center, the fact that APA managed to grow fat and stodgy while migrating from one makeshift presold slum to another is enough to rule out a diagnosis of Edifice Complex here.) And, the Robert Joffrey Ballet, which stepped into the Balanchine company's shoes at its old barn of a City Center, has emerged as America's most exciting and adventurous dance troupe. The Joffrey Ballet doesn't presell subscriptions. When it does sell out the house, it sells out one night at a time—which, it seems, stimulates a grateful, almost electric, rapport between audience and performers.

Whatever the evils of preselling in all the arts, it is in the theater that "insuring the property" most directly overlaps artistry and affects a play's ability to get on the stage at all. Even off-Broadway, "No producer in his right mind will take a new script unless he can get the subsidiary rights," according to Dorothy Olim, who provides managerial assistance to small-scale theatrical entrepreneurs. It used to be said that "the play's the thing," but now it's a distant relation, twice or thrice removed from man speaking to man.

[III]

The musical comedy used to be America's most distinctive art form. It isn't now. Instead of creating a *My Fair Lady* or an *Oklahoma!* or something of comparable quality at least once a season (and we used to!), we import a *Pickwick* or an *Oliver!*, British-made bastardizations of Dickens. With grudging admiration, Broadway director Alan Schneider labeled *Oliver!* "the kind of prepackaged, presold musical you whistle the songs from as you are going in, that paradoxical phenomenon of our commercial theater: the synthetically manufactured, yet genuine, *smasheroo!*"

American lyricists, librettists, and composers haven't all deteriorated or gone West, but in Broadway's emphasis on musical "properties," the talent has been spread thinner and badgered harder. For in the musical-comedy pressure cooker, there is a powerful new force comparable to and sometimes outweighing the Golden Dozen: *the original-cast album.*

In one form or another, show recordings have been with us ever since the 1920's, when Sir Louis Sterling of Columbia Records waxed excerpts from London hits on 12-inch 78-r.p.m. discs. In 1940 Decca Records hired Ethel Merman, starring in Cole Porter's *Panama Hattie* on Broadway, to perform four songs from the show. They were packaged in a souvenir album with performance photos. In 1942 Decca recorded selections from *Porgy and Bess* and *This Is the Army,* but sales were not remarkable.

The birth of an institution, however, came in 1943, when Decca waxed a six-disc album "featuring members of the original New York production" of *Oklahoma!* Released nine months after the premiere, the *Oklahoma!* album sold more than a million copies at $5, and show recordings became the folk songs of our time.

At first, show albums were regarded by Broadway producers as mere late-in-the-run promotional gimmicks to prolong the life of a hit. They were grateful to the record companies for paying the cast and musicians for the extra work involved. *Finian's Rainbow,* in the late 1940's, marked the first time Broadway producers realized they were sitting on a pot of gold. Lee Sabinson and William R. Katzell made Columbia Records negotiate for rights and pay a cash advance. Soon after, it became customary for record companies to make token investments (up to $25,000) in the shows they recorded. In 1949 the miraculous new long-playing record had been on the market for months but had not yet caught on. Then Columbia released *South Pacific*—the show you couldn't get tickets for—both ways: on *seven* standard discs and on *one* LP record that was three dollars cheaper. Overnight, in one enchanted evening, LP records were *in!*

In 1956 the Columbia Broadcasting System put up the entire financing for *My Fair Lady* and reaped a bonanza. But Columbia Records, a CBS subsidiary, made an even quicker killing by recording the show in one day at a cost of $22,000. Do you remember *that* summer when, everywhere you went, *that* record was playing? You could walk down the street where you lived and hear the rain in Spain tinkling into every living room. Dwight Eisenhower and Adlai Stevenson, rerunning for President of the United States, went virtually unheard. The *My Fair Lady* album's 4 million sales earned more cash than the Mark Hellinger Theater's box office took in during the first four years of the show's run. Only Herman Levin, the producer, felt shortchanged. For the record companies, he protested, "the album rights are a license to print money." Rex Harrison, who had a percentage of the show, earned $300,000 from just the album—scarcely petty cash for one day's extra work.

(Ever since Harrison talked his way through his songs, Broadway musicals have been afflicted by nonsinging actors like Maurice Evans in *Tenderloin* and Julie Harris in *Skyscraper*. In the theater, if you hear them at all, they sound colorless. You buy the album to hear what you've missed. Their voices have been souped and tuned up electronically. You wonder if you left your ears home the night you went. In addition, singing actors who replace nonsinging actors in musical hits are often required to speak their songs in order to satisfy the owners of LP records.)

Thanks to *My Fair Lady*, the Gold Rush was on. Columbia and its competitors rushed in foolishly where even Broadway's angels feared to tread. Just to get first crack at album rights, they invested in shows that otherwise might never have set heavy foot on Broadway.

Decca, which had pioneered the whole phenomenon, withdrew from show-album competition in 1959 with this explanation:

"Everyone seems to be trying for the jackpot. Decca believes in being prudent. We're willing to invest in shows where we consider the risk a fair one. But how many companies can put up the amounts now being asked for by producers?"

The answer was, at least three. On September 25, 1961, the New York *Times* proclaimed on its front page: "RECORD COMPANIES TAKING MAJOR ROLE AS THEATER ANGELS." Below the headline, Arthur Gelb reported that Columbia, Capitol, and Victor Records had put up more than 50 percent of the backing for eight impending shows:

> The alliance between the record companies and Broadway musicals has reached an apogee of investment frenzy . . . and is gradually changing the structure of Broadway financing.
>   . . . One leading producer, for example, recently conceded that he would have been unable to mount his costly show had it not been for major financial support from a record company.
>   . . . The success of an original-cast record album, according to several producers, can directly affect the longevity of certain musicals. Potential theatergoers, they maintain, listen to the album and then buy tickets to the show.

That season, Columbia Records lost an estimated one million dollars by underwriting four disasters: *Kean, All American, Bravo Giovanni,* and *Subways Are for Sleeping.* Since it was his *My Fair Lady* album that started the inflation, Goddard Lieberson of Columbia remarked: "We are the victims of our own Frankenstein monster."

None the less, with film-company subsidiaries like M-G-M Records and ABC-Paramount eager to fill the breach of disenchantment, the symbiotic relationship between Shubert Alley and Tin Pan Alley solidified. In 1963 Capitol Records handed over $3 million to the producing firm of Feuer and Martin (*Guys and Dolls, Can-Can, How to Succeed*) as a "revolving fund" for future projects in return for their making album rights available to Capitol over a five-year span. In 1966 RCA Victor invested $1½ million in David Merrick's productions in exchange for first call on album rights. To partake of the Barbra Streisand boom (she records for Columbia), Capitol Records financed her biggest hit, *Funny Girl,* and made the album. Capitol even gave Hillard Elkins, a producer with a relatively undistinguished track record, $250,000 for "first refusal" of album rights to his next three shows.

"It's blackmail by the producers," said one record-company official. "If you want a crack at the original-cast album, you have to invest in the show."

When music moguls play angels, they tend to spread their wings. Far, far backstage, even before shows are written, there is pressure for a hit song, preferably a title song like *Hello, Dolly!* or *Mame,* that will add a good 50 percent to album sales regardless of whether it has any real relationship to the plot. The producer joins in the clamor, for every time the title tune is played on the jukebox, it's a singing commercial for the show. Harold Rome's penchant for fitting hard-sell lyrics to his title tunes—e.g., *"Wish you were here, wish you were here, wish you were here,"* and *"Fanny, Fanny, Fanny, Fanny,"*—may have earned him the trade nickname of "Harold Rome-Rome-Rome," but it also helped two weak sisters stay alive on Broadway. Why did David Merrick change the title *Dolly—A Damned Exasperating Woman!* to *Hello, Dolly!* shortly before the premiere? A few years earlier, ticket hunters had searched in vain for a Merrick musical called *What Kind of Fool Am I?*—which happened to be the hit song in *Stop the World—I Want to Get Off.*

Richard Rodgers, a composer who resents record-company backing as artistic interference, uses his own money to finance his shows. "I wouldn't want a record company or a network telling me how a show should be produced or how I should write a song. The companies, being commercially oriented, work through intermediaries. I want to please only one man— the one who buys his seat in the theater."

A few years ago, a much-married musical-comedy genius needed ready cash to buy a Riviera villa. Strapped by his alimony obligations, he heeded the siren song of a record company, which put up the cash in exchange for the album rights of his next show, not yet written. He did this without consulting his collaborator or producer, who, when they heard he had given away rights in which they shared, required him to compensate them handsomely. The show, written and produced amid creative disharmony, proved to be one of the most tuneless and listless disappointments in Broadway history.

How does all this backstage maneuvering affect the consumer out front? To begin with, it has spawned at least two new breeds of pest: 1) The armchair critic, who can and will give you critiques of all the latest shows. Should you think to ask whether he has seen them, he'll reply: "No, but I've heard the albums";

2) The sing-along-with-Liza buff who has memorized the score of *My Fair Lady* or whatever show you're seeing and croons it disconcertingly from his theater seat behind you. In general, after a show album has been on sale for a few weeks, the audience not only comes *into* the theater humming the music but applauds certain tunes in the overture or when they begin.

With *Oliver!* David Merrick presold the show by recording and releasing its album during a lengthy pre-Broadway tour. Since then, most major original-cast albums have been recorded while the shows were still trying out prior to Broadway in order to have the discs on the counters immediately after the reviews hit. Perhaps they ought to be labeled "aboriginal-cast albums." In any event, one can wonder how many producers would allow a director to improve a musical, either before or after its album is waxed, by removing a potential Hit Parade song that slows down the show.

"I'm looking for the best record company that will give my shows the greatest possible advertising by promoting the albums heavily," Merrick told me before making his deal with RCA Victor. And with characteristic benevolence, the record companies have passed on their toll to the consumer, who subsidizes the mammoth advertising budgets and guarantees and higher royalty scales and investments with which the record moguls woo producers. Why do original-cast albums now retail for a dollar or two more than symphonies? The presidents of Capitol and Columbia conceded to me in separate interviews that we the people are paying for their frenzied competition.

What is the artistic toll? One music critic has complained that many original-cast albums are "less performances of scores than a notable song or two surrounded at 'album length' by what the audiences have to sit through to hear them." In earlier times, these songs would have comprised one 78-r.p.m. single. Nowadays, though, when so much of the Broadway economy revolves around the Golden Disc, the two songs are sometimes the justification not merely for the album but for the show itself.*

---

* RCA Victor, which invested in four 1967–68 musicals to obtain album rights, has recently diversified further by putting up front money that would enable movie producer Roger Lewis to assemble a "creative package" for a film musical based on H. G. Wells' *The Man Who Could Work Miracles*. When the movie materializes, RCA Victor will have sound-track rights.

One Broadway show out of four used to be a musical. At this writing, twenty-two shows are currently on Broadway. Twelve are musicals. There is so much album money to be spread around that it's easier, cheaper, and less risky for a producer to mount a mediocre $400,000 musical than a good $75,000 one-set drama.

Don't get me wrong. Good new American plays conceived for the stage, not for subsidiary sales, still are done well on Broadway, but under adverse conditions. Frank D. Gilroy's *The Subject Was Roses*, which won the Pulitzer and every other prize in sight, had to open *after* the drama customarily shuts down for the warm months; theater rentals were cheaper then. Even so, when the preview excitement seeped out, the fledgling producer and playwright of *Roses* had to resist offers to take over the "property" and replace its gifted cast of three with "star names." Tad Mosel's dramatization of James Agee's *All the Way Home* almost closed before the judges who awarded it the Pulitzer Prize could get to see it.

The theater parties and theater clubs, after all, favor big musicals. So do the ticket brokers. Their most visible means of support—the tireless businessman on an expense account, the visiting fireman and his little woman—are bursting to see *Mame* and never heard of *The Subject Was Roses*. For, thanks to original-cast albums and excerpts on Ed Sullivan, the well-heeled folks in Lake Forest or Schenectady or, for that matter, Glen Cove are nothing if not *au courant* with what's really happening in the American theater today.

[IV]

The case of *Camelot* is a classic example of the pressures engendered when a show is "fortunate" enough to have both the Golden Disc and the Golden Dozen behind it. When the first advertisement for *Camelot* appeared one Sunday in March, 1960, the show had not yet been written. Nevertheless that single ad attracted checks and money orders for $400,000. In addition, some 200 theater parties were booked.

Camelot, due on Broadway eight months later, was a glittering magnet. Its guiding lights were the triumvirate that had made *My Fair Lady* glow—Alan Jay Lerner (book and lyrics), Frederick Loewe (music), and Moss Hart (director). This time, they would serve as their own producers. Their stars were Richard Burton as King Arthur and Julie Andrews as his Guenevere. All the financing (which eventually amounted to a whopping $673,000) would come from CBS, whose subsidiary, Columbia Records, had the album rights.

Clearly, cart-before-horse thinking had already entered the picture when Norman Rosemont, general manager for the producers, said that his organization considered *the record album as important as the show itself!* Rosemont went on. "We chose Columbia because it came up with the best deal. . . . Lerner and Loewe got the highest authors' royalties ever paid. We also feel that producing a cast album is not merely a duplication of the show. It is an art in itself, and Columbia is one of the best at doing it."

Unborn and unseen, *Camelot* could scarcely miss. Toronto was selected for the pre-Broadway premiere on October 1, a date that loomed large on every Toronto social calendar. In September, a want ad appeared in the *Globe & Mail:*

ATTENTION CAMELOT FIRST NIGHTERS. Two first nighters, female, with ensemble but without tickets, would happily accompany two first nighters, male, with tickets. Box 699. Globe & Mail.

By then the creators of *Camelot* were beginning to suspect that they were in deep trouble. "Seldom in my memory," Lerner recalled later, "and never in my personal experience has any show undergone the trials that this one did. Illness, at one point even death, plagued it from the very beginning of its creation. . . ."

The costume designer, Adrian, had died. And *Camelot* itself, running more than an hour too long, was dangerously over-weight. Back stage, it was nicknamed "the uncut *Götterdämmerung*" and "*Ben-Hur* with music." Half jokingly, half apologetically, Moss Hart warned Toronto's lucky ticket holders to hire baby-sitters who could stay up late. "If you have small children at home, you'll find them ready for college when you get back."

The Canadian first-nighters rooted hard but began turning into drowsy pumpkins toward midnight. Their reaction was reflected in the next day's Toronto headlines: "CAMELOT

CHARMING, BUT THERE'S WORK TO BE DONE" and "IT HAS AN EM-
BARRASSMENT OF RICHES."

True, *Camelot* possessed enough virtues to stock a couple of
Broadway hits: a gifted cast, including a handsome newcomer
named Robert Goulet as Lancelot; Fritz Loewe's silken score;
Oliver Smith's majestic scenery; and the basic tale of the Round
Table. On the other hand, Lerner's libretto was indecisive and
draggy. The whole show needed a month of drastic trimming,
pacing, and rewriting.

That was as of October 1. The following week, however,
Lerner was immobilized by a bleeding ulcer, and Moss Hart's
ninety-seven-year-old father died in Miami. The director was
too essential to *Camelot*, however, even to attend his father's
funeral.

When the doctors said Lerner would be hospitalized for at
least ten days, Hart postponed the Broadway premiere from
mid-November to early December.

"CAMELOT DELAY HITS PARTY DATES," was *Variety*'s headline.
There was now $1,350,000 in benefit bookings.

On October 14, an overworked and grieving Moss Hart,
fifty-six, suffered a heart attack in his Toronto hotel room. He
was incapacitated for the rest of *Camelot*'s tryout and died a
year later.

Alan Jay Lerner came out of the hospital the day after Hart
went in. Lerner immediately assumed *Camelot*'s two heaviest
burdens—play doctor and director. His collaborator, Loewe,
had survived a heart attack two years earlier and was now per-
ilously close to exhaustion. Before *Camelot* left Toronto, even
the theater manager was hospitalized—with an ulcer attack.

Still, north of the border, Lerner managed to eliminate a
number called "The Quests," make other fixes, and deny rumors that *Camelot* would fold on the road. He told Morris
Duff of the Toronto *Star*: "The ladies in the theater parties got
a bit hysterical and started spreading rumors. . . . That's where
it started."

The wounded giant of a musical staggered into Boston, where
not a single ticket was left. "A BOX-OFFICE COUP UNPARALLELED
WITHIN THE MEMORY OF THE OLDEST RESIDENT OF BACK BAY OR
BEACON HILL," its grandiose flack wired the New York press. The
Boston reviewers had less enthusiastic messages: "CAMELOT

NEEDS WORK. GORGEOUS, BUT BOOK DULL." and "CAMELOT PROMISES
SPLENDID FUN AFTER PERIOD OF POLISHING."

A two-thirds-of-a-million-dollar investment was four weeks
away from its Broadway showcase and still a crude, unfinished,
diamond in the rough. Alan Jay Lerner's twenty-hour-a-day
labors were herculean, but a doctor is seldom his own best
surgeon. Nobody has less perspective on a play in distress than
its author. After a while, he is incapable of rational self-criticism.
In the final throes of production, a playwright needs guidance,
and a director needs detachment. The ailing Lerner tried to
summon both.

The first postponement had evoked protests and premature
obituaries. Another was likely to generate panic. With advance
orders of $3 million in the box office and another $1¼ million
from the record stores, nobody in *Camelot's* brain trust dared
to risk further delay. Ready or not, *Camelot* came to town on
December 3, 1960—a floundering whale of a production that
almost swallowed up the tender, subtly shaded King Arthur of
Richard Burton. Performances started at 8:25 sharp and ended
blurrily toward midnight.

New York was less than rapturous. Several critics liked *Camelot* in moderation, but not Walter Kerr (then with the *Herald
Tribune*).

"Once there was a fleeting wisp of glory!" cries Richard
Burton as he awaits the last curtain alone. And there was.
But, for *Camelot* as well as for Arthur's court, it is the
glory of a steadily setting sun.

Eight days after the premiere, Howard Taubman brooded
in his Sunday *Times* drama column about what went wrong.
"*Camelot* merely hints at what it might have been," he began,
citing failures of conception that could have been remedied in
several ways. Then Taubman went on to say:

Clearly no expense has been spared. And here we arrive
at a clue to the insuperable hazards Broadway sets for its
children once they put a big production in motion. With
costly contracts signed, countless theater parties spoken for,
innumerable commitments involving hundreds of thousands of dollars made, how is it possible to pause in To-

ronto or Boston or Philadelphia? Who has the courage to take stock and say the point of view is muddled and the show must be redone, even if it requires a year?

Blame Broadway for this, if you like. But remember that Broadway has seen to it that *Camelot* need not fret about financial security.

Cushioned initially by the Golden Dozen's parties and then by Columbia's slickly alluring album, *Camelot* survived some of the worst word of mouth in Broadway history. Then, after five or six months, the word of mouth began to sound like a tug-of-war; people who loved *Camelot* and people who hated *Camelot* didn't seem to be arguing about the same show. Toward the end of its two-year run, I went back to see it for a second time.

Richard Burton had gone East to make *Cleopatra*. Robert Goulet had gone West to make a Sandra Dee movie. Julie Andrews had gone to Disneyland to impersonate Mary Poppins. And to make matters worse, *she* was now being impersonated by a long-lost and best-forgotten movie star, Kathryn Grayson. Nevertheless *Camelot* now bubbled with the tang of an interesting new wine. Two songs had been dropped.* Ten minutes of dialogue had been deleted. Production numbers had been tightened. The entrances of Arthur's illegitimate son, Mordred, and his scheming aunt, Morgan Le Fey, had been rearranged. A more upbeat ending (a short speech by King Arthur addressed to modern audiences) had replaced the original shrug of a finale (the king turned and walked offstage). A few new lines had been written.

All of these commonsense improvements could have been conceived and executed by *Camelot*'s professionals in less than a week. But nobody had been afforded the chance to think rationally until, after the Broadway premiere, Alan Jay Lerner had escaped to Switzerland for a vacation. On his return, he had belatedly transformed the oafish heir to *My Fair Lady* into one of the best damn operettas Broadway has ever seen.

The Golden Disc and the Golden Dozen can and do claim

---

* "Then You May Take Me to the Fair" and "Fie on Goodness," both of which you can still hear on Columbia's Broadway-cast album, not to be confused with the sound-track album of the subsequent 1967 movie version.

some credit for keeping *Camelot* alive. But why was *Camelot* born in such pitiful condition? Who induced the premature delivery that was so nearly fatal? The Golden Dozen, midwives brandishing silk purses, and the Golden Disc, technology spinning an irresistible siren song. Put them together, and they spell neither M-O-T-H-E-R nor his master's voice but the almighty presell strangling Broadway in its own prepackaged web of insurance.

The Fourth Commandment of the Culture Vultures:
Don't knock the schlock, for it may be
by Irving Degas.

4
The Art Mart,
or Adventures in the Skin Game

[1]

The lecturer on "Skin Art" was, appropriately, a naked blonde. The model perched on the table beside her was a real brunette—slimmer, less bovine, and a little less undressed thanks to lipstick, nail polish, and a fuming cigarette. The eight of us—myself and seven other men—had shelled out $6 for our two hours of skin painting on the Friday before Thanksgiving, 1967, so we paid close attention to our lecturer as she droned:

"Now let's say you aren't very inventive. Say you just want to draw straight lines. Well, you can still exercise your artistic imagination by alternating colors—like this. Or you can make 'em slant—like this. Or you can draw them over each other— like so. Or you can make a blue square, for instance, like this, and later fill it in with different colors to achieve a stained-glass window effect. Like this!"

While she spoke, she had been dabbing paint onto the obliging model's back. Now the model suddenly erupted in a shudder, a cloudburst of smoke, and an outraged squeal. "Jesus, Doris! There's something running down my crack!"

"It's just blue paint," the lecturer assured her. "Now how

would one of you boys like to make some patterns on the front of this young lady?"

The scene was an overheated walk-up studio in the garment district of Manhattan, and the eight perspiring art lovers had answered ads in the Village Voice *and other local newspapers (though not the New York* Times, *whose advertising acceptability department had rejected the copy) that ran along these lines:*

Now . . . New

SKIN

PAINTING

Try your own designs

directly on our female

FIGURE MODELS

Here is an entirely new phase of art initiated by a celebrated nationally known artist. Paint the model—not on canvas—but by brushing or spraying the colors directly on the model to achieve spectacular and stimulating artistic effects. Learn the techniques of this process. . . .

We furnish the paints,

brushes, the model, & the

studio.

You bring your artistic

talent and try your hand at

skin painting.

BEGINNERS WELCOME

Studio Open Every Thurs. Fri. & Sat. From 1 to 9 P.M. $20 hr.: $12 for one-half hour. Rates include private studio and selected model of your choice.

SKIN PAINTING CLASS . . . Fri. Nov. 17, 7 to 9 P.M. $6

In the topless bistro and pornography publishing trades, spiels like the naked lecturer's are known as "RSI"—legal shorthand for the Redeeming Social Importance that is crucial nowadays in the event of a raid and then a court test. But what we are seeing here and will see throughout this Cook's tour of the art mart is something more than hard-core voyeurism wrapped in the flimsiest of cultural garb. If my night at the skin art studio recurs throughout this chapter, as it will, this is not only because it was both grubby and grabbing. It is also because, on its own primitive level, it was grasping and greedy enough to serve as a valid metaphor for the whole pretentious highbrow-middle-brow, op-pop-slop-schlock art scene that runs rampant through our museums and galleries and emporiums today in the much-maligned name of culture.

Skin art, for instance, is the logical debasement of the boom in do-it-yourself Sunday painting. America, says economist Arnold Mitchell of the Stanford Research Institute, has "as many Sunday artists as hunters"—15 million of them! *Dun's Review* exults beneath the banner headline of "BOOMING MARKET IN MASS CULTURE":

> There's a whole new world of sales for companies that cash in on Americans' urge for self-expression. . . . [On] drugstore shelves, paint-it-yourself kits now vie for the customer's dollar with aspirin, sulfa, and toothpaste.
> . . . This mass boom in culture, probably the first of its kind in history, gets its impetus from sources that reach even into the White House. Harry Truman's piano-playing, Dwight Eisenhower's efforts with brush-and-easel, John F. Kennedy's innovation of a live poet at his Inaugural . . . Truman . . . was widely known to favor classical works. . . . Eisenhower, his sucessor, found satisfaction at the easel—and thousands followed his suit.

By 1964 there was a museum of Sunday paintings—the Accademia delle Belle Arti in Montecatini, Italy—where you could either buy an admission ticket or fork over a sculpture or painting of your own making. Notable contributions on permanent display include a rugged marble sculpture carved by the late Spencer Tracy, assisted by Katharine Hepburn; a rakish drawing by Douglas Fairbanks, Sr.; and paintings by the Queen of Denmark, the President of the Italian Senate, and Anna Moffo. Still others have been promised by the Shah of Iran, the Prince of Liechtenstein, Prince Rainier and Princess Grace of Monaco, and General Eisenhower, who passed through Montecatini in World War II. The town's tourism has been vastly enhanced by the museum, according to its founder, Dr. Dino Scalabrino, who also heads the local Association of Mud Baths and Curative Waters.

Arnold Mitchell predicts that "the conspicuous consumption

of yesteryear may turn into tomorrow's conspicuous esthetics,"
but highbrow prophet Jacques Barzun says, "The otherwise
commendable do-it-yourself movement, represented by the Sunday painter and the Friday evening singer or player, contributes
to the dissipation of the artistic tradition; high art is not made
for these uses." It degenerates into a hobby and then an activity.
"MAKE AN OIL PAINTING IN AN HOUR! EVERYBODY A REMBRANDT!
NO TALENT NECESSARY!" screams the daily calendar at the fabulous Concord Hotel in the Catskills. Or, as Marshall McLuhan
contends with one categorical pun: "Art is the enema of the
people." McLuhan has also said, "Art is anything you can get
away with," a definition that has led some cagey entrepreneurs
from the cash boom in Sunday painting to the instant creativity
of spin art (the customer pours paint on a "small" cardboard
for 65 cents, "regular size," $1.25, or "large economy," $2.25;
steps on a pedal; watches it circulate; and leaves happily ever
after, clutching his creativity and feeling like Jackson Pollock)
to the penultimate reality of skin art.

On another front, General Eisenhower, the uncle figure of
Sunday painting, was speaking in his own inimitable style about
abstract art when he asked a question which also bears on the
collage of corruption detailed in this chapter.

"When we see movies and the stage and books and periodicals
using vulgarity, sensuality, indeed downright filth, to sell their
wares, you think that our spirit—do you say America has advanced as much as we have materially when we see our very art
forms so changed that the works of Michelangelo and Leonardo
da Vinci are scarcely spoken of in terms of a piece of canvas
that looks like a broken-down Tin Lizzie loaded with paint has
driven over it? What has happened to our concept of beauty
and decency and morality?"

Program note from a 1965 exhibition of "Yes Art—the Cultural Miracle":

> Jasper Johns once said, "Sometimes I see it and then
> paint it. Other times I paint it and then see it." Although
> this statement was made only five years ago, it sounds
> archaic when repeated today. A YES ARTIST opposes that
> type of either/or restriction, so he doesn't necessarily have
> to see anything or paint anything to create a painting. A

work of Art can be made merely by coming across an object that strikes an artist's fancy, and by signing it, he can make it into art. After all, art is made by artists and no one else. The preconceived notion that for something to be art it has to be a copy of something is utter nonsense and as outdated as Jackson Pollock. Most people who buy Brillo boxes couldn't care less whether they were made by the National Brillo Corporation or by an artist. That a Brillo box has been signed by an artist is what's meaningful and artistic.

The calculated placement of art in galleries and museums creates still another artificial barrier between artist and consumer. . . . The Fitzgerald Gallery by offering S&H Green Stamps with the purchase of paintings does a great job in removing the false atmosphere of the gallery. Selling much of the work by the pound is another bold and dynamic step towards lifting the false barriers set up between the artist and the public. YES ART in the final analysis is affirmative. It will eliminate the preconceived notion that art is anything more than whatever it turns out to be.

On display were a Brillo Mondrian (with the steel-wool insignia set inside one of the rectangles) that sold for $450 (4,500 Green Stamps); an S&H Green Stamp insignia painted in oil on canvas for $667 (6,670 Green Stamps); and "Oldenbird," a nineteen-inch-high mechanical, moving, talking parrot spouting some gabble about modern art for $100 (1,000 Green Stamps).

The Fitzgerald Gallery is on Madison Avenue. The ARTerie is in Detroit—another of the American economy's outposts that thrives on built-in obsolescence. "WE'VE STRUCK OILS!" a sign proclaims outside the Quonset-like former auto sales office on Woodward Avenue. Inside, every inch of wall space and much of the ceiling is covered by some 500 original oil paintings, mostly bought up by the batch in Europe. They are priced from $4 to $2,000, including the frame, with the majority below $100. They can also be rented for as little as $6 a month because the ARTerie operates on the orgiastic premise that (according to the adman who conceived it) "the true test of whether a painting is worth *your* hard-earned dollars is whether *you* . . . want to *live* with it, now and in the future." To which the ARTerie's brochure adds: "And, if you later decide to buy the painting which you have rented, every penny you pay in rent applies toward the purchase price!"

From the outset, the ARTerie's hottest gimmick was its huge red couch, on which six or eight supine browsers could take their ceiling art lying down. "After five days in business," *Time* reported, "114 paintings had been rented, while more than 100 pieces of art, including an African circumcision mask, had been sold." When I got there six months later, however, business had slowed perceptibly. Two small boys were using the couch as a trampoline while their mothers made small talk with one of the owners. But the management was getting ready to reactivate the cultural boom in Detroit by throwing in a free car wash with each art purchase.

If the ARTerie has indeed struck oil, its success won't be due to its gimmicks so much as to America's benign acceptance of the myth that *if it's original—and particularly if it's European, too—then it's got to be art.* This thinking provides the most visible means of support for a Common Market of Italian hired hands manufacturing watercolors of Venetian canals for a Long Island distributor to retail at $5; elderly Continental hacks turning out "European imports by tomorrow's famous artists" with assembly-line precision for a San Francisco packager to market at from $3.99 to $99.95; and a steady stream of "original oil paintings arriving daily from Spain and Holland. Only $19.95 each. Major credit cards honored." Even so, says one such American entrepreneur, "supply just can't keep up with demand."

"I wonder if hotcakes are selling like art these days," a New York art dealer remarked not long ago. Painting sales at the world's three leading art auction houses—Parke-Bernet in New York and Sotheby's and Christie's in London—have virtually doubled since 1960. The big buyers are largely Americans. Each year, Americans in all brackets are spending at least $200 million on paintings, prints, color reproductions, art materials as well as another $300 million to finance art museums. As the pop philosopher Tom (not Thomas) Wolfe has noted in one of his more lucid moments:

For untold thousands of intellectuals today Culture, not church, is the favored form of religious rejection of the world. Young men and women may be seen riding to work on the subway each morning in New York with volumes by Rilke, Rimbaud, Herman Hesse and LeRoi Jones or somebody like that in their laps as if to say, This filthy train, this filthy office, this rotten Gotham and this roaring ratrace are not my real life. My real life is Culture. Prints and paintings are on every wall today like ikons. Renoirs are virtually unobtainable; they are clutched like Columbus' bones.

Whatever the thrust behind this, it deserves better than the cheapening, coarsening, flattening, and degrading of taste that pervades so much of the art mart today.

Wolfe, like *Dun's Review,* finds it significant "that the 1961 Presidential Inaugural ceremonies included a succession of Roman Catholic, Protestant, Jewish, and Greek Orthodox clergymen reading prayers, followed closely by Robert Frost" trying to read a poem. A great deal of junky art—particularly of the ilk assembled for tourist traps like the Washington Square Outdoor Art Exhibit—has commemorated President Kennedy and his wife as a couple of cultural messiahs, largely because the President appointed an Adviser to the Arts, who went around telling the natives that culture was good.

That adviser, August Heckscher, now New York City Parks Commissioner, put this legend into perspective not long ago when he was introduced at a banquet as "President Kennedy's 'Mr. Culture' himself." Heckscher winced and then, as graciously as he could, reminded his audience that President Kennedy was a man whose personal tastes ran to Ian Fleming, Frank Sinatra, and Chubby Checkers. Heckscher went on to say, "John F. Kennedy was not and never pretended to be a connoisseur of ballet, painting, opera. Privately, he protested some of the things his wife dragged him to. But he had a lively mind and an appreciation of all forms of excellence. Toward the end of his life, he seemed to feel that through the arts, one could sense what was at the bottom of the strivings and aspirations of an entire people."

Speaking at Amherst a month before he died in Dallas, President Kennedy declared: "Art establishes the basic human truths which must serve as the touchstones of our judgment. . . . We must never forget that art is not a form of propaganda, it is a form of truth. And as [Archibald] MacLeish once remarked of poets, 'There is nothing worse for our trade than to be in style.' "

[II]

The first skin artist who volunteered to paint the nude model was a husky young man with close-cropped blond hair. He stood up, removed his leather jacket, and squared his shoulders.

"What're you gonna do, wrassle?" asked a friend he had come in with, dressed almost identically.

The volunteer said nothing. He picked up a paintbrush, dipped it, and then gingerly circled the model's right nipple in red. She puffed away nonchalantly at her cigarette, saying nothing. He circled his red circle in green. Then he circled his green circle in blue. Still no response.

The naked instructor, however, droned on encouragingly. "He's following and emphasizing the natural roundness of the breast, which is very important in figure art."

The volunteer asked the model: "How'm I doing?"

"Just fine," she answered uninterestedly.

"You're not too cold, are you?" he persisted.

"Naw."

His buddy couldn't stand it anymore. "I can paint rounder curves than that!" he boasted. Taking up a brush and the model's left breast, he coated it with blue circles.

The lecturer continued. "It takes about half an hour to paint a complete model."

The next man up darted forward and painted a tattoolike heart between her breasts. This elicited a coo from the model. "That's sweet!"

The next customer drew an intricate network of wiry lines connecting up all the model's more personal parts. The next man to try his hand was a pudgy, fatherly man with a prissy mouth. He immediately painted the outlines of a frilly brassiere around the model's chest and back. In fact, he did the same to the three other models he had a chance to paint that night. The

*third time around, I asked him if he was in the lingerie busi-
ness. "Certainly not," he replied, "I'm a chemical engineer."*

*The sixth man, who had a receding chin, was so nervous that
he splattered his white shirt as well as the model. "Don't worry,
Jackson Pollack," said the lecturer, "it washes out."*

*"Everyone's gonna know where you've been!" the first volun-
teer taunted.*

*"If you go to the art shop because you want to paint some-
body," said our naked schoolmarm, "be sure to ask for a water-
base paint, preferably tempera. It comes in jars or cans. Now
who hasn't had his chance?"*

She looked straight at me, so I stepped forward.

*"There isn't much canvas left," the instructress said apolo-
getically. "We'll bring in another model when you've all had a
chance to paint this one."*

*"Please don't paint my pubic hair," the model grumbled to
me. "It's murder to get paint outta there."*

*I picked up a brush, dipped it in blue paint, and kneeling
before my first live figure model, painted a big blue question
mark that wrapped around her navel. I dotted it just above
the area she had told me was off limits and started to sit down.*

*"Is that all you're gonna paint?" the second volunteer asked
me, outraged.*

*"An artistic statement can be made briefly or at great length,"
our naked cultural arbiter intoned. But the controversy my
skin art generated had piqued the model's interest. She glanced
downward and said to me: "What are you, a wise guy?"*

*Still aiming to please, I picked up the brush again, dipped
it in brown, and flanked my blue question mark with two flat-
tering exclamation points and then a plus sign and a minus
sign. As I did so, I felt a sudden tingling in my scalp. The model
had returned my compliments by using my hair as an ashtray.*

I must have had hair on my brain because the very next
morning I found pubic hair at Macy's. It was all over an exhibition of oils, prints, and sculptures by Philip Sutton, a thirty-
nine-year-old Briton described by Macy's as a "close friend" of
Albert Finney, the actor, and much of it belonged to Sutton's
wife, Heather. His themes were described in the program notes

as "happy ones; of his family, especially his children, views from his studio windows, his studio walls and beautiful luxurious nudes. . . . And his sculptures are almost a tribute to Matisse with stress on forms and primary colours."

Macy's used to have an eighth-floor art department run by a man named Stanley Cornfield, who was also the mirror buyer. It made news back in 1965 when Macy's announced that limited editions of signed graphics by Braque, Cezanne, Chagall, Picasso, Renoir, and Rouault were being reduced for clearance at "20 to 50 percent off regular or original prices," ranging from $59.95 to $1,500—a tactic that outraged many legitimate dealers.

Writing on "The Strange New Art Market" in *Harper's* magazine, Milton Esterow tells about a lady who went into Macy's around that time and said: "I'd like to buy a Rumbrandt."

"You mean a Rembrandt."

"Yes, Rembrandt. Do you have an original for under one hundred dollars?"

The clerk said no. The very same day, he also said no to a suburban matron who asked if Macy's was going to carry the "Mona Lisa," then touring the country on loan from the Louvre. "Why not?" the woman protested. "Macy's carries everything."

Sensing a craving for higher things among its clientele, Macy's revamped its art operation in 1966 and brought in Eugene Ivan Schuster of Detroit, an art historian and faculty member at Wayne State University, to launch a permanent professional gallery on the ninth floor. Schuster, who had formed a touring art organization while on a Fulbright to the University of London, inaugurated his London Arts-Macy's Gallery with a Picasso Retrospective and followed it with "Graphics for Fall Collectors," shows of Braque, Rouault, German expressionists, art nouveau, Jacob Epstein, Horace Brodzky, and a Mediterranean Art Show (to tie in with a Macy's Mediterranean Festival) before confronting Herald Square shoppers with Mrs. Philip Sutton's pubic hair.

Woolworth's recently featured original watercolors and Gainsborough "Blue Boy" reproductions for $6.95 as well as a Gainsborough original for $24,000 and a Dali for $75,000. And in a prize-winning New York *Times* article, "REMBRANDTS BY MAIL AND CUT-RATE PICASSOS PROVE ART IS GOOD BUSINESS," Virginia Lee Warren told of the gallery director at Sloane's furniture store who was asked on the same day, "Don't you have any nice bedroom pictures?" and "Don't you have any basic things? You know, little nothings in art."

There was also the crowd that stormed Stern's for a showing of "fine art." One man made twelve quick selections and then turned to the director for help. "I can buy only eight. Tell me which four not to take."

A woman tucked a $375 picture under her arm to keep anyone else from getting it while she shopped around and made up her mind. "I've already had two sold out from under me."

The chairman of the New York City Bar Association's art committee recently visited one store's art collection and saw a statue with plaster inside and bronze outside. It was labeled as a Degas. "Irving Degas?" he wondered.

The burgeoning frontier of department-store art was pioneered from the West in 1962 by Vincent Price, the movie actor and art collector, who assembled a selection of his own choice, bank-rolled by Sears Roebuck. Originally conceived as a prestige- and attention-getter for Sears, the Vincent Price Collection, unveiled in Denver, proved such big box office that it toured more than eighty cities and inspired Sears to open permanent galleries in its Los Angeles, Dallas, and Chicago stores. By 1963, Price was commissioning Salvador Dali to paint a series of madonnas and children to be sold exclusively in Sears stores. Soon after, when I visited Price—who calls himself "only a second-hand millionaire"—at his Bel Air home, he was averaging close to a thousand art purchases a month and was soon to rank (with William Randolph Hearst and J. P. Morgan) as one of the three most prolific collectors of the twentieth century.

A suave performer whose acting has been known to reek of vulgarity, Price nonetheless majored in art at Yale and insists that it was an honest contest when he tied Edward G. Robinson in art on television's *$64,000 Challenge*. He oozes enthusiasm for his new role as an art buyer. "Imagine walking into Sears and buying an original etching by Rembrandt, one of the greatest artists who ever lived. I've been shooting my mouth off for years about art. Now this is bringing fine art out of isolation to people in their homes. . . . And we find something like eighty-two percent of it is charged on the easy-payment plan."

At Price's, huge turtles grazed on the lawn, the buzz of bees

filtered in from the apiary, and my wife and I were kept waiting
for fifteen minutes, during which time we were privileged to
overhear Price persuading a customer on the phone about the
merits of a Rembrandt etching. Suffice to say that Price's silky
salesmanship did wonders for Rembrandt.

A less privileged cultural exchange—between Price and his
art associate, Harry Sundheim—was printed by Atlanta columnist Norman Shavin at a time when Price was buying up as
many as 450 paintings a day. The dialogue concerned a work
for which he paid $200, and Shavin says it went about like this:

PRICE: "I think we ought to buy it."
SUNDHEIM: "If you think it will sell."
PRICE: "Well, Harry, it's a nun, and you know how big nuns are
this year."
SUNDHEIM: "Okay, so nuns are big. We got a nun."

And the art mart has the phony cult of personality that
Vincent Price represents as well as the wholesale buying and
cynical selling that characterize department-store merchandising.

"When a store sells a clothespin or a zipper or a plastic
garbage pail," says John Canaday, art critic of the New York
Times, "it can apply the test of salability as a test of quality
because people know when clothespins or a zipper or a plastic
garbage pail work and when they won't. But when people are
offered art to buy, the seller has a responsibility to make some
kind of valid preliminary judgment for them and, above all, he
must not offer trash alongside quality in the hope that the quality will sort of seep down."

Vincent Price says that no matter where his collection goes,
most buyers come into Sears knowing what is current and chic.
The most lucrative area, he has found, is greater Philadelphia.
"I don't know why, but we do extremely well there. Some parts
of California are marvelous, too. Los Angeles is good, but not
as good as San Diego. San Francisco has always been a notori-
ously bad town for the sale of pictures." Cultural-news editor
Milton Esterow adds, "A Boston dealer, who has opened eleven
galleries in major cities in the last four years, keeps a card file on
the vagaries of taste throughout the country. Boston: nudes
don't sell, but seascapes are big; Denver: paintings of mountains
don't move; St. Louis: favors Italian and riverboat scenes and

landscapes; Chicago and Louisville: broad tastes so long as the subject matter is colorful and happy; Minneapolis: generally conservative."

The net effect of this mass merchandising of art is that new buyers, ranging from multimillionaires to the masses, are being peddled an awful lot of junk. "The art market today," said dealer Charles Alan, "is terribly unhealthy. People are buying not what they like but what is fashionable. People are actually buying things because they are expensive." Sidney Janis, one of the more successful Madison Avenue dealers, actually raised his prices in the early 1960's to attract brand-name buyers who didn't trust anything that wasn't expensive.*

Several of Manhattan's better galleries have gone private— open only to selected customers and those they recommend. And in 1965, not long after she was approached by a Texan who drawled, "Honey, Ah want you to make me up an American collection," a major art dealer went underground. Edith Halpert, who gave Ben Shahn and Jack Levine their first shows, relocated her Downtown Gallery in the substreet level of the Ritz Tower Hotel on a by-appointment-only basis. Explaining that she was fleeing the madding crowd of "off-street traffic" and people "who come in just to use the telephone or the john," Mrs. Halpert went on to tell *Newsweek*:

"When something becomes too accessible, it's no good. Art is being vulgarized every time a 'fine painting' is sold over the counter at Woolworth's and in department stores. Nowadays some kid makes a *spritz* on canvas, and he gets a museum show. We have no more standards. Fashion and style have taken over. Even the Museum of Modern Art admits that the op fabrics came before the painting."

Vulgarization and *accessibility* are ladylike words for what's going on. Art appreciation, in a word, has been schlocked to death. (*The Random House Dictionary* defines *schlock* as "something of cheap or inferior quality; junk.") Mass reproduction has put art not only within the reach of laymen but also within the grasp of promoters, the shrewd but untalented Irving Degas' who prosper by putting Michelangelo on commemorative coins, Matisse on coasters, and El Greco on cufflinks. ("By exclusive

---

* According to Charles Alan, quoted in *Time*, November 24, 1961, p. 65.

agreement the Museum Gallery offers this distinguished new gift GREAT MASTERPIECES OF ART CUFFLINKS reproduced in all their majesty of color & framed in Sterling Silver or 24kt. gold" for $10 plus tax, says an ad in the Diners' Club's magazine.)

Their highbrow counterparts have no qualms about using Picasso as a loss leader to stimulate hard-cover magazine sales ("FREE PICASSOS! WIN ONE OF 201 ORIGINALS IN ART IN AMERICA'S PICASSO POTPOURRI!") or reducing Rembrandts to museum miniatures that you lick like postage stamps and paste into albums. Art cinemas across the nation justify their three-letter title by dishing out art for sale along the stairway as you wend your way from Jane Fonda to the espresso or the john. The Yonkers Cinema recently advertised:

PUSHBACK SEATS   ART GALLERY
ACRES OF FREE PARKING

and then, in smaller print:

On our Giant Screen. . . .
Tony Curtis in
"Arrivederci, Baby!"
in color

The perfection of Ektachrome reversal film, circa 1950, triggered a boom in art books, but much of it merely involves American publishers buying into European publishers' output and bringing it out here under their own imprint. Our home-grown moguls have been known to place a Gainsborough "Blue Boy" next to an El Greco red Cardinal, causing both to blush purply. In another instance, *Time* noted: "One standard way for a dealer to promote an artist is to get a book written about him, but there has been at least one case in which a book contained nothing but fakes, all reproduced in glorious color."

Chock Full O'Nuts uses the "Venus de Milo" to remind you that its cream cheese sandwiches and brownies are untouched by human hands. A Newark supermarket chain salutes the arrival of the "Mona Lisa" in America with a full-page ad. Half the page is devoted to the painting, engraved in the wretchedest black and white imaginable. The other half page explains:

WHAT REALLY BROUGHT
THE MONA LISA TO TOWN?

As most Americans know, the world famous painting of the Mona Lisa, by Leonardo da Vinci, is now on exhibition in the National Gallery in Washington, D.C. . . . We saw the painting this past Sunday in Washington! As we stood there and gazed upon her beauty, and her contented smile, we couldn't help but dream. . . . Perhaps she crossed the Atlantic just to come to Shop-Rite! Certainly many people are known to travel for miles to save at Shop-Rite, the food stores that are high in value and low in price, to keep your cost of living down! Perhaps that's why the Mona Lisa is smiling.

With a little more logic, mayhap, a Pennsylvania chemical manufacturer advertises: "If Da Vinci worked at Air Products . . ." Offering full-color reproductions of "The World's Great Art" for $6.95 with every $50 deposit, Christmas Club, or loan application, the Manufacturers Hanover Trust Bank catches the eye with this friendly admonition: "HANG VLAMINCK IN YOUR LIVING ROOM."

Art on corporate walls and lawns has become the newest status symbol. Regan's Office Furniture in New York startled *its* window shoppers one morning with a display of two sculptures grappling behind glass: "MUSEUM APPROVED REPRODUCTIONS $11–$75." An official of Seagram Distillers was complimented about "that pop art print on your wall," which was, he informed his visitor tersely, his bulletin board.

"Too much art in too many places," says Jacques Barzun, "means art robbed of its right associations, its exact forms, its concentrated power. We are grateful for the comprehensive repertoire which modern industry for the first time puts within our reach, but we turn sick at the aggressive temptation, like the novice in the sweetshop."

The even greater long-range danger is that thanks to our daily gorging on schlock, we may be mistaking it for the real thing. And nowadays, when a slightly nebulous cultural explosion is assuming all the proportions of a religious revival, this would be tantamount to mistaking a soapbox atheist for God.

[III]

After I sat down, there was only one untried skin artist—a chap in his thirties with black beard and blue beret. Now he approached the model with the buckety lurch of a Park Avenue window washer and began to paint every uncovered patch he could find.

"Hey!" cried one of the early volunteers. "You're gonna embalm her pores."

"Don't hold back," said the naked lecturer. "She won't get blood poisoning like in Goldfinger."

"Next time I go first," Blackbeard muttered.

He did—on the three other models our class painted that night. In each case, he confined his colors to various mixtures of brown, orange and red and his locales to the various orifices. He created remarkable effects of blood gushing, coursing, or tricklin from them, and the instructor complimented him on his work.

"You don't paint like a beginner."

"I'm not," said Blackbeard. "I used to paint my wife."

"A lot of women say getting painted releases tensions and makes them tingle all over," said the instructor. "What does your wife think?"

"She's not my wife anymore," Blackbeard said succinctly.

The instructor gave a back-to-the-drawing-board sigh and told the rest of us not to wait for Blackbeard to finish his work on the model before him. "We can paint around him. We're all going to collaborate on a group painting, like they would in one of the old masters' studios."

A novelist I was writing about had to go to a fund-raising reception in his honor and invited me to come along "so there'll be someone I can talk with." My wife could come along, too, so his third wife would have someone to talk with. The party was up in Westchester, but it would help endow a distant cultural center that was threatening to dramatize one of his works. Each invited guest had paid $1,500 to rub elbows with this great American novelist, or so we thought until we had been there for fifteen minutes.

Our little foursome stood, otherwise alone, in the center of our wealthy host's drawing room. Occasionally our host passed by with a reassuring nod, but he was too busy shepherding his entourage to do much about us. For we quickly realized that virtually all the guests had paid their $1,500 apiece to view the host's home and art collection. The only people who bothered with the great American novelist after the initial introductions were a man who came back to find out why "none of you fellows has written a morality play against smoking" and a Helen Hokinson lady who deliberately extinguished her cigarette on the great American novelist's dinner jacket in order to clean him off with motherly delight verging on rape.

Throughout the evening, our strained chitchat was mercifully punctuated by the guided tour passing by. "Those are our Paul Klees," our host would purr silkily. "My wife and I kept them in our dressing room until we found out that Klee was Somebody."

The great American novelist shifted his weight occasionally but minded his own business and refrained from sardonic comment about the passing parade. He was almost relaxing with his third champagne when the host, without breaking his stride, admonished him, "Please don't lean against the Giacometti."

He wasn't leaning, but he sidestepped obligingly, spilling his champagne and almost colliding with a massive Rodin. The Helen Hokinson lady rushed over to clean him off again. This time, she had the great American novelist all to herself, for his third wife, a very loyal girl who'd been around, had pivoted belligerently and planted herself in the host's path.

"It's all right," she insisted with a wild logic of her own. "We *know* Giacometti." [At the time, the sculptor was alive.]

"You mean," said the host, pursing his lips, "you *knew* Giacometti."

"I know him," she said. "I saw him in Paris this year."

"Then you must have the wrong Giacometti," said the host with tour-must-go-on impatience, "because everybody in my collection has been dead for at least a decade."

"Then *you* must have the wrong Giacometti," said the third wife, her voice rising to a screech that made our host blanch.

"Calm down, darling," said the great American novelist, taking her arm. "It doesn't look like a fake to me."

"It's not a fake!" she said. "It looks like authentic lesser Giacometti, but he's alive!"

For once that evening, our little foursome was the center of attention. While the host phoned his art dealer at home for confirmation, a murmur of "fake" and "minor" and "Jack of who?" and "What a shame!" enveloped us like cigar smoke.

I sauntered off and caught a glimpse of our host, hanging up the telephone. He was crestfallen, and for a moment, I could have sworn I heard him sob. Then he glanced up at his Giacometti with new eyes, pulled himself together, marched up to the great American novelist's third wife, took her by the arm, and said effusively: "Well, well, you must tell us all about Signor Giacometti. What's he like? How does he . . . ?"

This expedition to darkest Westchester is probably as close as I'll ever come to the soul of big-money art collecting, although one occasionally catches a glimmer of it in items like *Newsweek's* visit to a gas and oil man's collection in Bradford, Pennsylvania. Or when Mrs. Robert Scull, the pop art collector, auctions off some newly acquired De Koonings and Barnett Newmans because "my pictures are like children to me and I hate to part with them, but we're selling them off to buy paintings by some of the younger artists," we see that the art world has become a place where children may not live to grow up.

S. N. Behrman's book, *Duveen,** is a classic biography of the culture dispenser who at first for better, but ultimately perhaps for worse, brought much of this about. *Duveen* is a gallery of vignettes: Henry Clay Frick in solitary splendor, glancing up from his *Saturday Evening Post* to contemplate old masters while an organist played "Silver Threads Among the Gold"; Samuel Kress, trying to wheedle Duveen into a discount for his buying art in bulk; H. E. Huntington, who bought the "Blue Boy" from Duveen for $620,000, complaining that it wasn't as blue as the reproduction in the Gainsborough Suite on board the *Aquitania*; Duveen and four other dealers presenting Henry Ford with a privately prepared three-volume set of reproductions, *The Hundred Greatest Paintings in the World* —the originals of which they hoped to sell to Ford in one vast

---

* Berhman, S. N., *Duveen*. New York, Random House, 1952.

transaction—and being sent away with: "But gentlemen, what would I want with the original pictures when the ones right here in these books are so beautiful?"

Joseph Duveen, later Baron of Millbank (1869–1939), was the art dealer who revolutionized American taste in art and who over five decades established the United States as the place where the art money was and the great paintings went. Before Duveen, American millionaires tended to collect "sweet French" and English "story" pictures. But Duveen, says Behrman, "forced American collectors to accumulate great things, infused them with a fierce pride in collecting, and finally got their collections into museums. . . ."

Duveen and the events of 1913 changed the face of art in America forever. On February 17 the Armory Show, the most important art exhibition in American history, opened at the 69th Regiment's headquarters on Lexington Avenue, New York, and brought modern European painting to our shores. Marcel Duchamp's "Nude Descending a Staircase" was its *cause célèbre.* On February 25, with the adoption of the sixteenth Amendment, the first federal income tax went into effect. Thirty-four days later, J. Pierpont Morgan died, but not before—in anticipation of an increase in British death duties—he had shipped his art collection from England to America. Morgan was able to leave an estate valued at $128 million, almost half of it in art, without his heirs paying one cent of federal estate tax. They did have to pay $3 million in New York State inheritance taxes. (Today the combined federal and state taxes on such an estate would exceed $100 million.) And on October 3, thanks to the efforts of lawyer John Quinn, a sponsor of the Armory Show, the tariff laws were altered to permit free entry of original paintings and sculpture.*

"In that watershed year of 1913," writes one historian, "when the dollar was worth far more than it is today, Benjamin Altman paid almost a quarter of a million dollars for Rembrandt's glorious *Toilet of Bathsheba,* now owned by the Metropolitan Museum; Henry Clay Frick paid more than a quarter of a million for a Rembrandt portrait of a merchant and [with Duveen's

---

* Tax data in this chapter is drawn largely from the definitive article "Art and Taxes," by lawyer Jerome S. Rubin (*Horizon,* Winter, 1966, pp. 5–15), who is working on a book on the subject.

guidance] commissioned the architectural firm of Carrère & Hastings to build his Fifth Avenue town house, where the Rembrandt resides in good company; and Arabella Huntington paid more than $400,000 for Velázquez's portrait of the Duke of Olivares, which hangs in the Huntington Library in San Marino, California." (Arabella Huntington was the wife of H. E. and the widow of his uncle, Collis. She and H. E. were married in 1913.)

Duveen would tell his clients: "I can't possibly sell a Rembrandt to a man who owns no other pictures. The Rembrandt would be lonely."

And Behrman comments:

> When the American millionaires of the era said, "I don't care what it costs," as they often did, they were silently adding, "So long as I have something to show for it. . . ."

"You can always make more money," Duveen would tell them, "but if you miss this picture, you'll never get another like it, for it is unique."

In the early years of the federal income tax, a citizen with a taxable annual income of $1 million was liable to the Internal Revenue Service for a modest $60,000. (If his income remained steady, his tax obligation would have risen to a wartime peak of $915,000 in 1944 and dropped slightly in postwar years.)

In 1916 a federal tax graduated to a ceiling of 10 percent was imposed on transfers of property at death. (This ceiling rose to 25 percent in World War I, dropped off thereafter, rose to 45 percent in 1932, and now stands at 77 percent on that portion of the taxable estate in excess of $10 million.)

In 1924 a gift tax was enacted which thwarted the taxpayer bent on transferring his property to his family before his death. (The rate has varied, but since 1932, it has generally been three-fourths of the estate tax rate.)

All of these measures made it increasingly difficult for an individual to amass, retain, or bequeath a private fortune. Sandwiched among them, however, was the Internal Revenue Act of 1917, wherein Congress gave the philanthropically minded a decent break by sanctioning tax deductions for contributions to federal, state, or municipal governments "for exclusively public purposes" and to American organizations "operated exclusively for religious, charitable, scientific, literary, or educational purposes." Parallel provisions were built into the estate-tax and gift-tax laws.

"It was shortly after the First World War," Behrman writes, "that Duveen realized where his future lay . . . in selling the idea of assembling collections that would automatically insure immortality to his clients. Each of the Duveen millionaires wanted to get the particular intimation of immortality Duveen offered, and, if possible, to get a stronger intimation than the other millionaires were getting." By specifying that a painting bought through Duveen was to be left to a museum after his death, a millionaire could import it duty free, hang it on his wall, and as Behrman puts it, "in good conscience, circumvent oblivion and the Collector of Internal Revenue at a single stroke."

This was the beginning of art as a tax dodge, which was to get out of hand after World War II. But in laying the groundwork, Congress and to some extent Duveen had the noblest, simplest, and most pragmatic of intentions. For Congress, the various exemptions were a way to attract much of the world's best art to America and into museums, thereby enabling the American people to see it here without spending dollars abroad. It is a scheme that worked, for as owners died off, their great art collections went public. Thus have we been blessed with the National Gallery in Washington and its Mellon, Kress, and Widener collections; Gertrude Vanderbilt Whitney's Museum of American Art; the Morgan and Huntington libraries at opposite ends of the country; the Guggenheim Museum; the Frick Collection; Isabella Stewart Gardner's Venetian Palazzo in Boston; and the Cloisters in upper Manhattan, among others.

Motivated by profit, Duveen's aims were nonetheless comparable to those of Congress. His clients needed to feel that although they were paying high for the priceless, they were getting it cheap. When Frick felt guilty about spending $400,000 on Velázquez's "Philip IV of Spain," for which the artist had earned a mere $600 back in 1645, he managed to convince himself—thanks in part to an elaborate computation of $600 at 6 percent interest compounded semiannually over the centuries—that he had bought the painting for less than nothing. And Duveen knew the terrain on which he manipulated his millionaires. "Do you realize," he would say, "that the only thing you can spend one hundred thousand dollars on without incurring an obligation to spend a great deal more for its upkeep is a picture? Once you've bought it, it costs you only a few hundred dollars every fifteen years for cleaning."

As Behrman writes of Duveen's clients:

> Their children made disastrous marriages, got killed in racing cars, had to pay blackmail to avoid scandal. But with the works of art it was different. They asked for nothing. They were rewarding. They shed their radiance, and it was a lovely soothing light. You could take them or leave them, and when you had visitors you could bask in the admiration the pictures and sculptures excited, which was directed toward you even more subtly than toward them, as if you yourself had gathered them and, even, created them. The works of art *became* their children.

Ever since Duveen, American millionaires and lesser philanthropists have been collecting art for a number of reasons, fewer and fewer of them aesthetic. The opportunities have been so great, says lawyer Jerome S. Rubin, that "especially in recent years, many persons with little or no interest in or feeling for works of art have passionately embraced art and have acquired and cheerfully disposed of paintings and objects primarily for tax advantages." Rubin claims that "the prearranged purchase and overvalued gift, the switched invoice, and other unsavory tricks" of the big-money art mart have not greatly affected the quality of the most important public collections in America. They were built with love as well as money and art. But art as a tax dodge has certainly inflated prices—to the point where an art dealer insists that "it's easier to sell a picture for a hundred thousand dollars than for ten thousand," and an art editor contends that "the enormous growth of interest in art that we hear so much about is, for the most part, only an interest in the *price* of art." *

Art critic Robert Wraight has complained of the new-style

---

* More than a quarter of a billion dollars changes hands in a year of art sales. Most of the purchasers in the $50,000-and-up-apiece bracket live in America.

American collector. "By comparison . . . Mellon and Morgan and Huntington were art-for-art's-sake aesthetes. This [new] sort of collector, more than any before him, has equated the possession of works of art with the possession of money, and his example has inevitably been followed in countries where no tax-dodging inducement is offered. He is a gift to those dealers who, now that the best old masters and impressionist pictures are nearly all locked up in museums, are promoting modern art and artists by every means known to modern high-pressure salesmanship."

There were so many tax wrinkles—installment giving, deductions based on a donor's actuarial life expectancy, mounting appraisals of a painting's "fair-market value," etc.—that in recent years, Congress has tightened these aspects of its revenue acts and placed limitations on the proportion of total income that can be written off as tax-exempt philanthropy. But ever since 1934, when the government lost a $3 million tax case against Andrew Mellon because of Duveen's testimony, the Internal Revenue Service has been reluctant to tangle with the well-endowed patron of the arts, his expensive lawyers, and the expert appraiser who works for a fee and is sometimes willing to give the fee payer the appraisal he wants.

The benefit of this doubt that the tax collector is willing to extend to the art collector nowadays was amply illustrated in a Texas tax case that was resolved in a federal court in February, 1967. A Houston oil widow had donated a fifteenth-century French painting (School of Avignon) to the Houston Museum of Fine Arts and taken $425,000 off her income tax. During the trial, federal lawyers said that while they considered the painting to be worth a mere $12,000, they had allowed her a tax deduction of $300,000 before dunning her for the rest.

Texas, as might have been expected, is a hotbed of indiscriminate art collecting, and whole museums are springing up just to house the acquisitions of its Big Daddies. In 1950 there were no local art galleries in Texas, just a few outposts of Eastern dealers. A decade later there were ten home-owned galleries in Houston, thirteen in Dallas, three in Fort Worth, two in Amarillo, one in San Antonio, and more on the way. In 1964 a dozen Texans formed a sort of mutual fund called Art Investments, Ltd. "To be a collector is to be marked as not only a man of means, but a man of taste and civic virtue, worthy of notice—perhaps even of being taken up—by desirable new friends," said John Bainbridge in his profile of Texas, *The Super-Americans.* "It's not just here," a Texan told Bainbridge. "All over the country, people are using art to promote themselves socially." Farther west, in the movie colony, fashions in artists change with the regularity of fashions in cars. "Picasso's passé, but Matisse is chic this year," I was told on my last visit to the Coast.

Even in more conservative communities, says Richard H. Rush in *Art as an Investment,** "the news does not fall on unseeing eyes that Paul Mellon, the Pittsburgh banker, purchased a painting for over $600,000, or that Henry Ford II purchased a Renoir for $200,000, or that Nelson Rockefeller sold a Braque for $145,000." Rush then outlines the deductive process that ensues:

1. These are the wealthiest families of the country. They must know what they are doing financially. They have an eye on the investment value of anything.

2. Why, then, don't I do the same thing, and maybe it will be a smart investment for me, too?

Postwar prosperity brought about a bull market in art and further tax dodging in the name of capital gains. From its outset in 1913, the federal income tax has been primarily a levy on income rather than on capital. Gains in the sale or exchange of capital assets are taxed at half the ordinary rate, and taxation is never higher than 25 percent of the proceeds. In his article "Art and Taxes," Jerome S. Rubin explains:

In a rising market, works of art have thus lent themselves admirably to speculation and have led to the formation of hastily accumulated and often as hastily sold portfolios of art objects. Leaping from one fad to another, capitalizing on every trend and subtrend, the postwar investor-collector has been able, with the right timing, to buy Action painting cheap and sell it dear, to jump in and

* Rush, Richard H., *Art as an Investment.* Englewood Cliffs, New Jersey, Prentice-Hall, 1961.

out of Pop with the same agility, and finally to hop into the dazzling world of Op.

One Manhattan art dealer published a handsome brochure to seduce new art lovers into playing the fascinating game of old masters with "that other avid collector, Uncle Sam." It takes the case of a Mr. Martin, a man in the 90 percent income-tax bracket, who bought a $30,000 painting a few years back and now finds it is worth $70,000. Should he sell it? No, says the brochure. If he does, he will pay a 25 percent capital gains tax on $40,000 and thus net a profit of only $30,000. Should he give it away to a museum? No, no, says the brochure. True, he will be able to deduct the entire $70,000, thereby saving $63,000 in income tax. But his profit will be only that $63,000 minus the original $30,000 cost of the painting, or $33,000. Then what should he do? *Sell* it to a museum for the original $30,000, the brochure counsels. Then, having recovered his original investment, he can still deduct the $40,000 loss he's taking and thereby save $36,000 in income taxes.

With a recession or two under its belt, Wall Street latched onto the notion of art as an investment, and brokers began recommending it as a form of insurance. *Fortune* carried a two-part series, "The Great International Art Market," with such tips as:

> The only thing likely to happen to Vermeer's value in the foreseeable future is that it will increase until, sometime not too far distant, it will be altogether priceless.

"DOES REMBRANDT PAY DIVIDENDS?" asked a writer for the *Commercial & Financial Chronicle,* and the answer was a resounding yes with the added intelligence that "the ownership of a Seurat is as good as a triple-A rating in *Dun & Bradstreet.*" "NO RECESSION IN ART" was the headline in the international coffee-table magazine, *Réalités,* which enumerated "a few market tips," including:

> A painting in red sells better than one in any other color.
> Portraits of women are worth more than those of men.
> Flowers sell better than vegetables or fish.
> Portraits of military personages sell badly.

"IN PAINTING, THE PROFITS ARE FOREVER," said the New York *Times* Economic Review. The common basic truth on which all these empires were being built seemed to be that in recent years, art prices were increasing faster than the dollar's value was decreasing. As art prices rose as much as 80 percent a year, *Pick's World Currency Report* indicated that only Liberty ships and quicksilver were more spectacular investments. And a new market tip sheet screamed: "HOW TO MAKE SUPER-PROFITS IN THE ART MARKET NOW: Your possible *rewards* are so UN*limited* that it might be more accurate to say that the risk you take is the risk of becoming RICH!"

This particular boom generated its own bible—Richard Rush's aforementioned *Art as an Investment*. For $10, it amounts to a 418-page performance chart and tip sheet. Rush is a Washington, D.C., investment banker who most recently made news testifying on behalf of the Texas oil widow when her painting was challenged as a $425,000 deduction by Internal Revenue. (The widow, incidentally, won her case before a federal court jury.) Judging from an occasional personal anecdote and the book jacket, showing Rush and his wife amid their art collection, Rush is a small Big Daddy who buys in the four-and-five-figure-per-painting bracket.

Rush rushes through seven centuries of great art like a million-dollar mogul in a five-and-ten-cent store. "We can dispense with" Michelangelo because there are so few authenticated paintings by him. Corot, Millet, Rousseau are up a couple of points because "they are very pleasing and wear well with the viewer, adding greatly to the charm and livability of a home." Closing prices on Grandma Moses indicate she is still "a factor in the market. There is a substantial demand for her paintings, and there are enough of them to give some liquidity to the market and at the same time provide a reasonably stable price level." And Modigliani has achieved a corporate identity because "his works are almost instantly recognizable . . . when a Modigliani hangs on the wall it advertises itself, and many of the viewers can recognize it. . . . As in the case of Modigliani, Rouault is instantly recognizable to even the less experienced eye, and this quality alone adds to his importance and to his value." Still seeking to reduce art to a science, Rush lumps

Cézanne, Gauguin, and Van Gogh together in a three-man parlay. In a prodigious feat of Dow Jones averaging, using their 1930 prices as a base of 100, Rush proves conclusively that the three postimpressionist giants were marketed at 177 in 1950, 566 in 1955, and 4,833 in 1960.

"It is hardly possible to emphasize the foolishness of investing a great deal of money in just one painting," Rush counsels, "and considering this one painting as an investment which may one day be liquidated at a good profit. Yet this is a prevalent view of the investment value of art among some art owners who are otherwise good businessmen.

"To own just one painting is like investing all of one's assets in one stock. Standard Oil of New Jersey is certainly a fine company and its stock is good, but there is merit to the attitude that it might not rise as surely as would a portfolio of selected stocks."

Rush even furnishes sample conversations for the beginning collector's first foray into an art gallery. One of them runs thusly:

"I would like to see some paintings, please."

"What artists do you prefer?"

"I don't know, but I have been reading a lot about paintings in the papers and magazines lately, and I thought I'd see what was being offered for sale."

"What School do you prefer?"

"School? Why, I don't know. What have you got?"

"In the American School we have John Steuart Curry here."

"No. That's not at all what I have in mind. You see paintings like that all the time. I want something modern. I have a new house with modern furniture, and I want something that's going to fit in."

"How about this John Marin watercolor?"

"Now that's more what I'm thinking about. How much is it?

"Twenty-eight hundred dollars."

If there is an aesthetic nugget to be discerned throughout Rush's hard-boiled cram course in art appreciation, it is contained in this passage:

The artist and the art dealers can extol a particular
School of Art or a painting all they want, but if the buying public is unimpressed, the School and the painting
go by the wayside, perhaps to wait generations, or forever,
in order to secure *that recognition which is spelled out in
the buyer's check.*

The italics are mine, for they spell out how totally the standards of the box office can apply. And this phenomenon is not
uniquely American. A Paris dealer tells of a customer who
ordered two Matisses by telephone.

"Wouldn't you like to come down and look at them first?"
the dealer suggested.

The voice at the other end thundered: "When I buy a hundred shares of Royal Dutch, I don't go and look at the oil wells!"

"The climate is such in the art market that the public wants
to be deceived," says one dealer. "There aren't enough Chagalls
for all the people who want Chagalls." What there is instead is
what the Attorney General of New York State calls "an alarming
increase in art fraud." * An international art expert says, "Millions and millions are spent on fakes by the public each year,"
and the Metropolitan Museum of Art is initiating a course in
fake detection.

"We use our own fakes for study," said a Metropolitan official,
who added: "When an institution is no longer self-critical and
honest, that's the end of it." Not long ago, a vast number of
Matisse "originals" were traced to a workshop in Japan.

In 1967 alone, there were at least three major scandals involving art forgeries. In the spring, a Texas oil millionaire
named Algur H. Meadows was informed by the Art Dealers
Association of America that of the fifty-eight works hanging in
his suburban Dallas villa, forty-four—including seven Modigli-
anis, a Picasso, a Degas, a Chagall, five Vlamincks, and fifteen

---

* Early in 1968 the State of California sued a San Francisco art gallery for
fraudulently inflating the value of an artist's work. The suit claimed that the
gallery, which was the little-known painter's exclusive representative, had sold
one of his works to a mentally ill "collector" for the record sum of $52,000. The
man was placed in an institution, and his relatives claim they advised the gallery
that his check would bounce; but the gallery nevertheless is alleged to have
delivered the painting, advertised its price, and sold lithographs of it for $150 a
copy.

Dufys—were fakes. Meadows was ready to shrug off the million-dollar beating he had apparently taken from a Paris art dealer. "I'm going to build a room in my house called 'Room of Fakes Bought by Mr. Sap.' Oh, well, this would have been really bad if it had happened to someone who couldn't afford it."

A few days later, in a separate case, a New York art dealer was arrested and indicted on charges of having painted forty-one oils, watercolors, and gouaches and sold them as works by Chagall, Matisse, and Picasso. The customers he is accused of bilking include the Hammer Gallery (one "Chagall" for $6,000), the Korvette department stores (two "Picassos" for $7,000), and various dealers and collectors. The assistant district attorney in charge of the case said that when Marc Chagall was shown some of the works attributed to him, he "became furious and said they were very poor fakes. He was on the verge of tearing one of them up, but we talked him out of it, saying we needed it for evidence."

Late last summer, the Society of London Art Dealers held an emergency meeting, and the London *Times* exposed what was on the agenda. As a result, thirty watercolors bearing the signature of the American portraitist John Singer Sargent were discredited, and Sargent's American-born biographer, who had authenticated all of them, later sued several of the parties involved in casting doubt on their authenticity. The case is still pending, but the owner of the gallery that sold fourteen of them called back the paintings and refunded the customers' money with interest. Christie's, which auctioned off thirteen of them, admitted that it "might have boobed." Sotheby's, the auctioneers who turned down what Christie's sold, said it was "considerably relieved" that "our man was right."

The gallery owner was philosophical about being out $15,-000. "No harm comes of airing these things from time to time. It acts as a deterrent." But the chief victim, he admitted, was the artist, for the scandal "now puts the whole position of Sargent's work in jeopardy."

Sic transit gloria Duveen! The Duveen Gallery in Manhattan and all its assets were sold in 1964 for $15 million to the Norton Simon Foundation of Fullerton, California. Simon is the Hunt Tomato tycoon who at last count also owns, controls, or dominates Wesson Oil, Ohio Match, Fuller Paint, Wheeling Steel, Knox Glass, Canada Dry, Fibreboard, Swift Meat Packing, American Broadcasting-Paramount Theaters, *McCall's, Redbook, Saturday Review,* and a $50 million art collection. His foundation, incorporated for general charitable purposes in 1952, has concentrated since 1963 on procuring works of art and lending them to museums for public exhibition.

Simon, a morose man with the pained expression of a dental patient, sleeps with six Cézannes at the head of his bed and a Mondrian on his sliding wall. Perhaps this exposure has made him a trifle more sensitive than most of today's cultural wheeler-dealers, for he is capable of an occasional articulation like: "When you become acquisitive about art, which I think every collector does at some time, it's just the same as chasing the mirages that you chase in business—more, more, more. And when this happens to me, I cut off the art. I get back to my business. If I'm going to chase something, I may as well chase it there."

On March 19, 1965, Norton Simon involved the scheming world of art collection in a brouhaha of Simon Says intrigue that might have mystified Machiavelli. The setting was one in which a nod, a pencil flick, a nose blow, a twitch, or a tic can mean almost anything—Christie's, a London auction gallery, on the day Rembrandt's "Titus" came up for sale.

Simon, who maintains to this day that he wanted to avoid publicity, arrived in the company of Dudley Tooth of the eminent London gallery Tooth & Tooth. As if this wasn't enough ostentation, Simon virtually demanded Fleet Street's attention in the early bidding on a Hogarth. At a stage where the rules required raising bids by 1,000 guineas at a time,* Simon raised by 500.

When Rembrandt went on the block, many eyes somehow were focused on Simon. The auctioneer, who had the superb James Bondian name of I. O. Chance, opened the bidding at 100,000 guineas, and it went to 500,000 in thirty seconds. Then Simon, who had been bidding openly by raising a finger and

---

* The pound was then worth $2.80 and the guinea (a pound plus a shilling) $2.94.

nodding his head, called out, "Six hundred thousand!" He was promptly topped by a bid of 650,000. At 700,000, one of the three remaining bidders dropped out.

Simon bid 720,000. Then David Somerset of the Marlborough Fine Art Gallery bid 740,000. All eyes swiveled to Simon. But Simon said nothing.

The auctioneer stared at tycoon Norton Simon for a long half-minute. Simon was a study in still life.

"For the last time," said I. O. Chance, not taking his eye off Simon, "seven hundred and forty thousand guineas against you."

When no answer came, Chance looked around the hushed room and said, "Seven hundred and forty thousand guineas. Any more?" Then he rapped his gavel and said, "Sold to Marlborough Fine Art!"

There were some patriotic cheers, for it looked as though one of Britain's dwindling supply of art treasures had been rescued from export, and even I. O. Chance permitted himself a smile.

From Norton Simon, however, there came a moan of anguish —and then the astounding proclamation: "I am still bidding!"

Chance wiped the smile off his face as he told the seemingly bumptious American: "I said quite clearly it was against you."

"You got my message, Mr. Chance," Simon shouted back. "You had an instruction to watch for!"

Chance was perplexed. Simon pulled a letter out of his pocket and tried to read it aloud. His hand shook so much, however, that he handed it to his dealer, Mr. Tooth, to read. Tooth was unable to make himself heard in the pandemonium. He handed it back to Simon, who read it in an uncustomarily booming voice. It was a secret bidding arrangement, written by Christie's, that Chance had overlooked. It read:

> When Mr. Simon is sitting down he is bidding. If he bids openly he is also bidding. When he stands up he has stopped bidding. If he sits down again he is not bidding unless he raises his finger. Having raised his finger he is bidding until he stands up again.

Since Simon hadn't stood during the bidding, Chance felt compelled to overrule the sale. Bidding resumed, and Chance hammered down the Rembrandt to the Norton Simon Foundation for 760,000 guineas, or $2,234,000.*

As the press milled around him, Simon explained briskly that the whole deception was designed to conceal his identity until he could lend his Rembrandt to the brand-new Los Angeles County Museum of Art to "hang there for a while. . . . I wanted to release the news in Los Angeles after I'd spoken to the museum directors." With that, he left by the back door to catch a cab to his hotel and then a plane to the States.

The Los Angeles County Museum of Art opened twelve days later, on March 31, 1965. A three-building complex with the exterior blandness of a bank, a motel, or a department store, it has nevertheless been attracting art lovers at the rate of 2½ million a year—thanks partly to "Simon's 'Titus,' " which is how some of its regulars refer to the tomato tycoon's Rembrandt. By local standards, the attendance figures make the Los Angeles Museum a better draw than the Louvre, the British Museum, or the National Gallery and four times as attractive as the Uffizi in Florence ever was. For as Robert Wernick remarked in *Life,*** "Los Angeles is a city built on the principle that the box office never lies."

In his saga of how a one-building project budgeted at $4½ million became a three-building complex that cost more than $12 million, Wernick has characterized the museum's patrons as "Instant Medicis . . . a corpus of art-loving, art-collecting, public-spirited, immensely wealthy benefactors . . . moved by all the passions and interests which have built up the great collections of art over the centuries—love of beauty, love of great paintings, love of display, love of power, love of social advancement, love of tax write-offs. They were self-made and strong-willed; they wanted immortality and wanted it fast."

Love of art and beauty, however, does not loom large in Wer-

---

* Two more bids of 20,000 guineas and the price would have surpassed the highest price ever paid for a painting—$2,300,000 by New York's Metropolitan Museum at Parke-Bernet Galleries in 1961 for another Rembrandt, "Aristotle Contemplating the Bust of Homer." In 1967 this record was broken when the National Gallery in Washington apparently paid at least $5 million for a Leonardo in a secretive transaction with Prince Francis Joseph II of Liechtenstein.

** Much (but not all) of the museum's history, which follows, is drawn from Wernick's article, "Wars of the Instant Medicis," in the October 28, 1966, issue of *Life.*

nick's harrowing chronicle of the Instant Medicis. The pioneer Medici was Norton Simon, who owned a mere handful of old masters back in 1954, when Richard Brown of the Frick Collection in Manhattan went West to head the new museum (not even on the drawing board then). After four years of diligent evangelizing, Brown made a knowledgeable, prodigious collector out of Simon and persuaded him to pledge $1 million toward building the museum of Brown's dreams in Hancock Park on top of the La Brea tar pits.

Brown was bolstered by the salesmanship of Edward W. Carter, a Western department-store magnate whose marketing tactics went thisaway: "It so happens that there is room on the Founding Benefactors' Wall for just one more name, in *Trajanic* lettering—copied from Trajan's Column in Rome, y'know. I think you'll want to be there, so I'm going to give you the first chance to leave your footprints in the community."

One day, Carter snared a $2 million gift from savings-and-loan philanthropist Howard Ahmanson. The stipulation, however, that the museum had to be named the Ahmanson Gallery of Fine Arts stirred up a tempest over just how much immortality Ahmanson thought he could buy for $2 million. Norton Simon abruptly lowered his pledge to $250,000. Another collector changed his will.

Finally a compromise was achieved. There would be three buildings instead of one: an Ahmanson Gallery, a Bing Center in honor of a real-estate magnate (whose widow gave $1 million), and a Lytton Gallery in honor of another savings-and-loan mogul. Bart Lytton, whose banks have also purchased more than $400,000 worth of art for display in their offices, has been hailed as one of "the new Medicis of art" by the New York *Times** as well as *Life*.

(Speaking at Stanford University, Lytton calculated that his $400,000 investment represented an initial cost of $3 per square foot of office space, plus a continuing cost of $27,000 a year that the money might otherwise be earning. "But," he concluded, "a

---

* Other corporate Medicis cited by the *Times*: CBS, Chase Manhattan Bank, Standard Oil of New Jersey, Johnson's Wax, IBM, all for "the spin-off benefits of investment, prestige-building, and public relations." Basic-Witz Furniture also earned a place on the honor roll by commissioning Robert Evett, a musician who earns his living as books and arts editor of the *New Republic*, to compose a concerto commemorating Basic-Witz's seventy-fifth anniversary.

thing of beauty is a profit forever. Even reasonably well chosen, it tends to increase in resale value, bring staff and customer satisfaction, and greater community acceptance.")

In an argument over a second story for his gallery at the Los Angeles County Museum, Lytton later trimmed his contribution from $750,000 to a mere $250,000, and his name was chiseled off its wall.* (At last roll call, the building was called the Special Exhibitions Gallery.)

Howard Ahmanson insisted that Millard Sheets, the local architect responsible for Ahmanson's own gold-facaded banks, have a hand in the design of the museum. Richard Brown, the director, countered with the name of Miës van der Rohe. The trustees settled for William Pereira. Next, Ahmanson demanded that his art collection be hung in the museum. Brown refused because he and several other experts doubted the authenticity of many of Ahmanson's treasures (which are attributed to Titian, Vermeer, and Velázquez). As one of Brown's staff remarked: "Who would work for a museum that would even consider hanging a fake Vermeer?" And perhaps the final straw came for Richard Brown when the museum's interior temperature, carefully regulated to preserve the art, was ordered changed for the personal comfort of one of the trustees.

Only a few weeks after director Brown's dream of a museum (somewhat overblown and compromised, to be sure) was opened in 1965, Brown resigned. The facts are murky; there was not even substantial agreement on whether Brown quit or was fired or was forced to quit. Several trustees accused Brown of "bad decorum," of "petulancy" and "insecurity," and of being a likely candidate to "see a psychologist," but eighteen of the nineteen trustees conceded that whatever happened wasn't mostly Brown's fault. Only Howard Ahmanson contended that Brown wasn't big enough for the job.

"There are many versions of what led to open conflict," Wer-

---

* In the spring of 1968, Bart Lytton—who had boasted of being one of the most successful businessmen in America—lost his position as chairman, president, and chief executive of the $500,000,000 Lytton Financial Corporation. Lytton had been unable to raise $2,800,000 to meet obligations to two creditors. Lytton, who had been paid a total of $217,050 in 1967, stayed on as a part-time consultant for $50,000 a year with a ten-year contract. Lytton said his personal fortune, once estimated at $25,000,000, had been "decimated and redecimated. I'm no longer a millionaire. Perhaps the relief chauffeur will have to go."

nick wrote in *Life*. "Ric Brown's is that he was set on by a pack
of maddened millionaires who continually interfered with his
operations. . . . Intent on doing everything himself, he let
trustees' pet projects pile up or go astray. Identifying himself
wholly with the museum, he tended to slight the arts of concilia-
tion and compromise. . . ."

Artforum, a magazine based in Los Angeles, points out, however:

"Dr. Brown's resignation came about as a result not of his
shortcomings, whatever they may have been, but of his virtues.
. . . The point has been, from the beginning, good taste vs.
bad taste, professional standards vs. amateur standards, qualified
museum personnel vs. trustees who have earned power in the
Cultural Establishment by virtue of economic or social power."

Outside of Los Angeles, where the box office reigns supreme,
most museums are measured by a worldwide double standard of
B. O. (box office) and O. M. (old masters). Put them together,
however, and they may not always spell BOOM. The Los Angeles County Museum, for instance, has plenty of both, but
virtually all of its old masters and one-quarter of its exhibits are
on loan from the Norton Simon Foundation. With Simon's
tutor, Brown, gone and Simon's treasures hanging in buildings
bearing names like Ahmanson and Bing, there are those who
wonder what would happen if Simon pulled out his paintings.
The empty museum might even sink back into the tar pits from
which it has never really emerged.

Another museum of art heavily endowed and patronized was
haunted by its trustees' concern with the greatest good for the
greatest number. They bedeviled their director with anxieties
about public approval. When they hired a polling agency to
ascertain whether the flood of visitors really liked what they saw,
he resigned.

By all standards, New York's Metropolitan Museum of Art
should and does reign secure. Its average attendance on a Sunday would fill Madison Square Garden twice over. With a dynamic and popular captain, Thomas P. F. Hoving, at the helm,
and room after room of old masters and other art treasures on
its decks, it should be enjoying smooth, dignified sailing and
setting an example for the rest of the art world to aspire to. But

in recent years, its greatest influence has been a fat young associate curator of American art named Henry Geldzahler, "the Metropolitan's ambassador to the scene." By 1966, when he was thirty, the Belgian-born Geldzahler had starred in a Claes Oldenberg happening and an Andy Warhol movie (called *Henry Geldzahler*.) He had modeled as a subject for Marisol, Frank Stella, Marcia Marcus, and George Segal, among others. He had been featured in *Life* as "the most 'in' and gadabout man in the art world . . . a household word in lofts, penthouses, and even the White House." He was ranked with critic Clement Greenberg and the Museum of Modern Art as one of the foremost powers-that-be. He was adviser to the Green and Castelli galleries, the two principal dealers in pop art. "When we see him coming," said one art dealer, "we practically roll the red carpet right down the block and wait on our knees at the end of it."

Writing in the *New York* magazine when it was part of the old *Herald Tribune,** Frances FitzGerald dubbed Geldzahler:

> the Telstar of the art world and all its subsidiary planets— a man so tuned in to all its wave lengths that he registers events almost before they happen. Scarcely a year after he came back to New York from his studies, he went with an artist and two dealers to visit the studio of two unknown painters—James Rosenquist and Roy Lichtenstein. Within the next few weeks, he had met Claes Oldenberg, Jim Dine, Andy Warhol, and Tom Wesselman. . . . When the great klieg lights of the mass media turned upon them, he was discovered in their midst. . . . To the schools of reporters and avant-garde hunters, he was . . . an art historian in touch, in the know, a hip Metropolitan curator, a young critic unhampered by a body of criticism who liked the new thing, and yet, if necessary, could talk about it in the old language. The same qualities made him extremely useful to the Pop artists.

And so the media beat a path to the Metropolitan, where their prime source sat beneath seven knights in English armor, to ask: "What's new, Mr. Geldzahler, what's new?" And no matter

* Frances FitzGerald, "What's New, Henry Geldzahler, What's New?" *New York* (November 21, 1965), pp. 14–20.

what he said, they amplified his reply so loudly and acted on it so swiftly that it came true overnight. Thus, in some opinions, was the cachet of the Metropolitan Museum of Art—already abused by the Book-of-the-Month Club to sell home seminars and postage-stamp reproductions—exploited to accelerate the debasement of American taste.

The strength of the established museums in America is so great that it would take a better man than Huntington Hartford to challenge their power structure. But Hartford, who has gone through the greater part of the $70 million A&P grocery fortune he inherited, was perhaps the only man around with enough resources as well as the desire to try. When he came to the conclusion that one museum, the Museum of Modern Art, was charting the whole course of American painting and much of European painting through its extraordinary control of reputations and publicity, he set out to erect a rival monument to his own comparatively Eisenhowerish tastes. He called it, rather pointedly, the Gallery of Modern Art.

It looked like a beautiful slab of white Swiss cheese out there on Columbus Circle in New York City—the world's tallest art museum, designed by Edward Durell Stone, ten stories high with intriguing portholes that made you yearn to be on the inside looking out—and it cost Huntington Hartford $7½ million when he opened it in 1964. It had taste and a point of view; its living-room decor made an imposing case for the Sargents and Constables that Hartford championed and hung there. And it had audacity, whether in a sprawling Dali exhibition or in the Kipling poem, "When Earth's Last Picture Is Painted," carved in marble by the elevators. On its ninth floor, it had the best Polynesian restaurant in New York, with tapestries by Gauguin and a view of Central Park. In its basement, it had a lively cinema.

The gallery caught on with a sizable public, particularly out-of-town visitors, and it was invariably well attended. "My museum represents the taste of the country more than any of them," Hartford said with pride. "It is the only one that is less extreme in the field of modern art."

Having just begun to prove his point of view with his museum, Hartford promptly gave up and tried to unload it.

Fourteen months after he had opened the Gallery of Modern Art, he was denying persistent rumors that it was up for sale. A year later, in 1966, he confirmed the rumors by offering his gallery to Fordham University as a downtown classroom building, or as the president of Fordham put it, "our exclamation point on the face of New York."

The deal was still up in the air at last inquiry, and so were the people who work at the gallery. From the bottom up, this promising new challenge had the jitters. The exhibitions grew indecisive and blurry. The movie department didn't know what, if anything, would be playing next month. The restaurant seemed hesitant to make reservations far in advance. And everybody spoke about the place in the past tense, although its shell was still standing tall and its *raison d'être* was as sound as ever.

This is what happens when you put an art form or a good idea at the mercy of a dilettante who is a patronizer, rather than a patron, of the arts.

[IV]

"If we run out of models, you get to paint me," the skin art lecturer had promised, and ten minutes before our two hours were up, that's what happened.

While Blackbeard bloodied her orifices and the rest of the old masters took up stations alongside the canvas they'd been looking at longest, the chemical engineer painted a quick brassiere on the lecturer and then pointed to the next room, where a tanned young nude was lolling around in black laced boots. "Why don't we get to paint her?" he whined.

"That's Maria," the lecturer explained. "She's on photo calls, in case anyone comes in and wants to take pictures. She does all the Playboy poses and anything else for the individual rate, plus a dollar an hour if you rent one of our Polaroids."

"What if a guy comes in and wants to paint her for twenty dollars an hour?"

"You can't paint Maria," the lecturer said protectively. "The first and last time Maria was skin-painted, she broke out in a rash."

By then it was almost nine o'clock, and the lecturer told her old masters: "Okay, boys. Three more circles apiece, and then you better dismiss yourselves or there won't be any hot water left in the shower for me."

On our way out, the gold-turtlenecked, crew-cut guy who ran the studio intercepted us. "Boys, have you met Maria?"

"We know all about her," the chemical engineer said, primly but hungrily.

"Tell you what, boys," the guy said, approximately half-jokingly. "For five dollars more apiece, Maria will kick you and stomp you as much as you want."

"THE second weaver," the emperor told the little boy, "looked a great deal like the first. But where the first weaver was bland, this one was clever. And whenever the first weaver would soothe me, this fellow would needle me. . . ."

"Needle the emperor!" the little boy exclaimed. "But how, Your Majesty?"

"I said *needle* in the most contemporary sense of the word," the emperor explained. "At the fitting of my velvet underdoublet, for example, the two weavers were both impelled to *oooh* and *ahhh* at the handiwork—"

"Which, after all, was theirs," the little boy murmured.

"—and while the first weaver was still gushing over it, the second asked me discreetly whether I really wanted velvet, since by the time of the procession, velvet would be on the way out and gold lace on the way in—which it was, I'll say that for him. Costly though it was, I shall always be grateful to him that I converted in time."

"From imaginary velvet to imaginary gold," the little boy observed. "And might I point out, Your Majesty, that the only reason velvet was out and gold in was that your switch to gold had been amply publicized."

"The rogue!" snorted the emperor. "How he used me! And to think that I used to encourage him to make something of himself! 'With your imagination,' I used to tell him, 'you ought to be a designer.' And he would say—almost snarling, I remember now—'I'm only a humble weaver, Your Highness, not a creator. And I'm content to be what I am.' "

"As well he might be," said the little boy knowingly. "For the second type of culture vulture is perhaps the more vicious and destructive and yet the less equipped for survival until he brings the real world down to his own level."

Part II:

THE CAREERISTS

---

careerism—devotion to a successful career, often at the expense of
one's personal life, ethics, etc.
—*Random House Dictionary*

The Fifth Commandment of the Culture Vultures:
Make nothing out of something,
for all else is beyond you.

5
Corruption of the Instinct:
The Critics

[1]

"IT'S harder to write a good review than a good play," said
Richard Schechner when he edited the *Tulane Drama Review* (now the New York *Drama Review*). When another drama
critic, Walter Kerr, was hired by the New York *Times* in 1966,
he received a bad notice in New Haven. Robert Brustein, dean
of the Yale Drama School and drama critic for the *New Republic*, proclaimed that Kerr's appointment "dooms the theater to
25 years of mediocrity." Later Brustein amended his estimate.
"Since Kerr is 53, we'll make it 20 years of mediocrity." Still
later, a rival New York newspaper sent a staffer to review Kerr's
first night as drama critic of the *Times*.

Reviewing, an auxiliary craft that belongs in the wings, has
taken center stage and now professes to be an art form in itself.
Its practitioners have become better known than the artists they
criticize ("Did you see what the *New York Review of Books* did
to Whatzisname's novel?") and are expected to be at least as
entertaining in their own right. This the critics could rarely
manage on their own, but fortunately for themselves, they have
the works under dissection to prey on, quote, or hold up to ridi-

cule. Small wonder, then, that even the best of the movies we long to see and music we yearn to hear and books we choose to read frequently strike us as distorted, anticlimactic, disappointing, or overly familiar.

"We are slaves to published criticism in this country," says Arthur Miller. "People are being told what to think."

A foreign journalist recently assumed a critic's post in America and was immediately appalled by the power he had been handed. "I have actually heard people here suggest that they thought something about a play, and then they read the paper the next day and they found they were wrong. They used this word: they were *wrong*. They didn't say they disagreed. . . . They said they were *wrong*."

If this were all, our arts still would have no trouble surviving the critics who fatten on them. But let us take an across-the-board look at what happens *within* various arts when those who nibble at their fringe are allowed to eat at their very fabric.

By definition and by recent history, drama reviewing affords the most dramatic illumination of the critic as *cause célèbre*.

Definition first. (Recent history next.) Little time will be wasted here in the diversionary swamp of distinguishing between criticism and reviewing. I am content to accept my battered *Webster's New Collegiate Dictionary's* definitions of *criticism* as "the act of criticizing, esp. unfavorable" and *reviewer* as "one who reviews or re-examines; specif., a professional critic of books." And the soundest job I know of defining drama criticism as a vocation was performed at Columbia's Graduate School of Journalism, when I was a student there in 1952–53.

Half of the course in drama criticism was one all-morning lecture/workshop conducted by Brooks Atkinson of the New York *Times*. Atkinson's morning quickly deteriorated into a chronic lament about that particular theater season's being the worst in memory. As proof positive, Atkinson ticked off the recent plays he'd walked out on before the final curtain.

The second half of the course was a similar morning, a week later, with John Chapman of the *Daily News*. Chapman's lecture went the same route as Atkinson's, although he was kindlier toward the season's bumper turkey crop. In the question period, a student asked Chapman how many of those plays he'd walked out on.

"None," Chapman replied. "I'm there for a newspaper. If somebody dropped dead on the stage or in the audience at a first night, that's news. I'd look pretty silly and so would my newspaper if I didn't mention it."

There was a commonsense lesson there, one that journalism schools had pretty much stopped teaching by 1952–53. The public had every right to expect its *daily* newspaper critics to double as police reporters and traffic cops, to describe what went on with a reasonable amount of detail and to divert potential customers from wasting their time on obvious bores and transparent junk. More leisurely observations and sober second thoughts could be reserved for Sunday drama columns or for essayists/ reviewers like Robert Brustein and Michael Smith, who cover second nights for the weeklies. The daily newspaper critic used to be a man the reader felt he could stop on the way up the aisle, ask how he liked the play, and expect a crisp, coherent reply. His review, after all, was due about an hour later.

Deadline pressure, in fact, spelled the beginning of the end for this kind of drama criticism. Even with 7 o'clock first-night curtains, the increased advertising bulk of the surviving American newspapers and their problems of megalopolitan distribution required earlier and earlier press times. Besides, the journalism schools weren't turning out critics capable of writing lucidly for a deadline. A few years after the Columbia Journalism workshop I described, Brooks Atkinson retired in his prime. He told his boss, assistant managing editor Harrison Salisbury, that he was quitting because he couldn't "do justice to the *Times*" in this age of increasing deadlines.

About the time of Atkinson's retirement, the Mansfield Theater on Forty-seventh Street was stripped of its fine old actor-manager's name and rechristened the Brooks Atkinson, an apt commentary on *whose* names are in lights nowadays. For by then, the most powerful drama critic in America was whoever covered first nights for the New York *Times,* a post that a news-magazine labeled "supercritic." The American theater meant Broadway, where the impact of the morning papers was more instantaneous than that of the evening papers. In the morning field, there were four newspapers by then. The *Daily Mirror* and *Herald Tribune* were dying lingering deaths, the *Daily News* was not read for its theater criticism, and the *Times'* drama critic reigned supreme in the hit-or-flop economy of Broadway. His influence extended far beyond Times Square, for any play he endorsed became a hot prospect for film and regional theater rights.

While keenly aware of his importance, Brooks Atkinson was a fair man and a qualified, responsible journalist who served with distinction as a war correspondent in between a couple of decades on the drama beat. He is most fondly remembered by many in the theater for having panned a play called *Mamba's Daughters*, starring Ethel Waters, and then, a few days later, writing a new notice in which he said it was a beautiful play to which he shouldn't have gone on opening night because he'd had a bad cold. By the time Atkinson retired, however, Broadway depended so slavishly on the New York *Times* to tell it whether it was any good that without a theater-party cushion, Mamba and her daughters wouldn't have been around by the time the second notice appeared.

Atkinson's successor, Howard Taubman, was a lackluster ex-baseball and music writer who met his job's deadlines and fulfilled its requirements drably but ethically. In mid-1956, however, it became known that Taubman was being kicked upstairs to critic-at-large, from which observation tower he would scan the hinterlands for signs of a cultural explosion. A six-month search for a successor culminated in the selection of Stanley Kauffmann, a leisurely essayist, not a journalist, whose weekly movie reviews made provocative reading in the *New Republic* and who was already the drama critic for New York's educational TV, Channel 13. Kauffmann was quick to tell his new employers that their arts coverage struck him as a "cultural dump," and he indicated that he expected his presence to improve the general level of daily newspaper reviewing "and thus possibly help the theater itself."

Broadway did not relish this favor, particularly David Merrick, who proclaimed Kauffmann's appointment "the greatest insult the *Times* could have perpetrated on the American theater. Stanley Kauffmann is a professorial type who has written some forty-five unproduced plays himself and would naturally be bitter toward Broadway." To distribute as evidence, Merrick bought several dozen copies of a particularly dreary novel Kauffmann once wrote. He also threatened privately to produce a festival of Kauffmann's plays as further documentation.

Vicious though this was, Merrick had a valid point to make. Art was being put at the journalistic mercy of a failed—and possibly frustrated—creative talent. True, this has been the case for centuries, and sometimes one's own past failures can intensify one's perception and appreciation of the work of others. Kauffmann, with the *Times* as his accomplice, promptly went history one better. Soon after his failings as a daily journalist became apparent, he sought to make a virtue of them and reshape the theater to fit them.

Kauffmann's initial first-night reviews verged on the unintelligible. Whether these represented new-job jitters or inability to cope with a nightly deadline will never be known. For after a few nights on the job, Kauffmann started going to previews, and his morning-after-the-premiere reviews grew lucid, readable, and insightful. This was the Stanley Kauffmann that *New Republic* readers knew! But to get this with breakfast, New York *Times* readers had to settle for a review of an unfinished performance. The play was no longer the thing; the critique was.

Even more alarmingly, Kauffmann, having built up a well-earned reputation as a full-time critic who stood *for* cultural uplift and *against* David Merrick merchandise like *Cactus Flower,** was at least as committed to his philosophy as a politician to his platform. And here the dangerous new math of the critic-as-public-figure is afoot. Let us assume that *Cactus Flower* is about to open on Broadway and is in moderately presentable shape at a semifinal preview attended by Stanley Kauffmann,

---

* "Why should a drama critic review *Cactus Flower?* . . . The present imperative for the critic to review every Broadway show seems to me a debasement of his function, a confusion of territories, and an invasion of a businessman's business rights. A man who manufactures popcorn has the right to sell it without interference, to anyone who wants to buy it. . . . Alfred Kazin does not try to dissuade anyone from reading Harold Robbins; why should a serious drama critic intrude on the mercantile projects that turn up on Broadway?"—Stanley Kauffmann.

who has been forced by his employers to review such trivia. And let us suppose that at this performance of *Cactus Flower*, Kauffmann cannot resist chuckling and laughing and maybe even slapping his beret against his knee. It can happen! And if he had to write his review with a deadline an hour away, mightn't he be inclined to give the play the rave it deserves from him? On the other hand, allowed almost forty-eight extra hours to equate his opinion with his past pronouncements, mightn't his enthusiasm be tempered?

One thing was certain. Much of Broadway was intimidated by Kauffmann, and not for the better. An innately cautious medium lapsed into apoplectic paralysis. A playwright who had written one smash-hit comedy and a couple of others that had achieved moderate success was startled when his producer turned down his latest play in early 1966. "It's the best thing you've ever done," the producer explained, "but nobody'll take a chance on investing in this because it's the kind of stuff that ------ Kauffmann's against."

The playwright swallowed hard and said: "What kind of play do you have to write to get by Kauffmann?"

"Phedre," said the producer, alluding to Kauffmann's rave for an off-Broadway revival of Racine. "But nobody's gonna do *Phedre* uptown, either. I don't know what *you're* going to do, but *I'm* low on anything that ain't arty-farty pretentious."

"I think Broadway *should* do *Phedre*," the playwright murmured. "But why can't it do *Life With Father*, too?"

Only David Merrick, who vowed that Kauffmann would "never get into a preview of mine," was defiant. But even Merrick seemed to capitulate when the *Times* requested preview tickets for his fragile little Irish import called *Philadelphia, Here I Come!* Merrick sent Kauffmann a pair, along with a cryptic note reading, "At Your Peril."

An ambush indeed was underway. On the night of the final preview, Kauffmann and a thousand other theatergoers showed up to find that the theater was dark.

"The performance was canceled because a rat got caught in the generator," said a Merrick spokesman, offering refunds or exchanges. "We got the rat out, so the formal opening will absolutely go on as scheduled."

It absolutely did—with Kauffmann up front and Merrick

out back, still sticking to his tale of an elusive white rat.* "I made my point," he moralized as smugly as any cat that ever gobbled a rat. "All sorts of technical things go wrong at previews that we can correct overnight."

In the next day's press, only one review was unfavorable— Kauffmann's. But the previous day's front-page headlines (in the New York *Times*: "THE DARK PREVIEW, OR 'AT YOUR PERIL' ") had negated his impact and in fact made him an embarrassment to the *Times*.

A dubious box office prospect at best, *Philadelphia, Here I Come!* ran eight months, which was about as long as Stanley Kauffmann lasted at the *Times*. For suddenly that summer, when the *Herald Tribune* folded on Forty-first Street, the *Times* seized the chance to retrieve its blunder (though not its honor). Firing Kauffmann and hiring the *Trib*'s Walter Kerr, the *Times* blandly announced:

> We are happy that we are able to offer the readers of The New York *Times* and former readers of The *Herald Tribune* a critic of such distinction as Mr. Kerr. Mr. Kauffmann leaves with our great gratitude for his services. . . . He has made and will continue to make an important contribution to American criticism. . . .

But elsewhere.** A *Times* official elaborated defensively. "We didn't want to boot Mr. Kauffmann out. We wanted Mr. Kerr for the New York *Times*." Stanley Kauffmann said his "feeling about the *Times* as an institution is that they behaved with less than entire good faith." And Walter Kerr, who was in Europe at the time, quoted Marlowe: " 'But that was in another country. And besides, the wench is dead.' "

As America's most articulate champion of a popular theater

---

* For those who cherish in-group symbolism, "The White Rat" is a West Forty-third Street nickname for a prominent *Times* executive who had some say in the hiring of Stanley Kauffmann.

** Kauffmann immediately rejoined the *New Republic*, this time as critic-at-large columnist, and Channel 13 as drama critic. Later he signed on with the *New American Review* as its film critic, although his initial contribution was a twenty-page firsthand account of "Drama on The *Times*: Experiences and Observations," in which Walter Kerr was mentioned as "my successor," never by name.

—a middle- or lower-class amusement, not an upper-bracket plaything or highbrow *objet d'art*—with all the foursquare vitality of Shakespeare and Chaplin, Walter Kerr has always been controversial. When Kauffmann was fired, you might have thought Kerr was replacing George Bernard Shaw. As a matter of fact, an English professor wrote in "with despair and disgust" to make just that comparison, while a journalism professor at Columbia congratulated the *Times* on "a great replacement for Brooks Atkinson."

Kerr proved to be an even more drastic reformer than Kauffmann. After a few weeks on the job, he did away with an indulgence that Atkinson had admitted to and Taubman and Kauffman had perpetuated: bending over backward to be kind to off-Broadway plays because of their impoverished circumstances and lofty aspirations. And even before flying home from Europe, Kerr remarked that he was alarmed by "the shrinking number of papers, about the fact that there are not as many voices. I like voices." And so, from Salzburg, Austria, he wrote a letter to his new employer protesting the monolithic tyranny of being supercritic.

> So long as there were six or seven reviewers with contending critical voices, it was always possible for a play to survive on mixed notices. But with the number of papers shrinking so, that is no longer going to be possible. . . . The theater could be thrown into even deeper trouble for lack of debate. It might be very valuable for The *Times* to become the vital center of debate through having at least two separate opinions, one daily, one Sunday.

Managing editor Clifton Daniel admitted that the *Times* was considering Kerr's proposal and might honor it, though "not next week, not next month."

Even if Kerr's proposal had been a mere gesture, it would have been a uniquely self-effacing landmark in contemporary criticism. But Kerr meant it.

At the end of Kerr's first season as supercritic, his request was granted. He became the *Times'* Sunday drama critic, and Clive Barnes became its daily critic. When the appointments were announced, Kerr and Barnes had never met, but Clive Barnes, the most conscientious and rewarding day-in-day-out critic practicing in America today, felt no compunction about saying cheerfully: "Between Mr. Kerr and myself, we are prepared to break the power of the *Times'* critic. We want influence, not power."

[II]

This was, in effect, no sooner said than done, thanks to the turnover (four different seat warmers in twenty-one months) and subsequent splitting of New York *Times* drama criticism. Besides, a new breed of cultural arbiter—the TV commentators with their thirty-second capsule critiques—were on the air before the *Times* had even gone to press and were chipping away at the fringe of power. The *Times,* however, retains the core of critical influence—and then some. And if responsible criticism does mean better or livelier theater, then the drama is in good hands with Clive Barnes on weekdays and Walter Kerr on Sundays.

Even if good criticism doesn't mean good art, both the *Times* and the drama had a narrow escape from Stanley Kauffmann's eight-month reign, during which a preoccupation with criticism had precedence over a preoccupation with theater or, for that matter, basic newspaper journalism.

From his prolific exile, Stanley Kauffmann (writing in the *New American Review*) greeted the split as "a questionable move . . . a political idea mistakenly applied to art. But at least it . . . puts Mr. Barnes in the position of immediate power. He will bring unwonted taste to the field of the New York daily theater reviewing."

What a relief it was to hear Clive Barnes himself (immediately after his appointment was announced) pontificating cheerfully on the theater.

"There is an enormous amount of garbage. The only time certain couples sleep together is when they go to the theater. Broadway has reached its lowest level. It can only go up. . . . I'm a sucker for all kinds of good plays. What I'm for is theater as an expression of man. That sounds terribly pompous, but I want it to move me, stimulate me, send me out screaming or shouting.

He made it clear that he is not one who thinks it is easier to write a good play than a good review.

"Some critics envy the artist. I know I'm an appreciator, not a creator. Anyway, who said critics are noble and good? They're bad guys."

Panning his first Broadway opening, a melodramatic fiasco called *Dr. Cook's Garden,* Barnes concluded:

"Oh, well, that was my first Broadway opening, and I survived. And in a job where people tell me they have to name a theater after you if you last out more than a season, this is no small consideration."

He went to every Broadway first night, some off-Broadway premieres, and Wednesday matinees of some long-running hits.

"Critics tend to forget they're journalists. . . . I plan to review or have reviewed all cast changes on Broadway, even when understudies take over for two weeks. Many more people have seen Herschel Bernardi and Luther Adler in *Fiddler on the Roof* than have seen Zero Mostel, and they've never been reviewed. Ads say 'The funniest comedy of the season' when a production may be in a complete state of chaos."

A baby-faced Briton, Clive Barnes, forty, has never taken long to establish his identity as the very model of a modern major-newspaper critic. Educated at Oxford, he covered the dance for the London *Times* and *Daily Express* for more than a decade until Clifton Daniel imported him to Times Square in August, 1965. As dance critic of the New York *Times,* he wasted no time in captivating his readers with the unpretentious, good-humored diligence* of an ardent fan who would venture uptown, downtown, and underground in pursuit of the dance. From a careful reading of his notices, it became apparent that he must have attended at least fourteen Christmastime performances of Balanchine's *Nutcracker* at Lincoln Center. And yet, at the end of his ordeal, he was incorrigibly cheerful though a trifle apologetic.

The dance world had a friend but a stern taskmaster in Clive Barnes, and so did the dance public. He was forever railing at

* As early as the fall of 1965, a buff who publishes a monthly love letter to the arts, Jerome B. Agel of *Books/,* was nominating Clive Barnes for drama critic of the *Times* in print and in a personal meeting with Clifton Daniel. A year and a half later, having selected first Kauffmann, then Kerr, and finally Barnes, Daniel acknowledged Agel's foresight with a thank-you note that ended: "We move very slowly over here."

unannounced cast changes and preselling of subscriptions by the New York City Ballet.

Barnes, who sees all, is anything but blind to where a practice like preselling for the dilettante dollar leads artistically. Reviewing a new ballet representing the work of eight composers, he found it

> a feeble ballet of more importance to the economic paraphernalia of ballet-giving than to the art of the ballet itself. Each season the self-styled patrons of New York City Ballet demand, Broadway-fashion, a certain output of new sensations.
>
> In the nature of things most of these new sensations must be trash. And that, sadly and somewhat inelegantly, characterizes John Taras' *La Guirlande de Campra.*

Even while defending the hard-core balletomane's artistic and financial interests, Barnes would sometimes take him to task. He concluded one weighty review with:

> . . . A point I would like to bring to the attention of my readers, especially those who tell me you cannot get tickets for New York City Ballet: For three nights in a row there have been unsold seats. Not many but some. Go on, try a little.

A few weeks later, Barnes remarked that

> I am still getting letters hinting, or more boldly stating, that one cannot, short of offering up either one's virtue or patrimony, obtain tickets for the New York City Ballet. Well, admittedly some tickets are difficult to obtain, and some of the occasional empty seats one sees at the State Theater are doubtless the result of some of the City Ballet over-subscribers' chickening out and going off to play pinochle . . . or merely, more innocently (and here I sympathize) having baby-sitter problems. But there are still tickets to be had for City Ballet performances, so please, please, do not write to tell me to the contrary. Furthermore, private research suggests that . . . it is the cheapest seats that are the easiest to buy.

Racing up and down the marble halls of Lincoln Center and other arts complexes across the nation, Barnes reemphasized the neglected critical function of reportage and, in doing so, caught a glimpse of the culture consumers' grim future.

"I think that we are going to be dealing with people who are not responsible to any arbitrator such as the box office or anything like that because they are going to have their money and [the treasury] is going to be full whatever they do. What defense will the poor box-office patron have if the management kicks him in his teeth? And bureaucratic managements *do* kick ordinary patrons in the teeth. It's no good writing letters to people. They never reply or, if they do reply, they never do anything about it.

"So the critic is responsible as a sort of an *ombudsman*, you know, the fellow who stands between everyone and tries to help a bit. . . . I don't think this can be left to highbrow or specialist publications. I think it should be discussed in newspapers at all levels of readership and all circulations."

One Friday night, en route to the ballet, Clive Barnes remarked that although he sometimes felt as though he had to write about *Swan Lake* eighty-eight times a week, "I would still try to say something about *Swan Lake*. I would say something about the performers inasmuch as how they illuminated the work."

It was a few days later that Barnes wrote:

"It must be three years or more since I last saw Violette Verdy in *Swan Lake*, and it was a pleasure to see her glowing dancing —here given perhaps more dramatic nuance than the other City Ballet ballerinas. She was partnered by André Prokovsky, who is having a good season but should perhaps guard against such mannerisms as waving to the audience on entry rather than to his colleagues."

When the notion of switching from dance criticism to drama criticism was broached by the *Times,* Barnes resisted it at first, but succumbed to what he considered "a challenge and a temptation. Inside most dance critics is a drama critic struggling to get out. I may be making the goddamndest mistake of my life, but I have to take the chance. On no account, though, will I give up dance—an overwhelming passion!" Thus Clive Barnes continues to cover as many ballets as he can and writes a Sunday column on the dance.

In 1966 two Princeton economists named Baumol and Bowen* completed a study for the Twentieth Century Fund that neatly dispelled the aura of the "cultural explosion." Without ever rebuking the wishful thinking that has lent credence to the blatant propaganda of the boom, they quietly observed that their "analysis of the record entitles us to conclude neither that the nation has entered a great cultural renaissance nor that it is lost in an artistic wilderness. Rather, as is often the case, one is forced to a comparatively colorless in-between position—that over the course of the last decade and a half, the over-all progress of professional activity in the living arts has amounted to little more than a continuation of past trends." In opera, "the number of professional performances by major opera companies has remained just about constant." In the theater, "it is clear that there has been no boom on Broadway." For symphony orchestras, "the increase in attendance has been slightly slower than the increase in population. . . . There is no obvious upward trend." The audience for all the arts is "drawn from an extremely narrow segment of the American population." Virtually all of the boom was talk—promising talk, exciting talk, the talk on which critics' futures are built, but nonetheless just talk.

There was one notable exception to Baumol and Bowen's statistics on the boom—*ballet.* "Here," they proclaimed in joyful chorus, "is a performing art in which there really seems to be a substantial rate of expansion."

The truth of this dances before our eyes. The existing companies are thriving on more seasons, longer seasons, and wider tours. New troupes blossom from adversity while Paul Taylor, Merce Cunningham, and even the venerable Martha Graham are dancing their way across the land and around the world. With burgeoning college and university circuits, a homeless dance troupe can live a reasonably comfortable life all year round.

---

* Baumol, William J., and Bowen, William G., *Performing Arts: The Economic Dilemma.* New York, The Twentieth Century Fund, 1966.

When you try to equate the presence of a Clive Barnes with today's flourishing state of the dance, both aesthetically and economically, you are playing the game of chicken versus egg, tail versus dog, cart versus horse. Though not balletomanes, my wife and I can testify that ever since Barnes joined our morning paper in 1965, our dancegoing doubled or tripled from its usual rate of once or twice a year. Even before then, what lured us was the high level of criticism practiced by two other dance reviewers: Jill Johnston of the *Village Voice* and Edwin Denby, an infrequent contributor to *Saturday Review* and other periodicals. The former makes the experimental dance scene come alive before your eyes. She can tell you what Merce Cunningham and his composer, John Cage, are getting at in such an explicit, dramatic way that should you attend a performance, you would wonder why you haven't always been on their wavelength. And Denby is a poet-critic, a peculiar hybrid, but perhaps the only creature that could transmit such esoteric intangibles as Margot Fonteyn's Sleeping Beauty or Maya Plisetskaya's shimmering swan in prose.

Jill Johnston, Edwin Denby, and Clive Barnes do their jobs so well that they make it imperative for you to attend any event that enchanted any of them. And while we still couldn't be enjoying a dance renaissance without choreographers like Robert Joffrey and ballerinas like Suzanne Farrell, we can be sure that they are being kept on their toes and upwardly mobile by the encouragement they draw from the high level of dance criticism in America today.

[III]

In coping with our other art forms, few influential critics even attempt to perform the basic rudiments of their jobs. In the November, 1965, issue of *Harper's* magazine, a review of Peter Matthiessen's *At Play in the Fields of the Lord* contained such an astounding plot summary that several readers wrote in. Two of them stated point-blank, as readers and authors often do, that the reviewer "demonstrates unmistakably that he hasn't even read the book." Now the story took an unexpected twist. In the January, 1966, issue, the reviewer, a *Harper's* regular named Roderick Cook, confessed: "There seems to have been more than one blackout in the Northeast this fall. I have just re-read the book I thought I had read, and am appalled that I could have blundered so carelessly in reporting the plot as I did. I would like to apologize unequivocally to Mr. Matthiessen and his publishers; and I would like to refer anyone who has been misled by my review to the better-informed reviews of this book that have appeared elsewhere."

Here was the book-reviewing mentality at its narcissistic worst. Note that Cook's otherwise abject apology referred the reader to "better-informed reviews," *not to the book itself!* The idea that people might go to the double trouble of reading him *and* the book he is reviewing occurs less and less to the modern critic.

The Cook caper also prompted a few spirited defenses of a reviewer's right *not* to read, including this scarcely facetious appraisal by Thomas Lask on the New York *Times'* editorial page:

> . . . For we live pre-eminently in an age of criticism. It is not enough to read a book today; it is far more important to know what so-and-so said about it.
>
> Turn to a literary journal and the proportion of criticism to original work is seven or eight to one—on a good day. Criticism that started out to illuminate the work of art has ended up by living off it.*

Criticism is a structure of words applied largely to nonverbal (e.g., symphonies) or partially verbal (e.g., drama) arts. Book reviewing, alias literary criticism, is the prime exception. The ease with which a critic can lift, quote, paraphrase, or translate literature into a prose review is the first reason why book reviewing today has more space, more prominence, more arrogance, and more carelessness than all other forms of reviewing combined.

The second element in literary criticism's prevalence is the academic world, in whose faculties are embedded a legion of critics all heeding the admonition to publish or perish. The universities nourish their tenure, and the mass periodicals flourish their ordure. This has made each Sunday's New York *Times*

---

* "What Are You Doing, Mr. Cook?", a "Topics of The Times" essay, January 22, 1966.

Book Review a dreary faculty club housing some of the most
jaded, incestuous criticism in the world. Its members commute
between backbiting and bootlicking, with the inevitable intermediate stop. Here a protégé receives a helpful pat on the back;
there a onetime mentor is nudged gently over the hill. Historians review statesmen's memoirs and economists review books
about money with clockwork regularity. We may one day pick
up the Sunday *Times* to find children reviewing juvenile books
and lifers reviewing murder mysteries. Until then, its liveliest
rewards are the academic scores that get settled in print. Recently, a number of historians competed for a grant to do a major
research project. When it was published, the winner's work was
panned in the *Times* Book Review by the man who had been
runner-up in the competition.

The *Times* Book Review is looked at by an estimated 20 percent of the newpaper's close to 2 million Sunday readers, which
makes it the best book-advertising medium there is at present.
Although its ads outshine the stodgy criticism they interrupt,
the *Times* Book Review can, with a concerted effort, pull itself
together and achieve some influence. An appealingly written
front-page notice *can* call public attention to an obscure novel,
as Chad Walsh did for Richard E. Kim's *The Martyred* and
Irving Howe did for a paperback reissue of Henry Roth's *Call
It Sleep,* which had gone neglected for three decades. A *Times*
Book Review hatchet job on Hannah Arendt's *Eichmann in
Jerusalem,* performed by an inflexibly liberal Gentile jurist,
maimed the book's sales, despite its cachet of advance serialization in the *New Yorker.*

A quieter way to destroy a book is not to review it at all. With
some 30,000 new books published a year, this happens for a
number of mundane reasons like lack of space, editorial judgment, editorial shortsightedness, and unpublishable reviewing.
The Autobiography of Malcolm X didn't get reviewed because
the *Times* gave the assignment to James Baldwin, who failed to
deliver. (A year later, when the paperback edition was issued,
the *Times* made partial amends by having another critic review
it then.) A review of the late Lenny Bruce's *How to Talk Dirty
and Influence People* was assigned to Kurt Vonnegut, Jr., one
of the livelier novelist/teacher/critics on the market. Vonnegut

delivered, but his notice was never published. Too racy, apparently.

Being an organ, however limp, of a *news*paper, the New York *Times* Book Review freely admits that timeliness takes precedence over art in its pages. When the great American novel is written, its notice may appear on page 69 if page 1 is reserved for an important university-press book on slums.

The great American novelist's best hope, then, may be the weekday paper's "Book of The Times" column, where a *full-length* rave review by Orville Prescott *for a novel* will mean a good 4,000 sales *if the book is in the stores when the review appears.* Prescott is generally credited in the publishing trade (and particularly in the houses involved) with skyrocketing 1966's *Secret of Santa Vittoria,* by Robert Crichton, and *Tai-Pan,* by James Clavell, toward the upper reaches of the best-seller stratosphere. But Prescott, whom Gore Vidal once christened "The Good Gray Goose," * is in semiretirement. He writes only twelve reviews a year for the *Times*—and not all favorable. "My scrapbooks," Prescott remarked recently, "seem like a graveyard of dead reputations."

Behind Prescott at the *Times* stands a faceless corps of ineffectual daily reviewers. And behind the daily and Sunday *Times,* our only semblance of a *national* newspaper, most other book-review media are given short shrift by book buyers and book advertisers alike.

The *Saturday Review* dropped the suffix *of Literature* a few years ago. Once you have left its editorial page, where head man Norman Cousins vehemes against such sitting ducks as nuclear weaponry and air pollution, blandness is all. *SR*'s relations with book clubs have always been close (*SR*'s Henry Seidel Canby and Christopher Morley were two of the first five Book-of-the-Month judges), and it has always served club members as an only slightly more acerbic shopping guide than the Book-of-the-Month Club *News* or the Literary Guild's *Wings.*

From generation to generation, *SR* has also been handed down as the bible of the overbusy culture consumer who wishes to know enough about a book to be able to discuss it without

---

* Vidal on Prescott: "He still gives marks to novels not for style or insight or wisdom or art, but for morality. Are these nice people? Is this a nice author?"

actually reading it. *SR* reviewers have long been encouraged to stress *what the book is about* and to give *detailed plot synopses* of fiction. Ever since *SR* was acquired by Norton Simon, the art-loving tomato tycoon (see Chapter 4), these virtues have, if anything, been accentuated.

Under Simon's ownership, too, *SR's* reviews concentrate on volumes of belles-lettres, literary criticism, social significance, and short stories, the last of which one *SR* executive termed "the most vigorous form of writing today." Here, too, the great American novel may well receive short shrift.

(Lumped by Simon with *McCall's* and *Redbook* in the Mc-Call Corporation, the *Saturday Review,* which always had a tendency toward chumminess with the literary power structure, has embraced a rather questionable togetherness with both the would-be-writer industry and Lincoln Center. *SR's* annual spring supplement on writers' conferences features an imposing array of ads for writers' workshops flanking passionate editorial paeans to the would-be-writer industry by such vested interests as critic Gorham Munson, who runs his own Florham Park Writers Conference in Madison, New Jersey. *Saturday Review* also snared the publishing concession at Lincoln Center, where *SR's* music editor, Irving Kolodin, moonlights as editor of the programs and writer of the program notes. Studying Kolodin's reviews with this relationship in mind, it is hard to discern any pulled punches amid *SR's* prevailing unexcitement. But don't wait around for him to denounce Rudolf Bing.)

Since the *New Yorker* pays as much as $40,000 for rights to a book, most authors would rather be serialized than reviewed there. The critiques, when they appear, are too often belated and inconsequential—except when an Edmund Wilson rises to exalt the life work of a Morley Callaghan or when a Dwight Macdonald smites down a possibly overpraised James Gould Cozzens as a racist prig, a muddy thinker, a grotesque stylist, and a pompous arriviste. And while the "Books" section of the *New Yorker* nowadays is less and less a maker or breaker of authors, it still remains a forum for some worthwhile literary reportage.

In the *New Yorker's* 1964 Fourth of July issue, a young newcomer named Renata Adler published an account called "Polemic and the New Reviewers." With twenty pages of massive documentation, she showed the *New Yorker*'s half million readers precisely what the self-avowedly influential *Commentary/Partisan Review/New York Review of Books* clique was up to.

> . . . There is a kind of reciprocity along the reviewing circuit that, while it occasionally imparts a pleasing continuity to critical discussion (the reader who suspects that the reviewer does not do justice to the book under consideration may be consoled by the knowledge that the reviewer has read at least all previous reviews of it), more often resembles nothing so much as a ticker-tape compendium or a caucus in an airless convention hall.

You can flounder in ever-narrowing circles as you try to keep track of these people cannibalizing and yet perpetuating each other. (Susan Sontag is their Natalie Wood, Jason Epstein their Robespierre, Vladimir Nabokov their Svengali, etc.) Miss Adler's devastating report was ostensibly a review of three books, one of which was Norman Podhoretz's *Doings and Undoings,* a collection of essays by the fierce young critic who edits *Commentary.* Podhoretz writes with a rhetorical authority that seems to grab the reader's ears as well as eyes and cannot be shaken off, no matter how banal his message. What grabbed Miss Adler was Podhoretz's piece on "Book Reviewing and Everyone I Know," in which he wrote:

> All these reviewers inhabit much the same intellectual milieu, and what they have in common, apart from talent and intelligence, is an attitude toward books and an idea about the proper way to discuss them. This attitude might be characterized as one of great suspiciousness: a book is assumed to be guilty until it proves itself innocent—and not many do.

And a page later:

> . . . Most of them, indeed, take the writing of reviews with the kind of seriousness that is ordinarily associated only with poets working at their verses, for on the whole they think of themselves less as critics than as writers and intellectuals. And it is as writers and intellectuals respond-

ing to the issues raised by a book—often even a bad book —that they approach the job of reviewing. Their reviews are thus neither intended as a service to the potential consumer who wishes to know whether or not the book under consideration is likely to interest him (which is how [the New York *Times* Book Review] conceives the function of a review), nor as a service to the author who wishes to know where he went right and where he went wrong so that he can do better next time (which is how no one but certain naïve journalists and sanctimonious novelists conceives the function of a review). If writers like these are performing a service at all when they review a book, it is a service to consciousness; a book for them is, quite simply, an occasion to do some writing of their own.*

It is no suprise, then, to find Podhoretz concluding that "some of the best writing done in America . . . and some of the most illuminating discussion of the life of our times" could be found in back issues of *Partisan Review* (circulation 20,000) and his own *Commentary* (circulation 60,000)** as well as in the brand-new pages of the *New York Review of Books.*

Podhoretz's "Book Reviewing and Everyone I Know" was, in turn, a 1963 salute to the founding (during a newspaper strike when the New York *Times* Book Review was shut down) of the *New York Review of Books,* now an Anglophilic fortnightly with a circulation at 75,000. The frighteningly articulate house organ of a self-promoting Manhattan coterie, it could easily be renamed the *New York Review of Each Other's Books.* And like many people who have chosen to dwell intimately with the printed word, the *New York Review* clique maintains a love-hate relationship with the art it serves. Hate often seems to be getting the better of it. "Her book is memorable to me," one review in it said, "only because halfway through reading it I was seized by a cramping suspicion that the novel as a viable literary form might after 300 years of life be ready for burial."

All of which bring us full circle to Miss Adler, who con-

---

* Podhoretz, Norman, *Doings and Undoings.* New York, Farrar, Straus & Giroux, 1964.

** It was once said, quite aptly, of Norman Podhoretz's prodigious talent and enthusiasm for whatever he is involved in: "If Mr. Podhoretz ever went into the plumbing business, we would soon have an essay on how the toilet bowl is replacing the book."

cludes, "The principles that unite the New Reviewing school are—if it is possible to call them 'principles' at all—an elaborate system of cross-references that amounts to mutual coattail-hanging; a stale liberalism gone reactionary in anti-Everyman snobbery and defeatist cliché; a false intellectualism that is astonishingly shabby in its arguments; a hostile imperiousness toward fiction that results in near megalomania on the part of expository writers; and withering condescension toward authors and readers that finds expression in a strident tendency to shout the opposition down. The New Reviewing is, more generally, a pastiche of attitudes and techniques vying to divert the attention of the reader from the book ostensibly under review to the personality of the reviewer. . . ."

Despite the odds that have been sketched herein, the great American novel may yet be written—for Roderick Cook to garble in *Harper's;* for the New York *Times* to ignore or bury; for Norman Podhoretz to get off some writing of his own. But, then again, it may not be written, simply because novelists, like most other people, prefer to go where the action is. Today's publishing action is in nonfiction rather than fiction, with criticism as the quickest route to fame, if not fortune.

If the pursuit of criticism should ultimately absorb the talents of potential great American novelists, fiction would not be the first art it has swallowed up. Our age of criticism stems, in part, from the decline of the essay as a publishable art form. Editors, buffeted by the nervous tempo of their times, their absentee publishers, and their vast readerships' needs for broad common denominators, stopped buying the reflective personal essay or taking a chance on the cheekiness of an unsolicited opinion. Frustrated essayists turned to criticism, using the latest books or movies as points of departure for some writing of their own. Even in the pages of the *New Yorker,* the bookish charm of Robert Benchley and E. B. White gave way to the cool-blooded *Grand Guignol* of Truman Capote and the frantic black humor of Donald Barthelme. Miss Adler herself broke into print with a documented essay craftily fitted into the *New Yorker's* book-review format.

Ironically, that one exposé of contemporary criticism immediately established Miss Adler as a critic to be reckoned with in American letters. It and subsequent *New Yorker* appearances led to her appointment, at twenty-nine, to replace Bosley Crowther as screen critic of the New York *Times,* effective January 1, 1968. Assuming she doesn't lose it at the movies, her immaculate perception should bring sorely needed first aid for a field that was surveyed thusly in *Holiday*'s 1966 special issue on culture: "Film criticism today seems the most malpracticed service in America."

Movie criticism has been called "yawning as a profession," but the definitive job description was written a few years ago by an anonymous bard in *Time.*

> In tireless pursuit of mediocrity and unreadability, the nation's run-of-the-film movie critics have transformed themselves into a group dispensary of tasteless, colorless, and odorless treacle, ignored on a wholesale basis by the moviegoer, sampled only by the movie industry itself, which is merely vigilant for any sign of recalcitrant tartness.

Movies being the most heavily advertised of all art forms, the goodwill of film exhibitors and distributors has grown more precious than ever to America's dwindling number of daily newspapers. Their critics are frequently policed by both advertisers and publishers. William Randolph Hearst, Jr., once memoed his ragged band of reviewers "not to be biting or sarcastic or bitter. . . . I don't believe our readers are interested in reading the personal likes and dislikes of our critics and I don't intend to waste our valuable space printing them."

The newspaper with the widest readership, the New York *Daily News* (circulation 2 million), simply *invented* its movie critic; Kate Cameron is a pseudonym instituted forty years ago by *News* publisher Joseph Medill Patterson. The first Kate Cameron was Irene Thirer, who later left the *News* to make a career as a critic under her own name. The second Kate Cameron was Miss Loretta King, a genteel spinster who commuted from Riverdale.

The New York *Times'* critic emeritus, Bosley Crowther, is a chunky Princetonian (class of '28) who used to write the bulletins flashed across the electric sign in Times Square and who became film critic in 1940. A self-appointed one-man legion of decency determined to safeguard moral rather than artistic standards, Crowther's pious vendetta against *Bonnie and Clyde* in Sunday column after Sunday column after daily review after Montreal film-festival review is credited with calling attention to that outlaw romance and making it one of the big winners of 1967.

What Crowther had only just begun to do when he was replaced by Renata Adler had been going on for several years in avant-garde criticism: *the corruption of the instinct.* Whose instinct? Yours! While the critic loved a brilliant director's sparkling comedy, *you* ought to boycott it (says he) because box-office success will tempt other serious film makers to turn out fluff. The tears we weep in darkened movie houses are fake tears, cheap tears. A poorly made spy thriller is really a beautifully conceived put-on or spoof of a spoof of a spoof. A movie can be "so bad it's good."

A handful of ambitious careerists (John Simon and Andrew Sarris come to mind most readily) have long been practicing this kind of witchcraft in a number of low-paying periodicals. They were spawned by the art-theater revolution (a dozen across the nation in 1950, more than 500 by 1960), which not only made Ingmar Bergman and Brigitte Bardot and Juan Valdez household words but also moved the fulcrum of critical power toward national periodicals, however small their circulations. The newspaper reviewers were left chasing after their daily nitty-gritty of Jerry Lewis comedies and Elvis Presley musicals while these quarterly pundits were free to get off some essays of their own about what *interested* them.

Today they even have their own film circle to dissent from prevailing reactions. Their most responsible member, perhaps the only one who seems to love movies more than he loves himself, is Richard Schickel, free-lance contributor to *Life.* And their Joan of Arc is a middle-aged frump named Pauline Kael, author of *I Lost It at the Movies.*

Wrapped in its seductive title and talked up by an articulate "cult of Kael," *I Lost It at the Movies,* a collection of Miss Kael's reviews, has sold more than 200,000 copies in hard-cover and paperback. Its publisher blurbed her as "considered by many the most influential critic in the United States today," a remarkable feat for a lady whose essays disguised as critiques had been appearing largely in such esoterica as *Film Quarterly,*

Kulchur, Massachusetts Review and *Partisan Review*. "It's nearly impossible for a serious critic to make a living wage in the United States," she once complained. "In ten years I made under two thousand dollars from film criticism." Those were the postwar years, when Miss Kael was underwriting her career as a critic by managing a movie house, composing program notes for film societies, and broadcasting on FM. But the boom in art cinemas rewarded her struggles, and her essays began appearing in *Vogue, Holiday, Life, Mademoiselle,* and the *Atlantic Monthly*. Her aesthetic postures were so consistent that they could be bound between hard covers with little fear of self-contradiction. And soon after *I Lost It at the Movies,* there came a call from *McCall's*, offering her the $20,000-a-year post of critic in residence for 8½ million women.

"From the beginning," Miss Kael said later, "I thought I was the wrong person for their readers, but they were willing to take the risk." And not being one to obey her instincts, she plunged ahead.

Like Joan of Arc, Pauline Kael heard voices—thrice in one column alone (March, 1966):

> "This spoofing is finished. It's time for the reality revolution." That's what I heard a teen-age boy say as he was coming out of *The Great Race.* . . .

Then, after suffering through *The Flight of the Phoenix:*

> and when the survivors finally make it out of the desert, a woman behind me said, "I never lost faith. I knew they'd make it." When the movie was over, I looked, and there she was, in blond mink, a woman in her fifties one might have expected to be rather sophisticated. Probably she's the kind of woman who will say pictures like this are great for kids. . . .

And finally, in another movie, Anne Bancroft took a fatal dose of sleeping pills. But Sidney Poitier, manning a telephone at the local suicide clinic, kept her talking while he deciphered her identity and whereabouts in the nick of time. And Pauline Kael wrote:

. . . *The Slender Thread* never deals with the irony that the audience is constantly soaking in: that the man at the end of the telephone wire is a Negro. At the end, when the woman's life has been saved and Telly Savalas, the decent, humane doctor, asks Poitier if he'd like to meet her, he thinks for a moment and then says: "No." Gulp. I was happy to hear a voice behind me in the theater: "They already met at the Academy Award show."

A couple of months later, Miss Kael's keen inner ear picked up sinister U-boats lurking beneath the Hallmark-card facade of *The Sound of Music*. She warned the women of America that they were being manipulated by "the Pavlovs of moviemaking," the evil geniuses who made the world's most popular movie. Comparing them to "the worst despots in history, the most cynical purveyors of mass culture," she labeled their product "the big lie, the sugarcoated lie that people seem to want to eat." Who on earth could *The Sound of Music* offend? Miss Kael asked rhetorically. "Only those of us who, *despite the fact that we may respond,* loathe being manipulated in this way and are aware of how self-indulgent and cheap and ready-made are the responses we are made to feel."

A torrent of mail convinced *McCall's* that 8½ million American women would rather be manipulated by movie makers than join in Pauline Kael's master race of moviegoers. And so, *McCall's* fired Miss Kael.

"I knew that she was extremely critical when I hired her," said Robert Stein, then the editor. "But her reviews became more and more uniformly unfavorable—not only to all films, but questioning the motives of the people who made the films."

Defrocked at *McCall's*, Pauline Kael sought sanctuary at the opinion-making *New Republic*, which took her in as its film critic.* With smaller circulation, smaller pay and greater egghead impact, she regained whatever she had lost at the movies, and the perils of Pauline started up again. She was next seen (or rather, *overheard*) being manipulated at a brand-new stand.

* The job vacated by Stanley Kauffmann in January, 1966, when he became drama critic of the New York *Times*. By taking in Miss Kael in the summer of 1966 and then Kauffmann-in-exile a few weeks later (as literary columnist), the *New Republic*'s Washington headquarters practically qualified for embassy status.

The new action-Western, *The Professionals* . . . has
the expertise of a cold old whore with practiced hands and
no thoughts of love. There's something to be said for this
kind of professionalism; the moviemakers know their business and they work us over. . . . The buyer gets exactly
what he expects and pays for: Manipulation for excitement.
We use the movie and the movie uses us.

In the same column (December 16, 1966), our Joan of Arc and
her voices took off after a French film called *The Shameless
Old Lady*.

. . . I wouldn't have minded the picture too much if the
audience hadn't been so audibly pleased with its capacity
to respond. I can hear someone saying "What snobbery!
She didn't like the picture because the audience enjoyed it."
And that's not too far wrong. . . . I experienced a groan
of recognition when the man behind me said happily, "It's
so French!"

Soon thereafter, the *New Republic* began to hear voices, too—
its readers'. When in her review of *Blow-Up*, Pauline Kael
dubbed Michelangelo Antonioni the product of middlebrow
moralists, there was a torrent of letters diagnosing her as "bor-
dering on an obsession" . . . a "lint-pick[er]" . . . an "in-
verted snob" preoccupied "with what's In and what's Out, what's
culturally and artistically fashionable and unfashionable, and
what's Hip and what's Square" . . . a masterpiece-suffocator
. . . "waspish, irrelevant, acutely self-congratulatory and un-
speakably vulgar" . . . "strident, shrill," and "smug." A man
from the University of Wisconsin wrote in that he was "beginning to think that she . . . has begun to write satire without
realizing it." A woman from Los Angeles wrote in, "Far too
often, Miss Kael tends to damn a picture for some preconceived
notion she holds somewhere (generally unstated) of what it
should have done. . . . The only utility she seems to find for
the film is to employ it as a club against all the critics who
disagree with her. She scarcely stoops to criticize the film at all.
In an age of non-books and anti-novels she stands high on the
list of non-critics."

This kind of outrage does more for the critic being attacked than for the movie being defended against her spleen. Most of the letter writers had already seen and loved *Blow-Up*, but Miss Kael had manipulated them into focusing on herself instead of the movie.* The moral of our cliff-hanger, then, is this: *Even if you can't shame all of the people all of the time into suppressing their own innate reactions (e.g., The Sound of Music), you can certainly anger them into pillorying you in print (e.g., Blow-Up), and maybe, one day at the movies, the next voice you hear will be denouncing* YOU!

A number of the voices we hear ministering to American creativity are shrill, waspish, and homosexual. While we read a great deal about the "pansy prose" of Edward Albee, the "man-taming women" of William Inge, and the "camp sensitivities" of Andy Warhol, we seldom read about the tastes of those who judge our arts for us.

Music criticism is possibly the most homosexual of the black arts today,** and this may have a little to do with how sterile and corrupt it is. Like homosexual waiters and homosexual book clerks, the homosexual critic tends to be distracted, flirtatious for his own ends, and subject to all the fickle passions of his peer group. Not long ago, I had occasion to sit behind a rather prominent music critic at a concert. As a student of criticism, I like to eavesdrop on reviewers (without disturbing them, of course) and learn how they operate. Do they jot notes with ball-point penlights? Do they take cognizance of their wives' opinions? Do they bring massive concentration to the event under review? The answers, in this case, were no. The critic in question was holding hands with the man next to him.

"But," said one music expert who ticked off a long list of names, "why shouldn't a lot of music critics be homosexual in an age when so very, very many of our top-ranked composers are?"

This was another chicken-versus-egg, cause-versus-effect question which people in the music world don't really answer; they

---

* A year later, Pauline Kael changed jobs again and became movie critic of the *New Yorker*—which seldom, if ever, publishes irate letters from readers.
** In seeking to verify this assertion, I queried a number of music critics, three of whom *volunteered* that they were homosexuals. One of them, speaking from experience, added that he had the same impression I do.

just take sides. Perhaps a number of highly esteemed American composers wouldn't be making the beautifully screechy music they make if they didn't have their problems and their room-mates to inspire them. Or perhaps they wouldn't be so highly esteemed. And very likely, if the field weren't so homosexual, composing might be more hospitable and appealing to young geniuses who also aspire to be family men or lady-killers.

Oddly enough, despite his pansy surroundings, the most powerful music critic in the field is an intensely undeviating tower of rectitude. This fact alone may have slowed contempo-rary music from a headlong rush into the grotesqueries of fashion, where designers shroud the female of the species in their contempt for her. On the opening night of the new Metro-politan Opera House, Harold C. Schonberg of the New York *Times* trumpeted a warning that was heeded for at least a while.

> Leontyne Price's dresses must have cost a fortune. It's too bad they were not becoming to her. Throughout the pro-duction her weaknesses rather than strengths were empha-sized. Miss Price is a noble artist with a great voice, but the way she was directed could have come only from the queer ideas current these days in certain circles of the Met-ropolitan Opera.

Schonberg didn't mean the Family Circle.

A dapper, scowling man who looks like David Merrick *sans* mustachios, Harold Schonberg trains like an athlete for a new opera at the Met. The glowing review he "tossed off" an hour after the curtain fell on Richard Strauss' *Die Frau ohne Schatten* last year represented three months of study, research, and inter-viewing on that one opera. But Schonberg is no Renaissance man like Clive Barnes. His attitude toward concert reviewing verges on arrogance. "I grew up in music from childhood. You get these artists who give a concert and they say, 'My God, I spent fifteen years preparing for this concert and this critic ruins me in fifteen minutes.' I think the critic should be in a position to say, 'Look, sonny boy, I spent thirty years pre-paring.' "

Preparing what? A symphony? A talent? Or a posture?

William Meredith, a poet who loves opera, remarked recently that Harold Schonberg once "criticized a production of *Lucia di*

Lammermoor for not being a great work, for being in fact a lesser work than *Don Giovanni* and *Falstaff*. Now . . . *Lucia* is in fact an opera worth Mr. Schonberg's respectful attention, but to read that column . . . which I have kept, yellowed among my souvenirs, I would think that Mr. [Rudolf] Bing had asked for an appointment with a great syphilologist and then turned out to have only crabs."

No matter how one reacts to Schonberg as a critic, it must be conceded that he is an honest broker of the tremendous power he wields. The music department of the New York *Times* has been handed a great responsibility, for a particularly unfair American musical tradition dictates that a beginning soloist must amass a set of New York reviews before he can hope for bookings elsewhere. Unless you win the Tchaikovsky Prize in Moscow or Leonard Bernstein takes a liking to you, you must hire a New York hall for hundreds or sometimes thousands of dollars. Given ample notification and press tickets, the *Times* will cover your debut. This requires a half dozen satellite critics to blanket whatever musical activity Schonberg cannot cover. Schonberg's crew includes one former Juilliard professor, one living lexicon of music, and a couple of ex-concert performers. (Once, at a continuous twenty-four-hour avant-garde concert, the pianist was late, and the *Times* critic on duty filled in for him.) All are now full-time journalists, for Schonberg insists— and the *Times* backs him up—that none of them can have concert or composing careers. A conductor might be induced to play a composition merely because it is by a critic whose favor he seeks. Schonberg's associates must clear all outside writing with the management. Writing program notes, signed or unsigned, for the Philharmonic (à la Irving Kolodin of *Saturday Review*) is grounds for dismissal.

This rigidity may have cost the world another Virgil Thomson (who doubled as composer and critic), but it preserves one unassailable bastion of virtue in a profession that too often operates like a male whorehouse.

The training ground for a good 75 percent of the people writing about music in New York today (as well as many now writing out of town) was a venerable monthly called *Musical America,* which used to hire young apprentices for $65 a week and free tickets to as many concerts as they could write up. But

Musical America used to sell advertising, particularly in its year-end issue, when everybody who cared what *Musical America* said about him took an ad. The bigger a singer's ad, the bigger (and often better) his notices in *Musical America.* As befits a periodical with such a show biz policy, *Musical America* was recently sold to the *Billboard* interests, which incorporated it as a section of their *High Fidelity* magazine. Its influence has waned, but the values it inculcated still thrive in the music world.

Musical Europe is not the proving ground for critics that it is for singers. After two centuries of powerful influence, European music criticism went into a decline with the rise of the Third Reich. In 1933 better than 90 percent of the major critics were Jewish, and now hardly any of them are left. Today in Vienna, once the citadel of music criticism, there is at least one major critic whose notice can be predicted. He works on a retainer from a prominent conductor. In Greece and Spain and much of France, there is only one way for a concert artist to be reviewed: he must pay in advance. Honest reviewing is the rule only in parts of Germany, in England and Switzerland, and in all of Scandinavia. Behind the Iron Curtain, music criticism is usually worse than negligible.

All this may explain why concert managers in New York and out of town require a notice from the New York *Times* before they engage an artist. In provincial cities, where the music critic's post frequently involves writing program notes for events he reviews, his publisher or publisher's wife is almost certain to be on the board of directors of anything he considers condemning. A Cincinnati critic lost his post in just such a situation, and a Louisville reviewer resigned in protest after a similar muzzling.

The occasional critic who is willing to outshout his master's voice earns fame beyond his territory—if he survives. Michael Steinberg of the Boston *Globe,* whose opinions are strictly his own, is just beginning to amass prestige outside New England. Paul Hume of the Washington *Post* achieved international repute in 1950 when he wrote that Miss Margaret Truman "cannot sing with anything approaching professional finish . . . she communicates almost nothing of the music she presents." The singer's father, then residing at 1600 Pennsylvania Avenue, wrote to Hume:

> Someday I hope to meet you. When that happens you'll need a new nose, a lot of beefsteak for black eyes, and perhaps a supporter below. [Westbrook] Pegler, a guttersnipe, is a gentleman alongside you.

But the President's daughter herself rallied to her detractor's defense. "Hume's a very fine critic," said Margaret Truman. "He has a right to write what he pleases."

As occupational hazards go, irate Presidents of the United States are few and far between. Much more devastating to the daily life of the music critic and his reader is culture fatigue, which has been sketched by Dr. Alfred Frankenstein of the San Francisco *Chronicle*. Dr. Frankenstein used to be art and music critic, but he recently gave up the music half of his job.

"You just can't write about Beethoven's Fifth Symphony after the thirty-fifth year," Dr. Frankenstein declared. "I defy anybody to do it intelligently. This . . . creates one of the worst situations and problems in music criticism. We do tend to emphasize what is the variable.

"Beethoven's Fifth is an invariable of the literature. The variable is that today it is being conducted by Mr. Toscanini and tomorrow by Mr. Koussevitzky and the third day by Mr. Bernstein, and the result is that we tend to emphasize almost exclusively that one variable, the one thing that is different from today's performance as against yesterday's—the interpretation. We tend monstrously to overemphasize . . . minor points which are really in the long run of no importance or interest to anyone and of no value.

"This is one reason why musical criticism becomes so desperately tired and why musical criticism is so ultimately desperately tiresome to read."

[IV]

There are still various art forms which survive quite cozily by riding roughshod over their critics—sometimes for the better (jazz), sometimes not (architecture), and sometimes merely by clearing out of town before the reviews hit the streets (TV). But there are others that have been completely warped and tyrannized by their critics, and one of these art forms is capital-A Art.

Most art criticism in America no longer explains coherently or evaluates; it merely espouses or denounces. A critic or his periodical becomes identified as spokesman for a period or movement. A critic belongs to a school of criticism just as firmly as an artist belongs to a school of art. After a while, the two overlap and only the artist seems dispensable.

"Today's critic is beginning to seem almost as essential to the development—indeed the identification—of art as the artist himself," says Gregory Battcock, a college lecturer in art criticism, at the outset of his anthology, *The New Art.** A paragraph later, Battcock takes his thesis a giant step farther. "The critic has, as it were, to paint the painting anew and make it more acceptable, less the threat that it often is. It is scarcely an exaggeration to say that the art of our time simply could not exist without the efforts of the critic."

It is a good life, that of the young art critic on the make. In his book, *The Art Game,*** veteran critic Robert Wraight looks back on the "perks" (or perquisites) that go with the job.

> Artists, even distinguished ones who have no need of the scrap of publicity he can give them, will receive him courteously, talk with him about their work as if he knew what they are talking about and perhaps give him a drawing or let him buy a painting or sculpture at a bargain price. . . .
> If he is the drinking sort he will be able to drink his fill almost every evening (and some mornings) of every month at parties given to launch the new shows. At these parties he will meet scores of people who think he can be useful to them and some who can be useful to him. He will talk in a loud, clear, authoritative voice and get himself invited to arrange an exhibition for some prestige-giving organization, or to judge a competition for some fee-paying, prestige-seeking industrial concern.

---

* New York, E. P. Dutton & Company, Inc., 1966 (a paperback original).
** New York, Simon & Schuster, 1966.

If all goes well, you will be seeing him on various learned TV symposia, where, as Wraight concludes with barely restrained ferocity—"he and four or five other self-esteemed pundits will pee lukewarm praise or insipid censure from their lofty height onto the achievements of their betters."

There are perils as well as perks. When a fad fades, the critic who is identified as its spokesman fades away, too. He must gather up his monographs and catalogs and anthologies and scurry for shelter to a university or museum, watching (usually in vain) for the tide to return or else searching for a new wave to leap aboard.

Nevertheless such moments in the sun seem well worth the darkness of exile. Thus the art world is so crowded with critics, each advocating a school of art, that the turnover in art trends resembles the surf at Malibu. A period or movement used to last a decade or two. Now, in the era of post-op-pop-slop, it is literally here today and gone tomorrow before you have time to duck or even to blink a responsive eye.

Harold Rosenberg, who coined the term "action painting," is remembered as the critic of abstract expressionism. Alan Solomon, former director of New York's Jewish Museum, is perhaps the ranking critic of pop art. Lawrence Alloway of *Art International* is the apologist for systemic art. Another critic, Lucy R. Lippard, beats her breasts for gray vinyl salamis as "eccentric abstraction." Clement Greenberg is *the* critic of postpainterly abstraction. (Susan Sontag, who deplores labeling as "the human substitute for thinking," has labeled him "for some years the art critic with the greatest influence.") Younger critics, striving for identities and looking around for trends to call their own, become neo-Greenbergians and anti-Greenbergians, etc. A hard-edge critic goes to live with a hard-edge artist, and they make beautiful right angles together. Certain critics review not the art on exhibit but the museum curator because "he is the *creator* of the exhibition."

Museum curators also double as critics, as the case of Henry Geldzahler (Chapter 4) makes clear. Recently, Edward F. Fry, associate curator of the Guggenheim Museum, was asked what the next new wave in art would be. He replied, "Cybernetics," meaning robotlike sculptures that will respond to heat and cold, light and darkness, in programmed ways. When Fry was asked who would become *the* critic of this new wave, he chuckled and said: "I am."

One leading critic practices "studio criticism"—visiting the artists whom he'll later extol, doubling as adviser to them, and tripling as talent scout for a dealer, who pays him a retainer and gives him first crack at writing program notes. Another critic, virtually a voice in the wilderness, deplores this "emergence of the art critic who wants to be a force in sales, and of the art dealer who wants to create styles, and of the blending of both into one lumpy entrepreneur."

Art criticism, which has wrought so much of the current art mart's current corruption and ephemera, began turning inward soon after 1878, when British critic John Ruskin expressed himself too explicitly.

> I have seen and heard much of Cockney impudence before now, but never expected to hear a coxcomb ask two hundred guineas for flinging a pot of paint into the public's face.

The painting in question was "Nocturne in Black and Gold— the Falling Rocket," and the Cockney coxcomb was the American artist James Whistler, who promptly sued Ruskin. In court, as is often the case, the artist was treated like the defendant. Critics are so much more reputable!

How long, Whistler was asked on the witness stand, did it take him to "knock off" his "Nocturne"?

"I knocked—it—off," Whistler replied scornfully, "possibly in a couple of days."

"The labor of two days, then, is that for which you ask two hundred guineas?"

"No," Whistler retorted. "I ask it for the knowledge of a lifetime."

Under cross-examination, Whistler was asked condescendingly: "Do you think you could make *me* see beauty in that picture?"

"No!" Whistler replied. "Do you know, I fear it would be as impossible as for the musician to pour his notes into the ear of a deaf man."

On the stand, Whistler made history's classic case on behalf of art for art's sake and *against criticism*. "The understanding of art is reserved for the artist alone," Whistler insisted. He won the verdict, despite a hostile jury that expressed its esteem for the whole squabble by awarding Whistler one farthing (a fraction of a penny) in damages.

Ruskin, until then the nineteenth century's greatest critic, was discredited. Having lost his wife, Effie, to another of those artist chaps, John Everett Millais, and now a farthing to Whistler, Ruskin went insane.* This left art criticism in the hard, gemlike hands of the perfectly unreadable Walter Pater and his later imitators. Over the next seven decades, art criticism grew less perfect and more unreadable. Whistler versus Ruskin had taught art critics a valuable lesson in freedom of expression: What is indecipherable can scarcely be actionable.

Who, for example, could be offended (let alone aroused) by such impenetrable critical prose as:

> The primary formal nucleus is a fissured ovoid form which incarnates the minimal, specifically sculptural articulation, connotes the promise of birth, the suggestion of death-in-life, of destruction, extinction.

Such phrases as "pullulation of disparate forms" and "violence of the urban junkscape" became standard critical language, as did mental stumbling blocks like "a sort of neo-Dada—pyrotechnic of lyric, earnest but sly, unaggressive ideologically but covered with esthetic spikes."

In Wilson Follett's *Modern American Usage,* an authoritative section is devoted to critics' words. Here it is writ:

---

* Whistler, too, was ruined—financially—by the long and costly trial. Afterward, customers and critics stayed away from him because he was controversial. He had to sell his paintings for groceries, but, stylish to the last, he put his bailiffs to work as servants when he went bankrupt. Encouraged by his victory over Ruskin, he also dissipated much of his remaining time and talent with eloquently vicious attacks on unworthy critics. When one of them complained that Whistler's "Symphony in White" was misnamed because it had other colors in it, Whistler's rejoinder was that he never expected such "profound prattle" to find its "place in print. And does he then in his astounding consequence believe that a symphony in F contains no other note but shall be a continued repetition of F, F, F?" With one final screech in F, Whistler concluded: "Fool!"

Nothing is more difficult than writing about the arts, literature included. To do so daily, weekly, or even monthly has proved a strain that the minds best endowed for this sort of work can withstand for only a few years. One ought therefore to be charitable to those who tell us every morning . . . what the gallery exhibition showed forth. But critics tend to ease their labors by fashioning for themselves vocabularies which are neither technical nor plainly descriptive, and which therefore must be reproved as jargon. . . .

The words cited are *crisp, firm, sensitive, sophisticated, alert, masterful,* and *structured* (some of which you'll find in this book, proving how deeply the enemy has infiltrated). Phrases cited are *deep-lying irony, wide context, dialectical tension, repeated insight, utter dispassion,* and *efflorescent ambit* (none of which you will find herein). "And still others," says Follett, "which begin by having a meaning, do not keep it long when turned to daily use: *apocalyptic, charisma, commitment, compassion, discourse, disturbing, empathy, epiphany, evocative, existential, identify, ironic, insightful, meaningful, perceptive, persona, sensibility, simplistic, stimulating,* etc."

While art criticism was becoming an art unto itself, speaking only to itself, something alarming was happening in a remote province. During the decade following World War II (which took in the McCarthy era of repression), a variety of psychoanalysts, sociologists, educators, and leftists infiltrated criticism as a forum for political and social ideas that were denied expression in their regular vocations. Comic books were literally analyzed to death by deadpan psychiatrists who linked them so doggedly to sex crimes that many funnies were withdrawn from the market. The sleaziest Humphrey Bogart, James Cagney, or Boston Blackie movies were renamed mass culture and given serious attention between hard covers. Sometimes they were assailed as kitsch, which one critic defined as "a Synthetic, Commercialized Pseudo-culture, deliberately manufactured to divert and distract. . . . [It] bears toward the genuine thing a relationship somewhat like that of a clever wax to a real fruit. It feeds on boredom without creating either the disturbance or satisfaction of genuine art, and it arises in response to the need for filling up the quantities of leisure time which industrial society has made available—but has not trained people to employ creatively." Critics went on and on like this in badly written tomes that intrigued the lonely crowd not because these books contained any new ideas (just new labels) but because of the spirited or spicy kitsch they quoted and analyzed.

Inevitably there was a backlash. While the mass culture vultures were dissecting Bogart and Cagney, another line of criticism began praising them as "so bad they're good," then as "the true folk artists of modern civilization," and ultimately as "high camp." Camp was a "sensibility—unmistakably modern, a variant of sophistication but hardly identical with it" that was defined by its bard, Miss Susan Sontag, as "dandyism in the age of mass culture." It had definite homosexual overtones, which Miss Sontag acknowledged.

> While it's not true that Camp taste *is* homosexual taste, there is no doubt a peculiar affinity and overlap. Not all liberals are Jews, but Jews have shown a peculiar affinity for liberal and reformist causes. So, not all homosexuals have Camp taste. But homosexuals, by and large, constitute the vanguard—and the most articulate audience—of Camp.

Apart from "a lazy two-page sketch" of Christopher Isherwood's 1954 novel, *The World in the Evening,* the concept of camp had "hardly broken into print," according to Miss Sontag—but nevertheless it was there, she insisted.

For a while, being essentially sterile, camp lived off the creations of the past: art nouveau, Tiffany lamps, and Busby Berkeley movies (*Golddiggers of 1937,* etc.). But gradually the demand for camp became insatiable, and all sorts of merchandise was created to gratify it—ranging from the ornate butterflies in the Papier Mâché store on Greenwich Avenue to the Truman Capote/John Huston/Humphrey Bogart movie, *Beat the Devil* ("would-be-Camp"—Susan Sontag) to Samuel Barber's opera *Vanessa* ("a piece of manufactured, calculated Camp"—Susan Sontag) to Miss Sontag's own celebrated "Notes on Camp." Miss Sontag, being a shapely young instructor at Columbia and a literary entertainer in her own right, kept camp going far longer than most Ephemera-of-the-Month.

Thanks to the mass-culture analysts and camp enthusiasts

dabbling in criticism, the tawdriest and most mundane objects were elevated to the stature of art—not high art, but pop art. And in a 1966 New York *Times* article headlined "LOOK! ALL OVER! IT'S ESTHETIC . . . IT'S BUSINESS . . . IT'S SUPERSUCCESS!" art historian Hilton Kramer wrote:

"While art critics provided Pop with the cachet of high-flown interpretation—still indispensable for the commercial success of an art movement—the work itself was as easy to take as the hamburgers and hot dogs that often figured as its motifs."

Pop was such a cinch for the mass magazines and color TV cameras that they descended on it in droves or, as one innocent bystander puts it, "like a team of anthropologists in a Stone Age village; under their observation, the art world has changed. Like the world of Society, it has become self-conscious, slightly paranoid. It roils in constant self-analysis and heaves under the very rumor of the 'cultural explosion.' "

All the elements of culture vulturism are to be found in art criticism today. Corruption of the instinct? Here is Henry Geldzahler, showing off a canvas by Robert Irwin that is fleshy pink and naked except for one straight line across the center. "When I first saw it in Irwin's studio, I looked at it for a long time and then was sick—physically sick. Then I went back to it, and I bought it. That's what usually happens to me. When I react very strongly against something, I usually end up by loving it." The debasement of taste? Here is a senior colleague of Geldzahler's at the Metropolitan talking. "Do you notice that people today say that paintings are *interesting* or *stimulating* and never that they are *good?*" The worship of ephemera? Here is art critic Alan Solomon bemoaning what happened to the pop he championed.

> . . . if you missed getting on the Pop bandwagon (money, power or sex wise), if you weren't clued in for Pop by the "Assemblage" show at the [Museum of] Modern [Art], this time you had the tip off with the announcement of "The Responsive Eye," [the Modern's Op exhibit]. The galleries timed Op shows to anticipate the Modern exhibition, timed shows to coincide with it, timed shows to catch the groundswell building behind it. In the end it all became a bore.

Art had become an instrument of fashion. We had been had. Obsolescence was built into the deal by the cynical clique, because the vogue for Pop was based on the kicks it provided and we know well that you have to feed a habit. So we've moved on from pep pills to LSD.*

Like op illusions, it happens much too fast even for its perpetrators. A generation lived through abstract expressionism and debated its merits; a teenybopper today has suffered through the birth and death of a half dozen art movements and couldn't care less.

The victim once again is art. Mexican muralist José Clemente Orozco once lamented: "The public refuses TO SEE painting. They want TO HEAR painting."

And Andy Warhol, who ought to know, purrs to the media that today's turnover in art is only the beginning. "There's going to be a day when no one will be famous for more than a week. Then everyone will have a chance to be famous."

The last great art critic was not an art critic at all but a German composer who once went to dinner with theater director (and drama critic) Harold Clurman at Charles Laughton's home in Los Angeles a while back. Clurman recalls:

"Laughton was very proud of a Renoir and everybody admired the Renoir. I love Renoir and I admired it [but] this irate, rude, excellent composer said: 'I hate it!'

"Everybody was astonished, and I said: 'Hans, why do you hate it?'

"And he said a very remarkable thing. He said: 'It's a butcher shop.'

"Now this picture was a picture of trees and flowers [but] he said it was a butcher shop. And I said: 'Hans, you are a remarkably fine critic. I don't hate it; I love the picture. But when you say it's a butcher shop, I know what you mean. You mean it's the quality of the painting, of the bark of the trees, of the leaves; it has something fleshly about it. And that means you don't like flesh. I like flesh, and therefore you have described yourself, and I can differentiate myself in relationship because

---

* Solomon, Alan, "The New York Revolution," *Playbill*, July, 1965.

I suddenly see it as a new thing by your description, which is very, very vivid—though it's harsh—and I know that you have really seen the picture. You have really seen it more than the person who tells me it is a masterpiece and something about the mixture of colors and the sense of the mixture of colors and the palette and this and that. You have seen it. You have given me an image which is vivid, which is strong, which also includes your own reaction, and your own personality.' "

The Sixth Commandment of the Culture Vultures:
Follow the leader fleetly, and one day
ye may pretend to be he.

6

The Dumb Intellectual, Esq.:
The Magazines

[1]

ON February 15, 1966, there was a happening inside the gray
flannel bowels of *Esquire* that went unreported in the
otherwise comprehensive pages of "The Magazine for Men." Its
wicked mastermind was a young lady who writes satire and sells
it, a remarkable feat in today's dwindling humor market. Purely
coincidentally, she had dated an *Esquire* editor, one of the
higher muckamucks on the masthead, from May to December
of 1965. What she called a "prolonged summer romance" (for
her boyfriend had a wife in the country) broke up shortly after
she learned that in order to preserve his editorial purity, he had
been vetoing her *exhibits* (*Esquire* inneroffice jargon for *manuscripts*) after first delegating them to lesser *communicators* (inneroffice for *editors*), some of whom had liked them.

Later she reflected ruefully that occasionally she and he had
encountered famous writers, each of whom had been put down
with a deprecatory ha-ha: "We have one of his exhibits in our
file. But I don't think we'll ever use it." (Writers in momentary
favor who *are* used, incidentally, are known as "The Group.")

Our heroine never appeared in the pages of *Esquire* (and

probaby never will now). But hell hath no more articulate fury than a woman writer scorned.

On February 9, 1966, while browsing in the household appliances section of Bloomingdale's, she encountered a couple of other creative types, one of whom remarked, "Everything's moving too fast! By the time we sit down and write, weave, compose, weld, draw, design, even *cook* anything, IT'S TOO LATE! DATED!"

Another remarked that the only new art form which seemed to be enduring rather than obsolescing was the happening. This ignited a spark of conspiracy, and six days later, under our heroine's direction, an army of some 200 artists, writers, and miscellaneous hippies surprised the boys who put out *Esquire* with a happening inside their very own editorial sanctum.

On Tuesday morning, to the rhythms of an eight-piece pachanga band, the Bloomingdale Group, as they called themselves, set up shop on 488 Madison Avenue's fourth floor, *Esquire* headquarters. Dancers performed a modern desk-top ballet called "Coffee Breakout." A tall Negro narrated a travelogue illustrated with slides. A female impersonator recited Kipling's "Danny Deever." Two yodelers and a Wall Street lawyer clad in a gorilla suit invaded the steno pool, and somebody tried to roast a pig over a portable hibachi. Improvisatory though the symbolism was, it was not inappropriate; *Esquire*'s America, the grotesque world of What's Happening as depicted in its pages, had come home to roost!

Harold T. P. Hayes, the boyish-looking editor in chief, who vaguely resembles *Playboy*'s Hugh Hefner, poked his head out of an office and asked: "What's happening?"

"It's a happening," he was told. Hayes withdrew.

One of the lesser communicators, however, panicked. Reaching for the nearest panic button, he succeeded in wrenching the office thermostat to zero.

In the chill that ensued, a masked happener asked a secretary where the safe was.

"I'm not sure," she replied sheepishly. "I'm new here."

The gorilla led the pachanga band in a march down the editorial corridor, where the doors all seemed locked. There was no response, no welcome, no question, not even a rejection slip. The Bloomingdale Group repaired to the reception area with the mournful chant, "Magazine for Men, come out, come out, wherever you are!"

A girl in gold leather spread a jigsaw puzzle on the floor, and a couple of ballerinas used it as a stage for pirouettes.

Shortly after 11 A.M., an *Esquire* official called the police because while fun was fun, "I don't know what these people are going to do!" Nine squad cars responded.

The police were greeted happily by the happeners, for they are part of most good happenings. The police, nonetheless, had their problems. How in hell can an honest cop tell a happener from a happenee? Uniformed cops and detectives wandered about, buttonholing various *Esquire* officials; an innocent male model who had an appointment; a chap from *Esquire's* "brother" periodical, *Gentleman's Quarterly,* simply because he was wearing chamois knickers; and each other.

Nobody was arrested, but the last to be evicted was the girl in gold, who took forty minutes to put together her jigsaw puzzle.

The press learned of it only when an *Esquire* official called one city desk to find out "just what happened here." Two days later, a man who had missed the event phoned *Esquire* to inquire if another happening was scheduled for the following Tuesday. He was told: "There must be some mistake. Nothing happened here last Tuesday."

Quixotically, our heroine agrees. "Of course nothing happened up there! How could it? There was nothing up there for it to happen to!"

That 1966 happening at *Esquire* is not being recounted here at this late date to right a journalistic wrong, to even someone else's romantic score, or because now it can be told. It is here because it expressed, however grotesquely, a valid intellectual protest against one of the most dangerous breeds of culture vulture—the trend spotter masquerading as pace setter. *Esquire* is neither the best nor the worst of our magazines. It is, however, the most extreme because it speaks with such ringingly convincing authority that it ends up actually doing what it began by merely purporting to do—molding (and hardening) men's minds.

In recent years, *Esquire* has grasped at the keen, growing intellect that feels just a little out of touch—for geographic, demographic, or psychic reasons. Grabbing this alert reader by the eyeballs with flashy covers, the editors of *Esquire* have proceeded to tamper with some of the finest minds of a whole generation, anesthetizing them with nerve-numbing charts of what's in and what's out, brainwashing them with the editors' own peculiar sense of *au courant*, and even lobotomizing many of their firsthand truths. The result is a composite reader—the Dumb Intellectual, Esq.—whose values and experiences revolve around one monthly bible that costs a dollar a copy. Thanks to prepublication in *Esquire*, he honestly believes that the new play about a one-breasted whore by Tennessee Williams (whom he thinks of familiarly as "TW") will be both the salvation of the American theater and the hottest ticket on Broadway.

Simply by reading *Esquire* religiously, the Dumb Intellectual is inclined, urged and led to believe:

. . . that such erstwhile contributors as Hemingway, Fitzgerald, Saroyan, Salinger, Wouk, Michener, Schlesinger, and Brock Brower were started on the road to fame and fortune in the pages of *Esquire* and did their best work therein before "being tapped by the Book-of-the-Month" or "graduating" to *Life* and the *Saturday Evening Post*. By then there are no regrets at *Esquire*, where "we shrug it off and look around . . . to try to uncover" another Tom (not Thomas) Wolfe, author of *The Kandy-Kolored Tangerine-Flake Streamline Baby*, or a Gay Talese, author of an *Esquire* article entitled " 'Joe,' said Marilyn Monroe, just back from Korea, 'you never heard such cheering.' 'Yes I have,' Joe DiMaggio answered." It is in the Tom (not Thomas) Wolfes and the Gay (a man's name in this case) Taleses that the Dumb Intellectual is led to believe that the future of American letters lies.

. . . that Mayor John Lindsay of New York is a "dull, earnest plodder" in whom "Jacqueline Kennedy would hardly have been interested." Questioned about his magazine's free-swinging, but often peripheral, hatchet jobs on Lindsay and Bobby Kennedy, Richard Nixon and John F. Kennedy, the editor of *Esquire* replied: "We are more interested in the reader who must make the judgments than in the man or idea about whom his judgments must be made." Questioned later in the light of this response, one Dumb Intellectual I know admitted that the judgment he makes is to boycott most elections. "From everything I read, it's usually one clown running against another clown."

. . . that, in the words of the president of Philip Morris International: "Good art can be good business. Art had to help us sell our products or ourselves. And our involvement in the arts had to be achieved within the same kind of budgetary guidelines as we apply to sales, or marketing, or manufacturing." These words were spoken during an *Esquire* symposium at Lincoln Center and rephrased thusly by the publisher of *Esquire*:

"In other words, the point was made, and nailed down in a dozen different ways, that culture is a significant and integral part of the business of business."

. . . that the "big names" of the Wall Street Establishment are Roy Cohn, Serge Rubinstein (listed as "deceased"), Ben Jack Cage (listed as "out of country"), Cyrus Eaton, Howard Hughes, J. Paul Getty, Jerry Finkelstein, the Sheik of Kuwait, Stavros Niarchos, and the Trujillo family.

. . . that Kate Smith, Joe Louis, Marianne Moore, Jimmy Durante, Norman Thomas, Helen Hayes, John Cameron Swayze, and Eddie Bracken are "The Unknockables," and what's more, "Knock them, and you're out of it."

. . . that London "has now become the best place imaginable to give the perfect cocktail party" and that the "best food in the world" is in London (documented by a list of five of the most skillful chefs in England).

. . . that "Shakespeare is still IN, but everybody else—with the possible exceptions of Bertholt [*sic*] Brecht, Pope John XXIII, and Adlai Stevenson—are [*sic*] OUT. Tennessee Williams is OUT but not as far OUT as Arthur Miller. Being sentimental about Marilyn Monroe is IN. Being sentimental about George and Martha Washington is OUT. Being sentimental about Lyndon and Lady Bird is not IN. Being sentimental about the future is IN."

(Oops! Sorry about that! The paragraph above is from an *advertisement* in *Esquire*—a four-page ad called "What's IN on Campus?" paid for by Kodel fabric fiber in the 1965 back-to-college issue. The text was disguised to look like *Esquire* editorial copy, which is one of the problems with *Esquire*; its advertising and editorial matter occasionally overlap.)

. . . that President Lyndon Johnson was "Corny Bird of the Year" and that the "Shortest Book of the Year" was Bill Adler's *The Johnson Humor.*

Once, introducing a list of "The 100 Best People in the World," *Esquire* carried a dialogue of instant disclaimer:

Q: "Is Not the Making of Such a List Extremely Presumptuous?

A: "Yes.

Q: "Who the Hell Are You to Decide Who the Best People Are?

A: "The Editors."

If the powers behind *Esquire* are particularly adept at transplanting their unnatural values onto living brain tissue en masse, it may well be because their origins and training and all their skills come from the world of fashion. The secret of *Esquire*'s success is that after more than three decades, it has remained—first, last, and always—a fashion magazine.

Esquire was, in fact, conceived in spite during a bitchy fashion war. Its founders were two brothers from Omaha, David and Alfred Smart, and a demon salesman named William Hobart Weintraub—who together were publishing a moderately successful trade paper called *National Men's Wear Salesman* and a more ornate stylebook called *Gentleman's Quarterly*, both based in Chicago.

As a promotional gimmick, the publishers decided to cover the Broadway opening of *Smiles* on November 18, 1930, and transmit—via the exciting new medium of wirephoto—pictures of what Otto Kahn and Florenz Ziegfeld and other Mr. First Nighters were wearing. The very next morning, haberdashers in the hinterlands could *show* their customers the truly latest New York fashions, thereby keeping Eau Claire *au courant!*

Fairchild Publications, the dominant giant of fashion-trade publishing (*Women's Wear Daily, Footwear News*, etc.), had the audacity to suggest that these instant images weren't hot off the wire at all. They were, Fairchild hinted, nothing but studio photos modeled and filmed and then mailed well in advance.

The Smarts smarted, but Weintraub suggested retaliation. Why not invade the fashion field with a gaudy periodical called *Apparel Arts* to race against the Fairchild stable?

Enter, at this crucial stage, the first editor of *Apparel Arts* and then *Esquire*—and today, almost forty years later, the publisher of *Esquire*. Arnold Gingrich was a young advertising writer whose sharp copy for Kuppenheimer Clothes had caught the Smarts' corporate eye. A man who knew him then describes Gingrich as "ambitious, but rather nicely pretentious. He didn't make older men feel old, the way so many other comers in their twenties did." Gingrich himself has confessed to a lifelong addiction to "hesternalgia," which he defines as "the hankering for bygone days."

Arnold Gingrich, like Ernest Hemingway, spent the best part of his youth in Michigan. And it must have been then and there that the gods of Grand Rapids decreed Gingrich's necrophilic love/hate affair with Papa. Gingrich, in fact, eventually married a onetime girl friend of Hemingway's. On the night Arnold met Janie—in Bimini in 1936—she was Mrs. G. Grant Mason, Jr.; they were both guests of Hemingway, and when Gingrich ungraciously declared that "Scott Fitzgerald draws the finest and purest tone from the English language of any writer now alive—in fact, *I* think, of any writer since Walter Pater," Janie hushed him with, "We don't say things like that around here." She warned him that what was good enough for Pater wasn't good with Papa, or as Gingrich put it, "I'd better not mention Fitzgerald or I might be out on my ear the next day." Instead, Gingrich kept quiet and heeded his new friend, Janie. "I hung around," he recalled later in an *Esquire* reminiscence called "Scott, Ernest, and Whoever," and we got to know each other a little bit better and in fact, almost 20 years later, and after four marriages to other people, we got married ourselves."

Gingrich's preference for Fitzgerald over Hemingway was strengthened in 1958, when Hemingway took legal action to prevent three of his vintage 1930's short stories from being reprinted, to his embarrassment, in an anthology called *The Armchair Esquire*. Two were withdrawn. Fitzgerald, on the other hand, spent his declining years grinding out the careless Pat Hobby stories for Gingrich on a monthly basis until his death, after which they still kept appearing. Gingrich's animosity toward Hemingway did not soften after the latter's death, as an unseemly handful of hesternalgia in a 1966 *Esquire* would indicate.

In his *A Moveable Feast,* published in 1964, Hemingway passed a one-sentence slur on Fitzgerald's genital equipment. Two and a half years later, this outraged Arnold Gingrich into defending Fitzgerald's manhood at four-paragraph length.

It seems that in 1935, eyewitness Gingrich went to Fitzgerald's Park Avenue apartment and found the great man working in his bathrobe. Fitzgerald greeted Gingrich with a courtly bow. "The one hitch," Gingrich divulged in 1966, "was that the cord of the bathrobe was caught in the grand downward swoop of the right arm, revealing all that F. Scott Fitzgerald had to reveal." It took Gingrich yet another paragraph to tell us that this was, in a word, "adequate."

All this enduring ephemera was yet to come, however, when Gingrich first joined the Smarts and Weintraub in launching *Apparel Arts.* Bound in hard covers, *Apparel Arts* sold for $1.50, but only to stores, which used it as a catalog. It featured merchandise that stores were unwilling to stock in the Depression but could easily order. On its pages were pasted actual samples of the latest woolens and tweeds.

"The idea," said David Smart, "was to give the customer something to consult so that he would not have to depend on the taste of the clerk or tailor."

The idea proved so successful that *Apparel Arts'* printings of 10,000 were quickly snapped up, and the stores' only complaint was that customers were stealing their copies.

Gingrich and the Smarts were visiting Manhattan in November, 1932, when, as Gingrich recalls, into their New York office came "an artist named C. F. Peters to deliver a fashion plate for *Apparel Arts.* He was the older and more established of two artists working at that time in New York with the same last name and the same first initials, so the other one, after some confusion, had changed his name to Peter Arno. Anyway, *this* C. F. Peters said he had just come from Rogers Peet, where he had delivered another drawing, and that they had said, now that this Depression might soon be lifting, that they wished they had something . . . that they could give away, or perhaps even sell, to their customers at Christmastime. They wondered if maybe we couldn't adapt something out of the fashion pages of *Apparel Arts.*"

Gingrich and associates couldn't in time for Christmas. But they tried dummying up a magazine that might sell for the princely sum of a dime—twice the price of established magazines like *Collier's, Liberty* and the *Saturday Evening Post.* When they were finished, according to Gingrich, what they had "didn't look worth a dime, and yet . . . it would have cost us more than a dime to produce. So within a matter of days we had worked up another, shooting this time for a fifteen-cent price. We liked it somehow even less. We felt it needed more sugar coating of entertainment around the central pill of men's fashions. But that meant it would cost more. Still, the next try, though aimed at a selling price of a quarter, was equally disappointing. It still seemed almost pansyish in its foppish concern with clothes. . . ."

As one of the partners remarked at the twenty-five-cent mark: "Who the hell would be caught dead carrying around a copy of a male *Vogue?*"

(The comparison was apt. Within a few years, to tell a man he looked "like a page out of *Esquire*" was to tell him he was truly in vogue.)

At the half-dollar mark, the partners agreed that they had at last planted enough hair on their baby's chest "to deodorize the deadly whiff that we thought emanated from [its] inner core of men's fashion content. . . ." What they had also done, as Huntington Hartford was to do better but later with his ill-starred *Show,* was to emulate the leading quality magazine of the day, *Vanity Fair.* In more recent years, *Esquire* has been credited with many of *Vanity Fair's* innovations, including full-color cartoons and illustrations and the daring notion of putting two entirely different features side by side.

"In most of the magazines of the times," one early *Esquire* staffer explains, "if a schoolteacher seduced a schoolgirl in a story, the facing page would show an illustration of the event. *Vanity Fair* broke that tradition, and when Gingrich went through its back numbers and picked up that trick, he made his new magazine look much faster-paced than most others."

Now Gingrich and the Smarts and Weintraub began to cast about for a name. *Trend, Stag, Beau,* and *Trim* were the initial choices, but each title search by a patent attorney in Washington resulted in the same report: The title had already been registered by someone else.

Ruefully reading over the lawyer's latest letter, David Smart noticed that it was addressed, with Dickensian formality, to "A. S. Gingrich, Esq."

Smart sat up straight and said: *"Esquire!* That's our title."

It was, the others agreed, a good working title, and the patent attorney said yes, too. Still, there was some doubt. Shortly before the first issue (dated October 15, 1933) was published in Chicago, a call came to Gingrich from New York. Two of the partners had decided on *Town & Campus* as the magazine's permanent title. Gingrich, who preferred *Esquire,* lied that the presses were too far along for the change to be made.

As a matter of fact, the new venture *was* hopelessly committed to the corporate image embodied by the *Esquire* title. Its initial pitch to advertisers had been:

> It is, as its title implies, a magazine for men. To analyze its name more closely, *Esquire* means, in the encyclopedia and dictionary sense, that class just below knighthood— the cream of that great middle class between the nobility and the peasantry. In a market sense, however, *Esquire* simply means Mister—the man of the middle class. Once it was the fashion to call him Babbitt, and to think of him as a wheel-horse with no interests outside of business. That's very outmoded thinking, however. For today he represents the New Leisure Class. . . .

This "new leisure" was a cornerstone of the early *Esquire.* Its first issue would contain an essay on "The New Leisure" by Nicholas Murray Butler, president of Columbia University, "as told to S. J. Woolf." And the prospectus for the as-yet unpublished magazine had declared:

> The New Deal has given leisure a new economic significance, and the five day week has become not merely every man's right but virtually every man's duty. . . . What more opportune occasion for the appearance of a new magazine . . . that will answer the question of What to do? What to eat, what to drink, what to wear, how to play, what to read

—in short a magazine dedicated to the improvement of the new leisure?

Even though the prospectus embodying this philosophy had arrived on advertisers' desks on March 6, 1933, the day President Franklin Roosevelt closed the banks, enough advertisers were intrigued to justify a 116-page first issue, and a thousand stores had preordered at twenty-five cents a copy to justify a printing of 105,000 copies. Each copy cost twenty-seven cents to produce, but the revenue from advertising put *Esquire* in the black from the very beginning.

The trend in clothing manufacturers' advertising was just shifting away from trade periodicals toward national consumer media, which was good for *Esquire*'s team. The only stumbling block was some advertisers' resistance to a fifty-cent price tag on a magazine they had never seen. Anticipating this, Weintraub would walk into an advertiser's office, and when the inevitable objection came, he would produce a nickel. Marching to the window, he would remark, *"Collier's* is a nickel," and toss the nickel out the window. Then he would produce a dime and, remarking, "The *Saturday Evening Post* is a dime," toss the dime out the window, too. After doing the same with a quarter for *Cosmopolitan,* he would take out a half dollar, toss it *on the advertiser's desk,* and declare: "I wouldn't throw half a dollar out the window. Half a dollar means something. And that's the kind of magazine *Esquire* is going to be."

Contract in hand, Weintraub would rejoin David Smart on the street, where his partner had been standing to catch the coins.

The first issue of *Esquire,* "The Quarterly for Men," contained fiction by John Dos Passos (an excerpt from his trilogy in progress, *U.S.A.,* illustrated with a watercolor by the author), Erskine Caldwell, Dashiel Hammett, Morley Callaghan, Manuel Komroff, Vincent Starrett, and Douglas Fairbanks, Jr. ("He tilted her chin upward, and after his eyes had gorged themselves on her face, he kissed her").

Esquire's nonfiction led off with "A Cuban Letter" from Ernest Hemingway, who had breakfasted on a glass of Vichy water, a glass of cold milk and a slice of Cuban bread, read the papers, walked down to the boat, gone fishing, and hooked a 468-pound marlin.

Arnold Gingrich had little trouble latching onto giants like Dos Passos and Hemingway for $300 an article or less. They had already made their reputations with ballsy, gutsy novels, but the prestige-periodical markets for fiction were women's magazines (which favored Fannie Hurst and Faith Baldwin) and the *Saturday Evening Post* (which favored Clarence Buddington Kelland and William Hazlett Upson). Theoretically, the true giants could earn $5,000 or $6,000 per story by knocking out whipped-cream fiction for the established magazines. Functionally, however, they were incapable of hacking. Even at their zeniths, the stories they wrote came back rejected, and so they welcomed the opportunity to empty their drawers onto the slick and lavish pages of *Esquire*.

Later, when *Esquire* was an established, thriving success, its fiction rates remained the same and these authors' gratitude cooled—sometimes turning to rage on realizing that *Esquire* had bought *all* rights, including the right to cash in on their names by reprinting their stories in anthologies. Arnold Gingrich has glossed over this by remarking in print, "There are authors who outgrow us, who reach a point where their least efforts are available only to the biggest magazines. Hemingway did. After *The Snows of Kilimanjaro* [August, 1936] he was really out of our league, though we printed him three more times, for a total of 34 appearances in our pages."

In its first issue, the corporate voice of *Esquire* was slightly more virile than the effete, bitchy tenor of today's "Magazine for Men." It growled rather than quibbled at the recurrent catechism that 85 percent of all consumer goods were bought by women.

> It is our belief, in offering ESQUIRE to the American male, that we are only getting around at last to a job that should have been done a long time ago—that of giving the masculine reader a break. The general magazines, in the mad scramble to increase the woman readership that seems to be so highly prized by national advertisers, have bent over backwards in catering to the special interests and tastes of the feminine audience. This has reached a point, in some of the more extreme instances, where a male reader,

in looking through what purports to be a general interest magazine, is made to feel like an intruder upon gynaecic mysteries. Occasionally features are included for his special attention, but somewhat after the manner in which scraps are tossed to the patient dog beneath the table. . . .

ESQUIRE aims to be, among other things, a fashion guide for men. But it never intends to become, by any possible stretch of the imagination, a primer for fops. . . .

And to make this plain, the highlight of the first issue and every issue thereafter for a decade was the Petty Girl, who may yet be remembered as *Esquire*'s major bona-fide contribution to American art. Air-brushed by George Petty into a balloonlike figure with no bones, she was a masturbatory goddess you could virtually touch and feel.*

The first issue of *Esquire* also contained a pledge to writers and artists that "at least as long as ESQUIRE remains a quarterly, every contribution will get the attention of the editor and one of the publishers." This was an easy promise to keep, for *Esquire*'s quarterly status lasted just that one issue. It was such an instant success that its newsstand distributor, who had placed an order for only 5,000 copies, sold out in five hours and clamored for more. There were no more. But Gingrich, Weintraub, and the Smarts took to the telephones and began recalling copies from the stores. They had hoped to sell 100,000 in the stores and 5,000 on the stands; instead, they did exactly the reverse with their first printing.

Esquire's second issue, dated January, 1934, proclaimed itself "The MONTHLY Magazine for Men." And for more than two decades thereafter—through a lingering Depression, a world war, a cold war, and into a Korean "conflict"—*Esquire* was content to shape itself to the needs and trends of the times. Its founders' instincts for fashion were sharp enough for *Esquire* to thrive most of the time or, at its lowest ebb, to survive. Of 1936's twelve issues of *Esquire*, Arnold Gingrich has remarked: "From front cover to back . . . the most newsworthy item was the announcement that you could now get beer in cans."

There were fewer and fewer proclamations about the new

---

* In January, 1965, one of *Esquire*'s Fourth Annual Dubious Achievement Awards went to the manufacturer of $49.75 inflatable Instant Party Dolls (5'5", made of soft, skinlike, extremely durable vinyl; 40"-20"-40") for people who need people—particularly for our boys in the boondocks of Vietnam.

leisure, for David Smart, *Esquire*'s publisher, was disclaiming any editorial policy at all. Conversing with another publisher, Smart had noted: "Your magazines have strong policies. How are they doing?"

"They're in the red," the man replied.

"Then we'll get along without any for the present," said David Smart. In peacetime there were autos and pinups (Petty Girls); in wartime, Westerns and pinups (Varga Girls). This "Smart thinking" was no more complex than today's *Playboy* philosophy. Stated succinctly rather than harrumphingly, it might have proved even more successful if *Esquire*'s brain trust had merely stuck to their guns. But in the 1940's, *Esquire* was jarred from its natural pattern of growth and development.

The first jolt was a censorship battle. *Esquire*, says a man who was on the staff then, "used to have a simple way of disarming obscenity charges. The more risqué the cartoon, the artier it got. If it was about a man hiding in a ladies' john, the artist would do it up as an oil painting instead of a black and white drawing."

This smut-evasion tactic worked until 1944, when the Postmaster General of the United States suddenly revoked *Esquire*'s permit to use second-class mailing rates (*the* crucial subsidy in magazine publishing) on the grounds that the magazine was "neither published for the dissemination of information of a public character nor devoted to literature, the sciences, arts, or industry."

It was an insensitive commentary on Hemingway's and Fitzgerald's old stamping ground, and the U.S. Court of Appeals unanimously overruled the Postmaster General a year later.

Even unsuccessful censorship persecutions, however, have a fearfully repressive power. They make fanatics, crusaders, or, more often than not, scared eunuchs out of their victims. A man rarely emerges from this kind of ordeal intact or as capable of doing his publishing job as he was before. In this case, says the ex-staffer, several of the key "liberated Puritans" at *Esquire* "thought in their heart of hearts that they'd always been obscene and were startled to find out in court that they weren't." Singed by the Postmaster General's effort to suppress them, they voluntarily dropped their gatefold. The Petty Girls and Varga Girls gave way to tamer and flatter pinups called Esquire Girls.

A virility void was being created on the newsstands, one just yawning for a clever young opportunist like Hugh Hefner to fill.

Furthermore, the founders were aging, and the magazine—as is often the case—was reflecting the interests of its owners and *their* contemporaries. There were recurrent articles about on-rushing senility, prostate complaints, and kidney troubles. Underlings chafed, but what else was there to assign when the boss came back from lunch with the word that everyone he knew had a sore back?

Esquire fell into the graceless postures of fun-loving middle age, with an emphasis on good clubs and hesternalgia that still persists in current series (e.g., "Great Clubs of America") and the recurrent reminiscences of Arnold Gingrich. But even in this small-bore league, *Esquire* was feeling a competitive pinch (though not yet the rapier thrust of Hugh Hefner). Where *Esquire* for years had reflected its founders' sporting interests, which consisted of ringside seats at prizefights and not much else, a new men's magazine called *True* hooked the reader who wanted to read more about baseball, football, and auto racing. As travel became a middle-aged pursuit, a magazine with *Esquire*'s postwar orientation toward middle-aged money should have been alert enough to leap into that breach. Instead, this gap was filled by a new magazine called *Holiday*, and it wasn't until a couple of months thereafter that *Esquire* hired Richard Joseph to roam the world as its travel editor. By then, it couldn't compete with *Holiday* or *National Geographic*.

With this hardening of the arteries went circulation trouble. Sales had approached three quarters of a million in the late 1930's; by 1950, they were plunging toward the half-million mark.

It was in 1952 that in desperation, *Esquire* embraced culture. "There was a brand-new audience of newly sophisticated and newly prosperous Americans," said Arnold Gingrich, "and we decided to go after them."

With what? First off, with the spoken word—complete texts of Brendan Behan and William Inge plays, plus Tennessee Williams' *Sweet Bird of Youth,* followed by a bottom barrel of inferior TW. There were also the filmed word (the screenplay of Paddy Chayefsky's *The Goddess*) and even the varely singable word (Gian Carlo Menotti's libretto for his friend Samuel Barber's opera, *Vanessa*). Many readers squawked (and still squawk) every time *Esquire* prints a play, but to hear Arnold Gingrich defend his policy, you'd think the protests were against Shakespeare. "Fortunately for the state of English literature," he said recently, "such people have always been in the minority, or some of its present chief adornments . . . would otherwise hardly have been heard of after four centuries."

The first issue of 1965 showed exactly where *Esquire* stands in the contemporary drama scene. The same editors who had once printed Chayefsky's *The Goddess,* the only significance of which was its cachet of gossip about Marilyn Monroe, voted a Dubious Achievement award to her ex-husband Arthur Miller as "Blabbermouth of the Year" for having unburdened his soul on the stage by writing *After the Fall*. And in that same issue, *Esquire* readers were treated, with utmost respect and fanfare, to a new one-act play by Saul Bellow, the best-selling novelist of the moment (*Herzog*), prior to the play's unveiling in Spoleto, London, Mineola, and New York.

In *The Wen,* Bellow, who is far more accomplished at prose writing than playwriting, told of an atomic scientist seeking out a childhood playmate, now a Hadassah matron in Miami, in order to revisit her birthmark, just inside the gateway to her *most precious possession*. By climax time, he has given away a military secret in exchange for going behind the sofa with her and a flashlight. . . . In *Esquire,* Bellow's *Wen* was subtitled: "If a great man explores the traumatic source of his genius, must lovely lady stoop to folly?"

Nine months later, Bellow was back in *Esquire* with a second play, *Orange Soufflé* (later presented disastrously on Broadway with *The Wen* and a third one-acter, all starring Shelley Winters). *Orange Soufflé* was about a middle-aged prostitute failing to arouse an eighty-eight-year-old millionaire with an orange soufflé. At the end, she said, "I can't understand what went wrong," and he replied, "You couldn't get it up."

In November, 1966, *Esquire* published a modest Broadway success imported from London, *The Killing of Sister George,* by Frank Marcus. Perhaps because Marcus didn't have the literary status of a Saul Bellow and *Sister George* had not yet been reviewed on Broadway at *Esquire*'s press time, Arnold Gingrich felt obliged to write this unasked-for disclaimer, which was the nearest thing to an editorial policy to be perceived in *Esquire* since it dispensed with the new leisure:

"As for the Lesbian aspects of *Sister George*, we can't get very excited about that. As a man's magazine, we're only queer for women. That's why we've never been able to understand fairies at all, and it probably explains why we've never really tried."

The covers of the new *Esquire* became another pseudocultural come-on. Conceived by an advertising artist, they sought and achieved the kind of double-take shock impact that made it next to impossible for a thinking man to filter past a newsstand without succumbing: Sonny Liston as Santa Claus; Svetlana Alliluyeva wearing her father's mustache; Rocky Graziano bussing Jack Palance while secretly holding hands with Raquel Welch (to announce a published, but as yet unproduced, Chayefsky play called *The Latent Heterosexual*); a trio of busty females in black cuddling up to James Bond's coffin; John F. Kennedy with a nation's tears superimposed on him; Elizabeth Taylor, lips pursed, enticing you to "See Elizabeth Taylor's Greatest Love"—her children; a football player kneeling in prayer (cover line: "Heaven help him—he's going to play 60 minutes of pro ball"); a composite face (one eye and bushy hair of Bob Dylan; one bespectacled eye and shiny brow of Malcolm X; John F. Kennedy's grin; and Fidel Castro's beard) of "4 of the 28 who count most with the college rebels"; Adolf Hitler, looking positively cherubic (cover line: "This month I will be 76 years old. Can I come home now?"), and Lyndon B. Johnson in shining armor, soon to be tarnished on an inside page.

The June, 1967, cover of *Esquire* featured a composite photo (of the ilk that the late Senator McCarthy brandished to "prove" Communist affiliations) of Jacqueline Kennedy with her arms around Eddie Fisher. "Anyone who is against me will look like a rat—unless I run off with Eddie Fisher. . . ." the cover lines trumpeted in black, echoing an unfortunate utterance made by Mrs. Kennedy during the literary/legal battle over William Manchester's history of her husband's assassination. Inside, on the Publisher's Page, Arnold Gingrich gushed unapologetically:

"We won't wait for you to tell us that there are three Kennedy-angled features in this one issue, nor that this is the third straight month that there has been something about the Kennedys on the front cover. . . . Kennedy has become Literature, and that's a fate beyond death, for in the classic definition laid down long ago by Ezra Pound, 'Literature is news that stays news.'"

The most shocking sequence of covers, however, had already come in September and October, 1966. On the first, the back-to-college issue, a debonair young man was dabbing his mouth with lipstick.

The cover line, as usual, minced no words: "HOW OUR RED-BLOODED CAMPUS HEROES ARE BEATING THE DRAFT: For 37 other ways, see page 125."

Regardless of how one felt about the American presence in Vietnam or the way Selective Service is run or the whole principle of conscription, the draft was probably the most pressing concern of any male collegian or otherwise eligible bachelor. *Esquire*'s cover therefore gave every appearance of being a crass, calculated, and strictly fiscal—but nonetheless valid—assault on What Every Young Man Wants to Know at one time or another.

Inside, however, was a trick cynical enough to make any draft dodger's bad blood boil. The one-page illustrated list of thirty-seven easy ways to achieve physical, mental, or moral unfitness was lifted largely from an Army publication, *Standards of Medical Fitness* (AR 40-501). A good many of the thirty-seven ways involved conditions the average reader could scarcely induce: too tall, too short, sole surviving son of a father who died of a service-connected injury, anemia, gout, etc. Other, more feasible, grounds for rejection had built-in limitations, ranging in seriousness from "chronic alcoholism" (booze on breath) to bringing an otherwise unwanted individual into the world ("wife plus one child") to incurring a police record that would almost certainly do lasting damage ("voyeurism and other deviations"). Encouraging the youth of America, however facetiously, to make passes at Army examining medics is a true public disservice.

The very next issue of *Esquire* dealt with another aspect of the Vietnam War. It featured the only cover in *Esquire*'s history without an illustration, just the words, in stark white on black:

"OH MY GOD
—WE HIT
A LITTLE GIRL!"
The true story of M Company.
From Fort Dix to Vietnam.

Inside, as promised, was John Sack's novella-length diary of a basic-training unit's baptism of fire. *M*, as it was called, was a literary and journalistic feat to be proud of.

Very little that is praiseworthy in *Esquire* goes unpraised in *Esquire*, so *M* came heralded by Arnold Gingrich himself, who ticked off these distinctions:

It was the second-longest piece ever published by *Esquire*; the longest was *Welcome to Our City*, a play by the late Thomas (not Tom) Wolfe.

It had the shortest title of any *Esquire* piece ever.

"George Lois, who designs our covers, has paid this story . . . the ultimate tribute, by substituting one single phrase from its context for any possible picture or design that might otherwise have graced this issue's cover."

The end result, said Gingrich, was "one of those landmark events of which there can never be more than a comparative few in the lifespan of any magazine. Probably *The Crack-Up* by F. Scott Fitzgerald and *The Snows of Kilimanjaro* by Ernest Hemingway would come to mind soonest, for anybody setting out to select the small list of such publishing events as would qualify from the pages of this magazine."

The most that can be said for Sack's novelistic reportage is that it was good enough to survive its This Month's Instant Classic merchandising. But *Esquire* wasn't finished promoting it. Its admen took the costly back page of the New York *Times* to proclaim: "We can state unequivocally that this is one of the most important pieces ever printed on the Vietnam war. So important that *ESQUIRE* is devoting 30,000 words to it in the October issue—making it the longest report ever to see print in the Magazine."

That ad in the *Times* was striking—as if the printed page were hammering the realities of life and death into the expense-account mentality of Madison Avenue, where *Esquire* dwells—until, after four more paragraphs summarizing Sack and quoting eloquently from him, the ad concluded:

"This is literary reportage that exploits all the dramatic possibilities of the language—and freezes the realities of Vietnam for a reader in a way nothing else he's read on the war can touch. And it *involves* him for page after page after page.

"*Involvement*. It's the mark of a great advertising medium."

Esquire's circulation passed the 1-million mark not long ago, and its hucksters bought up a chunk of back-page ad space in the *Times* to define "The Esquire Man." In a series of profiles, they identified him as Tennessee Williams (who said: "I can think of no other American magazine that is more identical with the moment we live in"); political prophet William F. Buckley, Jr. (who said: "If *Esquire* should fail, one gets the impression it's because American writers are failing, not because some formula or other has collapsed, or gone stale"); Commander Whitehead of Schweppes Tonic (whose grasp of reality is perhaps the most universally respected of the three), and "more than a million others like him. All esquires. All sophisticated men. Successful men. Men with a broad range of interest."

In still another ad, *Esquire* proclaimed that in the first six months of 1967, advertising was up 15 percent in pages and 23 percent in dollars. "Not bad when you consider that in 1966, *Esquire*'s rate of growth was 300 percent higher than the average for the industry." All this and other upbeat data was headed: "THE NAME OF THE GAME IS GROWTH."

Actually, the name of the game *Esquire* has been playing still is FASHION. It has simply widened its arena, not its outlook. In the pages of *Esquire*, the faddish lies cheek to jowl with the antiquated; the pseudo-hip lift pinkies with the dandified swish, and a curious democracy runs riot wherein an idea and an auto and a political posture and a swatch of clothing all have the same status—here one month, gone the next. Ring out the old, ring in the new! God is dead this year and Marshall McLuhan lives, and neither existed before *Esquire* listed them in its charts!

Each issue of *Esquire* has all the excitement and permanence of a Paris showing for men, which gives it an irresistible appeal. This isn't *all* bad, for too many magazines are written and edited with ponderousness belying their ephemeral nature. For better rather than worse, there is no *Esquire* style per se, nothing approximating the detached, passive voice that dominates

New Yorker prose or the gushy corporate voices of the women's magazines. Nevertheless, if you read the *New Yorker* or *Redbook* or even the *Ladies' Home Journal* over the years, you *will* find a consistent interest in and a civilized attitude toward the world around you. In *Esquire,* all you will find is a slickly run race toward the facade of the new. And the saddest truth about anything that's new is that inevitably it's old. Fashion itself is self-defeating, for what you are selling is obsolescence.

I talked to some people in fashion about this, and one of them, a man who runs a fabric factory, told me:

"What you're dealing with at *Esquire* is *men's* fashions, which are never noted for their originality. A woman dresses to be different from her group; a man dresses to be one of his group.

"The deep, deep secrets of men's fashions is that its fashion makers have no creativity at all. The fashion editor or fashion director of *Esquire* will go to the mills and get statistics on how many yards of what kinds of material the mills are running. If it's a certain kind of gray, then they'll go to the retailers and tell them all about Stonehenge Grey. The retailers will get all excited about the name and order it. Even if they don't, the poor slobs can't do anything about it because they can't get anything else from the mills. Meanwhile *Esquire* is writing about it. . . ."

This kind of reverse reportage can be applied not only to yard goods and fabrics but also to men's minds. At *Esquire,* the only idea whose time has come is one that works on the newsstands.

The man who runs a fabric factory took this thought full circle.

"Before *Esquire,* men's fashion editors used to be people who swam around jetties to see what was being worn in exclusive clubs. Nowadays *Esquire* is the club. At least, that's what I seem to read in *Esquire.*"

Two hesternalgic footnotes should be added here.

The first pertains to the new leisure that was *Esquire*'s avowed *raison d'être* back in 1933. Whatever became of it? *Esquire*'s answer was contained in an unbylined 1967 cover story, "The New American Woman: Through at 21," which began by summating "the L.A. Woman, henceforth to be known as the American Woman. She is sick, and she is also a sickness. The germs are already spreading out of Los Angeles across the country in the usual forms with the usual potency. . . . The American Woman Old-Style doesn't stand a chance; she will have to succumb to the overexposure if nothing else.

"The blame has to be shared by all of us. This is the bed we have made and these are the women who are sleeping in it."

Be that as it may, *Esquire's* moving but anonymous finger wrote in the same profile:

"Boredom drives her to hobbies. She is the result of 'the new leisure,' and so she takes up classes at U.C.L.A.—Spanish, television writing, acting. Leisure, normally a release from work, has for this woman become a terror; she now prays for work, as a release from leisure."

The second hesternalgic footnote pertains to Esky, "The Magazine for Men's" mascot, who appeared in every *Esquire* starting with the second issue. A dapper little dandy with a white mustache, a wistful leer, and a wandering eye, Esky used to hitch rides with newlyweds and dally with stenographers and showgirls month after month until he was deemphasized in the late 1950's.

Whatever became of Esky? On today's covers, Esky is merely the dot on the *i* in *Esquire*. He also appears on the contents page as the magazine's registered trademark. It ought to be noted in passing, though, that there has been a curious intercourse between art and nature. It is a touch of pure Dorian Gray. For Arnold Gingrich, who was only twenty-nine when he sired *Esquire,* has matured over the years into a senior citizen who looks much like Esky himself.

[II]

On the record, it would appear that *Esquire* owes its unparalleled recent success to Arnold Gingrich's bear-hug embrace of culture. But if we expand the dramatis personae of the *Esquire* success story by just one bit player—already mentioned in an offstage manner—it takes on a whole new dimension that makes us wonder whether *Esquire's* upgrading of pretensions wasn't in fact a costly blunder.

Deep in the bowels of *Esquire's* Chicago office in the early 1950's toiled a young father named Hugh Marston Hefner, writing circulation-promotion copy for the princely sum of $60 a week.

"I guess I've always been fascinated with magazines," said Hugh Hefner not long ago. "I read all the magazines there were, and I used to admire *Esquire* tremendously—the Petty girls, the sophisticated world it talked about. . . ."

Working for *Esquire,* however, was another matter. The young father had trouble finding enough drudgery to fill an eight-hour workday. And he wasn't happy at home, either; his marriage broke up around then.

In 1952, when Gingrich revamped his magazine's cultural outlook, *Esquire* moved the last of its offices from Chicago to New York. Hefner was offered a raise to $80 a week if he would relocate. He asked for $85 and was turned down, so he quit.

Hefner stayed on in Chicago, pasting up his dream of a new magazine that would and did outstrip *Esquire.* He admits that his vision of *Playboy* was a daydream that originated during his idle hours at *Esquire:* the *Esquire* formula (already in retreat, leaving the field wide open) carried forward with photographed nudes!

"Once this idea hit me," says Hefner, "I began to work on it with everything I had, and for the first time in my life, I felt free. It was like a mission—to publish a magazine that would thumb its nose at all the restrictions that had bound me."

Back in 1953, Marilyn Monroe was a *living* legend and so was the notorious nude calendar that had enabled her to live in her starlet days. Hefner went after it, and for $200—raised with a bank loan on his three-year-old Studebaker—he obtained the right to reproduce it in his first issue of *Playboy,* the McGuffey's Reader of the sexually literate.

Volume 1, Number 1 appeared shortly before Christmas, 1953, but it bore no dateline. Hefner didn't know whether there would be a second issue. Thanks to Marilyn, however, *Playboy* sold 51,000 copies at fifty cents. This was half the number of first issues that *Esquire* had sold at the same price back in 1933, but Hefner brought to the early *Playboy* the same cheeky vitality that had generated *Esquire*'s initial success.

The rest is history: a racy monthly whose circulation crossed the 4-million mark at just about the time that a "revivified" *Esquire* achieved 1 million; the nymphomaniacal Playmate of the Month, packaged with the prose of Nabokov, Malamud, Baldwin, Sartre* and—as second-generation middle-aging casts its shadow—J. Paul Getty and Hugh Hefner; the Friday night bacchanals in Hefner's Near North Side villa with its hot-and-cold running Bunnies, household staff of twenty-eight, kidney-shaped pool, including love nook called Woo Grotto, closed-circuit TV, electronic entertainment room, and, in the master bedroom, the potentate himself, running his $70 million Play-boy empire from a circular, revolving, vibratable motorized bed; the Playboy Clubs (fourteen in America, one in Jamaica, and one in London, at last count), emerging as the nation's largest booker of live talent; the Playboy Press (publishing); Playboy Models, Inc.; the Playboy Theater in Chicago; *Playboy Penthouse* on TV; the Playboy Jazz Festival; even a movie of Hefner's life with Tony Curtis as "Mr. Playboy," and in 1966, the conversion of the thirty-seven story Palmolive Building on North Michigan Avenue into the Playboy Building, crowned by a 2-billion-candlepower rotating searchlight, sometimes visi-ble 500 miles away, known as the "Bunny Beacon."

Anthropologists, theologians, and Hefner himself harrumph at great length about the Playboy phenomenon and what it all means in the era of Kinsey, the pill, and Ann Landers. Suffice to say herein that Hefner's onanistic world of look-but-don't-touch began with a magazine that undressed its girls better than anybody else had heretofore and still revolves around staying truer to both crotch and heart than its *au courant* predecessor, which might have grown four or five times as big and infinitely more honest if it had only stayed true to itself. Instead of going all the way, however, *Esquire* settled for seconds; it simply lay around, waiting to snap up potential Playboys who either re-jected the orgiastic Playboy philosophy or else outgrew it. And when this wasn't enough, *Esquire* performed a prodigious feat of mind bending and invented its own dear reader: The Dumb Intellectual.

[III]

Esquire does not have exclusive rights to the deceptive (some-times self-deceiving) illusion that What's Happening emanates

---

* This has occasioned the premature boast of a men's magazine editor that "the best writing in America is appearing between two breasts."

from its own editorial sanctum. Study the credits or copyright lines or publisher's page or backstage notes in the next issue of *Esquire* or *Look* or the New York *Times* magazine or *Harper's* and you may be able to fathom that often as not, the real blockbuster article is a chunk of a forthcoming book (either finished or in progress) that has been commissioned by some hard-cover publisher. It's a little hard to tell in the *New Yorker*, but rest assured that even if the article really is an article, its author is being approached to expand it into a book. And the next time the *Saturday Evening Post* advertises *its* exposés of Nazis or gangsters or CIA men in our midst, note how much of the spadework was done by writers with book contracts. Last Thanksgiving, when the *Satevepost* "shed new light" on the Kennedy assassination, all the digging it involved was buying up a book that met some fairly obvious November newsstand needs, excerpting it, and then blowing it up as news (and a potential best seller) simply because it was being serialized in a "major American magazine."

The ultimate in lucrative cannibalization is to be found in the June, 1967, *Esquire*, the one with Jacqueline Kennedy hugging Eddie Fisher on the cover. It features what Arnold Gingrich calls "a piece about somebody who is writing a book about somebody who wrote a book about Kennedy." What Gingrich is describing is a one-two-and-a-half punch. First, an article was written by Gay Talese called "The Corry Papers," which is about the adventures New York *Times* reporter John Corry had while covering the Kennedys' legal battle over *Look* magazine's serialization of William Manchester's book about the assassination. Second, Corry's own book, *The Manchester Affair*, was excerpted in the same issue of *Esquire*. And not quite third, the publication date of the book itself was postponed so that it could appear in *Esquire* first, which is the only way most major magazines will buy books.

What we have, then, are two powerful media whose strengths are not their own. It is a situation wherein too many books are created, commissioned, and published simply because the serialization prospects are bright. Conversely, too many articles are culled from books. The distortion that occurs in transmission is often horrendous; a good article can be padded to death at book length just as a good book can be fatally castrated and publicly damned on the basis of magazine excerpts. In either sequence, the occasional good work that is accepted for surgery receives enrichment and exposure, but not justice.

What all this is doing to book publishing was sketched by an editor who threatens to write a book called *The Deterioration of American Literature due to the Preoccupation of American Authors with the Best-Seller Lists*. Terming the charts themselves "souped-up, artificial," and confusing, this editor went on to say:

"Too many eager-beaver hacks are submitting outlines for books. They are ready to write a book on anything. This is deplorable. In the past, men spent years, wrote, polished, revised. Today we find ourselves buying from outlines, and in the last few years I've noticed the outlines become briefer and briefer, and at least fifty percent are hard-sell copy full of sales arguments rather than facts relating to the books under discussion. Deplorable!"

He said that the mortality rate on these outlines-that-try-to-be-books is high. "The authors have undertaken projects for which they are not equipped. What do authors talk about when they get together? Terms, options. . . . Authors are concerned with the deal, the best-seller list, promotion, publicity." Writing itself becomes a means to these ends.

What the subsidiary sources of income (book clubs, paperbacks, serializations, etc.) are doing to dominate book publishing has its grotesque counterpart in the magazine world, where the magazine publishers and writers *are doing it to themselves*. Small wonder, then, that there are only a few dozen free-lance nonfiction magazine writers whose primary income comes from magazine writing itself, even though 50 million American households read 5 billion magazines per year. Far too many of the bylines in our magazines belong to novelists out slumming in the real world or public relations men out planting in the media—and their sprawling, sloppy prose reflects this.

Inevitably the medium suffers from its own self-contempt. The Society of Magazine Writers' own monthly *Newsletter* carries a regular section devoted to "Book News" about members; scant attention is paid to one-shot appearances in magazines, only to book serializations. The Society of Magazine Writers, in fact, recently devoted one of its ten annual meetings to "How to

Make a Lot of Money from Books." The Pulitzer Prize people up at Columbia steadfastly decline to create an award for magazine journalism; after all, if John Corry deserves a Pulitzer for his Kennedy-Manchester reportage, he can be voted it in several newspaper categories and at least one book category.

This is too bad, not only for magazine writing but also for American letters. Back when a weekly magazine was something that lasted a week and not a minute longer, magazine writing used to be a very special here-and-now art form, as practiced by artists like E. B. White, Robert Benchley, H. L. Mencken, Bernard DeVoto, and (let's be honest about it!) H. Allen Smith. So was magazine editing, and it is only in a couple of the surviving weeklies that it is still practiced as such on occasion.*
Nowadays, however, when our nonmagazines amount to no more than glossy *Omnibooks* peddling their own private perversions of truth, it's enough to make Dumb Intellectuals of us all.

---

* At *Life,* I have found, to my surprise and delight, that the same artistic and technical care is lavished on text as on photos, although last-minute committee thinking is capable of undoing or diluting writers' and editors' best efforts. In the *New Yorker,* even the book excerpts are handled with such care that they sometimes surpass the book in merit. For documentation, see the book and magazine versions of Truman Capote's 1955 visit to Russia, *The Muses Are Heard.*

7
The Synthetic Society

[1]

BOOM!

"The Romantic worship of Art, having lost its purpose, heads toward self-extinction. The nations of the West now resemble those tribes that eat their gods to get the good there is in them," says Dean Jacques Barzun of Columbia University.

"The powerful devices of mechanical reproduction and high pressure distribution to which we owe the cultural 'awakening' necessarily distort and thus destroy. All the new media make arbitrary demands on the materials fed through them. And, because the public to be served is large and failure costly, it is important that the product suit—hence the endless cutting and adapting, re-working, and diluting, which end in travesty. . . ."

"To see the works of the Impressionists twisted into backgrounds for advertising perfume; to hear the melodies of Bach, Mozart, Berlioz, and Chopin re-handled by Tin Pan Alley; to listen to absent-minded hacks giving the lowdown on high art . . . all this is destructive in the same measure that it is communicative."

Bulk kills appetite, Barzun concludes.

"Symphonies in bars and cabs, classical drama on television any day of the week, highbrow paperbacks in mountainous profusion (easier to buy than to read), 'art seminars in the home,' capsule operas, *Chopin by Starlight*, *The Sound of Wag-*

ner, The Best of World Literature: this cornucopia thrust at the inexperienced and pouring out its contents over us all deadens attention and keeps taste still-born, like any form of gross feeding." *

[II]

BOOM!

Muzak, which the *Saturday Review* has defined with understandable admiration as "music to hear but not to listen to," is the most ubiquitous of the cultural foragers that Barzun is deploring.

There is Muzak in the air here, there, and everywhere. It wafts us from womb (labor rooms at New York Hospital) to tomb (Citizens Mortuary of Sacramento). It plumbs the lower depths (motel swimming pools, nuclear submarines) and permeates the loftiest reaches (jet planes, space capsules, chalets on Mount Kenya). It oozes into top-secret Pentagon conferences, featuring Muzak to confound wiretappers, and out of an upstate New York billboard advertising biscuits baked to music. Bland background melodies alleviate fear in dentists' chairs, tedium in beauty parlors, "driveway anxiety" in busy gas stations, typing errors at Lever Brothers, and absenteeism at Loft's Candy. Muzak hath charms in the Bronx Zoo reptile house, a mud-making plant in Houston, and the Federal Reserve Bank vaults. Every year, 546,000 miles of Muzak tape girdles the globe and helps the world unwind. Every day Muzak is heard, if not listened to, by some 60 million people in twenty countries and countless cities, ranging alphabetically from Aarhus (Denmark) to Zurich. The Strathcona Baptist Girls Grammar School of Australia recently subscribed, and a brothel in Stuttgart has applied for Muzak's "Light Industrial" programming.

At Muzak's headquarters on Park Avenue South, New York, I was shown an array of mood-stimulus curves for a typical business day. From 8 A.M. to 9, the programming is *"moderate:* to instill cheerful attitude at start of workday." From 9 to 10, *"moderate to bright:* to combat onset of potential tension."

---

* Jacques Barzun, "Romanticism Today," *Encounter* (September, 1961), pp. 26–32.

From 10 to 11, *"bright:* to counter maximum potential tension at period in morning when most critical." From 12 to 1, *"mild and restful:* to provide midday relief." A similar cycle starts in the afternoon, but the brightness is brighter and so is the moderation.

The *n*th degree of mood progression can be pinpointed by varying four elements: tempo (ranging from 58 to 131 metronome beats per minute); rhythm (fox trot, waltz, samba, quick step); instrumentation (strings produce the softest sounds, brass the loudest, and there are various intermediate combinations involving woodwinds); and orchestra size (Muzak uses groups ranging from six to thirty musicians). Thus Muzak's Tune Treasury (the company's term for its 10-million-dollar library) may include as many as five arrangements of the same song.

"Throughout the world," Muzak boasts, "a tune *designed* for playing at three in the afternoon is played at three o'clock."

Twice a month, Muzak holds a recording session at which twelve preselected songs are performed. Muzak's musicians include, or have included, Lawrence Welk, Richard Maltby, Lester Lanin, Bobby Hackett, Pee Wee Erwin and Urbie Green. At the session I attended, Richard Hayman conducted three-minute arrangements of "I Surrender, Dear," Leroy Anderson's "Saraband," Ernesto Lecuona's "Cordoba," Richard Rodgers' "Sixteen Going on Seventeen," plus a song from *Fiddler on the Roof* and four of Hayman's own compositions.

"I like to hear my own works on Muzak first," Hayman told me. "It's a great source of experimentation—a good middle-of-the-road framework on which I can later hang anything from an arrangement for the teen-age market to a Boston Pops orchestration."

I asked Hayman—who, as a composer, at least, is not the favorite of many—if arranging for Muzak was challenging creatively. He replied: "We have to temper our thinking. It's background music, not foreground. Don't get too wild, too vociferous, too startling. If a man's eating and there's a sudden noise, he's likely to lose his soup." Muzak arrangers avoid strong contrasts in tempo, volume, and range (no screeching trumpets or extremely low bassoons, organs, or trombones). Another taboo is extended solos. A lone instrument is rarely featured for more than two or three bars in a Muzak arrangement. Small wonder, then, that after Muzak has scientifically pasteurized Gershwin and Bernstein, they come out sounding like so much *ooby-ooby-doo*.

This dubious science falls under the heading of *ergonomics,* which the *International Labour Review* defines as "using engineered methods to humanize work areas." Ergonomy measures include air conditioning, lighting, and functional furniture, but hardly any can manipulate people as readily as *ooby-ooby-doo* does.

Musical ergonomics goes back at least as far as Ivan Petrovich Pavlov's experiments on conditioned reflex, whereby dogs were taught to salivate whenever a bell rang. The Muzak men first became aware of their product's ergonomic potential when their company was three years old. Muzak had begun in 1934 as a service that recorded medleys for restaurants and transmitted them over telephone lines. The name Muzak had been coined because it sounded catchy, easy to remember, and successful, like Kodak.

(Muzak, incidentally, was acquired in 1941 by William Benton, whose other holdings have at various times included *Encyclopaedia Britannica,* the Benton & Bowles advertising agency, and a United States Senate seat. Benton bought Muzak on the advice of economist Beardsley Ruml and paid slightly more than $100,000. In 1957 he sold it for many times that price to the Jack Wrather Organization, which also owns the *Lassie* television show, a hotel and monorail at Disneyland, a hotel in Palm Springs, and the Gilbert Toy Company. At last report, the Muzak division's annual income was 17 million dollars.)

Ergonomics and international Big Brotherhood were equated forever when a Muzak man named A. Oulianine told me: "When we first started programming for Buenos Aires, we thought special tapes were necessary, and so we sent sambas, tangos, and all Latin American tunes. But we found that they were just as attention-getting there as they would be here. We switched to the same tapes that people get in the United States. Since our music is functional, it makes no difference."

When I went to see Muzak's research manager, I expected to confront a fatherly, white-haired ergonomist. But Melvin

Cohen proved to be a diminutive young man working toward his master's degree in marketing management at City College of New York.

I asked Mel Cohen how far ahead Muzak's eggheads were thinking. He replied: "In writing, we go five years into the future."

What did the future hold?

"New markets," he said. "Every new phenomenon must be served. Trading stamps mean Muzak in redemption centers. Increasing longevity means Muzak in sanatoriums and rest homes. Emancipation of women means Muzak in billiard parlors, which have a growing female clientele. More leisure time means more Muzak in bowling alleys, racetracks, and swimming pools. *And hopefully, a continuing cultural explosion could lead to greater intellectual acceptance of Muzak.*"

The italics are mine. For a few minutes, I couldn't comprehend what Mel Cohen was getting at there—until I realized that at Muzak, among other places, *cultural explosion* has come to mean *cultural leveling toward the blandest common denominator.* When I picked Cohen's brains a little longer, he was inclined to agree.

For Muzak is the electronic music of a national march toward perfection through technical excellence. It is the same quest which enables the new breed of stereo lover to outrage the old breed of music lover by pointing out (with some justice) that a concert-hall performance cannot compare in quality with an engineered recording. Excellence and man's strivings have become the province of engineers, who have no use for the raggletaggle, caterpillarlike miracle called growth.

An interview with the Beatles or the Smothers Brothers— or, for that matter, with a guest on Margaret Truman's radio program—may be "open-ended." This means that interviewer and interviewee never meet; questions, or more often, answers are taped, and then room is left for the other ingredient to be supplied. In recent screen musicals, the stunning singing voices of Deborah Kerr and Natalie Wood and Audrey Hepburn all belong to an invisible recording artist named Marni Nixon. Ghostwriting and canned laughter are no longer accessories, but essentials. "Synthetics . . . are not new in films," writes Russell Baker in his "Observer" column. "They are as old as Bing

Crosby's toupee and Gary Cooper's stunt man. In those days, however, technical synthetics were merely crutches to help the act along. Nowadays they are becoming the act."

[III]

BOOM!

Discussing our conspicuous culture consumption, Robert Lekachman, professor of economics at Columbia, has written:

"When art becomes one more of the ploys of a bored society, the temptations placed before art's creators and servants are deeply subversive of art's purposes. The fashionable painter and the fashionable performer pander to their audiences. Even the writer, poet, or musician in dignified residence on the college campus is diverted from his proper work by lectures, conversations and demonstrations, and still more by the easy praise and adulation of the young."

And Karl E. Meyer of the Washington *Post,* writing in Britain's *New Statesman:*

"The remorseless feeding machine in Charlie Chaplin's *Modern Times* comes irresistibly to mind when one contemplates the culture boom in the United States. It is as if one were strapped into a Kulturvac 112B that spews forth classical records, paperbacks, poetry readings, Shakespeare festivals, little theaters, and big cultural centers. The machine is out of control, and at every turn one is pummeled by the artifacts of culture."

In greater Los Angeles in the spring of 1965, a family visiting there had a choice of attending no less than 851 community theaters (doing plays ranging from *Arsenic and Old Lace* to *Six Characters in Search of an Author*), 12 children's theaters, 63 art exhibits, 56 concerts, and 55 public lectures. Oppressed by all the possibilities, they escaped to the beach—and took advantage of none of them.

In New York, wander through Brentano's—"Booksellers to the World"—searching for a book, and you must make your way (on Thursday nights, at least) past a koto recital or a fencing match or a lecture on "Sex and the Teen-Ager" and (any day of the business week) a treasure trove of pre-Columbian jewelry; a sculpted Greek goat, 460/450 B.C., $15; malformed totems in the Gallery of Crafts; a reproduction of a fake fifth century B.C.

bronze horse, $75 (the news that the "original" was a twentieth-century fake stimulated business at both Brentano's and the Metropolitan Museum of Art); a bust of John F. Kennedy, ideal for culture centers and airports bearing his name, $50; stuffed animals; puzzles; automobile models; and red sweatshirts with black letters proclaiming: "TO THOSE OF US WITH REAL UNDER-STANDING . . . MUSIC IS THE ONLY PURE ART FORM."

[IV]

BOOMELAY, BOOMELAY, BOOMELAY, BOOM!

Culture being a sinew of the life we lead, what do all these man-made artifacts hold in store for us?

Welcome to the Synthetic Society, which just possibly *has* happened here.

Newsweek, for one, has sketched a slice of "The Good Non-Life" as an American lives it now:

> For breakfast he has non-caffeine coffee, meatless sausage, and the day's first nicotine-free cigarette. At the office he sits behind his non-working desk—a drawerless, paper-free form intended to look like a coffee table. At home, his wife has her wig, her false eyelashes, and a suntan from a bottle. His children are in school echoing the newest homilies of the teacherless teaching machine. After class his daughter practices the current non-dance, an over-all tremor requiring no movement of the feet. This is today's surrogate world, where man can have his cake substitute (made without butter) and eat it, too.

Russell Baker has portrayed "The Disposable Man for the Non Age":

> The child of the Nothing Generation is naturally swaddled in a disposable diaper. . . . His father lives in a no-down payment house and wears a wrinkle-free drip-dry wardrobe. . . . When the anti-hero wants to carbonate his stomach he takes a non-caloric soft drink. It comes in a disposable, no-deposit no-return bottle, or a throwaway can. For amusement he sits in dehumidified air watching non-actors perform non-dramas about non-people and absorbing

advertisements that tell how to take the misery out of wash-
day, the odors out of living. . . .*

You can wash down your flash-frozen gourmet dinner with
odorless vodka, supplement this diet with fuzzless peaches or
seedless grapes, and if you want to pretend to bake at home,
you can put some brown 'n' serve rolls in the oven. At workless
jobs, employees sign in and out with throwaway pens and do
little or nothing else all day to the sound of Muzak. At Sears
Roebuck, they're merchandising stingless bees for prudent bee-
keepers as well as art that has been attested to by Vincent Price.

Playwright George Axelrod (*Seven Year Itch*) insists, "We
are today an occupied country. The Toy People have taken
over." Axelrod conjures up a graphic picture of our Toy Sky-
scrapers crafted of "washable plastic blocks from a Build-A-City
Kit (Ages 9–14)" with Toy Restaurants (managed by Trader
Vic or Restaurant Associates) that take Toy Money (your Diners'
Club card). He sees Toy Sunburns (Mantan) and Toy Baseball
Teams (the California Angels of Anaheim), and this is only the
beginning of what Axelrod calls "Boobs in Toyland":

> They even have a Toy Book Publishing Company (Ber-
> nard Geis) with its own Toy Printing Press where they
> turn out Toy Books by Toy Authors (Art Linkletter). If
> you want a real case of the shakes sometime, go to one of the
> Toy Cocktail Parties they give at the Toy Restaurants to
> honor the Toy Author of one of the Toy Books. Only the
> martinis are real, to protect the innocent.
>
> Toy Movie Stars have always been with us. But that's
> okay. Movie Stars are *supposed* to be Toys. The thing is,
> they have Toy Real People now. And that's more sinister.
> Especially since they're so terribly *lifelike*.
>
> Once a week on television, you can watch a Toy Intellec-
> tual (when you turn *it* over it doesn't say "Ma-Ma," it says:
> 'Ambivalence') conduct a Toy Discussion. It's so cunning
> and *serious* you'd almost believe it was alive. And some-
> times, just to confuse you, it even has *real* Real People on
> with it. You can always tell them, though, by their slightly
> embarrassed expressions.

---

* "Observer" column, New York *Times,* June 28, 1964.

"The enemy," Axelrod concludes, "is completely indigenous to America in this century. It established, I think, its first serious beachhead with the advent of commercial aviation. All that Toy Food served on Toy Trays by what were (alas!) soon to become Toy Girls!" *

Axelrod, just like many professional social critics, can't conceal his own zest for what he is deploring. After you have lived with these costly "improvements"—be they meals and movies in flight, Plaid Stamps at the A&P, or seedless grapes in the fruit dish—it makes little sense, even economically, to go back to living without them. In the Synthetic Society, the question "Who needs it?" gives way to "Why should *I* be the one to give it up?"

The interplay of all our Toy artifacts with our more urgent moral and cultural values can be found every day in our newspapers. Just as critics corrupt instincts and magazines like *Esquire* lobotomize intellects, genuine social outrage can be supplemented and then replaced by instant synthetic protest. Vehement denunciations never uttered in House or Senate are inserted daily in the *Congressional Record*. When a white Southern scholar makes national headlines ("UNIVERSITY OF MISSISSIPPI PROFESSOR DECLARES HIS STATE IS 'TOTALITARIAN' "), news accounts of his angry outburst also mention that "an expanded version of the speech will be published as a book by Harcourt, Brace & World." A classified ad in the *Village Voice* proclaims:

> PICKETS WANTED: all types, both sexes, for varied lines in different parts of country. Must be prepared to defend or oppose controversial subjects. Good pay with bonus for extra risks due to local prejudices.

The talent agent who placed the ad is dead serious. His manpower pool includes unemployed actors, hippies, rednecks, rebellious college kids, and "an incredibly attention-getting cripple with a red beard."

In the age of disposable consciences and bloodless genocide, we have murderers who explain that they killed to make a name for themselves. We have Hell's Angels offering to terrorize

---

* © 1961, New York *Herald Tribune*. (Axelrod was guest columning for John Crosby at the time.)

any town a television network selects for $100 per Angel. And Latin America, which until recently led the world in Toy Dictators, Toy Armies, Toy Revolutions, and Real Starvation, takes a leaf from the Yankee catalog. In 1967, on an artificial island in the Florida Keys, U.S. Customs men surrounded, captured, and disbanded an army of exiles preparing to "liberate" Haiti and then Cuba. Early in the plot, CBS had dispatched a cameraman, a sound man, and a producer to work with the conspirators. The network had paid a four-figure sum to get in on the ground floor of the invasion.

Another artificial island was the principal eyesore of Princess Margaret's 1965 visit to America. Viewing the natural wonders of Arizona, she and her consort were taken for a boat ride on Lake Powell, a man-made lake formed by Glen Canyon Dam. On an "island" which used to be a lofty crag until man dammed the Colorado River and flooded the canyons) stood twenty "Hawaiians"—all from nearby Page, Arizona—including a purple "mermaid," a turquoise "mermaid," three plump housewives, and several children, all doing hula gyrations for the princess. The "island" itself had been "improved" with a grass shack of sorghum stalks, and its sandstone rock had been concealed by plastic flowers.

Synthetics don't *have* to be tacky, but it is here that one can detect the groundwork performed by such culture dispensers as the book clubs and schlock artmongers, plus such cultural arbiters as the critics and fashionable periodicals.

In the Synthetic Society's deluge of produce—largely trivial— an idea or a person must scream to be heard.

"A boy has to hustle," Truman Capote ("I'm a semantic Paganini") explained to the people who put him on the cover of *Newsweek*.

Mike Nichols says: "Our world has gotten to a point where the actual work people do seems to be almost secondary to publicity. Some people are famous and you're not even sure what they do. You just see them on magazine covers all the time. . . . If you're on television, people don't seem to care much whether you're good or bad. The important thing is that you were *on* television."

Shoddy craftsmen and inept repairmen are themselves the product of a society where the emphasis is on making it big

rather than on how you make it, for they—like our artists—
learn and work with one eye cocked for the big break. "People
in a hurry," says Eric Hoffer, "can neither grow nor decay.
They are preserved in a state of perpetual puerility."

Welcome to the Synthetic Society. CURTAIN GOING DOWN?

Interlude:
An Accusation in Court

"WHEN I think of the silver and gold I poured into those two rascals, I could weep," said the emperor. "And the money could have been used for so many better purposes."

"But that," said the little boy, "was only money."

"ONLY money!" the emperor exclaimed angrily. "I wanted the best that money could buy."

"When you sought to BUY a vision, you had already settled for less than the best."

Bristling, the emperor informed the little boy: "I do not like the accusing tone you are taking—with me, of all people!"

The little boy bowed so low that he almost hit his head. When he spoke, he said: "With all deference, Your Royal Highness, I cannot tell a lie. You yourself are the third culture vulture."

At this, the courtiers gasped and the emperor reeled on his throne. Then, while His Majesty pondered the meaning of these words, the little boy knelt on cold marble to await his fate.

Part III:

THE DILETTANTI

---

dilettante—1. a person who takes up an art, activity, or subject merely for amusement, esp. in a desultory or superficial way; dabbler. 2. a lover of an art or science. . . .
—*The Random House Dictionary of the English Language*

8

What Is Black and White and Gray All Over? Educational Television

A FEW years ago, I had the occasion to become a father, and while my wife was enjoying fourteen hours of air-conditioned labor, I was exposed to a day and a night of television in a darkened hospital alcove coyly labeled "Paternity Ward." The miracle of fatherhood, I learned there and then, no longer climaxes hours of cigarette smoking and miles of floor pacing. It simply marked the end of my absolutely passive broadcast day. Ever since then, planned parenthood to me meant having a baby on Sunday (when the programming used to be somewhat varied).

Fortunately, my only other child had made her entrance by the time I'd received word that she was en route and rushed to the hospital with the latest *TV Guide* in hand. Therefore, nothing so numbing as first fatherhood had happened to me until, suddenly one summer, I submerged myself in a full week of educational television-watching—at night, that is, after the day's diet of formal classroom teaching was ordinarily consumed.* Starting at 5:45 P.M. on five weekdays, I logged thirty

---

* I did subject myself, at other times, to several days' diet of Channel 13's School Television Service (which is used by 100 public and private school dis-

hours wallowing in what my hometown Channel 13 bravely, perhaps recklessly, calls "community programming . . . that lingers in your mind after you've clicked off the switch."

ETV, as it is known to its practitioners, is composed of some 124 American channels*—or approximately one out of five— wholly devoted to educational purposes, which are not permitted to accept advertising or operate commercially and which are licensed to nonprofit educational or civic organizations in order to serve the educational needs of their communities. ETV, at last census, was being used in homes *occasionally* (meaning at least once a month) by some 22½ million Americans, *regularly* (at least once a week) by 10 to 15-million, and *frequently* (four or five days a week) by 2 to 3 million.

Except for San Diego, Indianapolis, and Baltimore, every American city with over 500,000 people has an ETV station of its own, and all of these cities had ETV stations definitely committed to be broadcasting by 1968.** A total of 364 ETV stations are anticipated by the early 1970's.

Vermillion, South Dakota; Corvallis, Oregon; Waycross, Georgia; Dozier, Alabama; Monroe, Louisiana; Pullman, Washington; Carbondale, Illinois; and Durham, New Hampshire, already have their own ETV channels. So do Athens, Georgia, and Athens, Ohio. Florida has a network of six ETV stations, including one in Gainesville, where the founders were warned that the "only audience [is] alligators." Washington, D.C.'s station started in one room of a schoolhouse in nearby Virginia.

Merely by existing and surviving, ETV has proved itself a hardy, virtually indestructible medium. Milwaukee's was born

---

tricts in New York, New Jersey, and Connecticut), as well as the instructional fare in other cities. Where relevant, I will cite some of my findings. But for the purposes of this chapter, instructional television (ITV) defies widespread analysis because the medium is, like our sons and daughters, 1) *a prisoner of the peda-gogues*, who, for better or worse, comprise each station's curriculum committees and 2) *changing drastically* as videotape recorders, Time-Life and Encyclopaedia Britannica Films, and particularly 2,500-megacycle, multi-channel, closed-circuit, intraschool networks are moving into the classroom.

* A 125th channel, KVZK-TV, in Pagopago, American Samoa, was much admired by President Johnson on his visit to Asia in 1966 and *is* listed as an affiliate of National Educational Television of New York City, but it is not included in these statistics.

** Source: ETV Station Division, National Association of Educational Broadcasters.

over the opposition of the Hearst press and Senator Joseph Mc-
Carthy. Denver's came about despite chamber of commerce
hostility, a $500,000 fund drive that raised only $90,000, and a
"Who needs it?" attitude by the local press. (One reason for
initial opposition by the press to ETV is that even the most en-
lightened newspaper fears it as a threat to its own commercial
TV station. Later, because ETV's uncompetitive blandness
makes it so dated and passé and because its very presence keeps a
desirable channel out of a commercial competitor's clutches,
the newspaper tends to see the light.) Miami's antispending
forces—real estate, banks, utilities, and press, many of them involved with the Du Pont Corporation—waged open war with
WTHS with injunction suits, political pressure, and even an
attempt to have one of its founders indicted. Now Miami has
two ETV channels.

Only one ETV station has failed thus far: KTHE in Los
Angeles, an ultra-high-frequency station that went on the air
in 1953 and off the air in 1954, when its only substantial donor
withdrew his support. (This is still a potential hazard for much
or perhaps all of ETV, whose most visible means of support is
the Ford Foundation. Ford, which has thus far invested some
$130 million in ETV, is widely believed to be seeking to extract
itself from the unhappy medium with a series of forward-look-
ing, face-saving proposals for others to enact.) In any event, it
took almost a decade before Los Angeles tried again, and KCET
took to the air in 1963.

The young medium of ETV is still, chronologically at least,
in the insecure throes of adolescence. It is barely beginning to
come to grips with the problems prophesied by Dave Garroway
on NBC's *Today* show on May 12, 1953, the day commercial
television saluted the emergence of a brand-new poor relation.
As the first ETV station—KUHT in Houston—went on the air,
Garroway said:

"Let me say 'Welcome to the mushrooming television picture' and well-come in a big sense of the word, because you are
pioneering a brand-new and complex part of the television
picture. It's a new side and an unknown side, pretty much, to
television. No one really knows what educational TV can
do. . . .

"Television isn't anything in itself. It's nothing except a tool.

So many people in our branch of the business sometimes forget that. Television is only the copper wire in the telephone call; it's only the fountain pen, without the hand to move it. The ideas that can flow over it are the important things.

"The art form that is television is infinitely complex and hopeful, and a lot of people will expect you to grow up in thirty minutes. All other art forms had generations to grow up in, hundreds of years. But people will expect television, educational as well as commercial, to mature in another week or so. So take it easy—we try to—and good luck and welcome to the pool!"

The speech was pure Garroway as well as a position paper—commercial TV's understated attitude toward ETV: *sincere good wishes, so cool it and don't make it hot for yourselves or us.* But at least Garroway perceived what too many people in ETV have yet to discover: theirs is not just a medium, but an art form.

Now, with a quick twirl of the contrast button, let us try to glimpse the brave new world that loomed before the gray-eyed foundation visionaries who pioneered ETV.

"Like the Jeffersonian idealists who helped settle the West and who dotted it with colleges, churches, schools, and other outposts of literacy and culture, these traveling companions are impelled by an equally Jeffersonian dream: in the new land they would develop, every man should find pleasure for the eye, instruction for the mind, and refreshment for the spirit, in a common wealth of education, of culture, of communication—in a word [sic!], of Educational Television." *

Having given this Jeffersonian ideal almost a decade and a half to mature, I planted myself before Channel 13 for a week of educational televiewing to begin to answer my basic question: *What hath thought wrought?*

[II]

Channel 13 was operating only Monday through Friday. Earlier in the year, there *had* been a golden spell of a dozen Sun-

* Powell, John Walker, *Channels of Learning: The Story of Educational Television.* Washington, D.C., Public Affairs Press, 1962. When I interviewed Professor Powell in late 1966 at the University of Miami, he spoke wistfully and regretfully of how so many ETV stations "haven't created an image for themselves as a voice of the intellectual community."

days when the tube had been illuminated (drably!) by a cultural series called *Sunday Showcase,* thanks to a $250,000 grant from the Bristol-Myers Company (inventors of stomach acid for commercial TV) and the cooperation of Lincoln Center. But having inflicted ninety minutes each of Marshall McLuhan and Buckminster Fuller on me, as well as Mozart's deservedly forgotten opera *The Impresario,* Channel 13 had already withdrawn from Sunday programming.* So this was the week that was.

Each of my five weeknights began at 5:45 P.M. with the worst program for preschoolers that my two dutiful daughters have ever walked out on. It was called *Friendly Giant.* My two preschoolers stayed long enough for the opening titles, which were excellent. Then a somnolent voice droned, "Once upon a time not long ago and not far away, there was a friendly farm beyond the woods." The voice belonged to Friendly Giant, a torpid-looking grown-up who manipulated toy furniture for a moment, conversed for three long minutes with a couple of puppets, a faggotty giraffe named Jerome and a eunuchy rooster named Rusty, and then, for the rest of his allotted quarter hour, read an approved children's book while the illustrations were flashed on the screen and either the rooster or the giraffe interjected insipid comments or questions. The books were usually quite good as bedtime tales at 5:45 P.M. go, but Friendly's monotone had all the color and expression of Ed Sullivan's face. I defy you to imagine this voice delivering a punch line like, "Yippee, Mother, I'll never be Tommy Too Late anymore!"

Very few people in this world could have talked *down* to my two-year-old, but Friendly did it! The closing credits informed me that *Friendly Giant* was produced some time back by the University of Wisconsin Television Laboratory for National Educational Television (NET), about which more will be heard later. I was also advised to stay tuned for more "fun for children of all ages."

This fun consisted of a series called *What's New,* which also began with marvelous titles—an animated fife-and-drum trio spelling out its range of material, "In, Out, and Round-About Here, There and Everywhere"—and then went steadily down-

---

* A few months later, thanks to grants from Ford and the National Endowment for the Arts, some Sunday programming was resumed on Channel 13.

hill in the rest of its half hour. For three of my five nights, I watched a semidocumentary based on Joseph Krumgold's Newberry Award-winning children's book, *And Now Miguel,* from which I learned more than I ever wanted to know about sheep shearing in the shadow of the Sangre de Cristo Mountains of New Mexico. The narration was in dialect, which convinced me that Xavier Cugat had gone to work for March of Time: "Eet would be a great theeng eef I, Mee-gel, could breeng back the meesing sheep. Eet would mean [long pause for anticlimax]— much!" Thursday's *What's New* was a contrived adventure yarn about a lad named Viller Valle accompanying his dad on a UNESCO mission from Sweden to Tahiti. Friday's finale was a mishmash—ten minutes at the Bronx Zoo and twenty of gung-ho patriotism, with Pathé News films on Alexander Hamilton, Fort Ticonderoga, the Statue of Liberty, and Theodore Roosevelt while a sound track played "America the Beautiful" and "Over There." The Theodore Roosevelt film was a *Reader's Digest* model of cute compression. It lingered coyly over his role in spawning the teddy bear and then skipped him blithely from Governor of New York to President of the United States. It never paused to inform children of all ages that Roosevelt was elected Vice-President in between and that it took two bullets fired into President McKinley by an anarchist named Leon Czolgosz to accomplish this promotion.*

Every night, *What's New* signed off with the information— flawlessly executed by its animated fife-and-drum corps—that it, too, was a NET production. Further research indicated that NET beams *What's New* at the seven-to-twelve age group, the same mental-age bracket to which commercial TV is accused of pandering.

"EGGHEAD! SQUAREHEAD! FLATHEAD!" said the station-break announcement. "Educational television is none of these, we hope."

Then, at 6:30 P.M., for five nights running, my wife brought me sandwiches and beer while Channel 13 dished out its most

---

* Later, on a visit to Buffalo, where McKinley was assassinated, I saw a half-hour documentary of the event, produced by the local ETV station, WNED. Done with none of the resources that *What's New* had at its disposal, the local offering was relevant, accurate, enlightening, visual, gripping, and immediate— which once might have been what all of ETV was about.

consistently high-quality offering: *Living for the Sixties*, an interview program aimed at senior citizens "to encourage [them] to get more out of life." The hostess for the programs I saw was Kitty Carlisle (who alternated with Betty Furness). Her regular guests included a personable young man from Social Security, who talked benefits for no more than five minutes, and an energetic lady from the Y who limbered me up with five minutes of geriatric exercises—craning my neck, swiveling my head, and hissing "Yankee Doodle" in one breath while stretching my arms and marching in place without rising from my seat or, for that matter, choking on my delicatessen and beer.

Miss Carlisle's one-shot guests included the author of *Papa Hemingway,** discussing "When does a writer retire?"; a representative of the New Careers Program at Columbia University; Hal Holbrook, alias Mark Twain; Eugene Lyons, biographer of David Sarnoff, and "The Man From SPEC," who represented the Senior Personnel Employment Committee of Westchester. One night, Miss Carlisle, accompanied by a guitar offscreen and some Robert Osborn illustrations onscreen, read Osborn's essay *On Leisure.* It was, I realized later, the only glimmer of real wit that I witnessed all week on ETV. Another night, an expert on lipreading taught me her art, in case, as she put it so tactfully, I was trapped by a bore at a party while an interesting argument erupted across the room, or the audio on my TV set went dead, or my hearing was failing.

On still another night, the playful Kitty took on a boyish automation consultant named John Diebold in a memorable sparring match. She kept pressing him on whether he was in the business of automating *her* people into premature retirement. He kept talking his way out of clinches with anecdotes about the computer hooked up to an amputee's nervous system that activated his artificial arm and the checkers master who programmed a computer and hasn't won a game in three years. And

---

* It was on another ETV program, *Book Beat,* that the same author, A. E. Hotchner, confessed, "There is nothing in [*Papa Hemingway*] that came from a tape recording," a remarkable admission for the man who wrote on page 9 of his book: "Later on I augmented these journals with conversations recorded on pocket tape transistors that we carried when we traveled." For Hotch the bell tolls!

when Kitty counterpunched with a harrowing tale of an arrogant computer that unbalanced her bank account, Diebold blithely assured her, "They're doing away with checks, anyway."

The spectacle of the fiftyish heroine of *A Night at the Opera* trying to reach a fortyish young man who dwells in the future was not only a high point of my ETV week but also a rare specimen of the kind of programming that might make ETV a necessity rather than an echo. Although there is an audience of some 19 million people over sixty-five in this country, commercial TV is entirely geared to the young adult and very young generations with their potent consumer dollars. *Living for the Sixties*, produced by the State University of New York, answered a deeply felt need. Unfortunately it could be felt for only three weeks—the duration of the series. This is the story of too much ETV. Ideas are so cheap and money and manpower so scarce that worthwhile projects tend to die in infancy. *Living for the Sixties* was replaced by *New Jersey Speaks for Itself*.

Immediately after my first night's *Living for the Sixties*, I almost spilled my beer over this startling announcement: "CHANNEL 13 HAS SPONSORS! [*pause*] You, the local audience." Then came a pitch to "become a TV sponsor right now by sending a contribution" to Channel 13. This hard-sell onslaught continued all week, and judging by my conditioned reflexes, I could have been watching commercial channels 2, 4, 5, 7, 9, or 11. A five-minute program lull was filled in by Music to Write Checks By" (the overture to the Broadway show *Half a Sixpence*). Most shockingly for an educational medium, the misleading equation of $1.00 = $1.50 was flashed on the screen several times a night, between programs. An explanation followed. The Ford Foundation would add fifty cents to every dollar I donated, but I was continually distressed by this new math on ETV. Fortunately my children were exposed to it only once or twice before their bedtimes.

After *Living for the Sixties*, the nightly program content varied until 10 P.M., when New York's Channel 13 hooked up with ETV stations in Boston, Philadelphia, and Washington for *Interconnect*, an hour of news and interviews. Interconnection, via telephone wires now and communications satellites later, is the brave new hope of ETV for a "baby network." At present, most topical programs are filmed or taped and then shipped—

a distribution system with its own built-in obsolescence. A program seen in New York tonight may not be seen in Allentown, Pennsylvania, for eight or nine weeks.

Interconnect promised each evening's only breath of fresh news, but it proved as stale as last week's bread. Routine coverage of former Defense Secretary McNamara at a blackboard reassuring the press ("our thanks to ABC, CBS, and NBC for letting us tape their coverage of this") was interspersed with Vietnam newsreels that had been shown a day or more earlier on the networks. A film of a tightrope walker at Monte Carlo was followed by a coy promise to keep me posted "on marathon dancing and flagpole sitting." I felt vaguely futurized when the newscaster predicted "Tomorrow's Weather for Megalopolis" and then definitely chagrined when he failed to mention what today's weather in New York, Philadelphia, Boston, and Washington had been—a matter of utmost interest to any poor soul trapped in Megalopolis during the summer. I went from chagrined to patronized when news of Mr. Frank Sinatra's changing relationship with Miss Mia Farrow was followed thusly: "As good educational TV watchers, you should be above all this. But, if you're interested, Frank Sinatra is a singer and Mia Farrow acts in a TV serial called *Peyton Place,* which is not written by Henrik Ibsen."

The *Interconnect* interviews were standard fare at excruciating length: two Congressmen saying nothing; Dr. Ralph Lapp on flying saucers; four Marine pilots on helicopter warfare; David Astor of the London *Observer* on genocide; the president of the American Jewish Congress on his trip to Hungary; a Boston psychiatrist and a New York civil-liberties lawyer analyzing that week's mass murder, and three more Boston psychiatrists on—so help me!—"integrating the ongoing evaluation of mental health implementation into the mainstream of medicine without undue feedback." The emphasis was on split screens and megalopolitan universality rather than on preparation, thrust, liveliness, or even news. And all of this was "made possible by a public service grant from the Shell Oil Company."

Only two segments of *Interconnect* were worth watching in that week that was. One was a waspish five-minute verbal rape of Miss Elizabeth Taylor ("terrible, rotten, unripe") by a smirking critic named John Simon (of the *New Leader*). Although

Simon was clearly reading a review of *Who's Afraid of Virginia Woolf?* intended for publication elsewhere, his appearance had a certain melodramatic interest. The other highlight was an interview in which an incisive Washington newsman named Douglas Kiker stalked an unctuous West German lobbyist— who came on like S. Z. "Cuddles" Sakall and decomposed rapidly—through the labyrinth of Congressional influence. The program ran fifteen minutes overtime as the lobbyist disavowed his own status as "registered foreign agent" and pleaded, "I would like to be called a political consultant." It was precisely the kind of open-ended confrontation in depth that can scarcely be expected of commercial TV. It should occur more than once a week on ETV.

So much for the week's eleven and a half hours of regular nightly programming. What happened on Channel 13 in the fifteen hours a week between *Living for the Sixties* and *Interconnect?* And in the wee hours or quarter hours after 11 P.M.?

There were three and a half hours of adult education, three hours of which gave me my first peek at what other ETV stations were producing.

From KQED in San Francisco came two half-hour *Folk Guitar* lessons taught by Laura Weber, a pretty girl with a reedy voice and a smoky, intimate way of convincing the male beholder, at least, that he and she could make beautiful music together—if only he had a guitar. She was particularly effective at 11 o'clock at night.

KQED, alas, also furnished a grim half hour of *Koltanowski on Chess.* George Koltanowski, world's blindfold champion, had me checkmated from the outset when he began an illustrative anecdote with: "I have told this story many times with no success, but I am going to tell it anyway."

From WTTW in Chicago came a half-hour Italian-language lesson, *When in Rome,* wherein the instructor used so many archaic, stilted textbook phrases conversationally that he made both Italian and English seem as living as Latin. With a TV camera dwelling on a bedroom, there is no need for the teacher to tell us, first in English and then in Italian: "This is a bedroom." The Italian lesson was several light-years behind daytime ETV's beguiling *Parlons Français,* in which Madame Anne

Slack teaches French with hardly any English at all. She says *"Bonjour,"* points at you, and you say *"Bonjour"* back at her. She shows a film of children chatting in a French schoolyard at recess. Then she reruns the film, sentence by sentence, stopping it to have you practice the dialogue and repeat it, line by line. In fifteen minutes, she has taught you most of the words in that film. Words you already knew are reinforced, and brand-new words are defined by the acting. Then she runs the film at normal speed, and *voilà, vous comprenez!*

Madame Slack started out with ETV in Schenectady, where she taught school. She now originates from WGBH, Boston's ETV Channel 2.

It was syndication from WGBH on Wednesday night that furnished me with the only evening prime-time star ETV has produced: a jolly woman who looked like Margaret Rutherford in a mad scientist's laboratory and who began on a note of hysteria that she sustained for an entire half hour.

"If someone's drowning," she began, brandishing a skillet, "you'd hardly throw him this stainless steel lifesaver. But if someone's dying of hunger [pause to remove top of skillet], you'd throw him this fillet of turban of sole. This is *French Chef,* and I'm Julia Child."

With that, she taught me how to make a mousse. "Be sure that the fish smells good—in other words, not fishy," she admonished, working while she talked. "Too many people don't like fish because they don't select it carefully. If it smells fishy, take it back. Now, by mousse, we don't mean moose with antlers. *Mousse* comes from the *mousseux,* which means foamy."

Before she was done, even though I had just finished my beer and sandwiches, I was so hungry I could have eaten a mousse.

(In ETV circles, Julia Child—who has won an Emmy Award and has been carried on 104 stations as well as the Thanksgiving cover of *Time*—is known somewhat disdainfully as "Our Great Popularizer." Her voice has been described by the New York *Times* as "two parts Broderick Crawford and one part Elizabeth II," but newspapers across the nation carry her recipes the day after they are enacted on local ETV. Butchers and grocers subscribe to their ETV stations' monthly program guides and stock up accordingly when her topics are listed as "Speaking of Tongues" or "Lest We Forget Broccoli." In

Washington, when the local ETV station interrupted her to carry President Johnson live, its switchboard was jammed with complaints for an hour. For she is queen of an affluent society whose middle class can afford TV, Teflon, and truffles.)

From WENH in Durham, New Hampshire, came a somewhat patronizing lecture on "Collecting Furniture" by an antiquarian who used the phrase "of course" twenty-three times in thirty minutes. And from the State University of New York Law School in Buffalo came "In the Law Library," a stodgy, very formal lecture with what the lecturer had the nerve to call "visual aids." In the case of Escobedo versus Illinois, for instance, the visual aid was the words "Escobedo versus Illinois" flashed on the screen. Apparently it hadn't occurred to anyone in the law library to take a trip to a newspaper library, where a photo of Danny Escobedo—whose disallowed confession altered the course of crime and punishment in America—was readily obtainable and might have enlivened the proceedings.

There were three hours of documentaries, all presented under the auspices of National Educational Television.

Actually, there were two and a half hours of material, but a half-hour program called *Local Issue* on Wednesday at 7:30 P.M. was repeated on Friday at 7. ETV generally is very good at giving you more than one chance in a week to catch a "special," although most stations vary the times more sharply than Channel 13 did. Elsewhere, a program that is on at 7 one night may be repeated at 10:30 another night, to oblige the viewer who cannot get to his set at one hour or another.

Unfortunately, of all the documentaries on view that week, *Local Issue*'s was the least deserving of repetition. "The Last Menominee," it was called, and it was about the shutdown of an Indian reservation. A production team had gone all the way to Menominee, Wisconsin, for a series of unaffecting stand-up interviews couched in the bloodless jargon of the Washington bureaucrats who were "terminating" the Menominees while trying to "upgrade" and "acculturate" them.

The same criticisms, to a lesser degree, applied to "The Cities and the Poor," an hour-long part of NET's *America's Crises* series, and "At the Moment of Impact," a thirty-minute post-mortem on a three-year-old *DC-8* crash that killed all 118 passengers aboard.

"At the Moment of Impact" was followed by a far less promising documentary, "The Uprooted," an affectionate tribute by the English journalist James Cameron to America's immigrants, "the flotsam of Europe . . . who built America and, in so doing, became Americans." With nothing more than still photos and player-piano music to bring his subject to life, Cameron delivered a moving, throbbing half hour of Americana that was the highlight of my week. He never strayed from simplicity and directness ("The *young* immigrants grew up Americans. It was the sons who taught the fathers. And the uprooted had set down their roots at last"). His stills were more pictorial and vivid than almost all of the documentary film footage I had witnessed during the week that was.

That week, there was an hour and a half of science, all under the auspices of National Educational Television.

Again there was one repeat, so the ninety minutes were really a stretched sixty. *Science Reporter* was presented from 8:30 to 9 P.M. on Wednesday and repeated at 11:15 P.M. on Thursday. And like "The Last Menominee," it did not bear repetition. It was devoted to "Returning from the Moon" and bringing our Apollo astronauts back alive. The reentry problem, like so many of the subjects tackled and then evaded by NET that week, had its own innate fascination, which was promptly dissipated by tours of two factories, one in Virginia and one in Massachusetts, and stand-up interviews with scientists who *told* what science and industry were doing. The host, billed as "John Fitch, M.I.T. Science Reporter," asked provocative questions, but his guests were not about to give him one lively answer.

The other science half hour was part of a series called *Survival in the Sea: A Study in Marine Ecology.* This particular episode was entitled "Man the Predator." But it was nothing like what it purported to be. It was simply a filmed workday (a particularly uneventful workday, I would suspect) in the work life of two Bahamian fishermen. They sat in a dinghy and demonstrated six basic ways of catching fish in tropical waters. At the end, the host, Dr. John F. Storr, justified the title by proclaiming, "Man the predator must be controlled by man the conservator." But his program might better have been called "The Romance of Fishing" or just "Go Fish!" By any name, however, it was deadly dull.

There were three hours of music—an hour apiece on Monday, Wednesday, and Friday—and there could have been much more. There was no jazz, no opera, no ballet.

What there was, however, was nicely varied. On Monday night, Channel 13 reran its own snappy little seventy-five-minute revival of Harold Rome's 1937 Broadway musical revue, *Pins and Needles*. It was a little more stagy than televisual, but appealing nonethless. Almost in passing, it gave me a moment I never expected to see on black and white television in a million years: boy (white) serenading girl (Negro) with a love song called "In One Big Union for Two."

Channel 13 also produced Wednesday's hour, a concert of American music performed on one piano by Jean and Kenneth Wentworth. Friday's music hour came to me through the courtesy of NET. It was the Minneapolis Symphony, conducted by Stanislaw Skrowaczewski, in a concert of Russian and Polish music. The camera work was particularly imaginative and knowledgeable.

That week on ETV, I also saw two hours ABOUT *the arts.*

One of those two hours was about film, but only twelve minutes of it were used to show film. On Thursday night's *The Art of Film*, after twenty minutes of interesting chitchat about a film that hadn't been released, critic Richard Schickel, the host, showed us an eight-minute excerpt. The next night—same time, same station—NET's *Creative Person* followed a similar format. A half-hour program on director King Vidor's fifty years in moviemaking was divided between a screening room, where critic Arthur Knight interviewed Vidor, and an incredibly dreary tour of Hollywood landmarks. Vidor *shlepped* Knight from supermarket parking lot ("This one used to be the set of Griffith's *Intolerance*") to supermarket parking lot ("This one used to be Vidor Village") to Griffith Park ("Everyone used to be 'on location' here. . . . Remember the saying, 'A rock is a rock. A tree is a tree. Shoot it in Griffith Park'?". When it was over, words almost failed poor Knight. But he did manage to gasp, "Thank you, King, for that marvelous tour!" and rewarded my patience with four minutes of excerpts from Vidor's *Our Daily Bread* and *Solomon and Sheba*. Vidor's 1925 masterpiece, *The Big Parade*, was not represented.

Book Beat at 9:30 P.M. on Friday was entirely talk—with Leonard Mosley, author of a book on Emperor Hirohito. The talk, however, was stimulating. The host, Robert Cromie of the Chicago *Tribune,* is a first-rate interviewer. Unlike many people who read books for a living, Cromie retains a healthy respect for what he reads. His guests are selected for liveliness of personality as well as subject matter, which may explain why *Book Beat,* like Julia Child, has achieved some impact outside ETV. Produced by WTTW in Chicago, it is watched by the book trade everywhere and has some influence on bookstore ordering and perhaps sales.

The comic highlight of the week was unintentional: NET's *U.S.A.: Writers'* half hour on Philip Roth. The novelist was interviewed in his Greenwich Village home by a tricky little critic who asked what Roth meant by assigning the name of Klugman to a character in his novel *Goodbye, Columbus.* The critic, who is not Jewish, explained to Roth, who *is,* that "the word *klugman* has two meanings in Yiddish—a clever fellow and also a mourner, a sad fellow."

This was news to Roth, who replied that he called his man Klugman because he "just wanted a Jewish name that wasn't obvious, like Cohen." Yiddish, Roth added puckishly, was something his parents spoke when they *didn't* want him to understand.

Armed with insights, however, the zealous critic was not to be put off. He compared Roth's background (native of Newark, B.A. from Bucknell, M.A. from Chicago, writer in residence at Princeton, etc.) with Dostoievski's and Gogol's and then asked Roth portentously if he thought Saul Bellow's Herzog was an extension of Roth's Paul Hertz in *Letting Go.* There was, after all, this remarkable similarity in names. . . .

Roth dismissed this idea for what it was worth simply by expressing his admiration for Bellow as an original thinker. His interviewer, undaunted, went on to take a random potshot at Herman Wouk and *his* Jewish protagonist, whom he called "Marjorie Morningsickness."

To add an element of farce to this drawing-room comedy, Roth poured himself a glass of Danish beer at the beginning and didn't offer his interviewer any. (I suppose this was prearranged, rather than the overt snub I'd like to think it was.) For the rest of the half hour, Roth could be glimpsed sipping beer and, with only partial success, squelching a belch.

Despite its high laugh content, this was bad TV from every standpoint, starting with the initial camera work. For the first five minutes of a program ostensibly about Philip Roth, his interviewer sat in the foreground while Roth himself sat in shadow, virtually offscreen. Nevertheless, simply because it showed me Philip Roth as an easygoing young man with grace in the presence of folly, the program held my interest from beginning to end. This gave me some inkling of the massive effort it takes to make the rest of ETV as dull as it is.

Aside from baiting a literary lion, there were two hours of sports on my ETV that week.

The men's singles finals of the New England Amateur Tennis Championships—which had been held four weeks earlier at the Newton, Massachusetts, Squash and Tennis Club—was the final event of my ETV week that was. And I must confess that shortly after the first of its two hours, I fell asleep. Perhaps my inherent interest in a tennis match between two Harvard men named Ned Weld and Chauncey "Chum" Stele was limited. Whatever suspense the match possessed was dissipated by the certainty of the result, which could always be checked in the back sports pages. And something within me rebelled against televising a tennis match at the ungentlemanly hour of 11 P.M. And perhaps I'd just had enough ETV for one week.

In any event, when I awoke at 3 A.M., the screen was mercifully blank.

I have an additional confession to make. I lost two and a quarter hours of TV time on Tuesday night, when I was called away from my set by a trio of Puerto Ricans. They appeared on my doorstep because they heard I had an obsolescing electric drier for sale. It took all of two hours to negotiate in Spanish and English a $25 transaction and for the four of us to remove the drier. As we carried it down two flights of stairs, the youngest and burliest Puerto Rican urged me to "move your ass, Daddy-o" because he was "missing plenty of good TV."

"Where? Where?" I gasped.

He mentioned *Peyton Place* (on ABC) and then, at which

point I damn near dropped my end, a CBS special on Stravinsky. On the street, I asked him if he ever watched ETV, and he said: "I used to when they had Casals.* But I gave up on Channel Thirteen a long time ago."

He left me brooding—not only about the cultural horizons of Puerto Ricans but also about why the hell an ETV station in a city with 730,000 of them didn't beam English lessons at them or Spanish lessons at us. The young Puerto Rican's father and older brother *no hablaban inglés*.

Upstairs, *TV Guide* told me I'd missed two NET offerings —a *U.S.A.: Artists* half hour with Barnett Newman, the painter, and a 100-minute BBC production of *Wuthering Heights*, starring Claire Bloom. I made up *Wuthering Heights* the following Tuesday by watching Miss Bloom in the NET/BBC presentation of *Anna Karenina* (115 minutes).

(*Anna Karenina* also afforded a glimpse into the New York ETV mind's awareness of its times. Vronsky was played by movie star Sean Connery—known to the world, if not to Channel 13, as James Bond. Announcing his appearance in a press release, my hometown ETV harrumphed, "Mr. Connery in the past has been almost exclusively a Shakespearean actor.")

I had already made up my missed *U.S.A.: Artists* program by watching virtually the entire series on previous Tuesdays— from pop artist Jim Dine to sun sculptor Richard Lippold. Most were like *U.S.A.: Writers* on Philip Roth: bang-bang interviews with little craftsmanship and no more than a day's filming behind them, but with the same repellent fascination. "The Sun and Richard Lippold," however, was and still is the best thing I have ever seen on ETV!

It was a work of art in its own right: an attempt to explore the inner life of wire sculpture with the intimacy of a camera. In his studio at Locust Valley, Long Island, Lippold played Bach on an organ. Without a word of narration to distract him, the viewer *experienced* the kinship between Lippold's glistening suns and Bach's mathematical purity. After a brief and otherwise silent tour of Lippold's work, the producer-director (Leo

* Pablo Casals' *Master Class* was a series featuring the cellist and his pupils. Although the instruction was highly specialized, it had a wide ETV audience— not just musicians, but laymen yearning to sit at the feet of genius. A guitar series with Andrés Segovia has achieved comparable results on ETV.

Hurwitz) stated his intention of exploring "our common sharing of the power of the sun as it lives inside all of us who spend some time on this planet earth." With no further fanfare, the cameraman (Manfred Kirchheimer) went directly to Lippold's source of inspiration to illuminate his work. The film became a photographic hymn to the sun: a celluloid mosaic of light and shadow fighting for an underpass, a bee embracing a flower, grapes ripening on a vine, a spider weaving its web, a boy toying with a mirror, a sandpiper skittering along the seashore, light diffused by raindrops, puddles, Venetian blinds, and the Brooklyn Bridge before ultimately giving way to moonlight and the lamps of night. The film ended with another simple statement, almost a cliché: "The mind of the artist is an iceberg of memory [which] holds a lifetime of submerged experience." In New York, one is frequently confronted by Lippolds: in Lincoln Center, the Metropolitan Museum of Art, the Pan Am Building lobby. Once you have seen that film, it is impossible to pass one by.

It occurred to me, too, whenever I recalled "The Sun and Richard Lippold," that *virtually everything else I had seen on ETV in what is called the "cultural affairs" category had been peripheral. It had all been* ABOUT *art, rather than artistic in itself, after-the-fact rather than factually enlightening, aural rather than visual, amiably distracted when it could have been sustained or even slashing.*

[III]

On the basis of watching ETV in New York City casually over a four-year span and intensively over that thirty-hour week, one could have felt qualified to deliver a few further generalizations on the state of the medium.

It lacked excitement, timeliness, humanity and, worst of all, elementary showmanship. And behind this bland facade, one could perceive a contempt for all of these essentials, plus a willingness to forgive its own blunders because its intentions were so honorable.

It possessed an unmessianic emphasis on reaching the already

reached, rather than the passion needed to woo the uninitiated.
One could perceive no willingness at prime-time hours to approach the blue-collar worker or the Puerto Rican who had missed out on what we call a formal education, who seldom went to theaters or museums or concert halls, who had been untouched even by the cultural explosion, but who was still willing to experiment with twirling the dial past commercial Channel 11. ETV, which is constantly surveying itself with narcissistic pride, insults these people even as it files and forgets them under the remarkable label of "blue-collar deviants." Furthermore, as leisure time increases, it is likely that ETV's future will be in the hands of the blue-collar deviants and not the cultural elite to whom it now panders. The so-called "Mr. and Mrs. Culture," of whom we hear a lot at fund-raising cocktail parties, are often right there at the parties, talking about themselves. They can afford to attend concerts, and they do attend concerts—mostly or partly to hear the music but also to be among people like themselves. The Boston Symphony on ETV is not going to keep them home from the local symphony or cultural center. They are precisely the people whose attitude toward any TV is that they can take it or leave it—and they are more likely to leave it. Thus ETV's courtship of them is essentially self-defeating.

What was on view in New York City (and what you will see in many large cities, including Miami) was a five-day-a-week medium that shuts down on weekends—just when the mind at leisure craves stimulation. Much of this, I learned later, stems from the educator's addiction to a short working day, a five-day week, and a long summer vacation. This may be tradition, but it's not television.

It was totally enmeshed in the unimaginative and arbitrary trappings of commercial television. True, there were no paid advertisements. But the programming reflexes were strictly commercial. Where an NBC affiliate would have inserted two or three ads into a station break, my ETV channel plugged it with misleading $1 = $1.50 hard-sell pitches. All but one or two programs were packaged into the fifteen, thirty, and sixty minutes that a network sponsor buys. Why should educational television salivate like commercial television? If *Koltanowski on*

Chess would make an enlightening seven minutes, why shouldn't it be compressed to seven minutes instead of strung out (by bad jokes and repetition) to thirty? If the documentary on the air crash required thirty-seven minutes to make its point, why did it have to run thirty with its mystery being unraveled by an off-screen voice? Perhaps none of us could ever master the habit of tuning in from 8:11 to 8:38 for *Book Beat* one week and from 8:05 to 8:55 the next, but why couldn't it start at 8 o'clock both times and be followed by a short film or a musical number or a preview of coming attractions on ETV or a commentary on current events by some cerebral humorist like Paul Krassner of the *Realist* until *French Chef* came on at 9? Merely by taking advantage of the freedom it was born with, ETV could flex a hitherto unused muscle—surprise!

Arthur Miller once remarked that he had refused his plays to television for a long time because TV tends to digest, rather than adapt. "If you cut *A Doll's House* in half, as television has done, what you get is a *Reader's Digest* version of *A Doll's House. . . .* I can see where some plays should be no more than forty minutes and not padded to an hour. On the other hand, some ought to be an hour and twenty minutes. It will be a great day when television can let that clock rest." When that day came for Miller, with lengthy adaptations of his *Death of a Salesman* and *The Crucible,* it was on commercial TV, not ETV. Similarly, when the why-didn't-someone-think-of-it-before innovation for Christmas Eve finally happened in New York—three hours of nothing but a picture of a Yule log burning to the accompaniment of recorded carols, no commercials—it happened not on ETV (which was dark that night) but on the *Daily News'* hard-sell WPIX. In September, 1967, it was hard-boiled ABC, not ETV (which was dark that night), that devoted four hours one Sunday evening to a comprehensive program on Africa that was well worth the time (and 2 million dollars). Segments that were worth four minutes were given four minutes; segments worth forty minutes got the full forty. Later, this massive documentary was rebroadcast in smaller chunks on weekday mornings for classroom use.

What one didn't see were, just to begin with, an iota of good children's programming; satire or more than a flicker (Osborn's

On Leisure) *of wit; foreign movies and American art films, which could be the answer to commercial TV's numbing procession of bowdlerized, fragmented Hollywood hand-downs; any insight into current events; any athletic events of reasonable promise at a reasonable hour; any business or consumer education; any ballet, opera, music, or drama that was created FOR the ETV medium.* Nothing, but nothing, was originated, for ETV in a city that is one of the world's talent centers has yet to acquire that much basic self-respect. And the transplants from the concert and musical stages were less—quantitatively and qualitatively—than one could have found on commercial TV that week.

Furthermore, all that was sampled in five evenings had less meaningful content and entertainment value than a typical morning and afternoon of school programming on Channel 13. In one nine-to-five day of instructional television, one could witness (along with other programs not worthy of mention): a British documentary on Antarctica; a Negro barber demonstrating the arts of shaving and haircutting; *Parlons Français*; three elementary, but exciting, science programs; *Children of Other Lands;* a folk-sing-along show; a tour of American historical shrines; Clifton Fadiman lecturing on Dickens with illustrative scenes enacted on Encyclopaedia Britannica Films; *Sounds to Say; Letters to Learn,* a delightful quarter hour on the letter P, illustrated by a menu of pork, potatoes, peas, pepper, and pudding (but no pumpkin pie!), a toy circus with a polar bear, pelican, peacock, panda, pony, puppy (named Pepe) and parakeet (named Patrick) and concluded with a homework assignment to "cut out things beginning with the letter P and bring them in to your teacher," and a literary program on *Puritan versus Cavalier* that had Sir Ralph Richardson reading John Donne in the study of his own home, Chaucer's Wife of Bath recounting her five husbands, Paul Rogers strolling the country with Raymond Massey's daughter Anna and reciting Marlowe's "Come live with me and be my love" to her, and an excerpt from *Pride and Prejudice* that almost tempted me to give Jane Austen another try.

Thus, if Channel 13 were to be declared the disaster area it is, the first emergency measure might be to make day into night and show its instructional programming at prime-time hours.

[IV]

Most of these generalizations will be disputed by readers in Boston and San Francisco, who are blessed with ETV stations that have achieved strong local identities. One good measure of an ETV station's impact is how the natives refer to it. If they call it by an impersonal channel number, it could be just another network affiliate or a way station on the dial. If they call it by its call letters, then perhaps it has achieved some of the strong local flavor and personality of its own that radio's KDKA and WHN and WHDH used to have and that ETV *should* have.

In New York, Channel 13 is known as Channel 13.

In Boston, Channel 2 is known as WGBH.

In San Francisco, Channel 9 is known as KQED.

A more inflammatory test came on a Saturday night in 1961, when WGBH's studio burned down. In Monday morning's mail, there was $50,000 in gifts to its rebuilding fund. School-children went from door to door, collecting more, and when the campaign was over, some 50,000 Bostonians had contributed well over $1,000,000.

Now ask yourself if, in the event of fire, anything comparable to this response could be achieved by *your* ETV station— or if many people would even know that it was missing.

WGBH doesn't merely solicit the attention of a small army of local viewers; it generates their love. Boston cannot live without WGBH precisely because WGBH has injected itself into Boston's cultural life stream. It took the Boston Symphony, a dowager's delight, and made its televised concerts a suburban ritual. It took Louis Lyons, the Nieman Foundation's outspoken curator, who had been sounding off at Harvard for years, and made him into a local pundit without blunting his wisdom. And it made a very civilized knock-down, drag-out program called *Eliot Norton Reviews* into an event that should no more be missed while in Boston than a meal at Durgin-Park or Locke-Ober's.

Norton, the dean of Boston's dwindling faculty of newspaper

critics, does far more than mouth his printed review on ETV. His guests are the people he is criticizing: a director, an author, or an actor involved in a current play. Since most plays in Boston are undergoing pre-Broadway tryout agonies, the tension is high even as the guests enter the studio.

The Odd Couple, a sparkling comedy about two divorced men living together in a bachelor apartment, had just opened in Boston. The next night, Norton's guests were Neil Simon, the playwright, Mike Nichols, the director, and Art Carney and Walter Matthau, the costars. Norton reiterated the complaint he'd made in his otherwise favorable notice: Didn't the third act "run down"?

Nonsense, said Nichols, who went on rhetorically. "How does *Private Lives* end? How do *Lysistrata* and *The Importance of Being Earnest* end? I don't remember how most classic comedies end. This is a built-in problem of comedy. You paint people into a predicament, and then you have to get them out and wrap it up as neatly as possible."

"I'm not complaining about your resolution," Norton shot back. "I'm just looking for one more big scene before it happens."

Neil Simon, who is the most successful and just possibly the most skillful American playwright practicing today, was more inquisitive than argumentative. He wanted to know exactly *what* Norton missed in the third act. Norton protested that he wasn't a playwright. But after some interrogation, he admitted: "I was thinking about those two English sisters who have a wonderful scene with Mr. Matthau and Mr. Carney in the second act. When the third-act curtain went up, I felt badly about those two girls not being around anymore."

While the others rose to the playwright's defense, Neil Simon himself could be seen meditating onscreen. I later learned that for forty-eight hours after leaving Norton's studio, Simon secluded himself in his room at the Ritz-Carlton and wrote a whole new scene bringing back the two sisters.

Thus had ETV in Boston done something in thirty minutes that it hadn't done in my thirty hours of it in New York. *By serving as perceptive observer of the world around it, it had changed that world*—and, most rewardingly in this instance, it had improved the level of laughter. In the process, the viewer had seen something vital and educational: the creative mind at work. This was something I *hadn't* seen on NET's *Creative Person* or *U.S.A.: Writers.*

At the other end of the continent, KQED in San Francisco has this kind of excitement going for it, whether it features the rambling philosophy of Eric Hoffer or a stripper named Tempest Storm, purring, "What I like about KQED is, it's so-o-oh educational" or a homegrown debate between Dr. Edward Teller and Dr. Linus Pauling on the perils of nuclear testing or a dealer in voodoo equipment citing the uses of bat's blood.

KQED takes what it can get from the Ford Foundation, but it also reaches out to its audience with an annual auction that lasts as long as six days and brings in as much as a fifth of KQED's annual budget. Guest auctioneers have included such prominent local citizens as Bishop James A. Pike and Shirley Temple Black. The *objets d'art* that have been donated for auctioning range from a thirty-day East African safari for two (valued at $4,800) to elephants, ashcans, a fully equipped kitchen (which went for $1,400), a week's service by a private detective (which, interestingly enough, went begging), girls' ties made from bed sheets slept in by one of the Beatles, and lavender bed sheets slept in by Kim Novak, "guaranteed unlaundered." *

"We think of KQED as a library," Channel 9's program director told a *Look* interviewer, "with each program representing one book. You take out the book that interests you. We have a great variety of books, including children's programs, public affairs, art, music, great thinkers, and adult education— everything from speed reading through skin diving to how to watch a football game. If each member of our potential audience watches only one program a week, we will have fulfilled our purpose."

The syndication of KQED's excellent series *Japanese Brush Painting,* for which it sells the necessary supplies, has made ETV the largest importer of Japanese brushes anywhere in the

---

* The auction has become THE fund-raising gimmick of ETV. In one city, when I asked, "What are your ETV station's outstanding programs?" the only local show mentioned was the auction. In New York, Channel 13's 1966 auction was as sedate and pretentious as the station itself. It was presented as an illustrated lecture on art auctioning direct from the Parke-Bernet Galleries.

world. Similar results have been achieved with music books to accompany KQED's *Folk Guitar* lessons.

[v]

In between these two coastal successes, there lies a vast waste-land of ETV (with exceptions in Denver, Pittsburgh, and Hershey, Pennsylvania), in which the thirty-hour week I witnessed on Channel 13 ranks as slightly better than average. Other viewers have characterized ETV as "a threadbare professor with terminal logorrhea droning on and on" and as a medium of "moderators with nothing to say," where "amateur raconteurs blink, gulp, betray noticeable tremors in voices, guides get tangled in their own wires, credits dissolve illegibly into the background, stagehands in checked shirts intrude, and sometimes the picture vanishes altogether." Perhaps the two most despairing comments I've heard about ETV are, "It's almost as boring as commercial television" and an innocent reference to "back in the golden age of educational television," which turned out to mean CBS's Sunday morning programming of the early 1950's.

ETV started out with every opportunity to be an art form and no right to be dull. Its Muzak-like sterility is hardly the *only* alternative to commercial television's opiated brainwash. Then why has it lacked, from the very beginning, so much newness and excitement?

This is only slightly the fault of the individual station managers, many of whom are the truest and most dedicated missionaries in all of today's cultural revival meeting. In the history of any ETV station, it was usually a dynamic station manager brought in from out of town who took it off the drawing board and put it on the air. Harried and overworked from that moment on, he could no more be held responsible for the quality of local ETV than a classroom teacher can be blamed for his textbooks and school system. Even the most energetic ETV station manager tends to obsolesce in his thirties, to think small, or to be reduced to chanting, "We just don't have the money."

One of them told me: "We used to give college-credit courses. But then we became more school-oriented because this was where the money was. And the colleges either lost interest or dropped by the wayside."

Another said: "The schools pay for their programming, and the Bar Association underwrites our Law Day coverage. But suppose we want to do a program on juvenile delinquency; who's going to pay for that, the juvenile delinquents? . . . We operate on a sound fiscal basis, but I don't feel like an ETV person when someone comes to me with a good idea—like an important regional horse show or a community meeting—that I'd like to do, but I have to say, 'Can you finance it?' . . . In the same situation, I know that commercial TV gives people runarounds. My approach is more honest, but it makes me act more like an M-G-M mogul than an ETV manager."

It is only slightly the fault of the authorities who have consigned much of ETV to the ultra-high-frequency limbos of channels 17, 24, 39, etc., for which, until recently, the average TV set was not equipped and which still requires suitable terrain and a special antenna for good reception. In one city whose ETV was behind a UHF curtain, when the station scheduled a nationally syndicated program on TV repair rackets, the head of the biggest local repair firm asked for a private screening in advance. The station obliged by showing him the text of the script, whereupon he demanded that it be canceled. The station refused. The man then said that his repairmen would no longer convert customers' sets to UHF. Finally the program was aired intact—but it was followed by a special appearance by the ETV station manager on screen to explain that none of the events depicted could possibly happen within his station's broadcast territory.

It is only slightly the fault of poverty, for with foundations and all kinds of government backing, ETV is not as poor as it looks. As Joseph Morgenstern of *Newsweek,* himself an alumnus of ETV, has pointed out, "Many budgets for individual [National Educational Television] shows are as high as they might be on commercial television. Poverty cannot excuse NET's negligence of children's programs—only fifteen of the two hundred sixty hours of new programs it produces yearly. Poverty cannot excuse the absence of truly unpopular, unsafe, or unexpected views in ETV's staple programming. Poverty cannot, but fear can. Local station managers are afraid of the wealth and influence represented by their local boards of directors. The members of these boards are afraid of pressure groups within their communities. . . ."

In October and November of 1966, the Carnegie Commission on Educational Television put me on its payroll as a $100-a-day consultant to investigate the problems of eight ETV stations in Florida, Pennsylvania, and upstate New York. Everywhere I went, I kept encountering virtually interchangeable Establishments of tired local aristocrats who sat on all the right boards, including ETV, with limited time for each. Less than a handful of them possessed the integrity or vitality of WGBH's Ralph Lowell. Some of them were still smarting with surprise, even annoyance, that their stations actually got on the air. In interviews with several trustees, I was appalled to hear them refer to ETV as a "philanthropy" or "charity." They clearly had no more hope for its future than they would for a pensioned retainer whom they felt obliged to keep small but respectable for the rest of his declining years. And they saw no more need to equip a station with its own mobile unit than to outfit their butler with his own station wagon.

One upstate political boss put it bluntly in discussing his hometown station's board of trustees.

"It's made up of people from the same segment of society that supports commercial television. Their ideas are already molded and not very progressive so far as educational television is concerned.

"Besides, any board of businessmen and educators is inhibited by the community interests to which they all have to appeal. Take the president of a small liberal arts college that's trying to exist here. He goes to the steel companies and doesn't want to get into trouble with anybody. The same is true of the lawyer who is chairman of the station's board and has to do business with the same people. It doesn't have to do with actual pressure being applied; it has to do with tiptoeing around to avoid pressure. The whole training of these trustees has been to conform to such interests. How much do you think they'll ever deviate from their norms?

"And any time you try to change things, you'll run into opposition. ETV *must* change things or else it's self-defeating. To begin with, I'd like to see some associate professors and guidance counselors on the board. . . . Educational TV, to me, is a full-time venture. Science has been magnificent to us on this achievement, and it's being thrown away."

The job of ETV in his city struck me as particularly urgent because on my first day there, I perceived that this was a blue-collar, branch-office town. Many decisions made elsewhere reached into the homes, pocketbooks, and destinies of local workers. With two of the three commercial TV stations absentee-owned and the third plugged into CBS virtually full-time, it seemed to me that ETV's local mission was clearly defined: *to explain and relate these remote ideas, concepts, and events to the somewhat powerless native.* The political boss agreed with me. The station manager agreed with me. Not one of the trustees I interviewed agreed with me!

From station to station, I kept running into similar patterns of community pressure and capitulation.

In a city where the three commercial channels showed a profit of $6 million in 1965, one of them is owned by the leading newspaper (the *only* evening paper). The paper, which is the one that viewers consult in their homes at night, has kept the local ETV station a well-guarded secret. Its programs are listed, but not with the hour-by-hour listings of the three commercial channels. The best official explanation for this segregation is the self-perpetuating one, "The station doesn't have the audience." But when the ETV station printed in its program brochure the slogan "NON-PROFIT, NO COMMERCIALS," an official of the newspaper phoned the ETV station's vice-chairman to protest that this was "hitting below the belt." The offending line was deleted.

In another city, a similar slogan flashed on ETV—"LOOK, MA, NO COMMERCIALS!"—occasioned a similar protest from the publishing empire that owns both newspapers and one commercial TV channel there. Since the head of the publisher's broadcasting division was also a trustee of the ETV station, the manager decided, "The better part of valor was to withdraw it for a while."

Elsewhere, a local ETV station was offered (by WGBH in Boston) a chance to tie in on its coverage of the U.S. Lawn Tennis Association tournament from the Longwood Cricket Club in Chestnut Hill, Massachusetts. The station decided, because of limited local interest and educational value, to televise only the finals—not the semifinals, quarterfinals, or eliminations. This was, after all, a factory city with a heavy blue-collar population. A woman member of the station's board of trustees, who was active in local tennis, called to protest this decision. When she received no satisfaction, her husband called three times to complain. At the next board meeting, the program and station managers suddenly were saddled with a special committee of trustees who would work closely with them on future programming well in advance. The station manager noted that the committee "sounded just a little more restrictive than helpful." The program manager noted that the tennis lady "jumped up right away and said she'd like to be on the committee."

A newspaper editor running for Congress resigned his job because of the conflict in public interests. But he kept his post on an ETV station's board of trustees. The station, as a matter of policy, had offered free air time for a debate by all three candidates, Democratic, Republican, and Conservative. The board member accepted immediately. His two opponents, understandably fearing an ambush on what they considered *his* station, declined because of "schedule conflicts." The ETV program manager was then pressured—by his board member's campaign headquarters and particularly by another board member working there—to write a letter certifying that the two opponents had refused to debate.

School board and university stations—for whom various elected, appointed, and academic authorities serve as the equivalent of trustees—are scarcely immune to what ails their community-licensed counterparts.

In 1965 in a major American city, the capable night manager of the school board station was summoned to the associate superintendent's office on an afternoon when the superintendent was out of town. There he was informed that because he was "incompetent, uncooperative, unimaginative" and didn't "get along with people," he was being relieved of his duties. After contacting his lawyer, he returned to his desk—only to find that it and his file cabinets were being removed by custodians and that his secretary had already been taken away from him. When the superintendent of schools returned, he reinstated the manager and *chided* the plotters who had fired him Saigon-style.

The most weak-kneed of all the stations I visited was the ETV outlet of a major university, whose president behaved like a sponsor. "One night I watched our station for one whole evening," the president told me. "I liked some of what I saw, but I blew my top at my director of broadcasting. I said: 'Who the hell does the viewer think is paying the bill? Damn it, I want people to know this station belongs to the university!' " What bothered *me* even more was that this station practiced an absurd policy of voluntary self-censorship. Syndicated programs received from such sources as NET or Encyclopaedia Britannica Films are occasionally submitted for prescreening to the "appropriate" university department, which then gives an opinion that is usually honored. A marriage-counseling program involving some profanity was deleted after consultation with the *political science department!* A series on child development wasn't satisfactory to the *home economics department,* and so the station didn't carry it.

A school board ETV station that receives State of Florida funds—as all of Florida's do—is subject to a 1957 statute entitled "246.13. Promotion of Political and Governmental Activities Prohibited." One Florida manager told me that when his station received a documentary (from NET in New York) showing Vice-President Hubert Humphrey campaigning in Minnesota for another candidate, "the opinion of our attorney was that we couldn't put this on, and so we didn't." Even commercial stations in Florida aren't always *that* subservient to legal caution.

Sometimes there is disturbing interplay between town and gown in ETV.

The president of a community-licensed station's board of trustees was running for the state legislature. His station's management was rooting ardently for him because, if elected, he would have to resign from the station. For this station president was also a vice-president of the city's big university, which had originally hoped to run the station. Failing in this, he sought, to quote the station manager, to "sabotage" the station whose presidency he had been awarded. Wearing his academic hat, he decreed that any involvement of university people with the mass media (including ETV) had to be approved by his office. "In other words," said the station manager, "when I want somebody from the university to appear on one of our programs, both he and I have to clear it with the president of our station!" The station manager, alleging other sabotage on the president's part, said he thought he knew why. "He's a fund raiser. We're going to exactly the same people he's going to on the university's behalf. He'd like to see us getting all our money from the government. When it comes to foundations, business, and industry, he's been downright uncooperative."

Outside of my Carnegie Commission beat, there are numerous examples of pressure on ETV. In 1963, when the station operated by the University of Georgia showed a Gina Lollobrigida film, the Georgia [commercial] Broadcasters Association protested unfair competition. "You are not educating, you are entertaining and amusing." In at least two Southern cities, ETV programs are prescreened by a citizens' committee hunting for objectionable outside material—particularly from Up Nawth.

When it came to censorship, however, I need never have left home. For sheer timidity, Channel 13 wins the coveted Casper Award (named after Casper Milquetoast) hands down. In the course of one year—1966—Channel 13:

. . . canceled a one-act play—*Neighbors,* by Arkady Leokum —dealing with a suburban white couple trying to sell their home to Negroes. The station president "explained" first that he had wanted "to seek reactions of persons highly experienced in matters of race relations" and then that he was worried about the play's possible effect. As TV critic Jack Gould pointed out in the New York *Times:* "A viable theatre does not flourish in the inhibiting environment of decision by committee, as commercial TV nightly attests. Moreover, Mr. Leokum is not to be confused with a propagandist for the Voice of America."

. . . cast aside a planned TV performance of *The Blood Knot,* a play by a controversial South African writer named Atholl Fugard.

. . . vetoed its program director's plans for televising a program about a clinic designed to help smokers break the habit.

. . . canceled a showing of a folk-rock musical, *The Golden Screw,* after taping it because its language was deemed in questionable taste for home viewing. The show had originated in a church.

After the last misadventure, the programming vice-president

was asked if he considered his position untenable. He replied: "Not at all! I feel it is the duty of the program director of a noncommercial station to keep pushing the margins a little further out." Three weeks later, he was dismissed by the station president.

The ousted program director, however, had the last word.

"The danger confronting educational television is that the medium will not realize its own potential and will settle for half measures. It should be bold and dynamic, perhaps even a little dangerous, if it is to be effective in the community and give a platform on which different ideas can be voiced."

It may well be, however, that ETV already *is* the puppet of a particularly gray Establishment—one that has been aptly described as a "coldbed of dilettantism." One trustee actually praised his station because "you can see that the handling isn't professional, which is sort of quaint, sort of nice, sort of European." Aside from an occasional go-getting businessman or sometimes an entire board, the liveliest ETV trustees are commercial broadcasters. They sit on ETV boards because their stations supplied local ETV with the secondhand broadcast equipment that put it on the air. Some of them did so in the hope that ETV would relieve the neuralgia and neuritis of justifying their licenses to the FCC with public-service programming. Whatever their motives, they sit as watchdogs, snarling at any attempt by ETV to brighten its picture or simply tell the world that it has no commercials. Their vested interest is to keep ETV the dull gray electronic blackboard it too often is.

[VI]

Much of what I've uncovered here points to ETV as a national scandal that is unfolding before our very eyes. Why doesn't somebody investigate it?

Somebody did—the Carnegie Commission on Educational Television, for which I worked as an investigator—and the Establishment can rest assured that no outrage over its abuses will ever be heard from *that* source. For the Carnegie Commission was truly a blue-ribbon jury of Establishment peers: five past or present college presidents (Killian of M.I.T., Conant of Harvard, Lee DuBridge of the California Institute of Technology,

David Henry of the University of Illinois, and Franklin Patter-
son of Hampshire College); at least five with commercial-broad-
casting connections (John Hayes of the Washington *Post* and
Newsweek stations, J. C. Kellam of the Texas Broadcasting
Corporation, which operates the TV interests of President John-
son's family, Oveta Culp Hobby of the Houston *Post* and
KPRC-TV, Joseph McConnell, former president of NBC, and
Robert Saudek of *Omnibus,* the Ford Foundation, and Lincoln
Center); former Governor Terry Sanford of North Carolina;
Edwin Land of Polaroid; Leonard Woodcock of the United
Automobile Workers (more respectable to the Establishment
than the Teamsters or Steelworkers); Rudolf Serkin, concert
pianist; and Ralph *(Invisible Man)* Ellison, perhaps the first
Negro writer since Booker T. Washington to achieve Establish-
ment stature.

The Carnegie Commission's fifteen-month job was to report
back to President Johnson in early 1967 with "an extensive
study of non-commercial television [and] recommend lines along
which non-commercial stations might more usefully develop
during the years ahead, taking into account technical, organi-
zational, financial, and programming considerations."

In the course of Carnegie's investigation, ninety-two ETV
stations were visited by various hired writers, including me.
We were paid $100 per day in each city as well as for each day
at the typewriter back home, plus travel and all first-class expenses. Novelist Mark Harris went to Sacramento and Redding,
California; Pullman, Washington; Moscow, Idaho; and Tempe,
Arizona. George Condon of the Cleveland *Plain Dealer* went to
see the Louisville Free Public Library's ETV station. A San
Franciscan named Leo Litwak took care of Utah. Gregory
Harney, on leave from WGBH in Boston to supervise these
station surveys, looked into South Carolina's ETV network and
National Educational Television, among others. And when
novelist Seymour Epstein (author of *Leah*) wisely defected to
Princeton, Greg Harney engaged me, sight unseen, to take over
the East Coast beat. Levy replaced Epstein on Yom Kippur,
1966.

My first inkling that something was wrong came when Harney
outlined the method of each station survey. My contact in each
city would be the local ETV station manager. Harney would

call him first because "I know some of these guys, and they would be offended if I didn't." The station manager would arrange my hotel reservations, itinerary, interviews, and interviewees.

It struck me that this was like having a prime suspect working as appointments secretary for the detective on the case. But Harney assured me that the station managers were "level guys" (which they were), and if there was anybody they didn't want me to see whom I wanted to see, I should feel free to make my own additional arrangements (which I did). Still, I was a little worried. . . .

In two months, I logged more than 4,000 miles (mostly by plane, but also by bus, train, rented car, and helicopter) and filed almost 300 pages of reports containing the good and the bad that I unearthed in my assigned territory. A few weeks after delivering a report, I would get it back—unedited but handsomely retyped, mimeographed, and bound in an impressive blue-gray cardboard Carnegie cover labeled "Confidential/Not for Publication." When my final report came back to me, a covering letter from Harney admonished me:

> I'm sure you're aware of this, but let me repeat it nonetheless since it has come up here lately. The interviewees have been granted anonymity; therefore, these copies of your reports should under no circumstances leave your possession. That's one of those silly things I feel compelled to say for you are an adult, intelligent, human being that [sic!] does not need to hear those words, but nevertheless they have been said.

I am also a journalist, and the rule of thumb I learned at Columbia Journalism and on the Louisville *Courier-Journal* is that nothing is off the record unless the reporter is apprised of this *beforehand*. This gives him a chance to say, as I often have, "Then I prefer not to hear it off the record. I'll leave now and find out for myself what you would have told me."

At no prior time had I been advised that my interviewees were promised anonymity. In fact, one or two of my interviewees had asked me: "When am I going to see my name in print?" I didn't reply to Harney's letter, partly because no reply was requested and partly because I don't respect ex post facto ethics.

My own ethic, I decided, would be 1) not to publish anything on ETV until the Carnegie Report was published, at which time I expected some of my own findings to be in the public record, and 2) to strive valiantly to protect the identities of my Carnegie interviewees—which I have done, although somebody *inside* ETV might be able to figure out which stations I have been describing.

This was at Christmastime, 1966. A few weeks earlier, just before Thanksgiving, I had flown to Boston to deliver my final manuscript to my Carnegie benefactors, whom I'd never met. At their headquarters on New Street in Cambridge, Harney introduced me to several of the staff people. He took me to an expense-account lunch at a Harvard Square inn called Yard o' Ale. Over red meat and vodka, he told me how much the staff members and commissioners liked my reports. I blushed but left lunch vaguely disturbed by two other pieces of news Harney had dropped. The first was that several of the staff members were dissatisfied with how soft the Carnegie Report was on commercial television. But, Harney added, this wasn't too surprising in view of who some of the commissioners were and the Lyndon Johnson family's television holdings. The other was that although the commission would be meeting in Cambridge the following week, its final report had been drafted and redrafted the preceding summer.

"Then what will this survey of mine and all the others I made contribute?" I had asked, quite distraught.

Harney assured me that a distillation from all seventy station surveys—quotes and excerpts running a total of about twenty-four typewritten pages—would appear as an Appendix to the Carnegie Report. In fact, he even offered me the job of doing the distilling, which I declined. Later, he told me that he and another staff member were doing it.

On the first working day in 1967, I received an urgent long-distance call from Harney. He asked if I could "take on two days of work for us that I think you'll like doing and won't involve your leaving your typewriter." It seemed that his compilation of quotes for the Appendix had, as might have been expected of something disembodied, very little life in them. Dr. Killian of M.I.T., the commission chairman, had vetoed it but suggested that since I worked fast and my findings had interested the commissioners, I should prepare a 3,000- or 4,000-word essay on the highlights of my own findings. This would be the Appendix to the Carnegie Report, and it would save Greg Harney's and Mark Harris' and Leo Litwak's and a lot of other people's labors, including my own, from going down the drain. I would be given a pay increase to $250 a day.

I consented—not only for these reasons but because there is nobody I enjoy rewriting more than myself. Harney's only admonitions were to "accentuate the positive because Killian doesn't like negative thinking" but to "be sure to include the lady cab driver and the station-in-the-bathroom episodes."

(The lady cabbie was one who, while delivering me to a studio, liked my voice and asked if I was going to have my own show on Channel 39. I told her no, and she in turn told me the tale of her conversion. "I watched this here *French Chef* at a friend's house, and she was making a soufflé. The moment she spilled some cheese down the side of the stove, I knew she was for me. All the other cooks on TV make me feel like a slob, but I'm a good cook, and sometimes the spilling's the best part. The repairmen have a racket around here, so it costs fifty or a hundred bucks to convert to UHF. No *French Chef*'s worth that, but the more I thought about it, the more converting made sense to me. With five kids in a family and both parents working, you're bound to let TV do a lot of baby-sitting for you. Well, you might as well let them learn some Spanish while they're watching. . . . You might say that our set's now permanently tuned to Channel Thirty-nine.")

("Station in the bathroom" was Carnegie Commission shorthand for an ETV poverty pocket in the basement of an ancient elementary school. Here the studio used to be a gym, its production office a dressing room, its photo darkroom a shower stall. Its master control room was and still is a boys' room; ten toilets and six urinals are in operation, but most of the sinks have been removed to make way for ETV. The station's mobile unit, parked outside, is painted an attention-getting school-bus yellow. It is as picturesque as all get-out! Most slums are picturesque if you don't have to live or work in them.)

I took the Appendix assignment on late Tuesday afternoon, January 3. My deadline was Friday morning, when Harney himself would catch the air shuttle from Boston to New York, fetch

the manuscript and have lunch at my house, and then shuttle
back to Boston.

My Appendix was ready for submission at 11:10 A.M. Friday.
At 11:15, Harney called and said he had come to New York the
night before and was stuck in a meeting. Would I mind coming
uptown at 12:30 and having lunch as *his* guest at an expense-
account restaurant on Third Avenue? That way, I could turn
over my Appendix to him, and he could catch the 2:30 shuttle
from LaGuardia Airport.

I shaved, donned a tie, and hurried uptown. At 12:40, after
fifteen minutes at the bar, I was joined by Harney and two
other men. Both of the newcomers were "public relations counsel"—New York publicity men handling the Carnegie account
and the impending problem of how to present it to the press
and the public.

Over a particularly coarse lunch of eggplant parmigiana and
a side order of spaghetti, I sat silently while Harney and the
two P.R. men concluded their discussion. As they talked about
"successive press conferences for the media" and how the commissioners on hand would have equal prominence on the platform while Killian outlined their recommendations, it sounded
like the most determinedly antivisual presentation ever envisioned for a report on television.* But what did I know?

Of the two P.R. men, one happened to have the same name
as a former Chicago Cubs relief pitcher but was otherwise undistinguished. The other was a pipe-smoking ex-newsman (for
the Washington *Post*) who dropped all the right Establishment
names and also let it be known that he had recently declined
the post of Assistant Secretary of Defense for Public Affairs, the
Pentagon's chief spokesman to the press, simply because, as he
put it to me, "If poor [Defense Secretary] McNamara could get
stuck in Bundy's war, what chance would I have?" (Former
White House adviser McGeorge Bundy, now president of the
Ford Foundation, is devoting his considerable talent and energy
to ETV instead of Vietnam.)

When his business with Harney was transacted, this P.R. man
—who kept identifying himself as a veteran liberal and whom I
identified as a Toy New Dealer—turned his attention to me.

---

* P.S.—it was.

He asked what I did, and Harney told him quite glowingly. In fact, Harney, who had been glancing at my Appendix, read the four of us my description of the station in the bathroom.

"Hmmmm," said the Toy New Dealer. "Do you write for business?"

"For business?" I said uncomprehendingly.

"Speeches for corporate executives to deliver," he explained.

My shudder was answer enough. When we parted, the Toy New Dealer gave me his calling card, which he informed me was "printed by Alger Hiss," lately in the stationery business.

The following day, Harney called me from Cambridge in a somber voice with an interim decision. He had been "pleased with the paper" but "concerned with its tone." His concern, he elaborated, "had to do with a conflict between my charge to you about the station in the bathroom and the way your report, while quite positive, tends to amplify some of the horrible situations that do exist in ETV—like the station in the bathroom." While I went around in circles trying to follow his reasoning, he added that this and the matter of the stations' being easily identifiable from my descriptions had been the crux of his conference about my Appendix with Dr. Killian. Harney said that Killian was "frowning more than ever on negative implications," and so it didn't look as if my Appendix would appear in the Carnegie Report.

I made a silent vow that it would appear in this book and went back to my work. Four days later, Harney called from New York—the Toy New Dealer's office on Third Avenue—to confirm the verdict. He said Killian had told him: "Look, I'm just going to have to make a very hard decision. I'm going to exclude everything to do with the station surveys, even though they have the most excitement and interest. They would create an improper image which we don't dare create." The image, said Harney, was that "ETV is a sinking ship."

I asked Harney if he felt bitter because so much time and talent had proved to be a well-paid waste. No, he said, because he thought many of our findings had influenced the commissioners' views and maybe resulted in a changed thought here or there in an already-drafted report. He said that I should consider his efforts and mine "experimental research that just hasn't worked out the way any of us would have liked—including Killian, who had to make a hard-nosed decision."

It was not my fault, he assured me, and he personally felt "the same way about this as I did [at Thanksgiving] about the commission's attitude toward commercial television, if you know what I mean." He added rather lamely, "It's show business." Then, ending upbeat, he said there was a possibility that after the Carnegie Report was published, National Educational Television [NET] would do a documentary on it, and "a couple of our reporters might be on it, including you, as performers." I told him I wouldn't count on it.

You may just be beginning to realize why educational television isn't as good as it should be, but I trust you have a fairly complete picture of why Carnegie's long-heralded White Paper wasn't going to change this situation very much. The Carnegie Report, when it came, was as skimpy and stodgy as an ETV documentary. (Bantam Books later published it as a $1 paperback, and still later, the Establishment's quasi-official publishing house, Harper & Row, did it up in hard covers.) Two noncommittal paragraphs straddled the sins of commercial TV, and three more summarized our visits to ninety-two ETV stations. ("The single theme in those reports that most impresses us is that of opportunity unrealized.")

With utmost fanfare, the fifteen commissioners huffed and puffed over the ailing patient they were studying and came up with a new label for it: *Public Television,* the title of their report. *Public* promptly became *the* snob word of 1967 in cultural circles. (When Joseph Papp's admirable free Shakespeare Festival in Central Park became a year-round operation, it opened winter quarters in the old Astor Library, added a $2.50 admission charge for its indoor activity, and called this new phase "Public Theatre.") And in case the word *public* didn't cure what ailed ETV, the Carnegie Commissioners proposed the old-fangled remedies of money, hardware, and continuing study, plus a new gimmick called the Corporation for Public Television. This would be "a federally chartered, nonprofit, nongovernmental" body to help put new ETV stations on the air, subsidize programming, and—to use the report's nonlanguage—enhance "the desirability of maximizing excitement, experimen-

tation, innovation and freedom for creativity in programming."
Half of the corporation's twelve directors would be appointed
by the President of the United States, with Senate concurrence,
and they would then elect the other six.

"The Commission considers the creation of the Corporation
fundamental to its proposal and would be most reluctant to
recommend the other parts of its plan unless the corporate
entity is brought into being," said the Carnegie Report, in what
struck me as a blunt exercise in self-perpetuation. I wondered
which three of the fifteen Carnegie Commissioners had decided
to bow out of the ETV picture. (As it was, when President Johnson later signed the Corporation for Public Broadcasting into
law, he immediately appointed Killian on the board.)

Then I began to wonder who would pay for this glorified
Carnegie Commission. Three pages later, I found out. *We the
public would pay a proposed 2 to 5 percent sales tax whenever
we bought a new TV set.* For those of us who have tried to stay
loyal to ETV, haven't we been punished enough? For those who
have managed to stay away from ETV, what price taxation
without representation?

If there was any humanity in the Carnegie Report, it was
compressed into an introductory letter from E. B. White.

> . . . I think television should be the visual counterpart of
> the literary essay, should arouse our dreams, satisfy our
> hunger for beauty, take us on journeys, enable us to partici-
> pate in events, present great drama and music, explore
> the sea and the sky and the woods and the hills. It should
> be our Lyceum, our Chautauqua, our Minsky's, and our
> Camelot. It should restate and clarify the social dilemma
> and the political pickle. Once in a while it does, and you
> get a quick glimpse of its potential.

To which the commissioners added lifelessly:

> Public Television is capable of becoming the clearest
> expression of American diversity, and of excellence within
> diversity. Wisely supported, as we conclude it must be, it
> will respect the old and the new alike, neither lunging at
> the present nor worshipping the past. It will seek vitality
> in well-established forms and in modern experiment. Its

attitude will be neither fearful nor vulgar. It will be, in short, a civilized voice in a civilized community.

A voice, not a vision! An essay, not an art form! Civilized, balanced, established, dull, gray, and challenging only in moderation.

The next day, numerous Establishment peers stumbled over each other reaching to pat the Old Boys from Carnegie on the corporate back. McGeorge Bundy of the Ford Foundation said it was "first class." A former Federal Communications Commissioner said it was "top notch." CBS pledged $1 million toward the kitty needed to endow the Corporation for Public Television. The rest of Madison Avenue was relieved, too, for there had been fear that the Carnegie Commission might consider taxing commercial TV advertisers instead of consumers.

The New York *Times* fired off several editorial salutes, and its star pundit, James Reston (who sits on National Educational Television's board of directors), proclaimed the Carnegie Report "candid and eloquent . . . one of those quiet events that, in the perspective of a generation or even more, may be recognized as one of the transforming occasions in American life." Dr. Killian was the *Times'* "Man in the News." The profile of him began, " 'He's the least anecdotal man I know,' a friend said recently." It was three weeks before the *Times'* TV critic, Jack Gould, had the audacity or perspective to refer to the Carnegie Report, almost in passing, as a "dreary" petition threatening "to take all the fun out of Educational TV."

[VII]

Harney's hint that a show-biz career on NET awaited me might have impressed me more if, in my thirty-hour stint of ETV watching, I hadn't become grimly aware of NET as a common source of grayness and infrequent illumination for 123* of the nation's 124 ETV stations.

National Educational Television likes to call itself "The Fourth Network." Largely subsidized by the Ford Foundation (to the tune of $6 million of its $8 million annual budget),

---

* The lone maverick, alas, is a particularly dismal ETV station in Minneapolis which has been described in three words: "Nuns teaching geometry."

NET supplies five hours of new programming a week to its ETV affiliates, who pay the bargain price of $100 a year. In addition, each affiliate has access to NET's program library of back tapes and other acquisitions at the rate of $5 per half-hour program.

NET is the originator, packager, syndicator, homogenizer, and common denominator of ETV. As the film and tape backbone without whose product few ETV stations could ever have gone on the air, it sets the style, tempo, and level for most of ETV across the nation.

"[ETV's] glamour shows come from NET, which is to ETV what NBC, ABC, and CBS are to the nation's commercial stations. NET deals in Culture with a capital C," says Kiplinger's *Changing Times* in fluent alphabetese. "It seeks to enrich while it entertains. . . . Programs are produced under the supervision of NET's staff, then taped and distributed to member stations. . . . With few exceptions,* most stations take [the NET] package." *Changing Times* adds parenthetically, "If they didn't, they'd probably find life on the airwaves a losing struggle."

The Educational Television and Radio Center, as NET was first called, was ETV's initial answer to a question that nags at all television: *How do you fill the time?* The Ford Foundation's Fund for Adult Education set it up in 1952 to start "building an inventory of programs on film for use as educational stations take the air." The strong man in its founding was the fund's president, C. Scott Fletcher, who insisted from the outset that the center should have no production equipment of its own—a position, an admiring history relates, that Fletcher maintained "against every persuasive pressure . . . and Fletcher held the purse strings." **

This was a costly mistake for which NET is still paying. Five months' rental of cameras and other film equipment usually involves spending as much as it would cost to buy them. I recently

---

* Aside from the Minneapolis maverick, a few Southern ETV stations have been unwilling to run NET's *History of the Negro People* and other programs with what they term a "Northeastern flavor."

** Fletcher is now with the National Association of Educational Broadcasters. When I met him in Miami recently, he remarked that without Ford, there wouldn't be any NET, for NET would not be capable of raising more than $1 million or $1½ million for itself.

visited an editing studio at 1721 Broadway, where an entire floor of little rooms, each equipped with a Movieola viewing machine, had been rented by NET. Each little room (I counted eight in use that day) was costing NET a basic rental of $80 a week. But $80 was just the beginning. Under various laws designed to keep nonprofit corporations profit-proof, NET had to pay the studio *an additional 10 percent above the normal rental, plus 10 percent of the salary of each NET employee working in each little room*—a surcharge of $30 to $60 per week per room!

(One of the expensive outside jobbing facilities used by NET belonged for a while to an NET producer, who was making more from NET as a landlord than as an employee.)

Because of Fletcher's Folly—the ground rules laid out for NET—this kind of waste could almost be justified as necessary expenditure. But waste breeds waste, and various visits to NET showed me a good deal of unnecessary waste. In quest of the talents that had made "The Sun and Richard Lippold," I was referred to 1790 Broadway, where NET had rented an entire floor for $5,000 a month. There were twenty-five rooms on that floor, and only six had occupants.

One block uptown, in the Coliseum Tower at Columbus Circle, NET's executive headquarters shares the twentieth floor with the National Association for the Advancement of Colored People's Legal Defense and Education Fund. NETville resembles a miniature CBS. In the upper-executive office area, the corridors are carpeted with pile and lined with antiques. For executive producers, there are cubicles with no rugs inside or out. For temporary talent and regular producers in disgrace, there are partitions that can expand or dwindle overnight. This "Doghouse," as it is known, is frequently occupied by producers who earn bad reviews or no reviews at all from Jack Gould of the New York *Times*. Although TV reviewing is perhaps the most impotent, after-the-fact form of criticism there is, NET dotes on it. Jack Gould is to NET what Trendex is to ABC.

All this squandering of real estate might be laughable if one didn't know that the free-lance editors in the little rooms with Movieolas and some of the outside talent in the Doghouse are laboring for half their usual fees just to work on "something worthwhile." And when you contrast NET's squandering with the poverty of some of the ETV stations it services, you have a real tearjerker.

The second strike against NET before it even started was the Ford Foundation. As often happens when an enterprise's most solid foundation is a foundation, too many of NET's first key staffers were prematurely gray pensioners from the grove of academe. Getting in on the ground floor, several of them gravitated (or were kicked) into various creative roles. Some were smarter or less pedantic than others, but hardly any were capable of the sharp black and white televisual thinking that the medium, whether commercial or educational, requires. For expertise on a music program, they would turn to a musician, not to a film maker.*

NET's first president, who concentrated on building and developing local ETV stations that would eventually display NET products, was Harry Newburn, former president of the University of Oregon. In 1959 he was succeeded by John F. White, a former college vice-president who had made a go of Pittsburgh's ETV station, WQED, and wanted to make the entire nation realize it couldn't do without ETV.

"Jack White is a dilettante with a lot of powerful friends," a former associate said. "If he meets one of these friends at a cocktail party who happens to have another friend who plays the piccolo, it's very likely that there'll be a piccolo concert on NET in the next few months."

White's regime has not been entirely inbred. He did reach out of his own world, but to where?

---

* Foundation support of ETV may have another disadvantage which wouldn't have occurred to me. Senator Philip A. Hart of Michigan, whose advocacy of truth in packaging led to cancellation of his scheduled commerical TV appearances when advertisers protested, was told by an ETV official that some of the same pressures applied in the noncommercial medium. "As he explained," says Senator Hart, "educational television may not have to depend directly on advertisers for financial life. But the largest contributors to the foundations which do feed their money to it are the major industries."

A still more serious indictment of the Ford Foundation can be found in the field of instructional TV, which I have largely neglected. Early in ETV, the Ford Foundation dispatched Dr. George Stoddard of the University of Illinois to evangelize schools on taking money ordinarily spent for buildings and spending it instead on mass TV teaching facilities. This led to such atrocities as 500 bodies crammed into an old Florida high school auditorium—not air-conditioned, with the temperature over 100 degrees—trying to concentrate on a televised lecture.

To big businesses. They were enthralled by a tax write-off that would enhance their corporate images while plugging, in a low key, their products and ideologies. For some $2 million, IBM underwrote an eight-part series, *The Computer and the Mind of Man.* Merrill, Lynch, Pierce, Fenner and Smith gave a grant toward a four-part series on investing. Humble Oil and Refining was outright proud to finance the importation of BBC's Shakespeare cycle, *An Age of Kings.* The FCC permits ETV to credit its public-service benefactors at beginning and end of a program, but never in the middle. NET maintains an official posture of utter scrupulousness about this, but its producers grope for ideas that have the broad appeal to win big-business backing. One producer was told by his superior: "Make this one good. It's for the client." And a facetious reference to Wheaties once was deleted from a script because NET hoped for a grant from General Mills.

To commercial television. Starting in 1964, there was an influx, particularly on the documentary side, of uninspired refugees from the networks. Those talents were no brighter than the earlier castoffs from the campus, and what they produced were hollow imitations of *CBS Reports.* White himself is reported to have described the new blood ruefully as "commercial scum." But a former NET writer, who spent most of his career in educational broadcasting, may have explained their failure most aptly.

> Of those who were hired away from the networks, many understood the problem as one of how to be slick with other people's material, but they could not always judge the material and they were usually slick about nothing. They tried to apply the formula of "Dragnet" to the politics of Jefferson or—equally sad to behold—feeling that they no longer had to prostitute themselves, they followed their own inclinations and discovered that they had always been whores.

The writer is Richard M. Elman, whose article in the *Nation,* on "The Timid Crusaders," * ought to be for NET *the* inside

---

* Richard Elman, "The Timid Crusaders" (March 1, 1965), pp. 217–221. Quotations from "The Timid Crusaders" reprinted by permission of the *Nation.*

hatchet job that *Only You, Dick Daring!* was for CBS. Elman was part of an NET team sent to unravel the mystery of two neighboring southern California towns, one of which tended to vote 3 to 1 Democratic and the other 3 to 1 Republican. On location, the team discovered a simple explanation that hadn't occurred to the brainstormers in New York: *Most of the Democratic town's people were Negro!* The producer then instructed his crew to "shoot around the Negroes."

Elman describes a never-never land where, as one official told him, "We don't have any gritty, gutty intellectuals making the decisions because that's not what they're good for," and where

> if you lack a firm opinion about something you hire a consultant to advise you, and if you disagree with him you find a second consultant, and a third, and a fourth, and a fifth. . . . If you are doing a program about education, your consultant will come from the educational lobby; if it's a program about South Vietnam, he will be a State Department adviser. If you intend to criticize a given institution, you first consult the institution to see if it objects to being criticized.

NET President White's rebuttal to this was: "If this network ever forgoes the responsibility to remain free, we had better get out of business, but that doesn't mean you have to be a damn fool. In programming, it's judgment and taste which count. It has nothing to do with courage. The way to succeed is to get substantial people who will fight for freedom. But you must have responsible people with judgment who won't bring something from out of left field."

This kind of Establishment consultant to whom NET turns often charges the going rate of $100 a day, plus expenses. Sometimes he appears on the program as an interviewee or even as the subject. In the closing credits, however, he is seldom identified as a man who had a hand in framing the documentary you just saw. CBS' *Twentieth Century* used to engage in the same practice but at least acknowledged it in the credits.

Small wonder, then, that NET has produced such spectacular fiascos as a six-part series, *The Population Explosion,** which

---

* At a cost of $600,000, expensive even by commercial TV economics.

never discussed birth control or the Catholic Church, and a documentary on auto safety that ignored Detroit's lobbying in Washington. And what I consider ETV's shining half hour, "The Sun and Richard Lippold," was made by outside talent on a contract with NET. The Lippold program came about for all the wrong reasons, I learned. It was commissioned largely because its makers had 7,000 feet of Lippold film left over from a previous NET effort* and was promoted within NET because it was to have a score by David Diamond, which was never used. A high NET official regarded the finished product as "not a very successful" effort, but the film's NET executive producer—improbably named Lane Slate and sometimes assisted by a cousin named Mallory Slate—did congratulate the cameraman on "some really crunchy images."

Names like David Diamond, a once blacklisted but now "safe" composer whose best works may well be behind him, excite NET's Establishment liberals far more than names like Julia Child, whom NET rejected for syndication. NET scrupulously avoids anything that threatens to *involve* the viewer—anything, that is, with humanity! If you look back over my chronicle of an ETV week, you will note that thirteen of my thirty hours— almost half!—bore the imprint of NET. Those thirteen hours contained, with a few exceptions, the most bloodless and remote hours of the week that was. Quite the opposite prevails at outstanding stations like WGBH and KQED. There the keynote of success is *involvement*. After watching a few dozen ETV stations across the country, I think I can lay down my own rule of thumb: *An ETV station's vitality varies inversely with the percentage of NET product in its programming.*

As of 1964, according to a Brandeis University study, the average ETV station was broadcasting fourteen hours and forty-two minutes of NET product a week. In some cases, NET provides as much as 60 percent of a station's programming. The average percentage of local programming on ETV stations, as of late 1966, was 20 percent and *going down*. By moving early into a vacuum created by time to kill and untrusting local trustees, NET had achieved a stranglehold on the baby medium of ETV.

The Ford Foundation's $6 million a year is simply the base

---

* "Essay on Death," commemorating John F. Kennedy's assassination.

for NET's virtual monopoly on the dissemination of ETV programs in the United States. Corporate gifts and grants from other foundations as well as various government agencies (Atomic Energy Commission, National Institutes of Mental Health, etc.) comprise an additional $2 million or more. As Richard Elman points out:

> The individual stations affiliated with NET may also receive grants from such sources, as well as grants from Ford and construction grants from the Federal Government. The net result is an interlocking directorate of powerful interest groups beholden to one another to preserve a common enterprise. The affiliates meet frequently under NET auspices, at which time programming decisions are made, and more or less binding policies are set forth.

"We've suggested a few programs to NET," one station manager told me, "but they haven't done any of them. And they've never suggested any for us to work with them on. Ninety percent of NET production money seems to go to a small number of stations—two or three of them. . . . There is getting to be an Establishment within NET. There are ten men who sit on all the boards, changing hats periodically, but never really changing. A few outside ideas and a little more abrasiveness in the decision-making process would do NET a world of good."

Joe Morgenstern of *Newsweek* insists that NET "is afraid of the Ford Foundation . . . and afraid of the very idea of getting good enough to compete with commercial television. So long as ETV remains a wistful cripple, the public will make allowances and the officers will keep their jobs."

Another station I went to was still hoping for an NET production contract for a relatively simple local project that it felt would have national interest.

"I suspect," the producer of the program told me, "that NET would want us to lend weight to it with an anthropologist and a sociologist instead of leaving the viewer to his own intellectual devices."

His station manager added, "I think NET and Ford money have had this influence on ETV programming: If we were given money to do something for NET, we'd be expected to lend this kind of weight to whatever we filmed. And I guess we'd go along with NET on it."

Another station manager blamed ETV's lack of decent children's programming on the fact that "NET, because of its relationship with Ford, feels it has to concentrate on public affairs. But I say you can do public-affairs programming for children, who are the opinion makers of tomorrow. These kids are being brought up with ETV; if ever there was an audience, this is it."

From the outside looking in, what we are seeing on ETV is a dilettante's view of the world. This view is respectable but not necessarily realistic. Early in the summer of 1964, for example, if a steadfast ETV viewer had been asked to name the probable Republican nominee for President, he might not have mentioned Senator Barry Goldwater—even though Goldwater by then had enough delegates in the bag for a first-ballot victory. But NET's campaign primer, *Of People and Politics,* had dismissed Goldwater with the observation that the unlikely event of his nomination would serve only as "a gratification of the death wish."

From the inside looking out, Elman's explanation: "NET's consultants, paid equally by Ford and NET, did not approve of the Arizona Senator."

Two weeks *after* Goldwater's nomination, the same NET film series followed a preselected delegate from Wisconsin through the Republican National Convention in San Francisco. This *typical* delegate was one of Pennsylvania Governor William Scranton's handful of supporters, chosen—according to Elman— "because he was a good friend of one of the consultants. . . . The Establishment had been crossed up by Goldwater's nomination, and so had its mouthpiece—NET."

Elman concentrated on public-affairs programming, which was his sphere. What hope is there for cultural affairs in NET's never-never land? Not much, when these guidelines are so solemnly laid down with a heavy hand for producers and directors:

> An underlying *seriousness of purpose* is indeed essential. This, however, does not preclude the light touch. Occasionally a serious theme can best be expressed by whimsey or

humor. (The comic drama is the obvious example here, though the statement applies to other performance categories and to nonperformance programs as well.) Nor does seriousness of purpose provide an excuse for snobbishness, preciousness, or pedantry. The intrusion of any of these will gravely impair an otherwise fine production.*

Which brings me back to my own initial guideline: *What hath thought wrought?* which perhaps ought to be rephrased *What hath Ford bought?* The answer is not a Fourth Network but a parody of the other three—an Establishment miscarriage that has been kept alive long enough to inbreed its own Establishment. To quote Richard Elman one last and most eloquent time:

> It makes no impact. No massive infusions of money . . . are likely to change that condition. . . . NET needs a new attitude and direction. It must find a massive base of support by providing the kind of service the public needs, and must be willing to suffer the consequences of its actions. Such a service cannot be administered from the top down; it must be a form of journalism, not mere pedagogy; it must be conscious of the tensions of its audience, responsive to the communities in which it functions—it must be "infinitely curious and incorrigibly patient and yet plastic and inflammable and determinable," to quote Henry James. Most important of all, it should not be a plaything for the middle-class** consumer of culture, but an instrument for social change, human involvement and individual betterment. It must criticize the established order, not rush to join its ranks, and it must constantly provoke and agitate, using first-rate minds as producers as well as consultants, for only then will it have a chance to educate. Will this ever be possible if ETV continues to be an extension of the FCC, the State Department and the Great Books Program?
>
> It strikes me as intolerable that we are prepared to allow the formation of one gigantic monopoly in Educational Television when we would be rightfully terrified if such a consolidation were to take place among the commercial net-

---

* This passage is quoted from *NET Program Philosophy and Purpose: A Guideline for Staff Planning*, published by NET in 1964. Italics are NET's.

** I beg to differ with Elman here. I found NET and ETV *upper*-class playthings.

works. In the next ten years, the NET apparatus may encompass as many as 200 stations, capable of reaching nearly every potential American viewer. There is talk that these stations will be interconnected. Many will be constructed with the aid of local legislatures eager to cut back on expensive teaching staffs, but their chief function will be adult programming. What will these broadcasts be like? As yet, there is no responsible criticism of educational programming. Grown lazy and fat from feeding off the Ford Foundation, which wishes to improve television but has no other outlet on which to expend its resources, NET will presumably function as a domestic version of "The Voice of America."

Elman and I are not alone in our despair. Maurice B. Mitchell, president of *Encyclopaedia Britannica,* has termed ETV "perhaps the most expensive and disastrous single failure in the history of educational technology. . . . Millions have been poured into educational television—by the government, by foundations, by business and industry, and by the people as individuals. Yet it is today a deeply disappointing, puny, unimpressive and minor instrument. . . ."

Senator Robert F. Kennedy has declared: "As a viewer, I am disappointed that educational television is so often ponderous and unnecessarily dull."

Even Julia Child seems to have given up on ETV—temporarily, at least. *The French Chef* has suspended further taping until color comes to ETV. Her explanation can be taken symbolically as well as literally: "I'm tired of gray food."

A while ago, even the president of the Ford Foundation conceded that while existing systems of ETV "are much better than nothing . . . compared to what this country deserves, they are *a depressing failure.*" The italics are mine, not his, for foundation people have a way of pulling their punches. And this is exactly what McGeorge Bundy of Ford did in his letter to the FCC.

This is not the fault of the talented and dedicated men who have worked their hearts out for noncommercial television. It is the fault of all of us—in that we have not yet found a way to give this work the resources it needs. It can well be argued that we at the Ford Foundation have

> contributed to this failure. When we give $6 million a year
> to NET, we seem to have done a lot. And for us it is a lot—
> it is our largest continuing annual grant. But the brutal
> fact is that our big gift is much too small.

Bundy not only prescribed the foundation man's all-purpose
cure—*money*—but sought to extricate Ford from its mammoth
gray elephant by recommending that commercial television's
profits be taxed to finance ETV. He envisioned this netting
some $30 million to $60 million a year for a network of timely
and professionally made ETV shows that could be transmitted
via satellites synchronized with the earth's orbit.

This proposal, known in the trade as "The Bundy Bird,"
outraged the commercial television trade, which was to be expected, and delighted the Establishment's house organ, the New
York *Times*. What seemed to nag at me was my own growing
distrust of the schizo-utopian vision of foundation apologists
and their obsession with money and hardware at the expense of
humanity. My contact with Carnegie had taught me how their
indefatigable pursuit of positive thinking can crowd reality out
of the retina, the black and the white out of an already gray
report with one cool appendectomy, and the life out of themselves and all around them. If this was the kind of thinking
that went on in the right clubs, I instinctively wanted out.

The more I brooded about the Bundy Bird, the better I was
able to pinpoint what really bothered me. It was the glib assumption of the Bundy letter (as well as of both the approving
and disapproving editorials) that NET was the logical vehicle
for launching the bold new venture of satellite ETV. Amid all
this long-range bigthink, it struck me that nothing would really
get far off the ground until ETV was called back to the drawing
board. Starting from scratch might even be more feasible than
overhauling a quasiofficial network of entrenched grass-roots
Establishments. Ford's futuristic proposal made no more sense
to me than selecting a basket case to be an astronaut.

The president of NET, of course, saw it entirely differently.
In fact, I felt as unprogressive as the first man who ever yelled,
"Get a horse!" at Ford when I read that Jack White called the
proposal "a giant step forward." White added, "NET is fully
prepared to accept the challenge and responsibility this proposal

would place upon us as the national network for noncommercial television."

The Bundy Bird was far off in the future, but in 1967 NET latched onto a $10 million Ford project nicknamed "Friendly-vision." The result, unveiled last November, was an obscene reprise of much that has gone before (particularly in this chapter) as well as an overture to what little lies ahead in the vast wasteland of ETV.

Friendlyvision was the brainchild of a fifty-two-year-old egg-head born Ferdinand Friendly Wachenheimer but better known as Fred W. Friendly. A vital figure in CBS' Edward R. Murrow era of the 1950's, Fred Friendly resigned as head of CBS News in 1966, a year after his erstwhile partner Murrow died. He left in a huff when CBS opted for rerunning *I Love Lucy* one morning rather than televising Senator William Fulbright's Foreign Relations Committee hearings on Vietnam "live," which NBC was doing. For Fred Friendly has long been a Totalitarian (not Toy) Liberal, willing to make any sacrifice to bring people up to his level of democratic thinking—even if it means depriving them of their freedom of choice.

Friendly has been described as both an example and a victim of a "Washington syndrome," which novelist Harvey Swados defines as "the seductive talk about the national purpose, the awe of the celebrity and the abject reliance on 'the world's leading authority,' the belief that the New York *Times* is the sole criterion not only for news, but for intellectual significance." To which an NBC official who professes to admire Friendly adds this severe reservation: "Listening to Friendly is like going to eight Washington banquets in a row. Behind all the high-flown talk resides the kind of belligerent lowbrow who is fascinated by technique and by the 'wisdom' symbolized by a handful of sages, and who knows nothing of an entire world of art and intellect."

To ETV's dilettantes—who only recently stopped boasting that they were in the business not of broadcasting but of "narrowcasting" to a small, select audience—Fred Friendly must have seemed like a professional breath of fresh air to invigorate their musty medium. Soon after his hasty exit from CBS, he became the Ford Foundation's TV consultant and Edward R. Murrow Professor of Journalism at Columbia University, where he originated the Friendlyvisionary idea of a three-hour comprehensive review of current events. It would be televised every Sunday night of the year over a telephone-interconnected network of all the NET affiliates.

Bolstered by an eight-figure grant from Ford and the label of Public Broadcasting Laboratory adapted from Carnegie, the Friendlyvisionaries set up headquarters on Madison Avenue with a hard core of high-paid professionals culled from the networks, a sixty-man editorial staff, and studio facilities rented from NBC. They hired newscaster Edward P. Morgan away from ABC as their chief correspondent. They engaged doctors, lawyers, sociologists, and political scientists as consultants. They followed Presidential possibilities George Wallace and Ronald Reagan around the country all summer. They turned Groucho Marx loose on Washington to interview public figures like Everett Dirksen. They launched a newspaper advertising campaign reminiscent of *Fact* magazine's, with teasing little titles and provocative, but oversimplified, one-sentence blurbs for episodes that looked solid at first glance over a printed page. Spread over "this Sunday, and . . . Sundays to come," they sounded as thin as raspberry jam.

So were reports from Friendlyvision headquarters, which would indicate that whores who no longer have to prostitute themselves are capable only of early retirement. The laboratory's managing editor, formerly with the Canadian Broadcasting Corporation, was dismayed to find some of his old TV hands reluctant to experiment. "Most of the people here know what they don't want to do. But finding out what they want to do is much trickier."

Several months before the Public Broadcasting Laboratory took the air, it was emasculated to *two* hours *twenty-six* Sundays a year because of the high cost of NET interconnection. And in the days and hours preceding its premiere, two nights before the November, 1967, elections, it lost 29 of the 119 NET stations that had agreed to take it. Its first broadcast, devoted almost entirely to America's Negro problems, was deemed too dangerous by a number of stations in the North as well as the South. The inclusion of a play about a Southern town that wakes up to find its Negroes missing also lost the laboratory the support of its own editorial policy committee, headed by the dean of Columbia Journalism. (Further pressure was felt two weeks later, when Walter Lippmann gave PBL an exclusive hour of his time, wherein—despite sloppy questioning—he managed to express his disdain for President Johnson and his preference for Nelson Rockefeller as the best-qualified Presidential candidate in 1968. It was hinted in Washington that the whole Corporation for Public Broadcasting might encounter appropriations trouble if PBL didn't muzzle itself.)

All this fuss and finance was over a drab spectacular that scarcely illuminated the home screen. It dwelled at some length on the mayoralty campaigns of two Negroes in Gary, Indiana, and Cleveland, Ohio, as well as a white-backlash lady in Boston, but it seldom told me anything I hadn't learned from watching the CBS *Morning News*. It set up its own studio shouting match in Chicago, where a carefully casted cross section watched and then discussed a filmed tour of a ghetto conducted by an angry black nationalist. The forum spoke for itself, but afterward, the Public Broadcasting Laboratory brought Harvard psychiatrist Robert Coles onscreen to tell ETV viewers what they'd seen. (The Negro militant, Coles noted, had "the ironic name, Russ Meek, obviously given to him by a white person.") The controversial play *Day of Absence* was more than two years old and draggily acted by Negroes in whiteface, many of whom were in the cast that did it much better when I saw it off-Broadway. It, too, spoke for itself, but it was followed by a Negro historian, who analyzed it.

The segments were punctuated by anticommercials. These were purring public-service messages cautioning us that the new 100-millimeter cigarettes had even more cancer potential than did the oldfangled ones and that the cheaper the aspirin, the better the buy, because they all do the same job, anyway. Coupled with station breaks and plugs for NET coming attractions, the Public Broadcasting Laboratory kept us salivating at the same tempo we maintain while watching ABC, CBS, and NBC —despite PBL's claim to be "completely free of commercial interruptions."

The next day's reaction across the nation was described in a news headline as "largely adverse." In the ETV Establishment's bible, the New York *Times*, Jack Gould found "far more moments of journalistic and theatrical ineptitude" than "flashes of provocative heat." That old pro Fred Friendly said his own review "was tougher than the one in the New York *Times*. But let's be fair. It was a beginning. . . . They can only go up from here."

But will they? And when? And how fast? And how far? The answers, on the basis of subsequent Sundays, kept coming up negative. And the future of ETV still belongs to genteel dilettantes like Jack White of NET, who had nothing but kind words for his and Friendly's PBL fiasco. White spoke, as people in ETV often do, of the "obligation to fail."

The Ninth Commandment of the Culture Vultures:
Hallowed be the self-fulfilling prophecy.

9
A Tale of Two Civic Clubs:
The Lecture Circuit

[1]

DIALING 608 connects me with southern Wisconsin, and
seven digits more take me into the home of Mrs. Hazel
Stewart Alberson on Euclid Avenue in Madison.

"Hello, Mrs. Alberson. You *are* the program chairman of the
Madison Civics Club, aren't you?"

"Yes, indeed," says a friendly, vibrant voice, "I'm the chairman for one more meeting, anyway. That'll be a week from Saturday." I ask who the speaker will be, and she replies: "Patsy
Mink, the Congresswoman from Hawaii. I'm counting the
days!" I tell her I'm investigating the lecture circuit, with emphasis on why and how women's organizations—nowadays, lecturing's most visible means of support—get the speakers they get.
Mrs. Alberson is delighted. She invites me to "come hear
Patsy," whom she's "never met, but I feel so involved that I
have a hard time remembering we're not on a first-name basis."

Dialing 612 links me with Minnesota, and seven digits more
put me on the line with Mrs. Lura Crounse, program chairman
of the Woman's Club of Minneapolis.

"Hello, Mrs. Crounse. The lecture bureau in New York tells
me you're having a speaker on the fifteenth. Is that correct?"

A dry, surprisingly Southern voice answers cautiously: "Is that a Tuesday?" Yes, it's a week from Tuesday. Mrs. Crounse says: "Then the answer is yes. We have a speaker just about every Tuesday in the season." The season, I ascertain, lasts from October through April. Mrs. Crounse asks if *I* happen to know who *her* speaker will be on the 15th! I say they told me in New York that it would be Commander Mendel Peterson, U.S.N.R., of the Smithsonian Institution. She checks her files and allows that this is so. I am probably welcome to attend, although "I want to clear you with my president. But, if you don't hear otherwise, it's all right. Now your full name is—?"

[II]

The Woman's Club of Minneapolis dwells in its own six-story clubhouse on Oak Grove Street, overlooking Loring Park Lagoon, in a part of town that has seen better days. This was a wealthy residential district in 1907, when the club was organized to provide "education, civic and social service, study and friendly intercourse." Today some of the fine old homes have been partitioned into rooming houses; others have given way to office buildings. Almost all of the 1,800 active (annual dues, $75) and junior (ages twenty-one to thirty-five: annual dues, $37.50) members live elsewhere, and the clubhouse operates at a deficit.

This is the pattern in many cities, where yesterday's silk-stocking district has become today's ghetto. Some clubs unload their buildings. Others move out to suburbia, where the action is. A few stay on and struggle, often in vain, to improve their surroundings. Still others try to build a bar business. The Woman's Club of Minneapolis, however, functions on a bring-your-own-bottle-and-we'll-furnish-setups basis. The clubhouse deficit has been offset by the club's fortunate portfolio of outside investments. Still, the clubhouse remains a remote, insatiable white elephant that must be fed an enormous diet of speakers, events, and activities to justify its existence. The auditorium holds 650 comfortably, but gone are the days when the overflow for a Charles Laughton or a Dr. Walter Judd* was seated on-

---

* Dr. Judd, the Minnesota missionary-turned-Congressman, was at his lecture-circuit zenith in the 1930's, when he was warning the world about Japan's wicked

stage or in the orchestra pit. Nowadays, lectures draw anywhere from 200 to an occasional 600. But even on the sparsest Tuesday, there is a serious parking problem.

Today is Monday, however, the day before Commander Peterson's talk, and I am sitting in an airy conference room with Lura Crounse, the stately, redheaded, Tennessee-born wife of an attorney, and the club's president, Gertrude Priest, the bluish-gray-haired wife of an eye, ear, nose, and throat specialist.

"Program chairman is a thankless job," says Mrs. Priest, who used to be one herself. "If there are two things in the club on which members seldom agree, they're the food and the speakers."

Mrs. Crounse sighs philosophically and adds: "You do most of your booking a year in advance; we've already lined up next year's. You tell the lecture agencies what dates you have open, and they tell you what speakers they have available in your price bracket. We pay anywhere from three hundred to eight hundred dollars a speaker, occasionally a thousand."

I ask how the Minneapolitans shop for speakers.

Mrs. Crounse replies: "Some of the lecture bureaus simply send brochures and descriptions, but the big ones, like Colston Leigh and Keedick, send their representatives. Leigh's contact here is Elaine Wallace from the Chicago office. Mr. Keedick comes out from New York himself. It's certainly better for them to come. They save us a lot of mistakes. We'll say, 'How about so-and-so?' and they'll say right away, 'No, he wouldn't be good for *your* club.' "

A little later, she adds, "It seems to us that we pay a very great deal for a forty-five-minute talk. But our speakers' expenses are high, I imagine: travel and food and hotels and time out from their work."

I ask why local orators—from the University of Minnesota, the Walker Art Center, and the Tyrone Guthrie Theater, for instance—can't be integrated into the Tuesday programs to provide occasional free speech amid the fee speech. I am told that at little or no charge, local speakers *do* address the ladies at morning and summer events. But, says Mrs. Crounse cheerily

---

designs. One senior lecturegoer recalls: "He said that the money we spent on silk stockings paid for the bullets he was digging out of Chinese war wounded. I for one wore cotton stockings for a year."

and resolutely, "On Tuesdays we try to give our members an afternoon that they can't go elsewhere in town to get."

This particular season began with "Betty Furness On the Record" and will end with the Russian-born Nila Magidoff (topic: "Have Speech, Will Travel"). Mrs. Magidoff is one of the true lionesses of the lecture circuit. Where almost all lecturers have achieved their fame, notoriety, or expertise elsewhere, Mrs. Magidoff, a veteran of Lubyanka prison and Siberian exile who married an NBC news correspondent in 1937, *talked* her way up to Madison Square Garden and Hollywood Bowl stature selling war bonds. The postwar Nila is advertised as "a combination of Bob Hope and Billy Graham." Her Boswell is her traveling companion, Willie Snow (Mrs. Mark) Ethridge, who has written two books about her, *Russian Duet* and *Nila: Her Story as Told to. . . .* The latter is published (and peddled at her talks) in an overpriced paperback edition ($2.50!) by Keedick Press, a subsidiary of her lecture agency.

In between, among others:

Winston S. Churchill (not the late, great Book-of-the-Month Club statesman, but his sandy-haired grandson, still in his twenties) spoke on "Africa and the Middle East Today."

Bernice Clifton, author of *Sight Unseen,* preached that "Adversity Can Pay Dividends" while being chaperoned by her seeing-eye dog, Karla.

Madame Geneviève Dariaux gave "Tips from a Paris Expert." A onetime oil executive spoke on "Beyond Arabian Sands," and a semanticist spoke on "The Art of Saying What You Mean." Boris Goldovsky demonstrated "Romance on the Piano." Alvin Toffler, author of *The Culture Consumers,* worried about "Federal Aid to the Arts?"

Before the clubwomen's very eyes, Carl Mose, the speaker on "Sculpture in Modern Life," transformed a mass of clay into a member's head.

Dr. Charles Gaupp, connected with the Denver Art Museum, drew the best crowd for his "Confessions of an Antique Dealer" but committed the lucrative *faux pas* of peddling a $2 pamphlet from the podium. Mrs. Crounse shook her head ruefully as she told me: "We never got him to tea afterward; he was so busy selling pamphlets."

There had been a couple of substitutions.

Two days before Miss Nemone Balfour of Dawyck, Peeblesshire, was to have given a slide talk on "The High Road to Scotland," she was laid low by illness. The Colston Leigh agency sent a substitute. Mrs. Priest furrows her brow. "Who was it? Isn't it funny how they all melt together!"

Mrs. Crounse looks up the answer: Beverly Younger, a character actress from Chicago, who impersonated famous First Ladies. "She was very good," Mrs. Crounse recalls, "but on such short notice, we had no time to get word to our members." Confronted by Dolly Madison instead of Loch Lomond, some of the audience had walked out.

The other defector was Kermit Roosevelt, who had to be in Asia when he should have been in Minneapolis, discussing "CIA and the American Way of Life." His replacement spoke on "The Impact of Science Upon Our Culture," which, Mrs. Crounse regretted, "threw our program a little out of balance."

Balance is vital to the Woman's Club of Minneapolis. A season that lacks something for everybody will run into opposition long before it is announced in the monthly *Bulletin*. First, the program chairman's selections must run two gamuts of approval: her program committee of eight ("They overruled me many times when I was chairman," Mrs. Priest recalls) and the club's twelve-woman board of directors, whose specifications are that programs must be "challenging and provocative as well as informative" with speakers "recognized as leaders in their fields."

Mrs. Priest explains: "The board considers each speaker individually. We say things like 'too controversial' or 'too biased in one direction.' Or, 'We've had this man and he was good, but this is too soon.' "

"Of course," says Mrs. Crounse, "if a speaker made a particularly good impression, we *can* have him back the very next season. We had an Indian gentleman last season and again this season." She glances down to identify him as "Dr. Amiya Chakravarty, a real intellectual with great compassion and understanding—"

"Which came right across the footlights," Mrs. Priest gushes. "He had sincerity and poetry and a little quality of the mystic— *and a different lecture this year!* On the other hand, there was another speaker that the board asked the program committee to reconsider. He hadn't been here for about fifteen years, and while his file card said he'd been good, his topic was the same now that it had been then. So we wondered if we could count on him to give us an up-to-date speech."

"Keeping a good file card is essential to a good program chairman," says Mrs. Crounse. "It doesn't have to be a formal critique, but just a note or two, like *well-liked* and *merits a repeat* or *doesn't merit a repeat*. The one with the best grades used to be Dwight Cooke, the commentator. Remember him? We had him year after year for maybe five years. We relied on Mr. Cooke to keep us up with world affairs. But then one year he said something about Red China that wasn't very popular here —nobody remembers what it was he said—and he was never booked here again."

The upheaval that one abrasive reference to Peking can trigger in Minneapolis jolts me into a reverie and a flashback—to the origins of the lecture circuit. In today's cultural euphoria, we forget (or never learn) that until less than four decades ago, lecturegoing used to be a robust family pursuit, and lecture programming wasn't always a bland matriarchy-cum-bureaucracy.

Americans have long possessed an indefatigable urge to be lectured, which may explain why so many earlier colonizers of the New World were missionaries. But it was not until 1826 that lecturing was put on an organized basis in Millbury, Massachusetts, with the founding of the first lyceum.

The word *lyceum* is derived from the walled garden of the Temple of Apollo Lyceus, where the featured speaker in the fourth century B.C. was Aristotle. Millbury's lyceum was a local self-improvement center which, when it exhausted the local talent, imported out-of-town lecturers. In nearby Concord, a second lyceum's well of free speech ranneth over. Ralph Waldo Emerson gave ninety-eight lectures there in the first few years without so much as suggesting a fee.

As America's thirst for the spoken word quickened, lyceums began to compete, and no self-respecting speaker would show up for less than a standard $5 "honorarium," plus all the oats his horse could eat. When Josiah Holbrook, founder of the Millbury lyceum, organized an agency to syndicate his lecturers, the rates went up—to an average of $150 an evening. Emerson's price was $500.

By 1842, when Charles Dickens came to America, Massachusetts and New York had their own state lyceum boards to regulate competition and promotion of lecturers. The going lyceum bureau commission for a "name" speaker was 40 percent to cover booking costs, travel, and other details. Still, Dickens' take-home fee from his lecture tour was enough to support his ten children, plus his scathing, sprawling *American Notes.*

Out West, lyceum arrangements were primitive but lucrative. When a West Coast manager wired Artemus Ward, "WHAT WOULD YOU TAKE FOR FORTY NIGHTS IN CALIFORNIA?" the humorist wired back, "BRANDY AND WATER." Ward, alias Charles Farrar Browne (1834–1867), a columnist for the Cleveland *Plain Dealer,* was a stand-up comic whose stock in trade were the pithy one-liner ("Let us all be happy and live within our means, even if we have to borrow the money to do it with") and a rambling lecture on Brigham Young ("the most married man I ever saw in my life") and the Mormons. The latter lecture proved so popular that Ward soon had a competitor: the nineteenth of Brigham Young's twenty-seven wives, crusading against polygamy.

Another Ohio journalist, David Ross Locke (1833–1888), editor of the Toledo *Blade,* assumed the reactionary character of Reverend Petroleum Vesuvius Nasby. By preaching for all the wrong causes, he made converts for many of the right ones, including liberty for women and slaves.

On many of the same podiums, the bogus Reverend Petroleum V. Nasby was followed by the real Reverend Henry Ward Beecher's liberal fire-and-brimstone preaching. By 1874. Negroes—but not women—had the vote, and the lyceum business was a thriving winter sport whose season lasted from October to May. November and February represented the peak months for indoor listening. But the warm season was a yawning cultural gap—until that summer. Into the breach—with an impact that virtually drowned the lyceum trade for half a century—swelled Chautauqua!

In upstate New York on the banks of Lake Chautauqua, Reverend John Heyl Vincent had organized a summer camp for indoctrinating Methodist and Episcopal Sunday school teachers. But *camp* was then, as now, a much-abused word. Back in 1874, it conjured up a vision of religious camp meetings—coeducational emotional baths with emphasis on dramatic conversions, however temporary. To avoid this image, Vincent named his camp the Sunday School Teachers' Assembly. He advertised two weeks of bonfires at the water's edge, community sings, study instead of sermons, good food, good lodging, good manners, and good morals—all for $6 per person.

After a while, Vincent's assembly took a nonsectarian path, but with an emphasis on morality and inspiration that characterized Chautauqua to its very end. Senators, statesmen and six Presidents of the United States (Grant, Hayes, Garfield, McKinley, Theodore Roosevelt,* and Taft) journeyed to speak in the big tent by the lake. Vincent's two-week assembly became a two-month season, and tens of thousands flocked to Chautauqua from all over the country. Hundreds of tents made it a true tent city. In their colorful history of Chautauqua, *We Called It Culture,*** Victoria and Robert Ormond Case wrote:

> The magnificent voice of William Jennings Bryan soared out over the water. Vachel Lindsay the poet and Evangeline Booth the Salvation Army girl told their philosophies and their dreams. College presidents and popular authors, leaders of reform, entertainers, Shakespearean actors, and the great humorists of the day held the audiences spellbound, collected their ever-expanding fees, and departed, much impressed with this new type of "American university."

Famous composers gave music courses. Violinists gave concerts. And ultimately, Vincent brought in the New York Symphony, conducted by Walter Damrosch, for a six-week engagement.

Such a success could scarcely resist packaging. At first there was tie-in merchandise: home-study courses for the winter months; *The Home* book, "designed to provide lessons for chil-

---

* Theodore Roosevelt pronounced Chautauqua "the most American thing in America." Later, years after the Chautauqua boom had ended, Franklin Delano Roosevelt came to Chautauqua, New York, to deliver his "I hate war" speech.

* Case, Victoria, and Case, Robert Ormand, *We Called It Culture.* New York, Doubleday & Company, 1948.

dren and young people, a home teacher full of pictures, puzzles, poems, and practical suggestions" (Chautauqua-Century Press, $3.75); a monthly magazine; a museum; a school of theology and a Chautauqua University, authorized to issue diplomas and confer degrees; and a line of children's books, featuring *Four Girls at Chautauqua* and *Chautauqua Girls at Home*.

In 1903 ambitious promoters took the show on the road, organized Chautauqua circuits across the nation, and cashed in up and down the line. As the Cases put it:

> The circuit managers brought their own pavilion, seats, rostrum, and programs, abandoned the vacation idea to set up their tents near Main Street, lost the old leisure but drew infinitely larger audiences. Now it was no longer a matter of vacation or home study, but a program of inspiration and culture right at the doorstep, where townspeople could flock in and out and farmers might attend an afternoon session, go home and do their chores, and be back for the evening.

The word *chautauqua* came to mean a week-long barrage of lecturing and entertaining in tents pitched, wherever possible, at lakeside beneath what the promoters called "God's green canopy." By 1924 more than 30 million American men, women, and children were attending some 12,000 Chautauquas. For many a mother west of the Hudson, Chautauqua Week was her one chance a year to afford her children and herself a glimpse of the culture of Boston and New York. Or as one of the faithful put it, "It was as though my great soul hunger had come to a feast."

Weeks in advance, "CHAUTAUQUA IS COMING" banners enlivened Main Street, and buttons reading "I'LL BE THERE" adorned the lapels of small boys. Each Chautauqua was a local promotion—typically, with all expenses underwritten by twenty or thirty local businessmen, who then presold season tickets at $2.50 apiece. They would have to sell close to 1,000 tickets to break even. Whether or not they did, however, a $2,000 guarantee had to be in the local bank, deposited to the Chautauqua booking bureau's account, by opening day. No cash, no Chautauqua.

These out-of-town booking bureaus made their heaviest profits from single ticket sales (75 cents per event, a dozen or more events per day), on which they kept all the proceeds. Some Chautauquas made money for their local sponsors; others were written off as deliberate loss leaders to enhance community prestige and bring in business from nearby towns.

"Mothers and grandmothers carried flat cushions and palm-leaf fans," one Chautauqua alumnus recalls. "The young girls wore white dimity dresses with sprigs of flowers in them, and the children who had been barefoot all day long put on shoes for the occasion."

Chautauqua was largely showmanship and evangelizing. There were music and juggling and wondrous prestidigitators and mind readers and Indian rain dance lessons for the boys and girls and Mother Goose pageants with audience participation.

Its most durable staple, however, was a type of lecture classified as "Mother, Home and Heaven," in which, according to one historian, speakers drew their morals from "the soldier lying on his hard pallet in the far-off Philippines . . . the sabbath sunrise at the edge of the Grand Canyon . . . the brave Salvation Army lassie who met a gang of hoodlums in the slums of a great city . . . the famous gambler lying at the point of death . . . the silver-haired old mother of five lovely girls who asked me this question . . . and the last words of the old infidel as his little granddaughter bent over his bed."

No Chautauqua worth its salt was complete without a second best known. She would come to town a few days ahead of her speech, look it over, and at her appointed hour, deliver a gentle but prodding sermon on "Our Town and How to Make It Better." If Nels couldn't make it, an architect or city planner or much-traveled man of the world would fill the role of community scold. In *Main Street* (1920), Sinclair Lewis of Sauk Centre, Minnesota, defined a lecturer as "a little man who kept his hands in his pockets and said Miles City should be ashamed to have dirty back yards." But it was in the community scold's wake that many a Miles City tidied its backyards, uncluttered its back alleys, and even removed an occasional civic eyesore.

My reminiscence delights neither Mrs. Priest nor Mrs. Crounse of Minneapolis, Minnesota.

"Some of our members would find this Nels Darling presumptuous," says the former, "even though others might agree with her."

"Many people don't like to hear their own faults," says the latter, verging on passion. "Some of our people don't like to hear what they've done wrong or what America's done wrong—even when the speaker *is* American. I suppose our membership is predominantly conservative. Certainly our liberal speakers get the most criticism—except for liberal Englishmen. They're very well received here for some reason."

I suggest, from past experience, that maybe their messages are unintelligible.

"Accents *are* a very unfortunate problem," Mrs. Priest concedes, "and not only with Englishmen. We've had several speakers with a great deal to say, but whose pronunciation left it unsaid."

"We always ask the lecture bureaus about this when they suggest a foreign speaker," says Mrs. Crounse, "but we don't always get a straight answer. Still, we can often check the grapevine. The speaker may have appeared at the St. Paul Women's Institute or at the university."

I ask why a woman's club can't book a speaker without going through a lecture bureau.

"The lecture agencies not only give you a good selection," Mrs. Crounse responds blandly, "but it's to our advantage when we can find a number we like from the same bureau. Some bureaus will give us a package deal: a little discount if we take a large number of their people."

"And the fact is," says Mrs. Priest, after recalling with horror an English journalist she once booked independently who stood her up, "that even the occasional speaker who isn't affiliated with an agency charges whatever the traffic will bear. He'll just pocket the commission that the agency would take, so there's no saving and much less reliability. At least the agency issues a contract usually saying that the speaker will be in town the night before the lecture and specifying what his additional responsibilities will be. In our case, he attends luncheon before and tea after his speech."

"It used to be," says Mrs. Crounse, "that we would meet their trains and planes."

"And entertain them and offer to show them around town," adds Mrs. Priest, "when they stayed long enough. Lately, though, they don't seem to want this."

"Even if they did, I couldn't fit them into my schedule very easily," says Mrs. Crounse. "But with the jets, the trend seems to be away from staying overnight either before or after the speech. No matter what the bureaus say, some of our speakers come to town on Tuesday morning and expect you to have a cab waiting during the tea."

"One speaker," says Mrs. Priest, "walked in here while we were finishing lunch and just when I was to introduce him."

Tomorrow's speaker, Commander Peterson, should pose no such problem. Instead of the usual lecture-bureau form, Mrs. Crounse has received what she calls "a personal note from Admiral Peterson." She shows it to me.

> I will be arriving in Minneapolis Monday . . . God and the weather permitting. I have some business with the Minnesota Historical Society at St. Paul, but will call you from there to tell you of my arrival.

"If he doesn't reach *me*," says Mrs. Crounse, "the secretary at the club will tell him to report at 11:45 A.M."

I ask if this will allow time for her to brief the speaker on his audience and to interview him about his background. No, Mrs. Crounse says, the Colston Leigh Bureau has taken care of all that. She shows me an all-purpose press release for Mrs. Priest to use in preparing her introduction of the speaker. It begins:

> History will come alive on _____ when Commander Mendel Peterson, USNR, of the world famous Smithsonian Institution delivers a talk, strikingly illustrated by color slides, at _____ under the auspices of _____.

Two pages of biography follow. "Sometimes," says Mrs. Priest, "I find these embarrassingly out of date. I'll say the speaker has two children when by now he has four." Then a blank is allowed for filling in which of Commander Peterson's four subjects the sponsor has chosen: "The Smithsonian: Treasure House of History," "History Under the Sea," "Weaponry:

From Rocks to Rockets," or "Render Unto Caesar: The History and Romance of Money." Tomorrow is Men's Guest Day, so the ladies have chosen "History Under the Sea" to appeal to the husbands. The topic, they explain unblushingly, is masculine, but not too masculine—as the weapons talk might be.

The next noon, having turned his slides over to a projectionist, Commander Peterson goes to lunch at a round table in a private dining room with Mrs. Priest, Mrs. Crounse, a dozen other club officials, and a handful of husbands, including Mrs. Crounse's. The commander is a gray-haired, very erect native of Idaho who speaks with a crisp Southern-fried purr peculiar to lecturers, Washingtonians, and service personnel. In the main dining room beyond the door, 200 of the ladies who will hear the lecture are eating the same $1.50 macaroni-soufflé-in-pink-shrimp-sauce luncheon, but without Commander Peterson's presence. Like a reluctant dragon, the commander dominates the round table—for the conversation is desultory, except for questions aimed at him. At one point, Mrs. Priest passes a dish of cottage cheese and asks playfully: "What would you do, Commander, if I dropped this in your lap?"

The commander's granite jaw makes a gallant thrust as he replies: "The show must go on—even under cottage cheese."

A committeewoman on my left gasps: "That man exudes power!"

The commander, who should be relaxing or tensing up for his speech, instead is expected to entertain his private-dining-room audience. Pumped for tales of skin diving and shipwrecks, he copes gamely and vividly.

"The important thing about a shipwreck is that it's a closed site. As I'm going to say in my lecture, a ship is an archaeological discovery made in an instant. Once you identify the ship and its year of sinking, you can study everything inside it with some certainty that it was actually in use in that year. I call a shipwreck an underwater time capsule."

By 1:20, when the commander takes an elevator down to the auditorium, he appears drained. He stops in at the men's room, but even there he has no privacy. One of the husbands ambushes him at the urinal with a question left over from lunch.

In the auditorium, a members' fashion show is in progress. To

the tune of "I'm as Restless as a Willow in a Windstorm," a
Minneapolis matron models "The Mondrian Look." At 1:35,
Commander Peterson and Gertrude Priest mount the stage, and
she announces: "It is a lucky man who can have adventure as
his vocation. . . ." On finishing her canned introduction, she
leaves the stage and joins the 400 other ladies present. (The president used to sit on the platform until short dresses came back
in.)

Commander Peterson's lecture is occasionally too fast (from
fifteenth century to himself exhuming a galleon in one slide)
and too cute ("Now pirates don't come to town to play parcheesi
and sip lemonade") and definitely too long (ninety slides lasting
an hour!). But on the lecture circuit nowadays, none of these
constitutes a serious flaw, and the commander's skill and passion
ordinarily would offset them. What does drag down the afternoon, however, is the innocent, yet debilitating, luncheon that
preceded it. Much of the same material I heard an hour earlier
is now delivered flabbily, almost apologetically, with little of
the off-the-cuff vitality it had in the private dining room. Because Commander Peterson runs overtime, the question period
is skipped, and he goes straight to tea. Mrs. Crounse says goodbye apologetically, for she must drive her husband back to the
office. On the receiving line, a woman who had squirmed
through the commander's lecture is still a dozen handshakes
away, but looking forward eagerly. "He's a regular James Bond,
isn't he?"

[III]

The Chautauqua bubble burst from overexpansion. The banner year of 1924 was, in retrospect, disappointing (its content
was spread too thin), and hardly anyone rebooked. The facade
was the last detail to crumble, but Chautauqua's historians, the
Cases, say that the kiss of death had been on it for more than a
decade. The automobile, the radio, and the movies had opened
new horizons for Chautauqua's public while Chautauqua itself
grew more inbred as it expanded.

The zealous promoters had sold three-day Chautauquas to
half-interested communities. As the circuits had expanded, an

act that would be meaningful in Bozeman, Montana; De Funiak Springs, Florida; Lithia Springs, New Jersey; and Albany, Oregon, had come to have very little relevance to anybody anywhere. Booking jams and close connections had exhausted the best talent and left the field open to amateurs and hard-boiled "Chautauqua people." Chautauqua no longer required any growth, any change in a speaker; in fact, his managers resisted any variables in a known quantity, and he could always be reassured by the sound of his own voice.

Glibness had created the first nagging doubts on Main Street. One Chautauqua devotee recalls a speaker who in 1916, when Europe was already at war, had lectured for two hours, "saying over and over again that the United States would never go to war. He bolstered his arguments with history, philosophy, psychology, and quotations from literature. We could see that he was absolutely sincere, and he knew what he was talking about.

"The United States declared war next spring, and of course Chautauqua was coming again in the summer. When we got our programs, we found the same speaker booked again. I think all of the men in town jammed into the tent to hear him explain where his history, philosophy, and the rest had slipped up. So we listened to another two-hour lecture on another subject entirely, with arguments bolstered by history, philosophy, psychology, and quotations from literature, and the man was absolutely sincere and knew what he was talking about. This time it sounded like sawdust. If he had made one single reference to his former speech, if he had said, 'Well, folks, is my face red!' or indicated in any way that he had been wrong once in his life, it would have satisfied us. As it was, nobody wanted to sign for Chautauqua again."

When the United States government clapped a 10 percent amusement tax on Chautauqua, its days as a cultural institution were numbered. Imagine, for comparison's sake, the future of the Golden Dozen if theater parties were to lose their tax exemption.

Still, on the surface, 1924 was a very good year—statistically, the best ever. Chautauqua looked as ruddy and expansive as its silver tongue, William Jennings Bryan. But three decades of Chautauqua—the first two stimulating him to new feats of ora-

tory and the last coarsening him, flattening him, emptying him
—had drained the statesman much as I was to see an afternoon's
repetition numb Commander Mendel Peterson, U.S.N.R.
In 1925, both Chautauqua and Bryan were dead.

The Depression hammered the final nail into Chautauqua's
coffin. In his own struggle to survive the 1930's, the American
male abdicated his cultural franchise, and lecturing lost what
rowdy virility it had. Only the middle-aged, well-to-do female
of the species had hands less than full. Thus the backbone of
lecturing became the Helen Hokinson ladies, fluttery gushers
named after the *New Yorker* cartoonist who immortalized them.
(Clubwoman to speaker: "But does Westchester want a strong
Yugoslavia?" Program chairman to committee: "It's the same
lecture, but for twenty dollars extra, he wears a leopard skin.")
Because they twittered so audibly and made themselves so visible, the Hokinson ladies were considered by many to be the
prototype of culture vultures, even though they were even
more preyed on than predatory.

After World War II, younger, more sophisticated women
seized the clubhouses. A portrait of one typical program chairman was drawn by Bernard De Voto in 1955:

> Marian . . . has been program chairman of the Bingville
> Women's Club for years and has bought all the books of
> every writer who has appeared on its platform during her
> term. . . . You inscribe them all 'To Marian' and sign
> your first name, for she is on terms of *tutoiement* with
> 'Ted,' who is Edward A. Weeks,* 'John,' who is John
> Mason Brown, and several dozen other circuit riders. You
> do not try to find out whether she has read any of them for
> there is no reason why she should have and at least she has
> wanted to meet you. More than half the delightful people
> who drop in don't want to; they are here because she is a
> power in Bingville. . . . Of the rest most think you are
> someone else. In my time I have been understood to be
> practically everyone from Brooks Atkinson to Gregory Zil-
> boorg. Once last year, when I came off the platform glowing
> with a conviction that this time I had been on the ball, I

---

* Then the editor of the *Atlantic Monthly*.

was collared by an elderly gentleman who asked angrily where my rope was. He thought I was Will Rogers.*

And do you think that Marian, as a pillar of the power structure in Bingville, would tolerate a community scold like Nels Darling on *her* platform? Whadayatalk! She doesn't know the territory doesn't know the territory pickalittle talkalittle cheepcheepcheep talkalot pickalittlemore! There may be trouble in River City, but not in Bingville.

"There is no juvenile delinquency," the lecture agent W. Colston Leigh reminds his lecturers before sending them out into the field. "It's all in the next town."

W. Colston Leigh, Inc., "America's Largest Lecture-Entertainment Bureau," has headquarters in a Fifth Avenue office building and branches in Chicago and San Francisco. Bill Leigh, the son of an eminent American painter, William Robinson Leigh, set up shop in the 1920's, while Chautauqua was crumbling. Amid the ruins, Leigh flourished with his first two talents: the Indian Princess Chinquilla and a Viennese monkey-gland miracle doctor. His stable expanded, but his big break came in 1933, when Mrs. Ernest K. Lindley, wife of one of his lecturers, inquired if he would be interested in representing Eleanor Roosevelt—"an honor," says Leigh, "that even a young whippersnapper like me would have been too embarrassed to ask for." He worked with Mrs. Roosevelt from then on (her regular fee was $1,500) and recalls that she once asked him: "After I leave the White House, do you think people will want to hear me?"

Today Leigh's active catalog lists more than 100 speakers, ranging from Cleveland Amory on "Who Killed Society?" or "TV: The Medium Medium" all the way to "An Evening with the Meredith Willsons," who certainly know the territory. Given enough notice and a fee from $200 on upward, Colston Leigh can set your home town cackling with Art Buchwald; surprise you with Jessica Mitford on "The American Way of LIFE" and Harry Golden on civil rights; show you "New Hampshire's Sugar Bush Country Through the Eyes of Drs. Lorus J. and Margery Milne"; share with you the secrets of "The Stories I

---

* De Voto, Bernard, "The Easy Chair." *Harper's* magazine (March, 1955).

Couldn't Write," by Eddy Gilmore of the Associated Press, "The Art of the Prima Ballerina," by Alicia Markova, "So Near the Great," by Winston Churchill's bodyguard, and "Science and Quackery in Nutrition," by Carlton Fredericks; furnish knowledgeable instruction by Louis Untermeyer on "How to Hate Poetry in One Easy Lesson," by Jim Bishop on "So You Want to Be a Journalist!" by Emily Kimbrough on "Listen While You Look"; and answer such questions as "Why Are We in Antarctica?" (Rear Admiral David M. Tyree, U.S.N., Ret.) and "Can We Trust the Germans?" (Mrs. James B. Conant) before you've even thought to ask them. Colston Leigh can even guarantee safe controversy; he packages a debate on any of several prechosen subjects by James A. Burkhart on the left versus Fulton Lewis III on the right.

The interior of a lecture agency is surprisingly sedate for a wonderland of negotiable earbending, where the speaker willing to talk on either "Help, There's a Rhinoceros in My Rose Garden!" or "The Emerging Nations of Africa" may well be offering the same speech; where last year's penologist on "Prisoners Are People" is replaced by this year's critic on "Authors Are People"; where novelist Harry Mark Petrakis—vended with customary understatement as "A Storyteller in the Great Tradition of Homer"—elects to confide, on the lecture platform, that he considers "Writing, Like Dying, A Private Experience"; where Vincent Price, who holds the Leigh bureau's record of fifty-seven speeches in sixty-one days, ranks second only to Mrs. Eleanor Roosevelt in esteem; where such pundits as Vance Packard and Betty Friedan are ranked as fair-to-middling speakers "whose material outweighs their style" but are seldom booked to address Jewish groups since they "require style as well as content and won't settle for a poor speaker because they themselves are good orators."

Lecturing is a multi-million-dollar industry today, despite competition from television's living-room intimacy and the explosion of new forms, new fads, new ideas, new culture complexes. Stodgy and unprogressive, lecturing has withstood its own erosion by eliminating the trappings of Chautauqua and concentrating on basics: the thirst of the American woman for self-improvement and somewhere to go. Some 100,000 "club lectures," as this oldfangled remnant of the lyceum trade is called, will be given this year for fees of up to $1,500. Ninety percent of the lecture business is outside the New York City area, where the citizens have so many opportunities to attend events that they take advantage of very few. While the lecturing scene takes in fraternal, business, professional, and university groups as well as town halls, the formidable matriarch of this landscape, more entrenched but more passive than ever, is the program chairwoman.

Whatever their degree of dedication, America's 15,000 Marians and Lura Crounses and Hazel Albersons have limited time and resources. They must depend, largely or wholly, on a handful of lecture bureaus based in New York or Chicago. A lecture bureau is a talent agency that auditions, represents, packages, merchandises and guarantees lecturers to clubs. Very few program chairladies know how a bureau operates or why speakers cost as much as they do. Most assume that the bureau pockets the 10 percent agent's commission that prevails in other arts.

Actually a typical bureau (such as W. Colston Leigh) takes a *35 percent to 50 percent commission,* depending on whether or not it pays the speaker's first-class travel arrangements. Under either plan, the lecturer must pay for his own food and hotel. The bureau prints brochures and other promotional materials advertising the speaker, but these costs (up to $200 or $300) are deducted periodically from his fees. If, however, the speaker has grossed $10,000 a year, the bureau pays these printing bills.

So far as the dozen lecturers I spoke with are concerned, W. Colston Leigh (abetted by a staff of thirty) runs such a smoothly meshed operation that none of them begrudged him his appallingly high commission. One speaker, just back from a tightly organized whirlwind tour, said he would "unhesitatingly nominate Colston Leigh for Secretary of Defense" on the basis of how he deploys his troops. An author-lecturer said he only wished his literary agent and publisher would do a fraction of the selling job that Leigh performs.

None of which impressed husky, tough-talking Bill Leigh, a supersalesman of sixty-six with close-cropped white hair and a broken nose. "My major concern," he said, "is to build a minimum of a million dollars in sales a year. . . . I live by the bible of what's going on and try to anticipate what'll happen."

When Leigh interviews a potential lecturer, he asks him:

"Are you interested in making money or making a crusade? If it's a crusade, go somewhere else. But if you want to make a buck, we'll do well by you and everyone within earshot."

One author, a crusader by nature, felt his heart sink. But then he responded that he wanted his lectures to sell his books, and he and Leigh were in business!

Several lecture agencies conduct annual spring "slave markets," for which hundreds of program chairwomen converge on New York hotel ballrooms to appraise the new talent. Notebooks in laps, they withstand, at ten-minute intervals, a dizzying succession of assaults (on safe targets like *Playboy* and Beatlemania), uplift ("I am forty-one and have learned that you must find your niche in fashion. I have good straight legs and good straight teeth. I make the most of them"), inspiration ("Beware of cavities in your courage!") and inside dope ("What I am telling you today I ask you to keep to yourself until next Sunday, when I shall break it on my program").

Bill Leigh, who frowns on complicated procedures that are "making the lecture racket into the lecture business," operates without formal auditions. A potential lecturer is asked to make an appointment with Leigh. When he arrives, he is ushered into Leigh's office. Waiting with Leigh are anywhere from twelve to twenty of the bureau's sales employees. Beside Leigh's desk is the only empty chair, and the startled visitor sinks into it. How he acquits himself in the next few minutes will determine whether he is to begin a career as a Leigh lecturer. "The people who evaluate you," Leigh explains blandly, "should be the people who'll be asked what you're like."

Leigh himself boasts that he has attended only two lectures in his life, one by Will Durant and one by someone whose name he forgets. Perhaps, I thought to myself, he would be less detached if he had tried for three with Mendel Peterson in Minneapolis. But Leigh must have thought I was thinking something else, for he plunged ahead rhetorically. "Curiosity? I have no curiosity. I delegate my curiosity."

By all rights, Colston Leigh's fees and attitudes should have earned him a stellar role in the first part of this book—among the Golden Dozen and other backstage Pied Pipers who package and peddle culture. Certainly, as a culture vulture, he has done his share to further a job that was begun in the last decade of Chautauqua—reshaping the American lecture from an inspired art into a synthetic, no-revolutions-per-hour, spoken-word record transmitted by ostensibly "live" stereophonic speakers.

But why belabor a disc jockey for the music he pushes? Anyway, at this stage of my research, Colston Leigh was merely a featured player. I was now hunting high and low for a culture consumer who would try to break the mold. I wanted to find out what happened when some intrepid dilettante sought to buck the tightly closed system. I realized that I had stumbled on that rare bird when I asked some of the people to whom Leigh delegates his curiosity: "Which agency booked Patsy Mink into Madison for the talk I'm going to hear on Saturday?"

Leigh's staff had to check with the Chicago office for an answer. A couple of hours later, an incredulous voice told me by phone: "Why, that Mrs. Alberson has gone into the booking business herself!"

[IV]

Hazel Stewart Alberson wears blue-rimmed glasses and reminds me of actress Mildred Dunnock. She is even more remarkable than I had been given to expect. Born in Iowa seventy-one years ago, she taught high school Latin and married a pilot who had suffered lung damage in a World War I plane crash. A few months apart, her husband, Oral, died of tuberculosis and their only child, eighteen-month-old Rachel, died of pneumonia. Alone, Hazel Alberson went back to school, took her Ph.D. at the University of Wisconsin, and designed her own one-story home on Euclid Avenue. The house went without wiring for several months because a wren had built its nest in a crucial spot, which Hazel Alberson refused to disturb until the baby birds had graduated to outdoor living. She calls her home Alberson Wrenstead.

She taught comparative literature at the university, where she became an associate professor in 1947, and later served twice as department chairman. When she retired in 1964, one former student wrote to her: "You give to your students the wonderful impression that we are worth your efforts. I shall remember your

example . . . long after I have forgotten what Confucius said."
Another mourned, "No one can duplicate your method or what
you had to say, for your courses were as much YOU as they were
the Greeks, the Indians, and Dante." Hazel Alberson, professor
emeritus, still teaches at the university's alumni seminars in the
summer.

She had been a member of the Madison Civics Club for only
four years when its board of directors, noting that this gifted
woman had a little time on her hands, selected her as assistant
program chairman for 1965, which meant automatic succession a
year later to the club's highest post, program chairman. And if
ever there was a woman qualified and willing to fight upstream
against the tide of canned superficiality that is the lecture racket
today, it was Hazel Stewart Alberson.

She was still assistant chairman when *Parade,* the Sunday supplement carried by the *Wisconsin State Journal,* featured a cover
story on the "most important woman in [Hawaiian] politics
since Queen Liliuokalani was dethroned in 1893 [and] the first
woman of Oriental ancestry to be admitted to the Hawaiian
Bar." Mrs. Alberson was in the market for an "outstanding
American career woman." She polled three or four of her dozen
board members by phone and then addressed a letter to Congresswoman Patsy Takemoto Mink, Washington, D.C.:

> Dear Madam:
> The picture of lovely you and the article in *Parade* has
> impelled me to write you hopefully about speaking before
> our Civics Club in Madison, Wis. As chairman of the Club
> of next year with the responsibility of setting up a five-
> lecture series for the year, I still have two dates open, _____
> and _____. I have one woman scheduled for February,
> Madame Rajan Nehru, and would love to have you for
> either date.
> This is a club which celebrated its 50th anniversary in
> 1962 and is composed of women, old and young, prominent
> in University and Civic life of the community and eager to
> welcome speakers who are active and wide-ranging in their
> interests. The meetings are always on Saturday: a small
> reception for the speakers and honor guests at 11:30, lunch-
> eon at 12, introduction of guests at 1, speech at 1:20 for 50

minutes, and a brief question session. The membership is 600 with a waiting list of 500, and the seating capacity for the luncheon is 750.

The fee we are prepared to offer is for $500 to $750, which must cover all transportation and expenses as well as the speech. We do make most contracts for lecturers through bureaus, but I have not seen your name listed on any of the brochures.

Obviously you are a busy woman, but because this date is a Saturday and flights to Madison very quick, I do hope it may be possible for you to consider it.

Cordially,
(signed) HAZEL STEWART ALBERSON
Associate Professor of Comparative Literature

The Madison Civics Club meets on Saturdays, Mrs. Alberson explained to me later, because this is best for career-woman members and downtown parking, not to mention husbands who baby-sit or tag along. It has no clubhouse but meets in the Park Motor Inn. This not only eases parking still further but also keeps the club virtually free to change addresses, as it has twice, with changing times.

("Several of the older members objected when we moved here from one of the *old* hotels," a fortyish hostess told me later at the Park Motor Inn. "But they're the ones who like this place best now. At the hotel, they used to have rectangular tables and straight-back chairs, and the old ladies used to fall asleep right after lunch. Here at the motor inn, we have smaller padded chairs and round tables, which keep the chitchat and the people alive.")

In retrospect, Mrs. Alberson realizes that she made one mistake in her letter to Patsy Mink. "I shouldn't have mentioned our price range. Once I'd admitted we could pay seven hundred and fifty dollars, it was certain we'd have to pay it. There isn't a single speaker who's worth the money we pay. But the bureaus set the price scale for the whole lecture business. I just won't let us go over seven hundred fifty dollars."

A month later, she received a very brief acceptance note from Congresswoman Mink. Mrs. Alberson wrote back, asking for biographical details and a publicity photo, suggesting "Duties,

Disturbances, and Delights of a Congresswoman" as a topic her members would enjoy hearing, and mentioning her pet project, a reading list:

> We place before the members at our first meeting in October a list of books, either by the speaker or related to the background of the speaker or the area of the speech. The City Librarian not only prepares this, but also sets up (at our beautiful new library building!) a book display. We would be very happy for any suggestions from you.

She concluded by reminding Mrs. Mink, "I need to ask what your fee will be" and urging that "you be in the city the night before so that we will not have 'jitters' about your arrival."

Mrs. Mink wrote back: "I shall be most happy to speak on the subject of 'Women in Politics' for 20 minutes at $750."

Hazel Alberson unleashed a small sigh of relief, for a price ceiling is often the bottom rung on which negotiations start. She wrote Mrs. Mink that price and subject were satisfactory, but the club members (who pay $13 for all five lectures and luncheons) and applicants and guests (who come for $3.25 per luncheon-lecture) expected a fifty-minute lecture. Mrs. Mink replied that she would go the full-length route and made a few suggestions for the reading list.*

Mrs. Alberson, who also wrote directly to Barbara Ward, Sargent Shriver, and John W. Gardner, only to be turned down by each, filled her other open date with Alvin Toffler, one of Colston Leigh's new faces, on "America's Cultural Coming of Age." The others, already booked through bureaus, were Madame Nehru on "The New Woman of India," the young Winston Churchill on "Changing Faces of European Politics," and Dr. Thomas P. Melady of the African Studies Institute in New York on "Africa and the Revolution of Color."

Madison's was not the balanced program for which the Woman's Club of Minneapolis had striven so mightily. But it met Mrs.

---

* *Hawaii Pono,* by Lawrence H. Fuchs, a social history of Hawaii; *Home Place: The Story of the U.S. House of Representatives,* by William S. White; *Modern American Career Women,* by Eleanor Clymer; *Ladies of Courage,* by Eleanor Roosevelt and Lorena A. Hickok, and *Understanding Politics,* by Louise M. Young.

Alberson's goal: "A series ought to have a theme—in my case, 'The Wide World'—that expresses the individual personality of the chairman. My Indian speaker represented my own love for India.* A speech on Africa was my way of getting into civil rights problems without talking about civil rights. Churchill! A dashing young Englishman who spoke understandable English and had a name that summoned up all my love for European literature and history. Toffler? Well, I must confess that I *used* him. I cannot understand why so many of our oldest members retire to Florida or Arizona and collect seashells or sit on cactuses or whatever they do. This includes our university people when they become emeritus. I wanted a young man who would remind our older members that they were lucky enough to live in a major cultural center which they would at last have time to enjoy.

"And Patsy was just someone who appealed to me. I suppose she was also my dainty little protest against the lecture-circuit lions, the stars of the bureaus, who have so little stature or depth and who are so infatuated with the sound of their own voices. Besides, she's a woman! The only balance I seek on my program is balance of the sexes.

"The important thing is to take what appeals to you and your interests. You can't go very far wrong on a speaker if he or she deals with an area *you* know and like. Being interested yourself, it's easy to interest your members in advance.

"I feel so strongly about the program expressing the chairman that even though I made a list of suggestions for my successor, I'm not going to show it to her for fear she'll be bound by it. Anyway, that's an advantage of our self-perpetuating board system. Having worked as my assistant chairman for a year, she must have learned the same lessons. . . ."

Once she had chosen and booked her talent, Mrs. Alberson had just begun to fight. "On this job," she said, "you're at the mercy of speakers, bureaus, transportation, snow, and bad weather."

When Dr. Melady sent word that his train was *due* to arrive

---

* In 1961, Mrs. Alberson went all the way to New Delhi for the 100th anniversary of the birth of Sir Rabindranath Tagore, the Nobel Prizewinning dramatist who died in 1941.

at 12:35 P.M. Saturday for a 1 o'clock lecture, Mrs. Alberson phoned his lecture agency and was told: "He likes to come in by train, do his work on the train in, and fly right out."

"Well, I have a contract that says he'll be in Madison the night before," said Mrs. Alberson firmly, "so tell him to fly in, and he can take the train back."

The agency yielded, but at 10:45 Friday night, Dr. Melady had not yet checked into the Park Motor Inn. Hazel Alberson called again at 9:30 A.M. Saturday and gave a sigh of relief when the Park Motor Inn told her: "Yes, he's in. Would you like to speak to him?"

"Certainly not," Mrs. Alberson replied, hanging up happily.

She and a vice-chancellor of the University went to the airport on Friday night to meet Alvin Toffler. But the speaker wasn't on the flight that Colston Leigh had specified. Mrs. Alberson and the vice-chancellor went on to dinner at the Top o' the Park Restaurant, where they'd reserved a table for three. There they sat, swapping stories about speakers, until a solitary diner at a nearby table overheard them and introduced himself as Al Toffler. The Leigh bureau had booked him on an earlier flight, and he had been wondering, ever since he'd checked in, what to do on a lonely night in Madison, Wisconsin.

The young Winston Churchill was tendered a Friday night dinner in his honor by some prominent local Anglophiles. His agency accepted but apparently didn't notify Churchill, who enjoyed Friday dinner in Chicago.

Two weeks before her date in Madison, Madame Nehru had a heart attack!

"Colston Leigh sent me a telegram canceling," Mrs. Alberson recalled, "which was a mistake on their part. They should have phoned and suggested a substitute. By the time they did, I'd spent two hours wringing my hands and then had called another bureau, Wide World, for another Indian speaker, Dr. Anup Singh, a Member of Parliament. I was told what train he'd be on. I went down to the railroad station, but he came in by plane."

With Madame Nehru scratched, the only female on Mrs. Alberson's program was her final entry, Patsy Mink. On the eve of the event, Mrs. Alberson showed me a copy of her last letter to the Congresswoman.

Dear Patsy T. Mink:

Everything is in readiness for your appearance here next Saturday. Publicity has been out for a week, the reservations are rolling in. . . .

She then reviewed the details about the club from her previous letters.

"It's important that you give the speaker a complete picture of what to expect," Hazel Alberson told me. "What you can't count on is that the speaker will read your briefing. A few years ago, Cleveland Amory came to Madison thinking we were a bunch of college kids. Fortunately, I suppose, he's a very fluent man, to say the least. He simply switched topics in midspeech." Her last letter to Patsy Mink concluded:

Unless you wish it I will not meet you at the airport, for I've had problems with every speaker this year! I will appreciate a call from you when you reach the hotel on Friday and will be happy to come in and chat, if you wish it. My telephone number is _____.

There will be a request from the afternoon newspaper reporter for an interview on Saturday morning for the paper goes to press while you are talking. . . .

It may be helpful for you to be briefed on the Honor Guests who will be sitting at the speaker's table with you. Governor Warren Knowles has sent a message for he has another appointment (in Washington!) for that day. The others who will be there are: Thomas Fairchild, Justice of the Supreme Court; Bronson La Follette, Attorney General; Wilbur Renk, a highly respected citizen active in politics; Shirley Abrahamson, a woman lawyer; Kathryn Clarenbach, Director of Women's Education; [Mrs.] Glenn Wise, first woman to hold constitutional office in this state; [Mrs.] Carolyn Wilds, president of the League of Women Voters, and two members of the board.

"The backdrop that you give a speaker makes a big difference," Mrs. Alberson told me. "It enhances acceptance if our women see him eating and perhaps chatting with local people. There's a rapport created. Just by being one of six hundred people in a dining room with him, you are, in a way, lunching with him. And perhaps it puts him at ease. If he'd rather be let alone, the people at the speaker's table will be sensitive enough to realize that, too. Another thing we do to help him relax comes during the question period. I ask the speaker to repeat the question, which gives him time to rephrase it, if he wishes, think on his feet, and answer it in his own way."

Her final speaker, however, had done nothing to relax Hazel Alberson. The last item on file was a notation that Patsy Mink would not leave Washington until Saturday morning, connecting at Chicago to North Central Flight 111, due in Madison at 11:02 A.M. She would leave Madison on a 3:30 P.M. flight, having seen little or nothing of the tree-rimmed lakes that shape Madison's geography, the university's sprawling waterfront campus, or the granite-domed capitol crowned by a famous statue, "Miss Wisconsin."

Hazel Alberson, however, could not have cared less about Patsy Mink's sightseeing. Taking the file back from me, she said: "If that young lady's plane is late, all this work can go into the wastebasket, and I'll have six hundred angry women on my hands. But she's a politician, so I don't think she'll stand up a crowd."

Toward 11:30 A.M. Saturday, when the preliminary orange punch reception is getting underway at the Park Motor Inn, a message comes from the airport, via the switchboard, that Mrs. Mink has arrived. The program chairman grows outright jolly. Her assistant chairman, Fay Little, protests: "But Hazel, I thought she was in town all along! You didn't even tell us there was trouble."

"It wouldn't have done your work any good if you'd been worrying about mine," Mrs. Alberson says calmly.

Enter Patsy Mink, wearing a mink stole. "Cute as a button!" says one of the hostesses. The newspaper interview is transacted. Hazel Alberson dutifully checks some biographical details. (She remembers the Han Suyin incident that embarrassed one of her predecessors. The glamorous authoress of *Love Is a Many Splendored Thing* brought along her new husband, who was not the man described in the lecture bureau's biography and introduced by the chairman.) The roast beef lunch is served on schedule to a near-capacity audience. At long last, after a member's public-affairs report, "Madison Greets the Space Age" (runway and terminal improvements at the Municipal Airport) and Hazel Alberson's introduction, Patsy Mink stands up to speak.

She begins promisingly by asking us, in a throbbing voice, why—according to a survey made in 1966—a *woman* seeking election starts out with an 18 percent disadvantage. But, alas, the rest is history—an impersonal, secondhand chronicle of women's rights from Anne Hutchinson the heretic to Ida M. Tarbell the muckraker. It is not a dull sermon, but it scarcely justifies the presence, let alone the 1,700-mile round trip, of Congresswoman Mink. Nor is it a fitting reward for the Madison Civics Club's $750 or Hazel Alberson's year of persistence. As I sit in that crowded ballroom, the noblest vision that Patsy Mink's words conjure up is teams of congressional researchers poring over history books in an effort to beef up her standard twenty-minute pep talk on "Women in Politics."

Even so, it lasts just thirty minutes. She closes with Jefferson's admonition that "institutions must change with the times." * Then, in the moment between lukewarm applause and question period, she lights a cigarette, thereby shocking several older members.

One of the younger women at my table, however, is already well along in her distress. Mrs. Kenneth Orchard, who preceded Hazel Alberson as chairman, tells me: "The Congresswoman made a common mistake of lecturers. *She underestimated her audience.* Our women are saturated with feminine-mystique preaching. They want nuts-and-bolts details, information from experience. What's it like, and how does it feel to be a mother in politics? Children are the big enigma. . . ."

What a shame! Congresswoman Mink, unfettered by lecture-bureau restrictions or, for that matter, commissions, had every opportunity to set a good example for the women of Madison and the lecture circuit in general. Thoroughly briefed by Hazel Alberson, she was fully capable of electrifying the Madison Civics Club with a rousing talk on "Duties, Disturbances and

---

* That Mrs. Mink is no mere civic-club crusader for women's rights was demonstrated early in 1967, when, brandishing a form invitation to all Congressmen, she showed up ready to work out at the all-male House gymnasium and was immediately ejected.

Delights of a Congresswoman" or on what it's like to be a "Woman in Politics." Instead she had simply lifted a leaf from Colston Leigh's handbook and delivered a syndicated, padded, prepackaged and largely impersonal background briefing.

What is operating here is an everyday principle that psychiatrists and philosophers call *the self-fulfilling prophecy*, which also cushions virtually every culture vulture we have confronted. This is how it works: If one or both partners in a marriage behave as though it is doomed, then it is likely to fail. If parents treat a child like a delinquent, the chances are he will become one. If a nation girds for war, a war often ensues. If the Book-of-the-Month Club picks a book as a likely best seller, it is likely to become a best seller, thanks to the Book-of-the-Month Club. If Henry Geldzahler says an unknown painter will attract attention, the art world immediately sits up and takes notice. And if Colston Leigh says you can't get better lecturing cheaper than from him, by golly, free-lance lecturer Patsy Mink isn't about to prove him wrong!

When the question period begins, Lorraine Orchard's hand is raised high.

"You have a daughter," she begins. "We know your life is very busy, and you have a high dedication to morality and public life. But what is your typical day like, as it affects your family? What are the problems? Can you give us some practical tips?"

Mrs. Mink's answer is halting, rambling, but warm and enlightening. She describes the uprooting of her family in 1964, when Hawaii's voters sent her to Washington; her scientist husband relocating at Johns Hopkins; her fourteen-year-old daughter coming home from a Washington junior high school around 4:30 and starting the dinner, with father joining her around 6 and mother "crawling in as soon thereafter as I can"; mother and daughter moving back to Hawaii for the fall campaign, and the daughter changing her own ambition in life from nurse to politician.

In the audience, there is a rustle of affection that has not been felt since the hopeful moment when Hazel Alberson said, "And now I give you Patsy Mink!" From the dais, Mrs. Alberson flashes Mrs. Orchard a look of gratitude. For she has wiped some of the egg off Hazel Alberson's face. Mrs. Alberson made all—

or almost all—the right moves and a few brilliant ones, but in the end, it is the speaker who makes or breaks a program chairman.

Mrs. Orchard, however, is not yet appeased by Patsy Mink. "She's still underestimating her audience," she tells me. "She didn't say whether she has a cleaning woman."

The Tenth Commandment of the Culture Vultures:
Settle for less than the best, and you will get
exactly what you deserve.

10

The Baby-Grand Tourists

grand tour—An extended tour of the Continent formerly commonly taken by youth of the British aristocracy as a part of their education; hence, any similar extended tour.
— *Webster's*

[1]

THE grand tour was conceived by Queen Elizabeth I as the climax of a liberal education. "There were always," wrote Sir Francis Bacon, "sent forth into several parts beyond the seas some young men of whom good hopes were conceived . . . to be trained up and made fit for such public employment and to learn the languages. This was the charge of the Queen, which was not much; for they travelled but as private gentlemen, and as by their industry their deserts did appear, so were they further employed or rewarded."

In his essay *Of Travel*, Bacon, who had never been farther than Paris, plotted the itinerary of a young British aristocrat's grand tour.

First . . . he must have some entrance into the language before he goeth. Then he must have such a servant or tutor as knoweth the country. . . . Let him carry with him also some card or book describing the country where he travelleth; which will be a good key to his inquiry. Let him also keep a diary. Let him not stay long in one city or town; more or less as the place deserveth, but not long; nay, when he stayeth in one city or town, let him change his lodging from one end and part of the town to another. . . . Let him sequester himself from the company of his countrymen, and diet in such places where there is good company of the nation where he travelleth. Let him upon his removes from one place to another, procure recommendation to some person of quality residing in the place whither he removeth; that he may use his favor in those things he desireth to see or know. Thus he may abridge his travel with much profit. . . .

The grand tour was a main current, perhaps *the* main current, in the flow of British culture during the seventeenth and eighteenth and much of the nineteenth centuries. "It was slowness, that is, time for leisurely travel, that made it what it once was," writes one contemporary historian. "The oafish and ignorant young English squire, setting forth . . . in the company of his sly clerical mentor, knew that he had at least a twelvemonth in which to wear off his rough edges and acquire the veneer of cosmopolitan manners. However rich his lordship might be, there was one thing he could not buy—speed. . . . Thus he became willy-nilly a part of the landscape over which slow transport compelled him to march with decent deliberation."

Soon the grand tour came to mean a circuit of France, Switzerland, Italy, Germany, and the Low Countries, lasting from one to three years. (After five years, it was safe to consider a grand tourist an expatriate.)

In 1641, toward the end of the Thirty Years' War, the young diarist John Evelyn set out for France just in time to participate as a volunteer, "taking careful note of military devices," in a siege by the French and Dutch armies. Then he made his way by water to Rotterdam to view his first elephant and pelican. In Leyden he was made an honorary student of the university. In Amsterdam he visited hospitals, asylums, and charitable institutions—and tarried unduly long at the cottage of a widow who,

"having run through 25 husbands, was under some suspicion."
Notebook still in hand, John Evelyn went on to Paris to re-
cuperate amid "all the collections royal and private" and in-
dulge his passion for gardens. He spent five months in Tours
and then went on, by horseback and barge, to Marseilles. Fearing Turkish pirates, he traveled by mule to Cannes and thence
by sea to Italy, where he visited all the chief towns "except
Parma, Piacenza, and Mantua, rendered too dangerous by *ban-
ditti*." He spent seven months in Rome, inspecting "every relic"
and attending "every religious ceremony," including midnight
masses and a circumcision in the ghetto; led the gay life of
Venice, where a "bath did so open my pores that it cost me one
of the greatest colds I ever had in my life"; studied anatomy at
the University of Padua; caught smallpox from unchanged bed
linen in Switzerland; was married in Paris to the British Ambassador's teen-age daughter on his way home, and landed in
Dover ready and qualified to undertake the life of a country
squire.

Later in that century, an ascetic youth named Joseph Addison
—future poet, critic, and essayist—went to Paris but withdrew
to Blois, more celebrated for the purity of its French. "All the
languages of Europe are spoken [in Blois]," Addison proclaimed,
"except English, which is not to be heard, I believe, within 50
miles of the place." Mastering French in Blois, he returned to
Paris, at last able to converse in its salons. Later, his grand tour
took him to Lyons, Marseilles, Genoa, Milan, Verona, Padua,
Venice, and Rome. Oblivious to wolves, bears, bandits, and
assassins, he made the usual loop to Naples, "going by road to
feel like Horace and coming back by sea to feel like Virgil."

Charles James Fox, the Whig statesman, made his grand tour
in 1768 with three friends, a typical odyssey summated thusly
by Fox's biographer, George Otto Trevelyan:

> Lads of 18 and 19, who had been their own masters al-
> most since they could remember; bearing names that were
> a passport to any circle; with unimpaired health, and a
> credit at their banker's which they were not yet old enough
> to have exhausted, made their Grand Tour after much the
> same fashion. . . . Travelling with eight servants apiece;
> noticed by queens; treated as equals by ambassadors; losing
> their hearts in one palace and their money in another, and

yet, on the whole, getting into less mischief in high society than when left to their own devices, they

> "sauntered Europe round,
> And gathered every vice on Christian ground;
> Saw every court; heard every king declare
> His royal sense of operas or the fair;
> Tried all *hors-d'oeuvres,* all *liqueurs* defined,
> Judicious drank, and greatly daring dined."

For some, the grand tour might have been renamed the rake's progress. Many young men returned home with broken health or empty purse, as snobs and scoundrels, or utterly unchanged, as evidenced by this extract from a letter home dated "Rome, May the 3d, 1753":

> Sir: I have been here now a month, and will give you an account of my way of life. Here are a great many agreeable English gentlemen; we are about nine or ten as smart bucks as any in England. We constantly breakfast together, and then either go and see sights, or drive about. . . . We meet before dinner at the English coffee-house; where there is a very good billiard-table and very good company. From thence we go and dine together by turns at each other's lodgings. Then after a cheerful glass of claret, for we have made a shift to get some here, we go to the coffee-house again; from thence to supper, and so to bed. I do not believe these Romans are a bit like the old Romans; they are a parcel of thin-gutted, snivelling, cringing dogs; and I verily believe that our set could thrash 40 of them. We never go among them; it would not be worth while; besides, we none of us speak Italian and none of these signors speak English; which shows what sort of fellows they are. We saw the Pope go by t'other day in a procession, but we resolved to assert the honour of Old England; so we neither bowed nor pulled off our hats to the old rogue. Provisions and liquor are not bad here; and, to say the truth, I have not had one thorough good meal's meat since I left England.

By the same post, the father received a letter of resignation from the French tutor accompanying his son. "I am either laughed at or insulted. Sometimes I am called a beggarly French dog, and bid to go back to my own country and eat my frogs. . . ."

Nevertheless, even the most cynical historian must concede that the grand tour shaped the ideals and character of the most influential citizens of England. "A young lord may have caroused through Europe, caring less for a great cathedral than for a cockpit at Shoreditch, but the mere fact that as a leader of society and of fashion he had made the long tours of travel was enough to make it seem worthy of imitation." Then as now, the imitators included not only his countrymen but also the foreigners in whose lands they journeyed. Anglomania even became fashionable for a while among the French, who drank tea, imported racehorses, dressed like English jockeys, formed stuffy clubs, read Shakespeare, and even experimented with cold baths.

The revolutions of the late eighteenth century began to erode the grand tour; a letter of introduction to a guillotined aristocrat was worse than no letter at all. With the steam railways of the nineteenth century, a British aristocrat's visit to the Continent became an annual event rather than the trip of a lifetime. And when the middle class wanted in, the grand tour gave way to the Cook's tour.

The travel agent is a middle-class invention, a nineteenth-century offspring of speedy mass travel and safety in numbers. In 1838 a British entrepreneur took a trainload of tourists from Wadebridge to Bodmin to witness the hanging of two murderers. "Since the Bodmin gallows were in clear sight of the uncovered station," writes one historian, "excursionists had their fun without ever leaving the open railway carriages." Three years later, a traveling Baptist preacher and book salesman named Thomas Cook was on his way to a temperance meeting in Leicester when, in a flash of inspiration, he conceived "the idea of engaging a special train to carry the friends of temperance from Leicester to Loughborough and back" to attend another teetotaling rally. He signed up 570 customers at a group rate of a shilling apiece for the twenty-two-mile round trip, which included a band to play hymns, a picnic lunch featuring ham, and afternoon tea.

Thus did Thomas Cook (and Son, later on) launch low-priced rail excursions through England in the 1840's. By 1856, Cook was advertising the first "Grand Circular Tour of the Continent" (London, Antwerp, Brussels, Waterloo, Cologne, the Rhine, Mainz, Frankfurt, Heidelberg, Baden-Baden to take the waters, Strasbourg, Paris, London). Italy was not a must for the Cook's tourist the way it had been for the grand tourist. "Gentlemen," Cook would counsel his clientele, "do not invest your money in diarrhea." By 1869, Cook was offering what one historian calls "the first middle-class Conducted Crusade to the Holy Land." *

Then, amid the smoke of the Industrial Revolution, the American tourist planted his banner in old Europe. Some innocents abroad, ranging from Mark Twain and President Grant, went under Cook's auspices. Others traveled independently with wives and children. Still others, with every intention of catching up later, sent their wives and children ahead to grapple with the centuries-old complexities and corruptions of Europe. Their Boswell was Henry James, who, before even unpacking his bags on arrival in Rome, scrawled in his diary: "At last, for the first time, I live." And no American tourist was ever more real than James' most charming but vulnerable creation, Daisy Miller of Schenectady.

As the fast transatlantic steamship opened Europe to upper-class and then middle-class American tourism, the grand tour in its classical form came to an end. And in today's jet age, when Fodor has replaced Baedeker and you're only two gourmet meals away from the Colosseum on Alitalia, certain important values have been sacrificed for speed. Young men do their grand tours in uniform and then are quick to settle down and raise families (even quicker when Selective Service is deferring married fathers). The grand tour has fallen into the antiseptic custody of travel agents, who apply the label recklessly to anything from a four-day-and-three-night Bermuda Commuter Holiday at the Elbow Beach Surf Club on up. And no matter what the setting and circumstances, the game is the same. "The traveler used to

* Historical material herein on the grand tour is drawn primarily from four sources: *The Grand Tour: A History of the Golden Age of Travel,* by Geoffrey Trease. New York, Holt, Rinehart & Winston, 1967; *Grand Tour: A Journey in the Tracks of the Age of Aristocracy,* edited by R. S. Lambert (particularly the essays by Mona Wilson). London, Faber and Faber, 1935; *The Grand Tour in the 18th Century,* by William Edward Mead. Boston, Houghton Mifflin, 1914, and *An Early History of Charles James Fox,* by George Otto Trevelyan. New York, Harper, 1880.

go about the world to encounter the natives," says Professor Daniel J. Boorstin in his essay on the lost art of travel.* "A function of travel agencies now is to prevent this encounter. They are always devising effective new ways to insulate the tourist. . . ."

Boorstin concludes:

> As a nation we are probably the most traveled people of our time, or of any time. What is remarkable, on reflection, is not that our foreign travel has increased so much. But rather that all this travel has made so little difference in our thinking and feeling
> Our travels have not, it seems, made us noticeably more cosmopolitan or more understanding of other peoples. The explanation is not that Americans are any more obtuse or uneducable than they used to be. Rather, the travel experience itself has been transformed. Many Americans now "travel," yet few are travelers in the old sense of the word. The multiplication, improvement, and cheapening of travel facilities have carried many more people to distant places. But the experience of being there, and what is brought back from there are all very different. The experience has become diluted, contrived, prefabricated. . . .

Boorstin's sentiments do not differ vastly from those expressed by Dr. Samuel Johnson two centuries earlier about certain grand tourists who "tell nothing, because their method of travelling supplies them with nothing to be told. He that enters a town at night and surveys it in the morning, and then hastens away to another place . . . may please himself for a time with a hasty change of scenes and a confused remembrance of palaces. . . ." Nevertheless Dr. Johnson approved of grand tourism properly done. He once berated a gentleman for not being better company and particularly urged him to travel in Bohemia. "Surely," said Dr. Johnson, "the man who has seen Prague might tell us something new and something strange, and not sit silent for want of matter to put his lips in motion!"

The final episode of culture vulturism to be explored in this book will tell of an odyssey by seventy American dilettantes,

---

* From *The Image: or What Happened to the American Dream.* New York, Atheneum, 1962.

mostly female, who took Dr. Johnson's prescription of Prague by
flying to the capital of old Bohemia and the new Czechoslovakian
Socialist Republic.

What used to be a month-long trip is now almost a weekend possibility.   —Conrad Hilton.

[II]

The very first nonstop jet flight* between the United States
and Communist Czechoslovakia landed in a downpour at
Prague on the Sunday after Easter, 1966. Aboard the chartered
Scandinavian Airlines System DC-8 were two alligators, seven
turtles, and seventy moneyed Friends of the Cincinnati Symphony Orchestra (an estimated forty-seven of them bona fide
millionaires or next of kin.) The reptiles, a good-will gift from
the Cincinnati Zoo to the Prague Zoo, had only a few kilo-
meters farther to go. But the people, all patrons of the arts,
would leave Prague four days later for Vienna, Budapest, Moscow, Leningrad, and then back to Cincinnati to complete their
twenty-one-day culture tour of Eastern Europe. For this adventure, each had contributed at least $500 to the Cincinnati Or-
chestra "to raise salaries for musicians" and at least $1,100 more
to the Lindblad Travel Agency of New York and Nairobi "to
raise money for Lindblad." **

At 8:02 P.M., some 70 of us were airborne. . . . Because
of air turbulence, no dinner nor even drinks were served
until 8:45 P.M. Our last American drinks were good and
plentiful, and the dinner of shrimp, tournedos, salad, vege-
tables and cake good, but not as outstanding as had been
rumored.—From the diary of Cincinnatian John R. Bullock, attorney-at-law.

---

* Source: Scandinavian Airlines System in Prague.
** Source: Mrs. Lars-Eric Lindblad.

Nine hours aloft had dissipated some of the tensions that might have made togetherness impossible in Cincinnati. Aboard flight #9346 were business, political, and social rivals; an outspoken critic whose dim view of Max Rudolf's conducting had cost him his job, seated across from the good gray Establishment lawyer who had participated in his ouster; a traveling *ménage à trois* of husband, wife and other woman, and an Episcopalian minister who had long yearned to visit Russia but whose Indian Hill parishioners could forgive such heresy *only* because he was traveling under the most respectable Cincinnati auspices. As it was, while packing their bags, two dozen tour members had been harassed by Bircher calls informing them that their money was financing the Vietcong. In the *Enquirer*, which solid Cincinnati reads religiously, they had been heckled passionately by letters to the editor:

> While Moscow Communists admit they are furnishing arms and supplies for the murder of American soldiers in Vietnam, certain Cincinnatians are preparing "to attend symphony performances, theater, ballet, and art galleries in Vienna, Budapest, Prague, Moscow, and Leningrad." This is roughly like a friendly visit with Hitler in 1943 to see his etchings. . . .

and somewhat impersonally by an anonymous editorial writer:

> Thus far, it would seem, the widely held hope that increased trade and broadened cultural contacts between East and West would improve the level of life for the captive peoples of Eastern Europe has not been a realistic one. Indeed, lightening the economic woes of East Europe's Communist governments has only seemed to make the imposition of tighter political controls easier.

In addition to dispatching its book and art editor and a society writer to cover the tour, the *Enquirer* had assigned a special writer as far as the airport to send the adventurers aloft with a funereal throb.

> Husbands (or wives) seemed matter-of-fact as they bestowed kisses of farewell. Children of tour members seemed to cling a bit longer in that last embrace and a few, among

those who watched longingly from the big windows of the passenger lounge, wiped their eyes quietly as the big four-jet plane lumbered from ramp to runway almost out of sight.

Despite this rugged send-off, the cast of characters was not teeming with virility or youth. Women outnumbered men by more than two to one. Only four passengers were under thirty— all young girls in their early twenties, whose parents had treated them to the trip. (One of the girls was getting over a divorce.) There were a dozen indefatigable "traveling ladies," sprightly sexagenarians and septuagenarians who are the backbone of any group tour nowadays. Throughout the journey, one had great difficulty telling the traveling ladies apart, even though each had her own distinction—such as comparing a red wine in Budapest with its opposite number in Addis Ababa. For immortality's sake, there was an editor of *Town & Country*, a Hearst monthly that numerous members, somewhat apologetically, swore by. (Later he was to write, in the perfumed prose of his periodical, "At the outset it is obvious that it was anything but 'on-beat.'")

Above all, there was the trip's driving force, the organizer who had quelled all doubt and dissent—Mrs. Fred Lazarus III.

Irma Lazarus, fifty, who sits on the symphony's executive board and conducts her own educational television program, *Culture Anyone?* is the hoarse-voiced matriarch of Cincinnati's aesthetic scene. The Lazarus family is probably the most powerful economic institution in Cincinnati and a billion-dollar-a-year* department-store dynasty to be reckoned with nationally. The Lazaruses are partners in Federated Stores, which include Bloomingdale's and Abraham & Straus in New York, Filene's in Boston, Burdine's in Miami, Foley's in Houston, and Shillito's in Cincinnati, among others. Irma's husband, Fred, who accompanied her on the tour, is chairman of the board at Shillito's.

Irma sweeps forward with regal thrust. Nobody who knew her was surprised when, two and a half weeks later in a Leningrad hotel lobby, a Russian bowed low and asked her in French if she was the Princess of Monaco.

---

* Mahoney, Tom, and Sloane, Leonard, *The Great Merchants*. New York, Harper & Row, 1967.

Irma Lazarus arrived in Europe with her right arm in a cast, having dislocated her shoulder while skiing. Undaunted, she had gone ahead with her every plan but one: setting her own hair, a chore that her rotund, twinkling spouse had taken over.

The continental breakfast was not particularly good fortification for the rain that greeted our arrival. . . . Customs check was perfunctory, except for passport inspection.
— John Bullock's diary.

Inside the terminal at Prague, a welcoming committee of six was waiting for the Cincinnatians to clear customs. Three were guides from Čedok, the government tourist service, which handles everything from visas and sightseeing to laundry and money changing (at a bonus tourist rate giving an American 125 per cent *more* for his dollar than a Czech gets at the official rate). Like several Communist nations, Czechoslovakia was racing to Americanize itself for the tourist trade and the foreign currency it brings in.* One of the men from Čedok was apologizing nervously for the weather.

Lars-Eric Lindblad, thirty-nine, whose travel agency was conducting the tour, gave a loud cackle and shoved his hands into the pockets of his blue raincoat. "It took me five years and a lot of gray hair," he said, "to learn that there was only one thing in the travel business I couldn't do anything about: bad weather. At least the plane is able to land."

Ten years ago, Lindblad, a Swedish-born alumnus of Cook's and American Express, went off on his own to specialize in what he calls "motivated group travel." Since then, he has dis-

---

* Pan American World Airways was already building an Inter-Continental Hotel in Zagreb and dickering for another to open in Bucharest in 1970, but plans for a Prague Inter-Continental were bogging down over bureaucratic insistence that the new structure conform to the prevailing neighborhood of its site —which happened to be in the old ghetto that the Nazis decimated. Bulgaria, which lagged behind the others for a long while, promised in 1967 "to offer Americans and Western Europeans the Hilton and Inter-Continental kind of service right down to the 'sanitized for your protection' wrapper on toilet bowls and glasses."

patched (to mention just a few groups) a planeload of Holy Rollers to the Holy Land; shutterbugs on a Leica tour of Germany; antiquarians to Abu Simbel; archaeology buffs to the cuneiform world of Mesopotamia, and an American Committee on Africa on a "Journey Through Independent Africa with Other Americans Sympathetic to the Wind of Change." He has run grand tours for hog breeders, yachtsmen, ornithologists, anthropologists, botanists, and garden clubs. Lindblad operates a network of "Wing Safaris" through Africa (hence a branch office in Nairobi) via Piper Cubs flown by former RAF pilots. In 1966, borrowing a 7,000-ton transport, a tugboat, and an icebreaker from the Argentine Navy, Lindblad took fifty-two tourists, including an eighty-six-year-old traveling lady, on the first private sightseeing expedition to the Antarctic (cost per person: $3,000). In the spring of 1967, he led the first tourist expedition to Easter Island ($1,500 per person). If there are new worlds left to package, rest assured that Lars Lindblad will place an all-inclusive price on them.

One of the first realms that Lindblad latched onto was the fund-raising cultural tour, ranging from twelve days in Mexico City and Yucatan for the Katonah Gallery of Westchester (cost per person: $850, including a $200 tax-deductible contribution) to twenty-five days in Japan, Hong Kong, Formosa, and Thailand for the Archives of American Art (cost per person: $2,450, including a $500 contribution). The Archives' grand tour is an annual event for Lindblad; over a six-year span, he has routed these artlovers to Greece, Egypt, Russia, Poland, Spain, Portugal, England, Holland, France, Italy, East Germany, and the Dalmatian coast.

This trip was the first for the Cincinnatians ("a benefit-with-a-difference!" gushed *Town & Country*). They had come to Lindblad on the recommendation of veterans of his Archives and St. Louis Museum fund-raising grand tours. Lindblad had taken out the map of Eastern Europe, for he considers the Iron Curtain countries "one of the last great travel bargains, perhaps the most rewarding. They're no less friendly than Paris or Vienna, maybe friendlier. The Western cities are hostile to Americans. It has nothing to do with foreign policy. Just saturation with tourists."

Waiting with Lindblad at the Prague Airport was his dapper

advance man, Fernando Maldonado, a wiry Argentinian who owns a home in Greenwich Village. Since the travel agent's job has been defined as "getting the tourist there without the experience of having gone," the Lindblad organization's hardest work is done well before its clients touch down at their destination. Everywhere a Lindblad tour goes, Fernando Maldonado goes first. Meeting and briefing local guides, he verifies that their English is fluent. He reconfirms each item in the printed itineraries (Tuesday's two castles, he discovered at Čedok, were closed, one for restoration, the other for movie making) and makes any necessary substitutions (two other castles). In each city, he prepares and mimeographs a fact sheet called "WELCOME TO—," which invariably leads off with a pronouncement about tap water: drinkable or undrinkable? Fernando also inspects and oversees hotel arrangements. Throughout a Lindblad tour, the first person to greet you on arrival at a terminal is Fernando with your room assignment and mail. This avoids hectic roll calls and milling around hotel desks.

The night before the group's arrival, Fernando and I had washed down a leisurely dinner of ham and eggs and caviar with the heady Pilsner beer that is one of the prides of Prague. We ate in a chandeliered dining room of the sprawling, comfortable Hotel International, for whose Stalin Gothic design every Czech I met promptly apologized. After plum brandies, we stopped at the hotel desk. Fernando asked the night clerk if she had the room assignments yet.

"Definitely not," said the clerk, a serious girl whose English may have been acquired from stage melodramas. "If I have told you once, I have told you thrice: Professor Hokeš [the tour's chief Čedok guide] will be arising at six of the morning to make up the list."

"Good," said Fernando. "I'll try to be there, too. But please don't forget about our VIP's."

"V—I—P's?" the girl asked with an ominous scowl.

Before her lay a roster of Cincinnatians in alphabetical order. On it, Fernando scrawled "*1" next to "Mr. and Mrs. Fred Lazarus III (Irma)"; "*2" next to "Mrs. Sarah E. Kahn," a dowager who had been on two of Lindblad's Archives trips; "*3" next to "Mr. and Mrs. M. Chester Martin (Helen)," and

"*4" next to "Mr. and Mrs. William Beckett (Fritzi)." Chester Martin is a prominent Taft Republican; Bill Beckett heads the Beckett Paper Company. Fernando's ranking is not the last word, but it does reflect the Cincinnati power structure as Lindblad had glimpsed it on a selling visit.

The girl was unimpressed. "And what may you want for your V—I—P's?"

"The best rooms," Fernando said softly.

The girl drew herself up. "You must be joking. Everybody is equal. There are single and there are double accommodations. Everybody gets one or the other."

"I know, I know," Fernando persisted. "But there are some rooms with a little nicer view and some that are too high up to hear the trolley cars." He and that idealistic girl argued for five minutes, she contending that all rooms were equal, he hinting that some rooms were more equal than others. Suddenly Fernando handed her a ballpoint pen imprinted with "LINDBLAD TRAVEL" and explained, rather unnecessarily: "I'm a travel agent. This is for whom I work. Good night, and see what you can do about those four rooms." He darted away before the dialogue between East and West could start up again.

Thus on Saturday night had the twain been joined. By Sunday morning at Prague Airport, the VIP rankings were official. Every list carried by Čedok people bore the *1, *2, *3, and *4 designations. So did every master list for the rest of the three-week tour.

The sixth person waiting at the airport in Prague was, as you may have deduced, myself. I had arrived in the capital of the true Bohemia a couple of days in advance—long enough to fall in love with that fortified yellow city of seven hills and a hundred spires; long enough to take a solitary stroll amid the blue raincoats and wet cobblestones of a misty night along the Moldau; long enough to attend a double-feature stage show of *Waiting for Godot,* as elliptical as ever in Czech, followed by Dixieland jazz at a wine cellar called the Viola; long enough to assure three anxious students that our own Bohemian bard, Allen Ginsberg, wasn't rotting in an American jail. (Ginsberg had recently been expelled from Czechoslovakia in an orgiastic political scandal.)

> dilettante . . . now often implies elegant trifling in the
> arts, but many still use the term to name the lover of the
> art rather than its skilled practitioner.—*Webster's*, under
> synonyms for *amateur*.

Once the Cincinnatians had boarded Čedok's waiting buses,
however, I would do what they did and see what they saw. I
was, to be sure, interested in whether cultural intercourse could
possibly be compressed in a five-cities-in-three-weeks jet odyssey.
I was interested in whether the Lazaruses and Martins and
Becketts and Bullocks were out to enlarge their artistic moving-
and-shaking potential. Having bought their tickets from the
Pied Piper variety of culture vulture (Lindblad), would the
seventy dilettantes prove to be victims or vultures themselves?
Most of all, I hoped that the next three weeks would tell me
*what happens when you use culture as a gimmick to raise money
instead of using money to promote culture.*

[III]

"Nonsense," said Melanie Lehmann, twenty-three, when I
began popping my questions. "They're here to have a party.
Cincinnatians love to party together—anywhere in the world."

Melanie, the most intense and articulate of the tour's four
young girls, went on to compare her fellow travelers to "the
Clutters in Truman Capote—insulated by the travel agent from
passports and formalities and everyday life, protected, yet utterly
helpless. Nothing will change them, so long as they survive."

It was Melanie's first day in Prague and my third, so I reserved
judgment. But the circumstantial evidence favored her partying
thesis. The first person off the plane had been the final member
of the Lindblad cadre, Kevin Patrick McDonnell, a rubber-
legged thirty-one-year-old bachelor who came bounding down
with this proclamation: "Gangway for the biggest bunch of
swingers I've ever taken across!" At least twice during the short
bus ride from airport to hotel, I heard the fun-and-games rally-

ing cry: "In Cincinnati, every night's a holiday, and Saturday night is New Year's Eve!"

These Cincinnatians did two things particularly expertly: photographing and partying. Occasionally they overdid one or the other. At the Vienna Opera, one of the lady shutterbugs outraged a boxload of Viennese by snapping pictures throughout the first act of *Der Rosenkavalier*. They admonished her. She ignored them. In the second act, they had her ejected from their box. Her reaction: "It's clear to me that there's a lot of anti-American feeling in Vienna."

If, through some miscalculation, none of her three weeks' photos materialized, she would undoubtedly have told solid Cincinnati what it may have wanted to hear: that Eastern Europe doesn't exist. For photography itself has become an objective, rather than a memento, of travel. Or, to quote another Cincinnatian as Budapest loomed up majestically on both sides of a hydrofoil skimming along the Danube: "It's breathtaking! I won't believe it until I see my slides."

The "Intourist Reunion" party was held at a pseudo-fashionable restaurant in Indian Hill. It features moving pictures of buildings that do not move and still pictures of people who do.—Early 1967 letter from Cincinnati.

Lantern slides and home movies having replaced diaries* as the art form of the grand tour, we must project a verbal carrousel of our cultural ambassadors from Cincinnati doing what they do best. Therefore, let us gingerly open the Pandora's box called "PARTIES, EUROPE: PRAGUE, BUDAPEST, MOSCOW, LENINGRAD."

In every Iron Curtain city they visited, the Friends of the Cincinnati Orchestra threw a party for thirty to fifty leading native artists and critics. Each guest list was compiled by the Ministry of Culture or the state tourist agency (Čedok in Czecho-

---

* Except for that of an occasional diehard like attorney John R. Bullock of Taft, Stettinius, and Hollister, whose lengthy journal of our journey to Eastern Europe is quoted periodically in this chapter.

slovakia, Ibusz in Hungary, Intourist in Russia) or the local House of Friendship—with Lindblad overseeing.

The first party was on the first night in Prague—a semiformal reception and banquet at the Ministry of Culture. One guest was a bushy-haired gentleman named Ilja Hurnik, a composer whose chamber music the Cincinnatians had heard or slept through (after partying all night on the plane!) that very afternoon. Hurnik was so touched by their candid apologies and a request for his autograph that he invited a dozen Cincinnatians home for lunch later in the week. It was his brand-new young bride's first meal for company.

Another gentleman was a prominent Czech musician who made it clear to us that he would like to and would be allowed to teach music in the United States for a year or two. Irma Lazarus said she would see if anything could be arranged at the Cincinnati Conservatory.

(Back home a month later, Irma didn't forget him. When a vacancy arose at the University of Cincinnati, she obtained a tentative invitation for him at her end and then an enthusiastic response from Prague. But a high university official vetoed the whole project with, "I won't have a Communist on *my* faculty.")

Phyllis Weston, who runs an art gallery in Cincinnati, asked around for the painter Ota Janeček, whose work she had seen in the Tate and Grosvenor galleries in London and in an American movie executive's home. He wasn't at the party, but as a result of her inquiries, she was invited to his studio—four stories high, reached through a back door of a Union of Artists gallery. Janeček opened up a bottle of Johnnie Walker Black Label, chatted freely, and later sent a "little drawing" around to her at the Hotel International. "It's worth at least one hundred dollars," Phyllis said later, "but I'll never sell it."

That first party at the Ministry of Culture evoked so much goodwill and good cheer that Irma Lazarus had only one small regret. Hardly anybody present, Czechoslovakian or Cincinnatian, realized *who* was giving the party. (The money came out of the funds the Cincinnatians had paid Lindblad for the trip.) "I think," said Irma, "that in Budapest, Moscow, and Leningrad, I'll make a little speech just to set the record straight."

Breakfast and all other meals at the hotel were served in
an attractive sunlit room. I had asked for scrambled eggs
and later for some ham. I got ham and eggs fried together, but they were good. We were intrigued that three
and four minute soft-boiled eggs were always served shelled
but otherwise whole   —John Bullock's diary.

The next morning, Chester Martin, the Republican bigwig
with the *3 rating from Maldonado, asked Irma to set him
straight on another matter. "Why the hell wasn't anybody from
the American Embassy at our party?"

Irma replied that it had been "a protocol slipup on our part."
The Cincinnatians had sent a letter to our embassy in Prague,
but not a formal invitation. Arriving on Sunday, they had been
unable to reach any American officials with personal invitations.
It would not happen again, she assured Chester.

Nevertheless, Chester felt that the embassy ought to take
more of an interest in "seventy American tourists paying their
own way to come look at Czechoslovakian culture," particularly in the off-season, when virtually the only other sightseers
in Prague seemed to be government-sponsored delegations of
workers from other Communist countries. On Monday morning,
with childlike innocence, Chester phoned the American Embassy and informed the ambassador's secretary that "our visit is
an event the U.S. government ought to make some hay with.
Tomorrow morning, we're presenting our alligators to the
Prague Zoo,* and I think somebody from your shop ought to
be on hand—maybe a photographer, too." The secretary remarked diplomatically that while she might be inclined to agree,
the cultural attaché would get back to Mr. Martin that afternoon.

Chester Martin never heard from the cultural attaché. On
Tuesday morning, Chester's wife Helen and Irma Lazarus, two
alligators, and seven turtles posed at the zoo amid a bobbing,

* Lest the ASPCA start dispatching irate cables, rest assured that the alligators
and turtles were already bedded down at the zoo prior to formal presentation.

delighted throng of apple-cheeked Prague school kids. But the
only local photographer on hand was a Czech who had come as
a personal favor to Professor Hokeš, the man from Čedok.

The matter might have ended there if our departure from
Prague on Thursday hadn't been delayed two hours by rain.
During the second hour, a flurry of airport activity prompted
Chester Martin to make inquiries. Kirk Douglas, the movie star
who made Van Gogh famous, was coming to Prague on a goodwill tour under U.S. State Department auspices. And the har-
ried-looking man supervising Douglas' red-carpet press reception
was none other than the embassy's elusive cultural attaché.

What happened next must be every bureaucrat's bad dream
come true.

"Boy, am I glad to see you!" said Chester Martin, introducing
himself to the cultural attaché.

The feeling clearly was not mutual, but after some squirm-
ing, the embarrassed diplomat offered to introduce Chester to
Kirk Douglas.

"No, thank you. I don't even want his autograph," said
Chester Martin, turning augustly on his heel and stalking away.

Eleanor Strauss, an architect's wife who happens to be Irma
Lazarus' twin sister, administered the *coup de grâce* by informing the cultural attaché:

"We have come to Czechoslovakia to share our culture with
the Czechs. Our only regret is that we've had no real contact
with your embassy, and we find your attitude toward us extremely shabby."

Later, aboard our Tupolev 104 jet, Mrs. Strauss added that
the Cincinnatians' four-day presence in Prague struck her as far
more useful to the Americanimageabroad (which is how, from
constant invocation, people now say it) than a whirlwind visit
from Kirk Douglas. Having crashed the actor's reception, I was
inclined to agree. Douglas, the former Issur Danielovitch of
Amsterdam, New York, had come striding off a plane from
Warsaw, looking more like Mayor John Lindsay (that year's
dynamic new image) than Lindsay himself. Owlishly, worldly-
wisely, the global celluloid god had looked over the small
gathering of Czechs before making his first goodwill utterance:

"Now, which of you is in charge of the bags?"

Impressions of Prague: Our hotel pleasant, but to say the
facilities, and particularly the washrooms outside of the
hotel and particularly outside of the city, are poor, would
be a gross misstatement. The people are very friendly, but
few of them speak more than a very limited amount of
English.   —John Bullock's diary.

Our next slides are from Fészek, the Artists Club of Budapest,
where the Cincinnatians' reception for "guests from Hungary's
cultural life" almost didn't take place.

The party was scheduled for a Monday afternoon. Some forty
Hungarians had been promised by the authorities. The American Legation, too, from the consul on down, had responded
eagerly to the Cincinnatians' formal invitation, for the ornate
threshold of Fészek had been uncrossed by Americans in recent
years. American diplomats in Budapest have lived a ghettolike
existence ever since the uprising of 1956. For a decade now, our
legation there has been blessed yet burdened by the refuge of
Joseph Cardinal Mindszenty on an upper floor.

Monday at noon, Irma Lazarus learned that there would
probably be no Hungarians present.

Lars Lindblad had been notified that the Magyar People's
Republic was frowning on growing contact between Hungarian
intellectuals and the West. Apparently, some had talked too
freely—and for publication. The official reason for declining the
Cincinnatians' invitations would be each artist's personal outrage over Vietnam. To avert such an incident, didn't Mrs.
Lazarus wish to cancel the reception?

"Let's go ahead with it," she told Lindblad. "We can still
have a pretty good party with seventy or eighty Americans. And
I think the legation people are sort of counting on it."

The party went on, as scheduled.

To everybody's surprise, more than forty Hungarians showed
up. Faced by Irma's fortitude, the government seems to have
decided that their absence would be a political backfire.

The cultural intercourse started tensely when a prominent
Hungarian composer entered the mirrored reception room and
was taken aback by an American diplomat speaking fluent Hun-

garian. The Hungarian turned away, only to come face-to-face with a Friend of the Cincinnati Orchestra named Sam Greenfield.

"Do you have any grandchildren?" Sam asked, flashing a wallet of baby photos.

The composer countered with a wallet of his own. As cocktail-party acquaintances go, he and Sam became fast friends. The next morning, he sent his wife around to the hotel to take the Greenfields shopping for toys.

Let's focus for a minute on Sam Greenfield and his blue-haired wife Miriam, for they are a new breed of grand tourist—comparison shoppers seeking the best buy in cultural enrichment from prefabricated travel. The Greenfields are not and never have been from Cincinnati, Ohio. They live in Brooklyn, New York, where he is an investment adviser and she is active in Hadassah. Having toured Europe before on their own and in groups, they had been searching for what Sam called "a tour with a purpose—not a rat race through seventeen countries in twenty-one days. About a year ago, a friend from Cincinnati mentioned this trip was in the works, and we liked it right away because it had a theme. We don't know much about the Cincinnati Symphony, but we sympathize with its aims, so as soon as the tour was official, we joined the Friends of the Orchestra and signed up."

Thanks to Sam, the party in Budapest loosened. It reached a climax of hilarity when Harriet "Happy" Williams, a blonde real-estate millionairess, raved about Budapest's "marvelous" public transportation to a Hungarian who had been telling of his trouble in obtaining a car. The Hungarian promptly accused Happy of being a Communist sympathizer.

Irma Lazarus, as she had vowed in Prague, made her little speech about who was giving the party and why. It was gracious and brief.

"Our trip is making it possible for the Cincinnati Symphony to raise more than twenty thousand dollars in order to give our musicians a larger sum of money, not to mention morale, just before they embark upon a concert tour around the world. And we come for another purpose as well. We come to see your beautiful city, how you make your music, how you raise your children, and what makes you tick. We have also discovered your food and will leave here tomorrow loving you—and five pounds heavier!"

The Hungarian interpreter who was supposed to translate Irma's speech didn't. She simply read off a list of those present. Later she "explained" that everybody present understood English, an assertion that was patently false.

Irma Lazarus' patrician chin, which she had stuck out so boldly at noon, was still jutting at nightfall. "In Moscow," she told me, "I'm going to stop after each sentence and wait to be translated."

This she did—at a vodka-and-caviar reception in Moscow's Hotel Metropole four days later. This time, her speech was translated, even though it fell on ears that understood it perfectly. For the "representatives of Soviet cultural life" on hand were a lackluster but affable and thoroughly English-speaking contingent of critics, editors, lecturers, and professional party-goers. Recruited by the House of Friendship (a goodwill sort of International House venture), they brought their built-in cordiality, but neither distinction nor depth, to a party they had clearly attended many times before.

After Irma had been applauded and toasted, a man from the House of Friendship made a speech. "We are glad," he proclaimed, "that on its world tour, the Cincinnati Symphony will make some money in Russia." Actually, the closest the orchestra would come to Moscow on its State Department-sponsored tour that summer would be Dubrovnik, Yugoslavia.

The party was well under way when a call came from Chester (*3) Martin's wife.

Helen Martin is a demon researcher who invaded every city armed with lists of better restaurants and nightclubs, plus their specialties. She even carried galley proofs of a unique guidebook—*Itinerary of Taste: A Guide to Restaurants Abroad with Notes on Markets and Modern Art*—that was published later in 1966 by, believe it or not, the E. F. MacDonald Company of Dayton (Plaid Stamps!) for $3.75 in cash. Woe betide Lindblad if he dared to tell Helen that the hotel had the best food in town!

Helen also came to town equipped with Xeroxed letters of introduction; the originals had been mailed weeks in advance. Thus the Martins were welcomed into private homes in Prague, Vienna, Budapest, and even Moscow.

It was at one of these, an elegant log house on a Moscow side street, that Helen Martin had just met three prominent Russian avant-garde artists. One of them, Oskar Rabin, thirty-eight, cut a wider swath in Soviet cultural life than all thirty of his better-fed compatriots being partied by the Cincinnatians at that very moment. A symbolist whose recurrent motif is a haunting black cat, Rabin has achieved an exhibition at the Grosvenor Gallery in London, a full column in the New York *Times,* a sizable public inside and outside Russia, and a denunciation by his own Ministry of Culture as a "miserable wretch who has gone astray in his ideas and in his art."

On the spur of the moment, Helen Martin invited Oskar Rabin and the other two artists to accompany her to the reception. To her delight, they accepted.

A cab was called. While they waited, however, Helen decided to phone the party and clear her invitation with Irma Lazarus or Lars Lindblad.

After some delay, she was connected with Lindblad.

There is some disagreement about what Helen Martin, who talks very fast, told Lindblad. She claims she said she had "three prominent artists" in tow. He claims she said "three people." Whichever way she phrased her question, Lindblad's answer was no. Intourist, he said, was "charging us ten dollars a head for each person at the party."

Helen Martin hung up with a disagreeable task to perform. The three Russian artists were already sitting in the cab, waiting to go to the party, when she disinvited them.

[At the] reception for Moscow artists and musicians . . . we enjoyed them, and I particularly enjoyed Mrs. [Lucy] Jarvis [of NBC in New York], the only woman television producer, who produced the commentary on the Kremlin and the Louvre. She is planning another one on the Kremlin. . . .   —John Bullock's diary.

After the triumph in Budapest and the fiasco in Moscow, the reception in Leningrad could only be a spectacular reprise of parties past.

Where Moscow had a *House* of Friendship, Leningrad had a *Palace* of Friendship. On hand were fifty Russians. The dignitaries, as usual, were so drably dressed that Miss Melissa J. Safford of William Howard Taft Road moaned: "I always wind up talking to waiters because they're the only ones who look like anybody."

The guest of honor was violinist David Oistrakh, who had doubled as conductor and soloist the night before in a stirring concert of Beethoven, Schubert, Mozart, and Wagner. Oistrakh and his son Igor had been Irma Lazarus' guests in Cincinnati. In Leningrad, Irma made her most eloquent speech of all, and it was translated sentence by sentence.

"Six months ago we had a dream. Mr. Oistrakh came to Cincinnati and not only gave us a beautiful night's music, but he spent the rest of the evening telling us about the beauties of Russia. We already loved the music of Russia, and I think it is safe to say that one-quarter of the classical music that is played in America is Russian. And we go back home tomorrow knowing that Mr. Oistrakh was not exaggerating. We go home tomorrow morning absolutely thrilled that *your* culture really belongs to your people. We see it in your museums and feel it in your concert halls. We only hope that some day in our New World, we will be able to say that our people enjoy our cultural heritage as your people do yours."

Over the loudspeaker, a dubious Russian tribute to the American musical world—a rock 'n' roll blast of "You gonna lewwwze dat girl!"—rattled Victorian mirrors and Venetian glass all around the palace. Later a Russian baritone stepped forth and sang Gershwin's "Lady Be Good" impeccably. The fun-loving Cincinnatians, sensing kindred spirits, tried to organize a Bunny Hop around the ballroom. But their hosts, fearing for their floors, asked them to desist.

Prior to Intourist's daily regimentation of tourism in Russia, the Cincinnatians might not have been prone to take *nyet* for an answer. But three drip-dry weeks of living out of suitcases at a jet age pace set by Lindblad and the state had worn down their resistance. Besides, for once they were outnumbered. Despite the glittering occasion, twenty-six of the seventy had elected to stay behind at the hotel—to pack or rest up or dress

up for the group's own private Farewell to Russia masquerade
ball later that evening.

> At the last minute, we decided to dress. Marion [Mrs.
> Bullock] made herself a hat from a Moscow subway system
> brochure and we, like many others, appeared as Russians.
> Two young musicians played the balalaika and accordion.
> The dinner was not up to the rest of the celebration
> (blintzes again) but this did not deter the gaiety of the
> party.   —John Bullock's diary.

Virtually all of the seventy Cincinnatians attended the masquerade. Some of them, one sensed, had come all the way to
Leningrad to see their fellow Cincinnatians as they saw themselves. The insights they gained might prove useful back home.
Chester (*3) Martin, the Republican bigwig, wore a paper hat.
Miss Melissa J. Safford of William Howard Taft Road dressed
like a Swiss dairymaid. Fred (*1) Lazarus III came on like a
brakeman doubling as dishwasher for the Baltimore & Ohio.

Is this what the grand tour of yore has become? A 10,000-
mile expedition to look into a mirror and return home with
some grotesque illuminations of oneself?

> Whether we seek models of greatness or experience else-
> where on the earth, we look into a mirror instead of out of
> a window and we see only ourselves.   —Daniel J. Boorstin.

Most people's travels are dictated by their economic status.
The infrequent traveler, whose three-week "trip of a lifetime"
may consume his life savings, can scarcely afford to gamble on
his own expertise—or so he has been led to believe. And this
becomes a self-fulfilling prophecy when, for instance, a headlined
"TRANSATLANTIC FARE REDUCTION FROM $300 TO $230" (New
York–London round trip) is actually only for groups of fifteen
who agree to fly to and from Europe together and book at least
$70 worth of tours and accommodations together. Or when Com-
munist bureaucracies like Čedok, Ibusz, and Intourist open

doors to seventy Americans that they might not open to one or two or four.

As true believers in democracy, perhaps we should rejoice that a planeload of upper-crust Cincinnatians, most of whom could afford an authentic grand tour, had chosen a middle-class mode of travel. But there was something more disturbing than democratic about watching aristocrats with the time and money for leisurely travel hurtling through Europe as though they had three weeks to live. My own middle-class morality was jarred by what the baby-grand scope of their grand tour said about how my fellow travelers saw the world and themselves.

For selling them this slightly cynical package, Lindblad was only partly to blame. He could, after all, make a quick killing by selling seventy people a three-week group tour; trying to persuade each to spend a year on his or her own would have been futile and suicidal. Besides, most of the Cincinnatians were too old for a truly grand tour. Thus, *their* grand tour, as defined by Lindblad, meant "best available hotels, twin-bedded rooms with private bathrooms, full (meat) breakfast, table d'hôte luncheons and dinner daily, except in Vienna, most tips, taxes, service charges, transfers, sightseeing, cocktail parties, receptions, and special dinners as detailed in itinerary."

Lindblad's selection of hotels and restaurants seldom left much to be desired (except by Helen Martin), for he is a conscientious and capable travel agent. To iron out the dents and wrinkles of Eastern Europe for his prestigious new account, Lars and his wife Sonja had made a dry run over the tour's route three months earlier.

When in the course of making a living, however, Lindblad hires the Argentine Navy to invade the Antarctic with sightseers or deploys such powerful energies as the Martins and the Lazaruses across the map of Europe in the role of cultural ambassador, he verges on practicing diplomacy without a license.

Diplomacy today, no matter how thin an occasional cultural attaché slices it, is too crucial an art to be entrusted to a travel agent peddling packaged reassurance and unctuous camp counseling for grown-ups. Lindblad's art is in fueling, feeding, bedding, and sightseeing. He is trained to think in terms of blandest common denominators (white bread rather than black bread, *Aida* rather than *Don Carlos*, groups rather than individuals), and his horizons are bounded by itineraries, connections, small print, and profits.

In the Moscow fiasco of the disinvited artists, Lindblad was as out of his league as David Susskind confronting Khrushchev. So was Helen Martin—but her instinct, at least, was to invite; her mistake, having invited, was to ask if she could. It was then that she came up against the travel agent's instinct to insulate. The result was a small international insult that ricocheted around Moscow's cultural grapevine for a day or two and was even noted by our embassy there.

Lest what I have said about creeping Lindbladism be construed as an attack on private enterprise, let me assure you that state-run tourism is at least as capable of diplomatic clumsiness. Throughout our stay in Russia, we were quietly joined by homesick Ghanians—homesick, at the very least, to hear English spoken. They would tag along on our guided tours or loiter among us in hotel lobbies. One evening in Leningrad, borne on a tide of English conversation, a smiling young Ghanaian drifted with the Cincinnatians into their private dining room. Diana Motch of Cincinnati and I were sitting at a table for three. He asked us politely but nervously: "May I be so kind as to join you?"

We knew that the young Negro didn't belong there, but I was happy to wave him to a seat, saying, "Be my guest," and Diana gave him a smile of welcome. Before our smiling guest could lower himself into the seat, however, the head Intourist guide hurried over and insisted that he leave.

First the smile and then the Negro vanished, leaving behind him two uglified Americans and one empty place setting.

[IV]

Thomas Wolfe called it *You Can't Go Home Again,* and the anthropologists call it *culture shock.* Mostly it afflicts young people, which is why, one day back in 1965, a thousand ex-Peace Corpsmen converged on Washington to talk about it with government officials and business leaders. They grappled with the emotional jolt a Peace Corps returnee experiences when, after two years of hard-working idealism amid the unspeakable poverty of Asia and Africa, he returns to confront the hard-nosed, self-seeking affluence of his native land. The conference in Washington didn't come up with any cure, but it did publicly identify the disease as culture shock, a term that now pops up often in our newsmagazines as well as in our learned journals.

Culture shock is a many-splendored trauma, however. Despite all their blunting of their own sensitivities with partying, drinking, and banding together, the mostly middle-aged friends of the Cincinnati Orchestra experienced culture shock going and returning.

Try, if you will, to put yourself in the mental posture of a Conservative Cincinnati capitalist who digests the *Enquirer* with breakfast and thinks of Eastern Europe as one vast slave labor camp with sullen, muzzled natives lusting to be liberated. Then off you go into the wild blue yonder, and when you touch down behind the Iron Curtain, virtually every Czech you meet seems glad to see you but not the least bit interested in stowing away on the boat you take out of Czechoslovakia—the hydrofoil from Bratislava to Vienna. Because the plane from Prague is late, you spend only an hour in Bratislava, but that's enough time for at least three surprises: on the banks of the Danube, an exhibit of Henry Moore statuary, handsomely displayed; at the Hotel Devin, the best *pâté* you ever tasted for lunch; and although everything is prepaid, should you want some extras like wine or souvenirs, the hotel honors your Diners' Club card.

Your thirty-six hours in Vienna, the tour's only destination outside the Curtain, gives you your first reverse culture shock. The Americanization of Europe seems to explode in your face. The Vienna Opera offers an ironic glimpse of musical America as disconcertingly as when you put the wrong end of your opera glasses to your eyes. That marvelous mezzo in *Rosenkavalier* is Claire Watson, an American girl, the first American singer, in fact, ever to receive the Bavarian Order of Merit. Forced by her shortsighted compatriots to make her name and her living abroad, she proves the contention of the New York *Times'* Harold C. Schonberg that most of the best American singers "are solidly entrenched in European opera houses." *

---

* Finally, on September 21, 1966, Claire Watson made her American debut with the San Francisco Opera, followed by an engagement with the Chicago Lyric Opera.

The Vienna Inter-Continental is indeed a home away from home. At this automated parody of a streamlined American hotel, the personnel go out of their way to be impersonal. The self-service elevators resonate with the sound of Muzak and the Anglo-Saxon banter of Hertz Rent-a-Car sales executives convening in a ballroom. Eighteen hours after checking in, one of the Cincinnatians forgets his room number and inquires at the desk—only to be informed that he isn't registered at the hotel.

It was still raining as we reached the beautiful Inter-Continental Hotel. We found we had a luxurious combined living and bedroom, and, unbelievably, wastebaskets in the room. . . . The Martinis were as good as could be obtained anywhere.   —John Bullock's diary.

Reverse reverse culture shock! Budapest—dazzling by day, glittering by night—is a summit on the cultural, political, and emotional roller-coaster ride your smoothly prefabricated tour is turning into. The Grand Hotel Gellert is a castlelike spa on the Danube. It boasts two swimming pools with artificial waves, bidets and balconies, marble-pillared lobbies connected by a staircase from which "His Majesty, the Emperor Francis Joseph" might be announced momentarily, and the old prewar Grand Hotel tradition of bowing-and-scraping personal service.

Milton W. Stulbarg, a Cincinnati lawyer, is oppressed by all the creature comforts of Marxism-Leninism, Hungarian style, until he spots a lineup of five cars at a gas pump on Sunday morning. He loudly calls this to the attention of all within earshot as evidence of Communist deprivation. As though such a spectacle could never be witnessed on a weekend in greater Cincinnati!

A few minutes later, you're in Budapest's Coronation Church. The mass, composed by Haydn, is being sung by a soprano who could hold her own in any opera house in the world and played on baroque instruments by an orchestra of philharmonic proportions. Every pew, every aisle, every alcove, and every doorway is jammed with Hungarian Catholics praying and tourists praying or just listening.

. . . many of our party stayed for the whole one-and-one-half hour mass. As Arthur Darack said, it is hard to find performances with a complete symphony orchestra, a fine conductor, several top soloists, and a chorus to equal our May Festival chorus. After a short visit, I preferred to walk around and got into a conversation with an elderly colonel's widow and her two grandchildren. They, like all the spectators, were intrigued by Marion's Polaroid camera, and we were surrounded by a crowd whenever she took a picture. —John Bullock's diary.

After the coddling of Prague and Budapest, Moscow offers the culture shock of an ice-cold bath. To a Cincinnatian, Moscow is as brusque and bustling and preoccupied as New York at World's Fair time. It offers the added discomforts of a difficult language, an inscrutable alphabet, and May Day impending. Stragglers and lone-ranging grand tourists find themselves on streets that are suddenly sealed off at both ends while they're in midblock. Whistles blow and sirens wail as tanks are moved into position for the May Day demonstration. The recurrent squeal of *"Nyet, nyet, nyet, nyet!"* is often directed at them!

There are two antidotes to culture shock for a Cincinnatian in the unaccommodating hurly-burly of Moscow. One is good ice cream. The other is the nightly cultural calendar: *Aida* at the Bolshoi Opera; *Cinderella,* with a bubbling score by Prokofiev, at the Bolshoi Ballet; a puppet spoof of the James Bond spoofs of spoofs. In the familiarity of the concert hall and the presence of art, the icy tensions of coping with an alien, seemingly hostile, environment are dissipated for a couple of hours. Then back to the siege of the Metropole Hotel, where the waiters actually throw plates at the guest in a sullen, determined effort to have him fed by midnight. It is, if you'll pardon the pun, disconcerting.

Remember that: *nye kulturni.* You'll find it extremely useful, because when these chaps are rude and you feel obliged to tick them off, it means not a whit to call them a bastard,

a son of a dog, but to tell him he's *uncultured,* that really
strikes home.—Advice to Americans, quoted in *The Muses
Are Heard,* Truman Capote's account of his 1955 trip to
Russia.

Disconcerted herself is a hard-swearing Cincinnati matron
who shall be nameless here. Mrs. Nameless has already distinguished herself by complaining, on a specially arranged backstage tour, that the Bolshoi is a dreary place (as what theater
isn't, between performances?). Later, in Leningrad, she will
deliver two memorable utterances in one gallery of the Her-
mitage: "Smells awful in here!" and "How do we *know* it's a
real Michelangelo?" But right now, Mrs. Nameless is between
the acts of the magical, luminously danced, spectacularly
mounted *Cinderella* at the Kremlin's glassy, sweeping Palace of
Congresses. Escalators have whisked many of the 6,000 ballet-
goers up to a dining room that is geared to feed all 6,000 a
sandwich and a drink apiece in fifteen minutes at stand-up
tables. This room at the top has not a pillar in it. It is sound-
proofed for the semblance of intimacy. Even when at least 2,000
pairs of high heels are walking on its parquet floor, you do not
hear a single clickety-clack. You don't even hear a din of voices
or the conversation more than six or seven feet away. But you
do hear the grating bellow of Mrs. Nameless cutting through all
this elegant atmosphere with an anguished question. "How in
hell are we gonna go back to Cincinnati and tell them everything's terrible here after we've seen this?"

"Well," Arthur Darack of the *Enquirer* murmurs to her,
"we'll just have to redouble our efforts to dislike everything,
won't we?"

Because the government really runs every business in the
country, and the total life of the people, they are dependent
upon decisions the government makes. Therefore, the government has gone to great pains to convince the people
of Russia that they can do a number of things better than
capitalist countries can, and that this superiority is due to
their central planning and central supervision of all activi-

ties. They accomplish this with symbols. One of these symbols is the cultural activities of the country—the ballets, operas, and concerts. There is no doubt that they are really superior to any but the very best companies in the largest cities elsewhere in the world. Every performance we saw in Russia was of uniformly high quality, even to the smaller orchestras and smaller ballet companies.

—Fred (*1) Lazarus III's memo.

In Leningrad, a very young bride and groom experience a rude cultural shock on their wedding day. You're in the Wedding Palace, a centralized marriage, catering, and florist's facility where some forty couples a day are united in solemn wedlock for the equivalent of $1.50 per couple. Approached in her dressing room by Intourist, the bride consents to have "some visitors from abroad" attend her wedding. Little does she realize that she is inviting an onslaught of some fifty Cincinnatians, cameras clicking, plus a dozen Japanese, flash cameras ablaze! Bride and groom are married beneath a photo of Lenin and amid a blinding barrage of flashbulbs. Mrs. Nameless runs out of film during the ceremony and explodes with a heartfelt "Son of a bitch!" Then, as the outnumbered and subdued Russian guests file out, a young Japanese gentleman and an elderly traveling lady from Cincinnati pose arm in arm in a grotesque parody of a wedding photo. And perhaps you wonder how soon the newlyweds are going to have their first quarrel. . . .

What we're seeing now in Leningrad was perhaps inevitable. The grand tour is ending neither with bang nor whimper, but with an ugly snarl, a barbaric yawp, and, as mentioned earlier, a masquerade ball. Our Cincinnatians have been jolted by a series of shocks as well as by the loss of perspective that occurs when accelerated travel robs you of gradual change in the landscape.

The hard-driving goodwill of Irma Lazarus, the incurably open mind of Arthur Darack, the newspaperman who moonlights as a professor of aesthetics at the University of Cincinnati; the grandfatherly humanity of Sam Greenfield from Brooklyn— all these are intact and, if anything, strengthened by their adventures. But most of their fellow travelers have stopped acting and started reacting. They see only what Intourist wishes them to see. A mission of cultural ambassadors has deteriorated into a tribe of hedonistic, hard-shopping, sightseeing but unseeing tourists.

Besides, as days together become weeks, people who might bore each other after an hour or two in Cincinnati prey on each other in Europe. They retell the same jokes, rub the same exposed nerves, and share the same experiences. The grand tour becomes a three-week honeymoon with seventy mates, not all of one's choosing. But you cannot explode, for you will have to live with them back home—at arm's length, to be sure, but in a tightly knit aristocracy. And so you vent your fury on the face-less (to you) natives through whose lands you journey and whose weddings and shrines you grace with your presence. Thus can group travel narrow instead of broaden.

Even Arthur Darack proves momentarily susceptible to the group's malaise. On a solitary stroll along the Nevsky Prospect, Leningrad's shopping street, where Tolstoy walked, Arthur loses his bearings and asks directions. Out of an uncomprehending throng steps a lissome young girl who gives him precise in-structions spoken in impeccable Oxonian.

"You must be British," says Arthur, paying a Cincinnati compliment.

"Can't I be Russian?" she says with a Gioconda smile that is slower than she to melt back into the crowd.

Indian Hill is consumed with curiosity about Russia. They see it as the one country that finally put labor unions in their place. —Picture postcard from Arthur Darack soon after return from grand tour.

Epilogue:
The Establishment's New Home

THE little boy felt ill at ease. But the emperor kept him on his knees to await his fate. He might have stayed that way forever if it hadn't been for the flurry and fanfare of two new arrivals at court. Both visitors looked familiar, sounded familiar, and said they were consultants on the arts.

"If it please Your Majesty," they said in unison, "you should build a huge new Establishment to house the cultural explosion."

"Establishment? Cultural explosion?" said the emperor. "Oh, yes. The cultural explosion must be contained, and it will take an Establishment to do it. But what will it require in the way of resources?"

"Money," chorused the two arts consultants.

"If that is all it takes," said the emperor, "I consider it a top-priority must. But what are your credentials to build it for me?"

The two arts consultants replied that they had erected many legendary wonders, including the Kennedy mystique, the American image abroad, and the national edifice complex. The Establishment's new home, however, would be their crowning achievement. It would take in a theater of the absurd, a citadel of classical music, with every seat within walking distance of a promenade, and an underground garage, easily accessible by Caldermobile.

With a snort of pride, the emperor gazed down condescendingly at the little boy and said: "How now? Who will ever afford to take your accusations seriously after they have looked in the reflecting pool and seen what these two geniuses and I have wrought?"

Smiling, the boy fell dead.

INDEX

Index